FREE APPROPRIATE PUBLIC EDUCATION

The Law and Children With Disabilities

SEVENTH EDITION

H. Rutherford Turnbull III
University of Kansas

Matthew J. Stowe
University of Kansas

Nancy E. Huerta
University of Kansas

LOVE PUBLISHING COMPANY®
Denver • London • Sydney

Published by Love Publishing Company
P.O. Box 22353
Denver, Colorado 80222
www.lovepublishing.com

Seventh Edition

Library of Congress Control Number: 2006926437

ISBN 0-89108-325-1

Contents

Part One:
Introduction to the American Legal System and Education and Related Laws   1

Preface

When my wife, Ann Turnbull, and I wrote the first edition of this book, our son Jay was just entering public schools. He had been in a private preschool in Durham, North Carolina, to which I drove him daily from our home in Chapel Hill. The program was operated by the Sarah Barker Center, a ladies' club, and directed by Evelyn Taylor.

Calling the Center a "school" was a euphemism, but one that was consistent with the time and place. It wasn't a school so much as it was a day-care center; it lacked highly qualified teachers, and there was barely any evidence-based intervention grounded in solid research for the staff to use. The Center was not publicly funded—Ms. Taylor had to raise the funds to operate it—and it was located in the basement of a church. In those days, basements, civic clubs, churches, and charity locations were the custom for preschool youngsters with disabilities.

Among the staff was Cordelia Bethea, a Black woman who took a special shine to Jay. I was separated from my then wife for most of the time Jay was at the Sarah Barker Center, and my work at the University of North Carolina at Chapel Hill required me to travel throughout the state on a nearly weekly basis. Ms. Taylor told Cordelia about my predicament: how to care for Jay and do my work simultaneously. Cordelia's response was one that I will never forget.

The day after learning of my situation, Cordelia greeted me at the entrance to the Center, reached out to take Jay from my arms, clasped him—a small White boy with blond curls—against her ample bosom, and declared, "Jay can stay with me and my family for as long as he wants. I'll treat him as if he were one of my own." He did, and she did, for nearly a year, except on weekends when he returned to be with me.

For most families and young children, early intervention in the early 1970s was a matter of charity and compassion. What I experienced at the Sarah Barker Center and with Cordelia was compassion that transcended race. Race was very much a part of special education then. It still is.

When Ann and I wrote the second edition of this book, Jay had entered public school in Chapel Hill, but his first two years were spent in a classroom in the administration building, far away from most other students and the school district's administrators. Needless to say, the only other students in his class were those with disabilities. I recall some of their names to this day: Bryant, Chip, Charles, Odell—most of them Black. I also recall Jay's teachers: Roger, Beth, Randy, and Julie. They were my first introduction to students and teachers in special education.

Before then, nearly everything I knew about special education I had merely read about or heard about from Ann or my friends Al Abeson and Fred Weintraub at CEC. I knew this much, however: Exclusion and segregation were wrong, and entry into a school of any sort was no longer a gift but a right.

As subsequent editions rolled off the presses, Congress continued to improve IDEA while state and local agencies continued to implement the law and also violate it. The law can never create perfect systems of human services. It can, however, enlarge rights, reduce wrongs, devise new remedies, and stimulate system repairs.

For most of his elementary, middle, and secondary school years, Jay was in segregated programs in our town of Lawrence, Kansas. He then attended the Walt Whitman High School in Bethesda, Maryland, where Ann and I were living on sabbatical. There, his teacher, Mary Morningstar, knew that there is a human instinct to kindness in all students, and she tapped it by arranging for Jay to be the assistant manager of the football team. He earned his letter and received resounding applause from his teammates and their families at the end-of-season banquet, eliciting praise and comments such as "Oh, so *that's* who that student is!"

At the end of the banquet ceremonies, three women came to our table. They introduced themselves as the mothers of the tri-captains and said, "Our sons want Jay to have a letter jacket. They know he will get one eventually, but not for several months. So they drew lots to see who would donate his jacket to Jay. Each of our sons wanted to 'win' that lottery. He'll be wearing a jacket come Monday morning!" Mary Morningstar, the football captains, and the parents knew what IDEA had always proclaimed: Integration has remarkable social value, not just academic worth.

Jay graduated in 1988 and, with the sponsorship of Jean Ann Summers and Ed Zamarripa at the University of Kansas, became a research clerical aide there. He moved out of our home and into one of his own—supported by graduate students who lived rent-free but contributed "sweat equity"—and established himself in our town as a resident. More than that, he became a living example of the nation's disability policies and of the fruits of capable teachers using imagination and evidence-based instruction. Jay began to prove that if he can have equal opportunity, he can also be somewhat economically self-sufficient, live independently but with support, and fully participate in his community.

And that brings us to this, the seventh edition. We focus on the 2004 amendments and continue the saga of this book's life as being parallel to Jay's. You will meet Jay in chapter 1, and you'll learn how he may have even had some influence on a president of the United States.

From charity and compassion through segregated and finally integrated education to valued outcomes, Jay has been the exemplar of what IDEA can produce if people comply with the letter and the spirit of the law. It takes all of us. So master the text in this book, and then cultivate the law's spirit as you carry out its letter.

Rud Turnbull
April 2006
Lawrence, Kansas

DEDICATIONS

Rud Turnbull dedicates to Ann, coauthor of the first and subsequent editions and partner in all that we have ever done and ever will do (Ann, you're right, you are the only one who'd have put up with me all these glorious years); to Jay, a first-generation IDEA beneficiary, who is my best professor (please, Jay, give me the course before you give me the final examination); to Amy, whose deep commitment to social justice is admirable and gratifying beyond my ability to describe (Amy, save the world tomorrow if you can't save it today); to Kate, whose muse of the theatre calls her powerfully to an interesting life and who permanently fascinates me (Kate, let your light shine forth before all the world); and to Rahul and Dylan, son-in-law and grandson, the two other men in my life who, together with my son, bring delightful levels of testosteronic energy to this aging old bull.

Matt Stowe dedicates to Ann Stowe (soon to be Dr. Stowe), my wife and partner, love and life, for her enduring ability to keep things in perspective, shatter stress with laughter, and remind me of the things that matter most (and pretty much everything else)—and also for being a wonderful mother; to Mattingly, whose indomitable spirit, unquenchable energy, and love of hands-on learning are a constant reminder to me that it is good to dream, but better to do; and to Jules, whose love and caring for others reveals a heart much too big to fit into such a little girl.

Nancy Huerta dedicates to the loves of her life: Mom, whose encouragement and strength is an unfailing inspiration; Dad, whose support and example gave me no boundaries; Sharon, my sister and my rock, without whom life would be empty; Jody, the man who loves me as I am (thanks); Marissa, for whom "buddy" says it all; and Scott, my best friend, reading books out loud to this happy 20th year.

Together, we three authors dedicate this book and our associated labors to the students, their families, and the educators whom IDEA is intended to benefit. We hope that this book makes it possible for them to understand and implement IDEA not just by the letter of the law but also by its powerful spirit.

ACKNOWLEDGMENTS

We acknowledge the following people:

Ann Turnbull, who, alongside Rud and while sitting at the Turnbulls' dining room table during Christmas and New Year's weeks in 1977, helped create the first edition of this book, who contributed significantly to each subsequent edition, and who supported her husband/partner at each stage of his work on this and related law and policy projects.

Mary-Margaret Simpson, the Beach Center's talented writer-in-residence and editor, who painstakingly attended to all of the grunge work related to format, grammar, references, tables and figures, tables of content, and the like; without whose diligence and attention to detail there would be a much less readable text; and without whose ebullient personality many a stressful moment would have occurred, not just in the writing of this book but in the writing of nearly every Beach Center product.

Suzanne Schrandt, a Kansas University law school graduate who, to our great satisfaction, has cast her lot with Matt and Rud at the Beach Center; who has been our Sherlock Holmes of citations, locating the missing ones and assuring each one's accuracy; who specializes in research on the legal, ethical, and social implications of the Human Genome Project; and who, we are proud to say, also teaches at various medical schools and knows how to burn the midnight oil, without complaint.

Lois Weldon, the Turnbulls' administrative aide and valued colleague, whose ability at the computer/word processor has resulted in saved, reorganized, and properly assembled text (in this and other books) and in the design and presentation of many of the figures that illustrate our text and IDEA's convoluted requirements.

Stan Love, the Turnbulls' publisher and friend of 30 years, whose pursuit of excellence in his work is matched only by his gentlemanly accommodations to his authors' quirks and support of their efforts to make a significant and sustainable difference by explaining IDEA to a wide audience.

The students who enrolled in Rud's doctoral class on special education law in the spring of 2006, namely, Rashida Banerjee, Jennifer Brown, Pam Epley, Donna Foy, Angela Galambia, Patty Gray, Jeff Green, Jennifer Harrington, Taeyoung Kim, Mary Jane Landaker, Linda Nobles, Rebecca Nunn, Susie Ostmeyer, Nan Perrin, Matt Ramsey, Joan Robbins, Sandra Salem, Luchara Sayles-Wallace, Amanda Tyrell, Joe Vitt, and Rebecca and Reneee Williams. Each contributed to the book by reading and critiquing it, and each contributed to the website by offering questions, many of which (as adapted by the authors of the book) found their way into the website. To teach is to learn twice. Rud is grateful to have learned from these students.

LIST OF FIGURES AND TABLES

Figures

Tables

Part One

Introduction to the American Legal System and Education and Related Laws

Chapter 1

Introduction to the American Legal System

Case on Point: Jay Turnbull

When Jay Turnbull was born at Johns Hopkins Hospital in 1967, his disability was apparent to all: His brain protruded from the fontenel in his skull, indicating that he had either hydrocephalus or megacephalus, both of which result in mental retardation.

Jay spent some of his early years at home and some in a private residential school. After he returned home, he was in separate, segregated special education programs for all but one of his school years, even though the federal special education law was signed when he was 8 years old. The one year he was not in separate schooling was his last year in high school. That year, he had a separate curriculum but was assistant manager of his school's varsity football team, which earned him a varsity sports "letter."

In his early postsecondary years, Jay was in a sheltered workshop and group home, then moved into supported employment and a home of his own. He has worked at the University of Kansas for 17 years, lived in his own home for 16 years, and participates as he wants in his community. In all of his work, residential living, and community participation, he has had the support of family, friends, and professionals. That outcome is unexpected but important, as the following story-within-a-case makes clear.

* * *

When Jay's father met with President Bill Clinton in 1995 to celebrate the fifth anniversary of the signing of the Americans with Disabilities Act, he told the president that, despite being advised to institutionalize Jay and to keep him in special education and sheltered living and work, he found that it was better for Jay, and for all of those involved with Jay, to integrate him as fully as possible with as much support as he needed.

He concluded by saying, "President Clinton, I want you to know that Jay Turnbull is now paying taxes and paying your salary. That's an outcome that no one predicted and that the law and a lot of careful support made possible."

The president responded with his familiar "Yes!", accompanied by his clenched-fist, arm-thrust-toward-the-sky gesture—a gesture that celebrates more than Jay's life. It is a testament to the power of law and practice.

THE PRINCIPLES OF FEDERALISM AND SEPARATION OF POWERS

In this chapter we introduce two principles of government that profoundly shape how students with disabilities—students like Jay Turnbull—receive their education. These principles are federalism and the separation of powers. Then we describe how those principles operate through legislation (who makes the law), regulation (who prescribes how to implement it), and interpretation (who adjudicates disputes about the meaning and application of the law). If you understand the two principles and how law is made, regulations promulgated, and cases decided, you will have the background to more fully appreciate our country's system for educating students with disabilities.

Federalism

The principle of federalism holds that the federal and state governments share responsibilities for governing. Thus, the term *federalism* describes the allocation of duties and responsibilities among federal and state governments. Two components are the reservation of powers and federal supremacy of the laws.

Reservation of Powers

Federalism recognizes that, under the Constitution of the United States, the federal government is limited and has only those powers that the Constitution expressly grants to it. Among those powers is the power, under the Fourteenth Amendment, to enforce the Constitution and its guarantees that everyone is equal under the law (the guarantee of equal protection) and that governments will deal fairly with people (the guarantee of due process).

> No State shall make or enforce any law which shall abridge the privileges or immunities of citizens of the United States; nor shall any State deprive any person of life, liberty, or property, without due process of law; nor deny to any person within its

jurisdiction the equal protection of the laws. (excerpts from the
Fourteenth Amendment, ratified 1868)

The Constitution, having limited the power of the federal government, then provides that all powers not given to federal government directly, including the power and duty to provide for the education of its citizens, are reserved by the states. This allocation of powers to the states is known as the *reservation of powers*. The states reserve for themselves the powers that are not granted explicitly to the federal government.

Federal Supremacy of the Laws

The federal Constitution and laws prevail over state constitutions and laws. This doctrine is called *federal supremacy of the laws*. The consequence of the supremacy doctrine is that state and local education agencies and other governmental entities must comply with the federal Constitution and federal laws when the Constitution and federal laws conflict with state and local laws. Accordingly, state and local education agencies are obliged to comply with the Constitution's equal protection and due process doctrines and with the federal special education and antidiscrimination laws that we describe in this and subsequent chapters.

Given the limited powers of the federal government, the reservation of powers to the states, the seemingly unlimited role of state governments for educating children, and the supremacy doctrine, the question nowadays is this: What is the federal government's role in educating students with and without disabilities? The answer lies in an understanding of the role of the federal government in enforcing the Constitution, which applies to all states, and enacting laws to enforce the Constitution.

Federal Laws

There are three kinds of federal laws.

1. The Constitution of the United States and especially, as far as the education of students with disabilities is concerned, the Fourteenth Amendment, which guarantees equal protection and due process to all citizens.
2. The laws that Congress enacts pursuant to its authority under the Constitution. The federal special education law, Individuals with Disabilities Education Act (IDEA), is one such law.
3. The regulations that an executive agency promulgates to implement the laws that Congress has enacted. That agency is the U.S. Department of Education, acting through its Office of Special Education Programs (OSEP). The Constitution justifies and is more powerful than federal statutes (IDEA), and those statutes in turn justify regulations that must not be inconsistent with the Constitution or the statutes themselves.

Three Types of Federal Laws

- The Constitution is the most powerful of all laws.
- It justifies statutes, which must not be inconsistent with (must conform to) the Constitution.
- They justify regulations, which must not be inconsistent with (must conform to) the Constitution and the statute they implement.

Likewise, there are three different kinds of state laws.

1. Each state has a constitution, which provides that the state may or must educate the children in that state.
2. Each state has a legislature that enacts the state's education laws, and an executive agency, often called a Department of Education or Department of Public Instruction (state education agency), that implements the law and regulates its application in the schools (local education agencies).
3. At the most basic level of government, local school boards (the local education agencies) derive their authority from state law but must comply with the federal Constitution, federal laws, and state laws.

Figure 1-1 illustrates the relationship between the federal, state, and local governments and their education agencies. Under the supremacy doctrine, federal laws prevail over state and local laws. Under state constitutions, state laws prevail over local laws. (See also pages 9 and 10 for more about hierarchies.)

Relationship of Federalism to Special Education

You may well ask: How does the principle of federalism relate to special education? The answer begins by recognizing that the federal government is a government of limited power and that the states have reserved to themselves all powers not granted

Federal	*State*	*Local*
Constitution	Constitution	Charter
Statutes	Statutes	Ordinances
Regulations	Regulations	Regulations

FIGURE 1.1
The Federal System

by the Constitution to the federal government. The answer then also recognizes that the tradition of local control of education persists even today.

Finally, the answer recognizes that the states and their laws are subject to the federal supremacy doctrine. Thus, local education agencies still have the duty to carry out the laws, face-to-face with students. But they must do so consistent with state law and, more to the point, consistent with federal laws and the federal Constitution as interpreted by the United States Supreme Court.

For example, when the U.S. Supreme Court, in *Brown vs. Board of Education* (1954), ordered racial desegregation in education, state education agencies (SEAs) and local education agencies (LEAs) were required to comply. *Brown* thus federalized education in the 1950s. It determined who will go to school with whom.

The issue today in special and general education is this: How much authority for educating students with and without disabilities should state education agencies (SEAs) and local education agencies (LEAs) have, and what should be the role of the federal government? Let's ask the question in a different way: What is the proper role in education, under federalism, for the federal government?

That question addresses the balance of federal and state/local power and responsibility. This balance is manifest in education issues such as whether the federal government may regulate school safety (for example, weapons or drugs near or on school grounds), the curriculum and how students will demonstrate that they have mastered it, and teachers' qualifications.

In special education, the current debate is whether the federal special education law (the Individuals with Disabilities Education Act, IDEA) or the federal general education law (the No Child Left Behind Act, NCLB) strike an acceptable balance for federal, state, and local control of education. As we will point out in chapter 3, these two laws govern a great deal about students' education. To a great extent, they supersede SEAs' and LEAs' power and responsibility in education, and they also impose responsibilities on the SEAs and LEAs. Both extend the federalization of education that began with *Brown*. Now it's not just a matter of who goes to school with whom (*Brown*) but where and how all students are educated (their curriculum and teachers' competency) and the outcomes they will achieve (IDEA and NCLB).

Let's relate these concepts to Jay Turnbull. When he was eligible to go to school at age 6, there was no federal law, such as IDEA, to assure that he would be entitled to go to school—that is, to be treated the same as students without disabilities (*equal protection*). There was no federal law to assure that his parents would be able to challenge an LEA that excluded him or, if it admitted him, segregated him (*due process*). And there was no federal law specifying the outcomes of his education (such as integrated work, residence, and participation).

As Jay grew older, Congress enacted IDEA and other laws that we will describe in chapter 3. Therefore, if Jay were born today, the state and local education agencies responsible for educating him would be governed by the federal laws as well as by their own laws. Jay would have a much better opportunity to go to school with peers who do not have disabilities and to attain, earlier in his adult years, the life that he finally now enjoys.

Separation of Powers

Under the principle of separation of powers, no single branch of government should have more power than any other branch. There must be a balance of power, or checks and balances, among the three branches—namely, the legislative, executive, and judicial branches at the federal and state levels. Figure 1.2 illustrates the separation of powers doctrine.

1. The role of the *legislative branch* is to authorize action that various governmental agencies may take and to appropriate funds so those agencies can carry

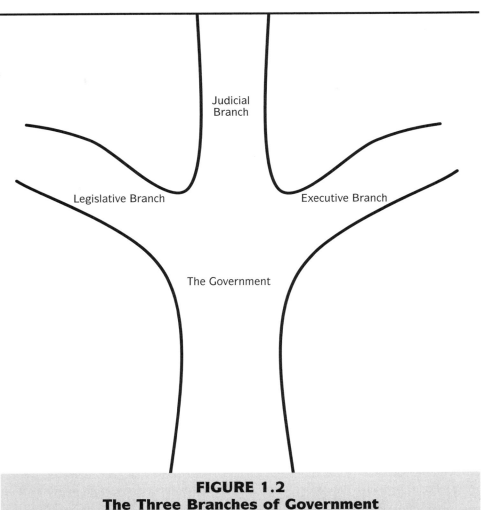

Judicial
Branch

Legislative Branch

Executive Branch

The Government

FIGURE 1.2
The Three Branches of Government

out their duties under the authorizing laws. Thus, for example, Congress enacts IDEA and NCLB and funds federal, state, and local education agencies. (We will describe the funding in chapter 3.)

2. The role of the *executive branch* (the president and the federal executive departments and the states' respective governors and their executive agencies) is to propose a budget (the legislative branch responds to the executive budget and appropriates whatever it believes is proper) and to promulgate and enforce regulations consistent with the authorizing laws. Thus, for example, the U.S. Department of Education and state education agencies promulgate regulations to enforce IDEA and NCLB.

3. The role of the *judicial branch* is to interpret and apply the federal or state constitutions and the federal or state laws. Thus, for example, the U.S. Supreme Court decided *Brown* under the federal Constitution, and it has decided various special education cases to interpret IDEA.

Relationship of Separation of Powers to Special Education

Again, you may well ask: How does the doctrine of separation of powers relate to special education? One answer is this: For you to understand how special education is provided and what its outcomes are, you have to know how these three branches of government operate (how they are "separate" but "equal" in their powers and responsibilities). A second answer is this: To understand special education law, you must understand the statutes that the legislature enacts, the regulations that executive agencies promulgate, and the decisions that courts make.

In this book we concentrate on the federal statutes and regulations (IDEA and, to a lesser degree, NCLB) and the courts' decisions (especially those of the U.S. Supreme Court). You will learn that the statutes, regulations, and decisions together constitute "the law," that there is a powerful interaction between Congress and the Court (separation of powers) and among these federal agencies and the SEAs and LEAs (federalism), and that you have to be able to read the statutes, the regulations, and the decisions to understand special education law.

The Hierarchy of Laws

Finally, there is a hierarchy of laws. Some laws are more powerful than others, as we pointed out on page 6.

1. The *federal Constitution*, as interpreted by the U.S. Supreme Court, is the most powerful of all laws. It governs the federal government and also the state and local governments.

2. *Statutes* (enacted by Congress at the federal level and by legislatures at the state level), the second most powerful laws, must derive their authority from the federal Constitution and from respective state constitutions. If there is a conflict between a constitution and a statute, the constitution prevails.

3. The *laws and ordinances* enacted by local governments, too, must not conflict with the federal Constitution or a federal law or with a state constitution or state law. If they do, the other laws prevail.

Rarely does Congress or even a state legislature enact a law that covers with sufficient specificity all of the individuals or entities to which it applies. Accordingly, executive agencies issue regulations to assist governed individuals and entities to know how to comply with a law. The agencies' power to promulgate regulations derives from the laws (statutes), and the regulations that they promulgate must be consistent with, and not conflict with, the statute they implement or with any applicable constitution.

Hierarchy of Laws

1. Constitutional law

   - Federal Constitution (especially Fifth and Fourteenth Amendments)
   - State constitution (especially provisions about education)
   - Local charter (especially provisions creating schools or school boards)

2. Legislature (legislative body)

   - Congress (e.g., IDEA)
   - State (e.g., equal educational opportunities legislation)
   - Local (e.g., school board policies establishing programs for children)

3. Regulations (executive agency)

   - Federal (Special Education Programs, Office of Special Education and Rehabilitative Services)
   - State (e.g., Kansas State Board of Education)
   - Local (e.g., director of pupil services or coordinator of special education)

"READING" THE LAW

We will demonstrate how to read the law through passages from IDEA and a court decision.

Reading IDEA

After Congress enacts a law and the president signs it, it is *codified*. That means it is placed into the United States Code, which contains all federal laws. That's where you will find IDEA.

How will you find it and, after you find it, what will you find? You must begin by understanding that the U.S. Code is organized by subject matter. All laws related to education are in Title 20. Thus, you begin finding IDEA by going to Title 20.

In Title 20 you will find still further categories. IDEA is in Title 20, Chapter 33. IDEA itself is divided into four Parts (A, B, C, and D), and each Part is divided into Sections and Subsections.

So when we cite (refer to) IDEA, we do it by Title, Part, Section, and Subsection, as follows, with the Title (that is, the volume of the U.S. Code) preceding the words "U.S. Code," and the Part, Sections, and Subsections thereafter. For example, here is the first citation to IDEA:

> 20 U.S. Code
> Part A, General Provisions
> Section 1400 [Short Title, Table of Contents, Findings, Purposes]
> Subsection (a) [Short Title] (Individuals with Disabilities Education Act)

As we said, IDEA consists of four Parts:

> Part A, General Provisions, Sections 1400–1410
> Part B, Assistance for Education of All Children with Disabilities, Sections 1411–1419
> Part C, Infants and Toddlers with Disabilities, Sections 1431–1444
> Part D, National Activities to Improve Education of Children with Disabilities, Sections 1451–1482

Having found IDEA and its provisions, how will you read and understand it? The simple answer is this: Every word carries a meaning, and every word is important. For example, read 20 U.S.C. Sec. 1400(c), "Findings," as follows:

> Disability is a natural part of the human experience and in no way diminishes the right of individuals to participate in or contribute to society. Improving educational results for children with disabilities is an essential element of our national policy of ensuring equality of opportunity, full participation, independent living, and economic self-sufficiency for individuals with disabilities. (IDEA, Section 1400(c)(1))

Having read that section carefully, you will conclude that it expresses these concepts:

- Disability is a natural, not an abnormal, part of human life.
- Disability itself does not justify limitations on people's rights.
- Among those rights is the right to participate in, or contribute to, society.
- Our national policy includes the improvement of educational results for students with disabilities; outcomes are important. The outcomes are
  - equal opportunities, including those to be educated;
  - full participation (the right to participate and contribute);

      ☐ independent living; and

      ☐ economic self-sufficiency.

If that is not what you gathered from reading the excerpt from IDEA, you did not pay attention to our admonition that every word in a statute carries a meaning and is significant and that you, therefore, must read IDEA carefully.

You will note that IDEA does not define the four outcomes we stated above. That's a problem. Sometimes Congress will define its terms. For example, it defines "special education" (20 U.S.C. Sec. 1400(29)). Sometimes, however, it will not, usually when it wants to declare general principles or outcomes and leave their meaning to be determined through regulations, research, or practice.

Similarly, the Department of Education regulations are codified into the Code of Federal Regulations ("C.F.R.") and, for IDEA, are in Title 34, Part 300, Section 300 *et seq.* ("and following").

Reading a Court's Decision

When lawyers talk about disputes that are in or have gone to court, they call those disputes *cases*. Thus, they speak about the case called *Brown v. Board of Education* (the 1954 school desegregation case). They call the people or entities involved in the case *litigants* or *parties*. Typically, they refer to the case by the name of the first party; thus, *Brown* refers to the school desegregation case and is always italicized when written to indicate that the author is referring to the case, not to any of the parties. Thus, they will talk about the *Brown* decision by referring to the family name of the person (party) who brought the case (sued the school board). Finally, they call the court's conclusion of who "wins" a *decision* or *opinion*.

Just as you have to read a statute carefully, paying attention to every word, so you have to read a decision/opinion the same way. Judges make that easier by, typically, organizing their decisions as follows:

1. Statement of the issue before the court
2. Statement of the facts
3. Statement of the law that applies to the facts
4. Application of the law to the facts
5. Statement of the court's *judgment* or *holding* (which party wins)

For example, in *Brown,* the *issue* was whether state and local education agencies that segregate students by race thereby deny the equal protection of the law to Black students. The *facts* were that state and local laws and practices required racial segregation and that the effects of segregation were to deny equal educational opportunities to Black students. The *law* that the Court applied was the Fourteenth Amendment's equal protection clause: No state shall deprive any person of the equal protection of its laws. In the Court's *application of that law to the facts*, it concluded that racial segregation violated the Constitution. The *judgment* or *holding* was that state and local education agencies had to desegregate with all due deliberate speed.

Judges often do not state the principle of the case—that is, the principle of law that their decision advances. That duty falls on lawyers and scholars. In *Brown,* the principle is that governments (state and local education agencies) may not use a person's unalterable trait, such as race (or sex or disability), as the basis for imposing a burden that they do not also impose on other people, or sometimes for unjustifiably granting a benefit that they also do not grant to other people. In this book, we will teach you about the cases—issues, facts, law, holdings, and principles—that interpret IDEA or other federal disability laws and that have been the most influential on schools and students with disabilities.

As is true for the federal statutes, so it is for the federal cases. They are *reported* in a *reporter* (a volume that includes the courts' decisions/opinions). For example, the decisions of the U.S. Supreme Court are reported in the *United States Reporter* (a publication of the federal government, cited as U.S.) and in the *Supreme Court Reporter* (also a publication of the federal government, cited as Sup. Ct.). Thus, with respect to the first IDEA case that the Court decided, the decision is cited as follows:

Board of Education v. Rowley, 458 U.S. 176, 102 S. Ct. 3034 (1982)

Likewise, the decisions of the federal courts of appeal, called Circuit Courts of Appeals, are reported in the *Federal Reporter* and are referenced as follows:

Rowley v. Board of Education, 632 F. 2d 945 (1st. Cir., 1980)

The decisions of the federal trial courts, called *district courts*, are reported in the *Federal Reporter* and are referenced as follows:

Rowley v. Board of Education, 483 F. Supp. 528 (E.D.N.Y., 1980)

Note that we italicize the name of the case, to make clear that we are talking about the decision, not one of the parties in the case. We call this the *Rowley* decision because that is the name of the student who brought the case against a board of education. And we place the volume of the reporter (458) in front of the abbreviated name of the reporter (*U.S. Supreme Court Reports*), the page at which the decision begins after the name of the reporter, and the date of the decision in parentheses.

The U.S. Supreme Court decides only a few cases each year. Most of the cases that interpret IDEA are decided by lower federal or state courts. Referring to the *Brown* decision, Figure 1-3 illustrates the court system, showing the lowest courts—called district courts—where the case is first heard (*tried* with witnesses), that the decisions there can be appealed to *appellate courts*, called *circuit courts*, and that those decisions can be appealed to the U.S. Supreme Court.

SUMMARY

Two principles that govern law-making are federalism and separation of powers. The roles of the legislative, executive, and judicial branches of government are,

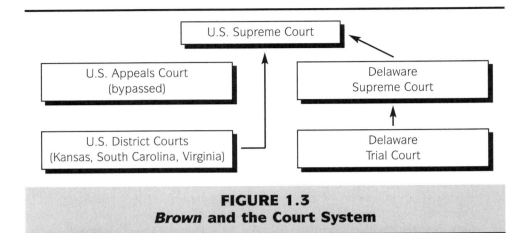

FIGURE 1.3
***Brown* and the Court System**

respectively, to enact laws, promulgate regulations, and interpret and apply laws and regulations to cases.

Four outcomes of federal disability policy are as follows:

- Equal opportunities, including those to be educated
- Full participation (the right to participate and contribute)
- Independent living
- Economic self-sufficiency

It is now appropriate for us to take you to the next stage of your education—an understanding of federal disability policy.

Before we do, let's return to the case in point. If Jay Turnbull were born in 2006 rather than 39 years earlier, he would be educated much differently than he was. The outcomes that he attained would be clear and advanced by policy, programs, and funding, from the beginning of his education, and not the result that his family and devoted professionals had to struggle to obtain.

Law can make a huge difference for anyone with a disability, but unless the person has advocates devoted to him or her, the outcomes may be elusive and, indeed, unacceptable. In Jay's case, law, advocacy, and outcomes have made all the difference.

Chapter 2

Federal Disability Policy

Case on Point: *Brown v. Board of Education of Topeka*
348 U.S. 886, 72 S. Ct. 120 (1954)

Before *Brown,* state and local education agencies could legally segregate students by race. Yet, that sort of legality seemed to many to violate the equal protection guarantee of the Fourteenth Amendment.

In *Brown,* the Court invalidated those laws and practices. The Court began by reviewing its many decisions authorizing separate but equal accommodations for White and Black students. The Court said that the issue is not whether separate and equal accommodations are constitutional simply because there is equalization. The Court "must look instead to the effect of segregation itself on public education." Taking that focus—namely, the effect of segregation per se—the Court proceeded to hold "separate but equal" to be a violation of the equal protection clause of the Fourteenth Amendment. Its reasoning was clear and applies to students with disabilities. For this to become clear, substitute "students with disabilities" for the Court's word "Negro":

> Today, education is perhaps the most important function of state and local governments. Compulsory school attendance laws and the great expenditures for education both demonstrate our recognition of the importance of education to our democratic society. It is required in the performance of our

> most basic public responsibilities, even service in the armed forces. It is the very foundation of good citizenship. Today it is a principal instrument in awakening the child to cultural values, in preparing him for later professional training, and in helping him to adjust normally to his environment. In these days, it is doubtful that any child may reasonably be expected to succeed in life if he is denied the opportunity of an education. Such an opportunity, where the state has undertaken to provide it, is a right which must be made available to all in equal terms.

Having ascribed such great value to education, the Court then asked: What is the effect of segregation on Black students (students with disabilities) in such a valued service? The answer was clear: To separate Black students (students with disabilities) from others of similar age and qualifications solely because of their race (disability) generates a feeling of inferiority as to their status in the community that may affect their hearts and minds in a way unlikely ever to be undone.

Given the importance of education and the stigmatizing effect of segregation, the Court then announced its holding:

> We conclude that in the field of public education the doctrine of "separate but equal" has no place. Separate educational facilities are inherently unequal. Therefore, we hold that the plaintiffs and others similarly situated for whom the actions have been brought are, by reason of the segregation complained of, deprived of the equal protection of the laws guaranteed by the Fourteenth Amendment.

Why is *Brown* relevant to your understanding of special education law? That is a question we will now answer.

BROWN AND ITS SIGNIFICANCE FOR SPECIAL EDUCATION

Undoubtedly, *Brown* was the most significant education-law decision ever written by the Supreme Court—or any other court, for that matter. This is so for many reasons:

- *Brown* illustrates the principle that the federal Constitution, as interpreted by the U.S. Supreme Court, is the supreme law of the land, is binding on all federal, state, and local governments, and is the precedent that all federal and state courts must follow in subsequent similar cases.
- *Brown* is a nearly perfect example of one of the major lessons of this book: All educational issues (such as the educational rights of students with disabilities)

are essentially political policy and social issues cast in the guise of constitutional litigation (Should those students be educated and, if so, how, with whom, and by whom?) and, because they are presented in the garments of the law, they ultimately are resolved by the courts.

- *Brown* demonstrates that the truly difficult educational issues also are fought on various civil rights battlefields. Just as *Brown* was the first successful case on the battlefield of racial desegregation of schools, so it was the seed that gave birth to other civil rights battles and to successful challenges to governmental discrimination against persons because of their unalterable personal characteristics (such as race, sex, and disability). *Brown* gave rise to the right to education for children with disabilities and to other rights for people with disabilities. The point—so obvious, yet so important—is that judicial resolution of educational issues on constitutional grounds becomes a precedent for judicial resolution of other civil rights issues on similar constitutional grounds.

- *Brown* gave immense comfort and support to civil rights activists, legitimizing their legal arguments and furnishing them with a powerful tool for persuading legislatures, particularly Congress, to enact entitlements and antidiscrimination laws. Case law frequently underpins legislation, and federal cases and legislation frequently precede state case law and legislation. Nowhere has this been truer than in establishing the rights of children with disabilities to an education.

- *Brown* demonstrates that, although the U.S. Constitution never once refers to a public education, the principles of equal protection and due process under the Fifth and Fourteenth Amendments have a significant effect on public education. This fact is crystal clear in the disability right-to-education cases. This is significant because the federal Constitution does not guarantee the right to an education. State constitutions do guarantee this right. But if a state denies (as many had) an education to some students, usually those with disabilities, but provides it to others (usually those without disabilities), the state violates the equal protection doctrine and, depending on the provisions of the state constitution, its own constitution as well (see chapter 1). The essential point of *Brown*, however, is that the states were violating the equal protection clause.

- *Brown* illustrates one kind of lawsuit—the civil action—that is typical of litigation between citizens and their governments. This type of suit is brought by a citizen who alleges that a government or a governmental official denied him or her rights or benefits to which the person is entitled under the law (constitution, statutes, or regulations). In this case, the plaintiff, Brown, sued the defendant, the Topeka (Kansas) Board of Education. A civil action is typical of the right-to-education cases. Criminal actions—in which the state prosecutes a person accused of a crime—are alien to educational law.

- *Brown* is almost ideal for teaching someone how to read a case and how cases are decided, particularly in the right-to-education area. If we substitute "disabled" or "students with disabilities" for "Negro" and "nondisabled" for "white" wherever those words appear in *Brown*, we can understand why

Brown is important to the education of students with disabilities and how the Fourteenth Amendment became the constitutional basis for the rights of students with disabilities to be educated.

What are the controlling facts of the case? In the language of the 1950s, Negro students are denied admission to schools attended by Whites under laws requiring or permitting segregation according to race, and racial segregation in public education is inherently damaging to the educational opportunities of Negro children.

What are the allegations? The facts prove a denial of equal protection of law as guaranteed by the Fourteenth Amendment because segregated public schools are not, and cannot be made, equal.

What are the issues of law the Court must resolve? The Court must determine whether the doctrine of separate-but-equal education and whether segregation, under that doctrine, violate the equal protection clause.

What is the Court's holding (answer to the issue)? Segregation solely on the basis of race in the public schools violates equal protection and denies minority (Negro) children an equal educational opportunity.

What is the Court's reasoning? Equal educational opportunities are denied when, in light of (1) the importance of education, (2) the stigmatizing effects of racial segregation, and (3) the detrimental consequences of racial segregation on the education of those against whom segregation is practiced, a state segregates by race. The effects of stigma—a negative connotation socially ascribed to a specific group of individuals and to all members of that group—are precisely the challenges that IDEA and other federal disability laws were enacted to overcome. Where there is stigma, there inevitably will be discrimination. Where there are laws that prohibit discrimination and entitle individuals (who are stigmatized and discriminated against) to be integrated, there are opportunities for equality and the removal of stigma and the elimination of discrimination.

What is the Court's order? The cases are to be argued again before the Court, and the argument should focus on the nature of the remedy the Court should order.

What is the principle of the case? State action in segregating the races in public education violates equal protection and, by extension, any state-required or state-sanctioned segregation solely because of a person's unalterable characteristic (race or disability) is usually unconstitutional.

What is the public policy in the case? State-created stigma or badges of inferiority based on race (or other characteristics, such as disabilities) are constitutionally intolerable because they mean that the state acts invidiously (i.e., discriminatorily, by denying equal opportunities) with respect to persons who have certain traits, such as race or disability. In brief, invidious (discriminatory) action is unconstitutional.

Whose interests are at issue? The interests or claims of Blacks to an equal educational opportunity are at issue.

Finally, what functions of government are at issue? At issue are the functions of education—namely, cultural assimilation, preparation for participation in the political process, and training so economic opportunities might become available.

Given the interests, the functions could not be parceled out or denied solely according to race.

Brown is worth an extended discussion here because it speaks directly to public schools, special education, and children with disabilities. The *Brown* plaintiffs and children with disabilities had undeniable similarities.

- Both proved that they had been denied equal educational opportunities.
- Both alleged an unconstitutional denial and based their arguments on equal protection principles.
- Both challenged segregation in education.
- Both found comfort in the holding of *Brown* and the right-to-education cases concerning denials of equality.
- Both were strengthened by the reasoning that relies on concepts of stigma and detrimental educational consequences.
- Both successfully advanced a public policy against invidious state action.
- Both had similar interests in obtaining an education.
- Both laid claim to the functions of the schools to educate meaningfully all students.

We have said that *Brown* is significant because it brought the federal government into public education, an area of government that had belonged almost exclusively to state and local education agencies and because it was the precedent on which students with disabilities relied to create their own right to an education. To make our point, we describe below the federal laws that affect students' education.

A BRIEF (RECENT) HISTORY OF FEDERAL DISABILITY LAWS

Brown federalized education in two other respects:

1. It caused Congress to enact various civil rights laws aimed at eliminating discrimination based on race.
2. It prompted Congress to examine just how inadequately state and local education agencies accommodated students' civil rights claims and to respond by improving the agencies' capacity to educate all students together, without regard to race or disability.

Federal Education Laws

Not until 1966 did Congress became involved in any major way in the education of students with disabilities. Thereafter, as Table 2.1 illustrates, Congress has enacted several important laws. The laws identified in the table assist state and local educational agencies in educating students with disabilities.

TABLE 2.1
Federal Education Laws Benefiting Students With Disabilities

Act	What It Did
Elementary and Secondary Education Act of 1965 **(originally 20 U.S.C. Secs. 3801-3900, now 20 U.S.C. 7801)**	
1966: Title III to 1966 ESEA Amendments (P.L. 89-750)	Established a program of federal grants to the states to assist them to educate students with disabilities
1970: Title III to 1970 ESEA Amendments (P.L. 91-230)	Replaced 1966 law with similar but updated federal grant-in-aid program
1974: Title VI to 1974 ESEA Amendments (P.L. 93-380)	Amended 1970 law; established goal of "full educational opportunities for all children with disabilities"
1994: Goals 2000: Educate America Act (P.L. 103-227)	Set national goals that led to postsecondary employment for all students
1994: Improving America's Schools Act (P.L. 103-382)	Provided for reform of public education, outcomes-based accountability and assessment of schools, and linkages between general and special education
2001: No Child Left Behind Act of 2001 (P.L. 107-110)	Established six principles for educating all students and for improving all schools (general education reform)
Education for All Handicapped Children Act of 1975 (P.L. 94-142), as amended, reauthorized, and renamed Individuals with Disabilities Education Act, 20 U.S.C. Secs. 1400 *et seq.*	
1975: Education for All Handicapped Children Act (P.L. 94-142)	Established full appropriate public education doctrine (FAPE) and six principles for educating all students with disabilities (see chapters 4 through 9 for discussion of the six principles)
1978: Education Amendments of 1978 (P.L. 95-561)	Provided statutory direction to schools funded or operated by the Bureau of Indian Affairs
1983: Education of the Handicapped Act Amendment of 1983 (P.L. 98-199)	Expanded incentives for preschool special education programs, early intervention, and transitioning programs
1986: Handicapped Children's Protection Act (P.L. 99-372)	Authorized recovery of attorneys' fees and undid the court's decision in *Smith v. Robinson,* 468 U.S. 992, 104 S. Ct. 3457 (1984) (see chapter 10)

TABLE 2.1
(continued)

Act	What It Did
1986: Education of the Handicapped Act Amendments of 1986 (P.L. 99-457)	Authorized Part C (infants and toddlers)
1990: Individuals with Disabilities Education Act (P.L. 101-476)	Guaranteed that all children with disabilities have available to them a free appropriate public education emphasizing special education and related services designed to meet their needs
1997: Individuals with Disabilities Education Act Amendments of 1997 (P.L. 105-17)	Established framework for current discipline provisions (see chapter 4) and preserved the right of the prevailing party to recover attorneys' fees (see chapter 10)
2004: Individuals with Disabilities Education Improvement Act (P.L. 108-446)	Reauthorized IDEA and significantly changed provisions related to discipline, evaluation, appropriate education, and procedural due process (but not parent participation)

Family Educational Rights and Privacy Act of 1974 (FERPA, P.L. 93-380, 20 U.S.C. 1232g)

Higher Education Amendments of 1998 (P.L. 105-244)	Provided for parental and student (at age of majority) consent related to access to and release of educational records; was incorporated into IDEA and therefore applies specifically to students with disabilities

Federal Antidiscrimination Laws

Other federal laws prohibit state and local governments and private-sector entities from discriminating against people who have disabilities, solely on the basis of their disability, if they are otherwise qualified to participate in a regulated activity, such as education.

Rehabilitation Act of 1973, as amended in 1974 (P.L. 93-651, 29 U.S.C. Sec. 794) (commonly called "Section 504"), prohibits discrimination solely on the basis of disability against any otherwise qualified individual with a disability in any program or activity receiving federal assistance.

Americans with Disabilities Act of 1990 (P.L. 101-336, 42 U.S.C. Secs. 12101 *et seq.*) prohibits discrimination solely on the basis of disability against any otherwise qualified individual with a disability in employment, public services, public accommodations, transportation, and telecommunications.

Federal Entitlement and Benefit Laws

In addition to assisting state and local educational agencies and prohibiting them and other government and private entities from engaging in disability-based discrimination, Congress also has enacted laws that create entitlements and grant benefits to individuals with disabilities. Table 2.2 illustrates this approach.

Justifications for Federal Laws

What justifies Congress's action?

1. *Brown v. Board of Education*: The federal government has the power and duty to enforce the federal Constitution, particularly the Fourteenth Amendment and its guarantees of *equal protection* and *due process*, through antidiscrimination laws.
2. The principle of *federalism*: Under that principle, as you learned in chapter 1, the federal and state and local governments share power, but the federal Constitution and laws are supreme in matters affecting all of the nation's citizens. As part of the sharing of power, the federal government assists state and local education agencies in educating students with disabilities, thereby complying with the federal constitution (equal protection) and their own state constitutions and laws.
3. Recognition that individuals with disabilities require special assistance, in the form of *entitlements and benefits*, so they can attain the nation's four disability policy goals of equal opportunities, full participation, independent living, and economic self-sufficiency.
4. The types of *discrimination* that state and local education agencies imposed on students with disabilities, the reasons for the discrimination, and the reasons why Congress appropriately enacted the federal laws.

An ancient legal maxim proclaims that if the reason for a law no longer exists, the law itself no longer should exist. Bearing in mind the reason-and-existence maxim, let's now turn to why state and local education agencies discriminated against students with disabilities.

PRELUDES TO IDEA: DISCRIMINATION IN EDUCATION

Types of Discrimination

When Congress first enacted IDEA (as P.L. 94-142, Education for All Handicapped Children Act—now renamed IDEA), it found as a matter of fact that state and local educational authorities had discriminated against students with disabilities in at least two significant ways.

1. *Exclusion.* The agencies had entirely excluded those students from school, not allowing them to enroll, much less attend school. This practice, known as *pure*

TABLE 2.2
Major Federal Entitlement Laws Benefiting
Individuals With Disabilities

Act	What It Did
Social Security Act (Title 42 U.S.C.)	
Title V (Maternal and Child Health Services Block Grant, 42 U.S.C. 701 *et seq.*)	Authorized federal grants to states to prevent disabilities and serve mothers and infants through family-centered, community-based, coordinated services such as immunization, genetic counseling, and rehabilitative services
Title XVI (Supplemental Security Income, 42 U.S.C. 1381 *et seq.*)	Authorized cash transfers to families and adults on the basis of poverty and severe disability
Title XVIII (Medicare, 42 U.S.C. 1395 *et seq.*)	Provided for federal health-care assistance to elderly and disabled individuals
Title XIX (Medicaid, 42 U.S.C. 1396 *et seq.*)	Authorized grants to states to maintain high standards in institutions for people with disabilities and to provide for home- and community-based care for them; Early & Periodic Screening Diagnosis and Treatment (EPSDT) is provided for in 42 U.S.C. 1396d; Katie Beckett waivers are authorized in 1915(c)
Title XX (Social Services Block Grant, 42 U.S.C. 1397 *et seq.*)	Authorized grants to state and local social service agencies to prevent inappropriate institutionalization, foster self-sufficiency in families, and prevent or intervene in cases of abuse, neglect, and exploitation
Title XXI (State Child Health Insurance Program, 42 U.S.C. 1397aa)	Authorized grants to states to provide child-health assistance to uninsured, low-income children and to provide preventive and primary care (immunization, well-baby, and well-child care)
Health-Care Programs	
Children's and Communities Mental Health Systems Improvement Act of 1991 (42 U.S.C. Secs. 290ff *et seq.*)	Authorized grants to states to provide for mental health services (individualized service plans, case management, multidisciplinary service coordination)
Children's Health Act of 2000 (42 U.S.C. Secs. 290bb-39 *et seq.*)	Provided for integrated treatment of children with co-occurring disorders (dual diagnosis)
Health Insurance Portability and Accountability Act (42 U.S.C. Secs. 300gg *et seq.*) and Employee Retirement Income Security Act (29 U.S.C. Secs. 1181 *et seq.*)	Restricted ability of insurers to prolong start of care for preexisting conditions and to disrupt existing care arrangements, provided for privacy of medical records, and provided for portability of health-insurance programs

TABLE 2.2
(continued)

Act	What It Did
Mental Health Parity Act (29 U.S.C. Sec. 1185a)	Required employers to offer or create comparable physical and mental health benefits
Emergency Medical Treatment and Active Labor Act (42 U.S.C. Sec 1395dd)	Required medical treatment facilities to provide stabilizing medical care and not to transfer patients to facilities incapable of providing appropriate treatment

Family Support Programs

Act	What It Did
Adoption Assistance and Child Welfare Act (42 U.S.C. Secs. 620 *et seq.*, including Promoting Safe and Stable Families Program, 42 U.S.C. Secs. 629 *et seq.*)	Authorized grants to states to provide programs of foster care, adoption, family support, and family preservation
Child Abuse Treatment and Prevention Act (42 U.S.C. Sec. 5101)	Authorized grants to states to prevent and treat child abuse and created presumption in favor of medical treatment of individuals (especially children) with disabilities
Family and Medical Leave Act (29 U.S.C. Secs. 2601 *et seq.*)	Obliged employers to grant leave to employees for medical reasons or for child- and family-care reasons

Employment-Related Programs

Act	What It Did
Rehabilitation Act (29 U.S.C. Secs. 701 *et seq.*)	Authorized federal assistances to states for vocational rehabilitation services, including supported employment and independent living
Workforce Investment Partnership Act (29 U.S.C. Secs. 2801 *et seq.*)	Consolidated federal job-training programs and linked them with Rehabilitation Act services
Ticket to Work and Work Incentive Improvement Act (42 U.S.C. Secs. 1320b-19)	Focused on eliminating work disincentives for people with disabilities

State Capacity-Building Programs

Act	What It Did
Developmental Disabilities Assistance and Bill of Rights Act (42 U.S.C. Secs. 15001 *et seq.*)	Authorized grants to states to create protection and advocacy agencies, university-based centers on excellence (service, training, and research), and state-level planning councils
Assistive Technology for Individuals with Disabilities Act (29 U.S.C. Secs. 3001 *et seq.*)	Authorized grants to states to create statewide programs for delivering assistive technology to individuals with disabilities

exclusion, was accompanied by yet another kind of exclusion, called *functional exclusion*—namely, the enrollment and admission of students to schools but the failure to provide them with any real benefit. Thus, the students were in, but not benefiting from, their education. They were in fact functionally excluded from school. The reasons for both pure and functional exclusion lie in the stigma that attaches to disability, the discrimination that results from the stigma, and the lack of laws and services sufficient to overcome the discrimination and counteract the stigma.

2. *Misclassification.* The agencies often misclassified students. Misclassification occurs when an agency wrongly determines that a student has a disability, when the student does not. It also occurs when an agency correctly determines that a student has a disability but wrongly describes the disability. Both forms of misclassification create the same result: the denial of an education based on a correct classification.

The agencies followed other discriminatory practices, but these two—exclusion and misclassification—were the most prevalent. Why, you might ask, did they occur? What were the reasons for the discrimination?

Reasons for Past Discrimination

The many reasons for the discrimination fall into several general categories. The categories reflect several ways of thinking about disability—that is, several "models" or frameworks that people use when they respond to disability (Turnbull & Stowe, 2001).

Human Development Model

The human development model reflects medical, psychological, and educational knowledge about human development. Traditionally, many educators assumed that students with disabilities, especially those with intellectual disabilities such as mental retardation or significant specific learning disabilities, were not able to learn and, thus, had no claim to be included in school.

Further, special education served as an escape hatch for general educators who did not know how, or want to learn how, to teach students with disabilities. The general educators referred students with disabilities to special education and, thus, were no longer responsible for educating them.

Public Studies Model

The public studies model addresses the public policy response to disability and subsumes law, political science and political philosophy, political economy, demographics, public administration, and social welfare. Traditionally, state law did not grant students with disabilities a right to be educated or, if it did, allowed for so many exceptions that many students with disabilities were excluded from the schools.

Further, special education, where it existed, was separate from general education and, for that reason, was relatively out of sight, out of mind, and easy to ignore. The cost of educating students with disabilities was higher than the cost of educating students without disabilities, and, to make matters more difficult, students with disabilities did not have sufficient political clout to secure a right to an education or sufficient funding for such services as might be offered (where they were offered). Where existing laws gave students with disabilities the right to be educated, they were rarely enforced and, therefore, essentially meaningless. Finally, insufficient numbers of special educators and other related professionals were prepared to educate the students. The public capacity was low.

Ethical and Theological Model

The ethical and theological model asks what is right from two different perspectives:

1. The ethical perspective, unrelated to any command by any deity
2. The theological perspective, grounded exclusively on a command by a deity

Far too many people (including especially policy makers and educators) simply believed that nothing was wrong from an ethical or theological perspective in not educating students with a disability. They believed that "less able means less worthy."

Challenges to Past Discrimination

These reasons for discrimination were challenged and changed because of several factors that are best understood inside the models just discussed.

The human development model was transformed in several ways. The science of disability—research on people with disabilities—began to prove that people with disabilities could learn and adapt to "normal" environments. As the science advanced, so did the claims of students with disabilities to be included in schools; there were no longer any scientific reasons to exclude them entirely.

The public law model also changed. Families of students with disabilities began to go public, coming "out of the closet" and describing their and their children's needs as well as the gifts that their children make to their families and others. The family-advocacy movement solidified, with organizations such as The Arc (then, the Association for Retarded Children) and United Cerebral Palsy Associates among the first family-advocacy organizations devoted to creating new services, improving existing services, and advocating at the federal and state/local levels for new policies and new practices.

Parallel to the parent movement, the Great Society programs of Presidents John Kennedy and Lyndon Johnson created new rights and programs for people with disabilities. The wounded veterans of the Vietnam War became powerful advocates for themselves and for everyone else with a disability, creating a hard-to-ignore constituency.

Simultaneously, the federal courts, and then Congress, recognized and acted to correct the deplorable conditions of state institutions and, in doing so, made it less likely that children would be placed into, and kept indefinitely in, the institutions and more likely that they would have to be admitted to school and served there, not in an institution. Federal and state courts increasingly recognized that exclusion, misclassification, and segregation in education violated students' rights to equal protection and placement in the least restrictive environments. The courts' decisions, in turn, spurred disability advocates to press Congress and state legislatures to create a right to an education and to fund that right.

The reality that people with disabilities were discriminated against in housing, transportation, employment, health care, voting, marriage and reproductive opportunities, and community living—the facts of their unwarranted confinement in institutions or correctional facilities, of their denial of the very basic rights that people without disabilities took for granted—caused disability advocates to launch a multipronged frontal attack on those policies and practices and then to use their victories in education as precedents for creating new rights in other arenas (and vice versa).

The cultural studies model addresses disability by studying how people with disabilities are viewed within society. It often merges with the other models because culture itself is an aggregate construct, not a specific one like the other models. Thus, there were new ideologies in law (the constitutional doctrine of equal protection), in politics (the theory of egalitarianism—that everyone should have an equal opportunity to participate in schools and society), and in human services (the theory of normalization—that people with disabilities should be treated as nearly normally as practicable). Further, the language to describe disability changed from "retardate" or "cripple" to "persons with mental retardation" or "persons with a physical disability." As the language changed, so did attitudes and laws.

The technological model is concerned with the "built" or "constructed" environment in which people with disabilities live (an architectural perspective), with the means by which people use technology to overcome the effects of disability (a perspective that takes into account matters such as computers and assistive technologies), and with the capacities of various professions to serve people with disabilities (a perspective that regards professionals as "human" or "soft" technologies). The technology of educating students with disabilities advanced—not just the "hard" technology of devices and curricula but also the "soft" technology of teachers' capacity to teach effectively.

Finally, *the ethical and theological model* changed. Crusading journalists, professionals in the field of mental and emotional/behavioral disabilities, and some policy leaders at the federal and state levels exposed the horrid conditions of state institutions and prodded Congress and state policy makers to reform the institutions and open school doors to children with disabilities. These revelations, the increasingly indefensible exclusion of students with disabilities from schools, and the growing sense that it would be simply "right" for public resources to be devoted to those who had been subjected to discrimination for so long undergirded many of the public policy responses and the right-to-education movement.

In light of all the reasons that agencies discriminated and all the reactions to their discrimination, you may wonder how Congress responded. Before we answer that question, let's consider the concept of a "right" and its corollary "duty." Once you understand about rights and duties, you will understand even better the laws that Congress has enacted.

THE NATURE OF RIGHTS

As we pointed out in chapter 1, and in this chapter, too, Congress responded to discrimination by enacting laws that assist state and local education agencies in educating students with disabilities and that prohibit discrimination. In addition, Congress enacted laws creating an individual entitlement. These laws provide that, if an individual meets certain standards (eligibility criteria), the person is entitled to certain benefits.

Often, these benefits are in the form of *cash transfers*—money the federal government pays directly to the individual, such as Social Security benefits. Cash transfers are often in the form of subsidies for services, such as health-care services. The question now is this: What is the nature of the rights granted by education, antidiscrimination, and entitlement laws? Let's answer that question before turning our attention to the details of the laws themselves.

Positive and Negative Rights

Classifying these responses by thinking in terms of negative rights and positive rights may be helpful.

Special Education and Entitlements as a Positive Right

A positive right confers a benefit. The right to go to school and to have an opportunity to benefit from education is a positive right. Likewise, entitlement laws—cash benefits or subsidies of health care, for example—are laws based on a theory of positive rights.

Antidiscrimination as a Negative Right

A negative right protects a person against the injurious actions of another person or entity. The right not to be discriminated against on the basis of disability alone is a negative right. Section 504 of the Rehabilitation Act and the Americans with Disabilities Act are good examples of laws based on a theory of negative rights.

Rights and Duties

It is axiomatic that there is no right without a corresponding duty. When individuals with a disability have a positive right to attend school, state and local education agencies have a duty to enroll them, classify them correctly, offer an appropriate education, place them in the least restrictive environment, guarantee them a fair (due) process when there are disputes involving their education, and offer them and their parents genuine opportunities to participate in making decisions about their education.

Similarly, when a person with a disability has a negative right not to be subjected to discrimination, state and local education agencies have two types of duty. The first derives from the federal education laws—the duty to carry out the laws to benefit the students. The second derives from the federal antidiscrimination laws—the duty not to discriminate and to offer a reasonable accommodation so the person can benefit from the policies, programs, and practices of the regulated entities.

"Rights and duties" has a nice ring to it. But what happens if an agency that has a duty to a student and the student or his parents disagree about the nature of the agency's duty and the student's rights?

A BRIEF (RECENT) HISTORY OF COURT DISABILITY-RELATED DECISIONS

As you learned in chapter 1, the doctrine of separation of powers means that legislatures (for example, Congress) enact laws but courts (for example, the U.S. Supreme Court) interpret the law when its meaning is in dispute between parties to a case. Table 2.3 illustrates the interaction between Congress and the Court as

TABLE 2.3
U.S. Supreme Court Cases Affecting Students and Adults With Disabilities in Education and Related Circumstances

Case	Related Circumstances
Goss v. Lopez 419 U.S. 565, 95 S. Ct. 729 (1975)	Held that a local education agency must provide at least a rudimentary hearing before disciplining a student (see chapter 4)
Ingraham v. Wright 430 U.S. 651, 97 S. Ct. 1401 (1977)	Held that the cruel and unusual punishment prohibition of the Eighth Amendment does not bar local education agencies from using corporal punishment.
Board of Education v. Rowley 458 U.S. 176, 102 S. Ct. 3034 (1984)	Held that IDEA's "appropriate education" requirement includes a process and an opportunity to benefit (see chapter 6)
Irving Independent School Dist v. Tatro 468 U.S. 883, 104 S. Ct. 3371 (1984)	Required local education agencies to provide the related service of clean intermittent catheterization
Smith v. Robinson 468 U.S. 992, 104 S. Ct. 3457 (1984)	Prohibited parents from recovering attorneys' fees in IDEA cases (Congress later enacted P.L. 99-372, former 20 U.S.C. Sec. 1415(e)(4), clearly authorizing attorneys'-fees recovery) (see chapter 10)

Note: The cases in this table are listed chronologically.

TABLE 2.3
(continued)

Burlington Sch. Comm. v. Massachusetts Dept. of Education 471 U.S. 359 (1985)	Required a local education agency to reimburse parents for the tuition of a private-school education if the local agency does not provide an appropriate education (see chapter 4)
Board of Education v. Arline 480 U.S. 273, 107 S. Ct. 1123 (1987)	Held that a teacher whose tuberculosis was in remission was entitled to the protection of Sec. 504 (the antidiscrimination provision of the Rehabilitation Act) because she had a record of a disability and was regarded as having a disability, and because tuberculosis creates a disability that significantly impairs a major life activity (work) (see chapter 4)
Southeastern Community College v. Davis 442 U.S. 397, 99 S. Ct. 2361 (1987)	Held that the college's refusal to admit a hearing-impaired person to its nursing program did not violate Sec. 504 (the antidiscrimination provision of the Rehabilitation Act) because, even with reasonable accommodations, the person would still be incapable of participating in the program
Bowen v. Massachusetts 487 U.S. 879, 108 S. Ct. 2722 (1988)	Held that states may use Medicaid funds to pay for education-related health-care services for students eligible for Medicaid (see chapter 4)
Honig v. Doe 484 U.S. 305, 108 S. Ct. 592 (1988)	Required local education agencies to adopt "stay put" practice, give hearing related to disciplinary action, determine whether disability is manifest in behavior, and resort to 10-day short-term suspensions as needed for "cooling off" period (see chapter 4)
Franklin v. Gwinnett County Pub. Sch. 503 U.S. 60, 112 S. Ct. 1028 (1992)	Held that a local education agency may be held liable for faculty-on-student sexual harassment (see chapter 10)
Florence County Sch. Dist. Four v. Carter 510 U.S. 7, 114 S. Ct. 361 (1993)	Held that a local education agency must reimburse a parent for tuition paid to a private school (to obtain an appropriate education) even if the private school is not state-certified (see chapter 4)
Davis v. Monroe County Board of Education 526 U.S. 629, 119 S. Ct. 1661 (1999)	Held that a local education agency may be held liable for student-on-student sexual harassment (see chapter 10)
Cedar Rapids Community Sch. Dist. v. Garrett F. 526 U.S. 66, 119 S. Ct. 992 (1999)	Held that a local education agency is the payor of last resort for a student's educationally beneficial health-care services (see chapter 6)
Zelman v. Simmons-Harris 536 U.S. 639, 122 S. Ct. 2460 (2002)	Authorized federal funds to be used to provide education vouchers that parents redeem for parochial education for their children (see chapter 4)

revealed in some of the Court's major cases related to special education. We will explain these cases in much greater detail in later chapters. For now, we simply make the point that the three kinds of laws that Congress enacts—special education access laws, entitlement laws, and antidiscrimination laws—invariably create disputes that the courts must resolve, just as the Supreme Court resolved a dispute over the meaning of the equal protection clause when it decided *Brown*.

To illustrate, let's leave *Brown* and consider *Board of Education v. Rowley* (1982), the Supreme Court's first special education decision. That case began when Amy Rowley's parents filed a complaint against her school district. Amy was deaf, and her parents wanted her to have an interpreter. Her school district refused to pay for an interpreter, and her parents alleged that the district did not comply with IDEA because it did not provide her with an interpreter, which would have enabled her to have a free appropriate public education consistent with IDEA. The complaint was heard (adjudicated) in a *due process hearing* at the local level by an *impartial hearing officer.*

When her parents lost their case before the local and then the state hearing officers, they appealed to the federal trial court. They won there, but the school district appealed to the federal court of appeals. That court sided with Amy, so the school district appealed to the U.S. Supreme Court, which resolved the dispute in favor of the school district (we will discuss *Rowley* in detail in chapter 6). *Rowley* involved a dispute about the meaning of "appropriate education."

Rowley also exemplifies how cases begin (at the due process hearing) and how they wind their way up from the local to a state hearing and then to the courts. Figure 2.1 illustrates that process, beginning with the trial (district) courts.

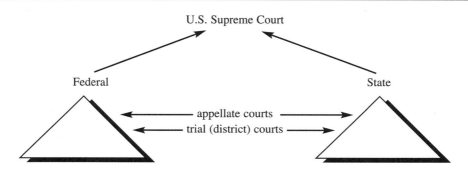

FIGURE 2.1
The Court System and Judicial Review Process

SUMMARY

In this chapter we have briefly reviewed the federal statutes related to the education of students with disabilities, especially IDEA, Sec. 504, and ADA, and we have given a short explanation of the justification for those statutes. We also have summarized the Supreme Court cases related to the education of students with disabilities, using *Rowley* as an example.

Next we will learn about the nature of discrimination and the types of rights that respond to discrimination. Before we do, however, let's return to the case in point. The law as it applies to special education involves the statute (the words Congress uses in the statute) and its interpretation (when parties disagree about the words or their application and the courts decide a case). Only when you approach special education law with a solid understanding of the interaction between Congress and the courts in creating the law will you be able to understand IDEA and apply it to students with disabilities.

Chapter 3

IDEA, Antidiscrimination Laws, and General Education Law

Case on Point: *White v. Western School Corporation*
1985 U.S. Dist. LEXIS 16540 (S.D. Ind., 1985)

Ryan White was a young boy who contracted AIDS as a result of receiving a contaminated blood transfusion. When his parents sought to enroll him in school after he had been diagnosed with having HIV, the local educational agency refused to enroll him. Relying on IDEA and federal antidiscrimination laws, his parents sued to have Ryan re-admitted, eventually winning.

If Ryan had lived, he would have entered school and benefited from IDEA and antidiscrimination laws and from another federal education law, the No Child Left Behind (NCLB) Act. Like IDEA, it is an education law, but it is a general education law, not exclusively a special education law.

How do these laws benefit students with disabilities? That's what you will discover in this chapter.

A BRIEF HISTORY OF IDEA

To gain an understanding of the Individuals with Disabilities Education Act, let's carefully examine its original purposes, more recent controversies, and the major criticisms that led to its reauthorization in 2004.

Original Purposes

Congress's purposes in enacting the Education of All Handicapped Children Act in 1975 (P.L. 94-142, 20 U.S.C. Sec. 1400(d)) were

- to assure the rights of all students with disabilities to a free appropriate public education,
- to protect the rights of the students and their parents in securing such an education,
- to assist state and local education agencies to provide for the education of those students, and
- to assess and assure the effectiveness of state and local efforts to educate those students.

In declaring these purposes, Congress also recognized a broader overarching purpose: to enforce the equal protection clause of the federal Constitution's Fourteenth Amendment (20 U.S.C. Sec. 1400(c)(6) [1975]). As you read in chapter 1, the equal protection clause provides that no state (and thus no local government) may deny anyone the equal protection of the laws. By excluding and misclassifying students with disabilities and thereby treating these students differently than students without disabilities, state and local education agencies were violating the equal protection clause.

Recent Controversies

Over the course of time, Congress amended IDEA, most recently in 2004 (P.L. 108-446). To understand the 2004 amendments, let's begin with a brief review of the 1997 reauthorization (P.L. 105-17), which was surrounded by controversy, principally over two issues:

1. *School discipline.* The debate was whether state and local education agencies have the power to discipline students with disabilities in the same way that they discipline students who do not have disabilities.
2. *The disputes between the agencies and the students and their parents.* The debate was whether the agencies should have to pay the lawyers who represent students and parents when the students and parents prevail (win) in court.

Major Criticisms Driving the 2004 Reauthorization

The controversies did not subside between 1997 and 2004. Indeed, they persisted. Other issues also arose and were expressed in two nearly identical publications: a book that proposed revamping special education for the twenty-first century (Finn, Rothermam, & Hokanson, 2001) and a presidential commission report on improving special education (President's Commission on Excellence in Special Education, 2002). The book and the Commission concluded that both general and special education were ineffective in serving students with disabilities. The book also charged that special education was a major disservice to many students with disabilities, preventing them from becoming effective adults.

The President's Commission announced several findings that reflect the major concerns from the book and that formed the basis for the 2004 reauthorization. These findings are summarized as follows:

- IDEA values process over outcomes and must be reformed to advance student achievement, reduce excessive paperwork, and ensure better outcomes for students with disabilities.
- The current approach to disability, in which schools wait for students to fail before intervening early and powerfully, ignores the value of prevention, early and accurate identification of learning and behavioral problems, and aggressive intervention using research-based approaches. Special education should be available only to students who do not respond to strong and appropriate instruction and methods, offered first in the general education programs.
- General and special education share, together, the responsibility for educating students with disabilities; the students' education is not separable and, indeed, students placed into special education are first and foremost general education students.
- Parents have little recourse and few options when their children with disabilities fail to make progress in special education. Indeed, they often do not feel empowered when the special education system fails their children.
- A "culture of compliance" has developed as a result of the many court cases brought under IDEA, and that culture diverts resources from the schools' mission of educating the students.
- Many students are misidentified because many current methods of identifying whether they have disabilities "lack validity."
- Teacher-preparation programs and inservice training of existing teachers are insufficient to prepare new teachers and to give all teachers the tools they need to identify students' needs early and accurately.
- Research on special education must be more rigorous, and schools' faculties do not sufficiently apply evidence-based practices.
- The culture of compliance and "bureaucratic imperatives" fail too many children and must be replaced by an emphasis on academic achievement, transition to postsecondary opportunities, and postsecondary outcomes.

Critics of general and special education (Finn et al., 2001) made one other important point: Special education was "teaching" students with disabilities that they were indeed unable to participate in mainstream American life, that they were, therefore, entitled to be treated differently than other students (such as by having special discipline protections), and that they should expect a lifetime of support from the federal and state/local governments. These critics alleged that the "dependency model" was the fundamental flaw in special education because it taught the wrong lessons and must be abandoned for a model that expects greater results and makes those outcomes possible.

Given this background, you will not be surprised by some of IDEA's provisions. Before studying them in detail, however, you will benefit from knowing how IDEA is organized.

ORGANIZATION OF IDEA

IDEA is divided into four Parts—A, B, C, and D. We will discuss each of these Parts here.

Part A (20 U.S.C. Secs. 1400–1410)

Part A relates to Congress's findings and purposes. It also guides us with respect to the terminology and definitions that we must use as we read and apply the law.

Findings and Purposes

Part A states the findings on which Congress acts—essentially, the justifications for the reauthorization—and the purposes of the reauthorization, which are essentially the goals that Congress sets for America's schools. You will recall (from chapter 1) that Congress found (Sec. 1400(c)) that

- disability is a natural part of the human experience;
- disability alone in no way diminishes the right of an individual to participate in or contribute to society;
- improving educational results for students with disabilities is an essential part of our national policy; and
- our national policy includes ensuring equal opportunities, full participation, independent living, and economic self-sufficiency.

IDEA and special education are the means for ensuring that students with disabilities will be educated to achieve these goals. Indeed, the desired outcomes of special education under IDEA and of reasonable accommodations under Section 504 of the Rehabilitation Act (29 U.S.C. 701, *et seq.*) and the Americans with Disabilities Act (42 U.S.C. 12010 *et seq.*) are that students with disabilities will have equal opportunity (relative to students without disabilities) to benefit from their education and thereby become sufficiently prepared to participate fully in communities of their own choice, live as independently as they can, and be as able to work as much as possible.

Congress did not limit itself to these findings. It further declared that, before IDEA was enacted (as the Education of All Handicapped Children Act in 1975), exclusion, misclassification, and underresourced special education were the reasons that students' educational needs were not being met. Since then, Congress continued, students have had access to a free appropriate public education and the results of special education have improved. Still, two factors impeded the implementation of IDEA and the achievements of the results it sought:

1. Educators' low expectations concerning the students and their capacities
2. Educators' insufficient focus on applying replicable research on proven methods of teaching and learning for students with disabilities

Accordingly, Congress offered the following eight solutions to these two barriers. IDEA declares that special education can be made more effective by

1. "Having high expectations for such children and ensuring their access to the general education curriculum in the regular classroom, to the maximum extent possible, in order to
   a. "meet developmental goals and, to the maximum extent possible, the challenging expectations that have been established for all children; and
   b. "be prepared to lead productive and independent adult lives, to the maximum extent possible" (20 U.S.C. 1400(c)(5)(A));
2. "Strengthening the role and responsibility of parents and ensuring that families of such children have meaningful opportunities to participate in the education of their children at school and at home" (20 U.S.C. 1400(c)(5)(B));
3. "Coordinating this title with other local, educational service agency, State, and Federal school improvement efforts, including improvement efforts under the Elementary and Secondary Education Act of 1965, in order to ensure that such children benefit from such efforts and that special education can become a service for such children rather than a place where such children are sent" (20 U.S.C. 1400(c)(5)(C));
4. "Providing appropriate special education and related services, and aids and supports in the regular classroom, to such children, whenever appropriate" (20 U.S.C. 1400(c)(5)(D));
5. "Supporting high-quality, intensive preservice preparation and professional development for all personnel who work with children with disabilities in order to ensure that such personnel have the skills and knowledge necessary to improve the academic achievement and functional performance of children with disabilities, including the use of scientifically based instructional practices, to the maximum extent possible" (20 U.S.C. 1400(c)(5)(E));
6. "Providing incentives for whole-school approaches, scientifically based early reading programs, positive behavioral interventions and supports, and early intervening services to reduce the need to label children as disabled in order to address the learning and behavioral needs of such children (20 U.S.C. 1400(c)(5)(F));
7. "Focusing resources on teaching and learning while reducing paperwork and requirements that do not assist in improving educational results" (20 U.S.C. 1400(c)(5)(G)); and

8. "Supporting the development and use of technology, including assistive technology devices and assistive technology services, to maximize accessibility for children with disabilities" (20 U.S.C. 1400(c)(5)(H)).

Why are these eight solutions significant? The first solution relates to NCLB: having high and challenging expectations for all students, including those with disabilities; educating students with disabilities in the general curriculum; and assessing them for their proficiency in its curriculum. Doing all that will enable these students to be effective adults who will achieve the four national-policy outcomes.

The second solution aligns with the NCLB principle of parent participation and is implemented by the IDEA principle of parent participation. The third solution specifically and generally aligns IDEA with NCLB and makes clear that special education is the placement that occurs only after a general education placement is demonstrably inappropriate for the student. The fourth solution relates to the IDEA principles of appropriate education and least restrictive environment. The fifth solution mirrors the NCLB principle of highly qualified teachers and focuses on developing the capacities of schools to be effective in educating students with disabilities.

The sixth solution also reflects NCLB by assuring that educators will carry out the interventions for students with disabilities; it also reflects the NCLB principle of evidence-based interventions such as reading, positive behavioral interventions, and early intervention.

The seventh solution addresses the complaint about too much focus on procedures and too little on outcomes by reducing paperwork and other noneducational requirements. The last solution refers to the Technology Assistance for Individuals with Disabilities Act (the "Tech Act" [P.L. 105-394]) and is found in the "related services" provisions in IDEA.

Your next questions should be: What are IDEA's purposes? How do they relate to the two barriers and the eight solutions?

In enacting the 2004 amendments, Congress declared these six purposes:

1. "To ensure that all children with disabilities have available to them a free appropriate public education that emphasizes special education and related services designed to meet their unique needs and prepare them for further education, employment, and independent living" (Sec. 1400(d)(1)(A))
2. "To ensure that the rights of children with disabilities and parents of such children are protected" (Sec. 1400(d)(1)(B))
3. "To assist States, localities, educational service agencies, and Federal agencies to provide for the education of all children with disabilities" (Sec. 1400(d)(1)(C))
4. "To assist States in the implementation of a statewide, comprehensive, coordinated, multidisciplinary, interagency system of early intervention services for infants and toddlers with disabilities and their families" (Sec. 1400(d)(2))
5. "To ensure that educators and parents have the necessary tools to improve educational results for children with disabilities by supporting system improvement

activities; coordinated research and personnel preparation; coordinated technical assistance, dissemination, and support; and technology development and media services" (Sec. 1400(d)(3))

6. "To assess, and ensure the effectiveness of, efforts to educate children with disabilities" (Sec. 1400(d)(4))

What is the significance of these six purposes? The first purpose links special education to the four national-policy outcomes. The second affirms that IDEA grants rights that, when implemented in schools, will lead to the outcomes. Thus, education should lead to designated adult-life outcomes. The third through sixth purposes develop the capacity of SEAs and LEAs, and parents, to educate students so that the national goals will be achieved.

Definitions

Part A defines the terms used in IDEA. This is, therefore, an appropriate place to list the terms that you need to know now, along with their significance. (We will describe other terms and their significance as we discuss other parts of IDEA.)

Child with a disability is one

- "…with mental retardation, hearing impairments (including deafness), speech or language impairments, visual impairments (including blindness), serious emotional disturbance (hereinafter referred to in this title as 'emotional disturbance'), orthopedic impairments, autism, traumatic brain injury, other health impairments, or specific learning disabilities; and
- "who, by reason thereof, needs special education and related services" (20 U.S.C. 1401(3)(A)(i-ii)).

There is no change from the prior law. This definition combines the *categorical approach* (listing the various categories of disabilities) with the *functional approach* (insisting that the disability causes the student to function in a way that requires special education intervention). The regulations define each of these categories of disability and provide that students who have deaf-blindness or multiple disabilities also qualify as students with a disability (34 C.F.R. 300.8(a)).

Free appropriate public education means special education and related services that

- "…have been provided at public expense, under public supervision and direction, and without charge;
- "meet the standards of the State educational agency;
- "include an appropriate preschool, elementary school, or secondary school education in the State involved; and
- "are provided in conformity with the individualized education program required under Section 1414(d)" (20 U.S.C. 1401(9)(A-D)).

There is no change from prior law.

Homeless children has the meaning given the term under the McKinney-Vento Homeless Assistance Act (42 U.S.C. 11434a(2)). That act defines a homeless child as one who does not have a regular place of residence (20 U.S.C. Sec. 1401(11)).

The 2004 amendments add accountability for schools to find and serve homeless children within the district. This expansion of services shows heightened awareness and responsibility on the effects of poverty on children and education.

Limited English proficient, according to NCLB (P.L. 107-110), means that the language that the child most uses at home is not English (20 U.S.C. Sec. 1401(18)).

Here, IDEA and NCLB align with each other.

Parent denotes a natural, adoptive, or foster parent, a legal guardian, an individual acting in the place of a natural or adoptive parent (including a grandparent, stepparent, or other relative) with whom the child lives, or an individual assigned to be a surrogate parent (20 U.S.C. Sec. 1401(23)).

This definition of "parent" mirrors the changing demographics of American families, recognizes that various people function as "parents," and expands the range of individuals who are both responsible and accountable under IDEA. The regulations clarify that "parent" refers to a person who is a biological or adoptive parent; a foster parent; a guardian generally authorized to act as the child's parent or to make educational decisions for the child; an individual acting in the place of a biological or adoptive parent (including a grandparent, stepparent, or other relative) with whom the child lives, or an individual who is legally responsible for the child's welfare; or a surrogate parent appointed by a state or local education agency to represent the child's interests in special education (34 C.F.R. 300.30). The regulations also make it clear that the biological or adoptive parent is presumed to be the parent when there is more than one person who otherwise meets the definition of a parent and that if a court order appoints a person to be the child's parent, then that person is the one who meets the federal standard for "parent."

Related services means "transportation, and such developmental, corrective, and other supportive services (including speech-language pathology and audiology services, interpreting services, psychological services, physical and occupational therapy, recreation, including therapeutic recreation, social work services, school nurse services designed to enable a child with a disability to receive a free appropriate public education as described in the individualized education program of the child, counseling services, including rehabilitation counseling, orientation and mobility services, and medical services, except that such medical services shall be for diagnostic and evaluation purposes only) as may be required to assist a child with a disability to benefit from special education, and includes the early identification and assessment of disabling conditions in children." The term "does not include a medical device that is surgically implanted, or the replacement of such a device" (20 U.S.C. Sec. 1401(26)).

A related service is available by right only if a child needs it to benefit from special education. The test is one of necessity, as under prior law. The regulations add that "related services" include "school health services and school nurse services, social work services in the schools, and parent counseling and training" (34 C.F.R. 300.34).

They also provide that related services do not include a medical device that is surgically implanted, the "optimization" of the device's functioning, the maintenance of the device, or the replacement of the device. Despite these qualifications, a student with an implanted device has a right to receive other related services. Accordingly, the LEA still has a responsibility to monitor and maintain devices that are needed to maintain the child's health and safety while the child is transported to and from school and while the child is in school. The LEA also may routinely check the external component of any device to make sure it is functioning properly. Those devices include a cochlear implant for a child who has hearing challenges or devices that affect the breathing, nutrition, or other bodily functions of the child (such as a catheter).

Special education is defined as specially designed instruction, at no cost to parents, to meet the unique needs of a child with a disability, including

■ instruction conducted in the classroom, in the home, in hospitals and institutions, and in other settings; and
■ instruction in physical education (20 U.S.C. Sec. 1401(29)).

There is no change from prior law. Note that the definition authorizes a continuum of service settings and thus gives some meaning to the principle of the least restrictive environment (see chapter 7). Under the regulations, "special education" also includes speech–language pathology services or any other related service if the service is "considered" to be a special education service and not a related service under a state's standards; travel training; and vocational education (34 C.F.R. 300.39).

Supplementary aids and services means "aids, services, and other supports that are provided in regular education classes or other education-related settings to enable children with disabilities to be educated with nondisabled children to the maximum extent appropriate in accordance with Section 1412(a)(5)" (20 U.S.C. Sec. 1401(33)).
This definition did not change from prior law.

Ward of the State means a child who is a foster child, a ward of the state, or is in the custody of a public welfare agency (does not include foster parent) (20 U.S.C. Sec. 1401(36)).
These new provisions protect the rights and interests of children who are wards of the state. This is important because access to due process remedies has been opened to "any party" under Section 1415(b)(6) and procedures are in place to appoint surrogates to act in place of the student's parents (Section 1415(b)(2)).

You will note that the definition of "child with a disability" above consists of two elements:

1. *The categorical approach.* A child has a disability if the child has one of the listed disabilities; those disabilities are described by "category."
2. *The functional approach.* The child has a disability if, in addition to fitting into a specific category of disability, the child needs special education and related services because of the disability. If the child needs special education, it is because the child's disability (the categorical approach) impairs the child so much that the child cannot benefit from general education; the child cannot function there (the functional approach).

Also note that, for the first time, IDEA defined two subsets of children/students with disabilities: those who are homeless and those who have limited proficiency in using English. We have said that the inclusion of "homeless children" is significant because IDEA now recognizes that poverty—which usually accompanies homelessness—is one of the reasons that students have disabilities and need special education.

What is IDEA saying, however, about "limited English proficient" (LEP) students? It deals with the *cause* of disability. It does not proclaim that LEP students need special education solely because they do not speak English. That fact alone does not mean that children have a disability, only that their language is not English. Instead, it declares that LEP students may need special education because they meet IDEA's categorical and functional definition of "child with a disability."

Language alone (language other than English) does not create a right to IDEA benefits, whereas meeting the categorical and functional definition does, without respect to the child's language. But a language difference (LEP) may contribute to disability because linguistic, cultural, and ethnic diversity themselves characterize many students in special education (those who meet the categorical and functional definition).

In acknowledging that poverty and linguistic diversity can be causes of disability, IDEA also acknowledges the theory called *co-morbidity* or "the new morbidity." That theory holds that when one or more of the following factors affect a child, the likelihood that the child will have a disability increases:

- Poverty
- Ethnic, cultural, or linguistic diversity
- Family structure (being a child of a single parent)
- Place of residence

Accordingly, IDEA is justified in targeting homeless and LEP students. Moreover, by targeting these students in particular, IDEA converts special education from an intervention that responds after the fact to the child's disability—that responds once the child has a disability—to an intervention that may prevent a child from having or acquiring a disability and an incapacity to function in general education. IDEA thus assures both intervention and prevention.

IDEA defines yet another subset of students and offers them special education and related services. Those are the students who, as infants and toddlers (birth through 2, also known as zero to 3) or as young children between ages 3 and 9, experience a developmental delay in one or more of the following areas of their development and who, by reason of the delay(s), need special education and related services:

- Physical development
- Cognitive development
- Communication development
- Social or emotional development
- Adaptive development

The regulations make it clear that a state may offer services to any "subset" of the children ages three through nine, that each state may define "developmental delay," and that the state must measure the existence of a delay by using "appropriate diagnostic instruments and procedures" (30 C.F.R. 300.8).

IDEA authorizes the state and local education agencies the option to use IDEA-supported programs to serve these developmentally delayed young students. It does not require a state or local education agency to serve them; it simply gives them the choice to do so. In that respect, IDEA reflects the principle of federalism: shared federal and state/local responsibility for the functions of government, with discretion granted by the federal government to state/local governments whether to serve these students or not.

Further, by authorizing services to young students with these delays, IDEA once again takes on two roles—that of authorizing interventions and that of preventing disabilities in the first place. Often, young children who receive special education and related services and who have developmental delays will no longer experience any delays. Now it is appropriate to explain in detail Parts B, C, and D, paying special attention to the ages of the children and students who benefit from IDEA.

Part B (20 U.S.C. Secs. 1411–1419): Services to Children Ages 3 through 21

These services include the following components:

1. *Authorization of assistance.* Part B authorizes federal assistance (basically, federal funds) to state and local education agencies so they may educate students who are between the ages of 3 and 21. (We explain that concept later in this chapter under the heading "Grant-in-Aid.") But IDEA makes a distinction between children ages 3 through 5 and children ages 6 through 21.
2. *Children ages 3 to 5.* Consistent with the principle of federalism (and its theory that federal law should grant some discretion to state and local governments) and consistent with the fact that some but not all states offered special education to students ages 3 to 5, IDEA provides that states may choose to educate students ages 3 through 5. If states do so, they must comply with IDEA's provisions. (In 2005, all states do offer special education to children ages 3 to 5. IDEA's provisions take into account the history that not all states did so.)
3. *Children ages 6 through 21.* Because all states have laws that provide for the education of students ages 6 and older, IDEA authorizes federal aid to state and local education agencies to serve those students. But, of course, it also provides that, if a state or local agency accepts federal funds under IDEA, it must comply with IDEA's provisions.
4. *Use of funds.* As noted above, IDEA provides that, if a state or local education agency accepts IDEA funds, it must comply with IDEA's provisions. Thus, IDEA is a conditional grant-in-aid statute: The aid is conditioned on state and local agencies' agreeing to comply with IDEA's provisions. We explain these provisions in chapters 4 through 9.

Part C (20 U.S.C. Secs. 1431–1444): Infants and Toddlers

In part because it is good public policy to prevent disabilities and to intervene whenever a person has a disability, Part C authorizes assistance to state and local education agencies to serve children from birth through age 2, also known as "zero to 3" or "infants and toddlers."

Consistent with the principle of federalism and state/local government choice and because some, but not all, state and local agencies offer services to very young children, IDEA provides that a state or local education agency may choose to serve these students. If it makes such a choice, it must, of course, comply with the provisions of Part C, and all states have elected to participate in Part C programs. We explain these programs in chapters 4 through 9.

IDEA's Six Principles

As we have described IDEA so far, we have only hinted at its basic principles. We did that by describing the types of discrimination that students with disabilities have experienced, IDEA's past and present findings and purposes, and its present use of funds. Now is the time for us to make those core principles absolutely clear. Each of its six principles is delineated below, and each principle will be explored in detail in chapters 4 through 9.

1. *Zero reject* reflects the process of enrollment and provides that every child with a disability (under IDEA) is entitled to a free appropriate public education. (See chapter 4.)
2. *Nondiscriminatory evaluation* occurs after the student enters school and when the school or others believe the student may have a disability and thus be entitled to IDEA's benefits. (See chapter 5.)
3. *Appropriate education* occurs when the student receives individualized programs that benefit him/her in progressing toward the national policy goals. (See chapter 6.)
4. *Least restrictive environment* reflects the presumption that the student's education will take place in a typical setting and with nondisabled students. (See chapter 7.)
5. *Procedural due process* is a way for parents to hold schools accountable for that education and for schools to hold parents accountable for their child. (See chapter 8.)
6. *Parent participation* ensures that parents and the student can be partners with educators in having a say about the student's education. (See chapter 9.)

These six principles have a satisfying seamlessness. The first four principles govern the processes that LEAs follow in order to confer on each IDEA-covered student the benefit of a free appropriate public education in the least restrictive environment. Zero reject commands each LEA to enroll each such student; nondiscriminatory evaluation requires the LEA to fairly assess the student's educational needs and strengths; appropriate education obliges the LEA to provide a beneficial education to the student; and least restrictive environment mandates that the LEA place the student in the most appropriate general education program.

The last two of IDEA's six principles are the procedures that the student and his/her parents use to hold the LEA accountable for complying with the first four principles and to be partners with the schools in the student's education. Procedural due process gives the student and his/her parents various techniques for resolving differences with the LEA, and parent participation buttresses the accountability provisions of procedural due process and also creates an opportunity for the LEA and the student and parents to be partners in the student's education.

Now that you know a little about IDEA's six principles, you may well ask: How do those principles and IDEA relate to general education and the No Child Left Behind Act (P.L. 107-110)? How does IDEA align with NCLB? How will special education under IDEA relate to general education under NCLB? Those are good questions. We answer them below.

Relationship of IDEA to General Education and NCLB

One of the purposes of the 2004 reauthorization was to align IDEA with NCLB. To determine just how well IDEA and NCLB align, let's begin by identifying the purposes of NCLB. In summary, they are student-focused, even though they, of course, address schools, educators, and parents. The six core principles of NCLB relate to its purposes, which are to

- reform American schools on behalf of all children;
- challenge the low expectations and illiteracy that affect many students; and
- increase students' academic competencies, especially reading in the early years.

To implement these purposes, NCLB rests on these six core principles:

1. *Principle of accountability*: Schools should educate all students in elementary and middle schools well enough so they will demonstrate proficiency in certain core academic subjects (English, mathematics, and others). The technique for achieving this principle is the standardized state or local assessments of student academic proficiency. IDEA provides that students with disabilities will participate in these assessments.
2. *Principle of highly qualified teachers*: Teachers, themselves, must be proficient to teach and thus must meet certain federal and state standards before they are certified to teach. IDEA requires comparable standards for those who teach students with disabilities.
3. *Principle of scientifically based intervention* (also known as evidence-based intervention): Highly qualified teachers will use research-based curricula and instructional methods. IDEA requires educators to use scientifically based methods in evaluating a student and then providing an appropriate education to the student.
4. *Principle of local flexibility*: State and local education agencies must have some discretion about how to use federal and state matching monies to secure the NCLB outcomes. IDEA grants some discretion to those agencies about how they use the IDEA funds.
5. *Principle of safe schools*: Effective teaching and learning can occur only in safe schools. IDEA sets out procedures and standards for disciplining students with disabilities.
6. *Principle of parent participation and choice*: The parents of all students should have the opportunity to participate in their children's education and to remove their children from unsafe or failing schools. IDEA grants rights and private-school opportunities for students with disabilities.

Knowing NCLB's purposes and its principles, you still may not be sure how IDEA and NCLB align with each other. In truth, they align generally but not exactly. That is because NCLB benefits all students, including but not specifically those with disabilities. Beyond this obvious alignment, there are others, best described in terms of IDEA's six principles as compared to NCLB's six principles:

1. The IDEA principle of zero reject, and especially its discipline provisions, relate to the NCLB principle of school safety.
2. The IDEA principle of nondiscriminatory evaluation has no close equivalent in NCLB.
3. The IDEA principle of appropriate education invokes NCLB's principles of accountability through assessments, highly qualified teachers, and scientifically based instruction.
4. The IDEA principle of least restrictive environment has no clear equivalent in NCLB.
5. The IDEA principle of procedural due process has no clear equivalent in NCLB.
6. The IDEA principle of parent participation invokes NCLB's principle of parent choice.

The NCLB principle of local flexibility does not fit into any of the IDEA principles, yet it, too, has become part of IDEA through that law's provisions that an SEA and LEA may use federal funds for general education students if the principal use of the funds is for special education students (see chapter 10, entitled "Compliance, Rights, and Remedies," and our discussion of the rule of incidental benefit).

Granted, the IDEA and NCLB principles are not as closely aligned as they might have been if students without disabilities had the same rights as students with disabilities (and there are many reasons why they should have comparable rights), but clearly, both by way of their respective principles and because Congress has reauthorized IDEA and provided for alignment of its and NCLB's approaches, these two laws make special education law somewhat more like general education law than ever before.

You are now at the point where you know something about IDEA (findings, purposes, use of funds, and six principles) and something about NCLB (purposes and six principles) and their relationship to each other. You are not, however, at the point where you have learned all you need to know about special education law. You need to know about one other set of laws—the antidiscrimination laws. We describe them next.

Antidiscrimination Laws—Section 504 and ADA— and Their Relationship to IDEA

You will recall that IDEA responds to discriminatory practices in education, protecting students with disabilities as they attend school but not protecting them in other aspects of their lives, such as employment and community integration and participation. Do these students need legal protection from discrimination in their lives outside of school? Yes. What laws protect them there?

You also will recall that IDEA defines "child with a disability" as one who "needs" special education and related services (the functional approach) because of the type of disability the child has (the categorical approach). Are some students with a disability not eligible for IDEA? In other words, does IDEA cover all students with disabilities, and, if not, what other laws protect them against discrimination?

The answers to these questions are found in two federal antidiscrimination laws that protect IDEA-eligible students outside of school and that protect IDEA-ineligible students in school: Section 504 of the Rehabilitation Act and the Americans with Disabilities Act (ADA). These civil rights laws differ from IDEA in several respects:

1. Section 504 and ADA prohibit discrimination in education against students with disabilities. To carry out their antidiscrimination, they create two related rights for students with disabilities:
   a. The right not to be subjected to discrimination based solely on their disabilities
   b. The right to reasonable accommodations in education
2. These laws do not authorize federal funds that can be used by state and local education agencies to educate students with disabilities. They are not grants-in-aid statutes, as NCLB and IDEA are.
3. A student with a disability may not qualify under IDEA as a child with a disability because, in spite of having a disability, the student does not need special education. Instead, the student needs reasonable accommodations in general (regular) education and nothing more. Section 504 and ADA provide that the student will receive those accommodations even though the student is not classified as eligible under IDEA. There are fewer IDEA-eligible students than Section 504/ADA-protected students.

Although Section 504 and ADA define "disability" differently than IDEA does, the 504 and ADA definitions are not inconsistent with IDEA's definition. As you may recall, IDEA uses a two-part approach to defining the children it benefits. First, the child must fit into one of the specified categories of disability. Second, the child must function in such a way that the child needs special education. Thus, IDEA uses both a categorical and a functional approach in defining its beneficiaries.

Section 504 and ADA have a three-part approach to defining the children who benefit:

1. The child must presently have a disability.
2. If the child does not have a disability, he/she must have a record of a disability; that is, the child must have a history of having a disability.
3. The child must be regarded as having a disability; that is, other people must be treating the child as if the child has a disability.

In addition, Section 504 and ADA require that the disability, the history of disability, or the regarded-as-being-disabled must significantly limit one or more of life's major activities. So far, following the precedent set by the U.S. Supreme Court in *Southeastern Community College v. Davis* (1999), the courts have treated education as a major life activity under Section 504. Note how similar the 504–ADA approach continues to be to IDEA's approach: All three laws require evidence of a functional disability, in that the student must not be able to function in education without IDEA benefits or without 504–ADA reasonable accommodations.

Why do the Section 504 and ADA definitions have a three-part approach? The first part—the person "has" a disability—is clearly justified: If the person has a disability, discrimination on that basis alone further disables the person and denies him/her equal opportunities and the equal protection of the law.

The second and third parts—the person has a "record" of a disability or "is regarded" as having one—are justified on the same grounds, but they address the problem that has plagued people with disabilities for a long time: They do not currently experience any effects of a disability and appear not to have a disability, yet they are treated as if they do, in fact, have a disability. Accordingly, Section 504 and ADA bar that kind of treatment.

Finally, note that the "regarded as" approach under 504–ADA is not part of the IDEA approach. Although IDEA clearly seeks to overcome educational discrimination by offering the student an opportunity for an appropriate education in the least restrictive environment, it does not deal nearly as directly with the effects of stigma—the negative connotation that attends "difference" that is so great as to be thought to be a "disability"—as Section 504 and ADA do.

Which students benefit from Section 504 and ADA? Stated another way, who are the students with disabilities who do not qualify for IDEA? The answer depends on the IDEA definition and in particular the part that says that, because of a certain type of disability, the student "needs" special education and related services.

Remember Ryan White, the Case on Point at the beginning of this chapter? He had HIV/AIDS. Other students do as well, and some of them will not experience any significant deleterious effects of that disease; they will not be so impaired by it that they cannot function effectively in general education and, therefore, they do not need special education or all the benefits of IDEA. Yet they may be subject to discrimination based on the disease: They have a disease, a record of one, and may be regarded as having a disability. Section 504 and ADA protect them against this kind of discrimination.

Still other students have disabling conditions that may lead state and local education agencies to discriminate against them but that do not require them to be placed into special education (they do not "need" it). For example, some students with attention deficit/hyperactivity disorder or with some health impairments (such as asthma) may need protection against discrimination and some accommodations in general education but still not need special education. Section 504 and ADA provide that a student who is protected under those laws also has the right to "reasonable accommodations" in general education. Some of the major 504 cases and the accommodations the courts have found to be "reasonable" are as follows.

Molly L. v. Lower Merion School District (2002)

For an elementary school student with a history of being hypersensitive to sensory stimulation (odors, touch, and loud noises), who has difficulty in staying in one position and rocks and rubs herself against her chair, needs support when she feels anxious and overwhelmed, is hypotonic, lacks balance when walking and walks slowly, has decreased muscle strength, and has severe problems with asthma and endurance, reasonable accommodations include (1) one-on-one classroom aid to help the student avoid asthma attacks, (2) the use of nonverbal signs to make her aware of when she is at risk for sensory overload, (3) an aide to make sure she does not injure herself during recesses, (4) preferential seating at lunchtime to minimize environmental stimuli, (5) an aide to assist her to enter and exit the school bus without being jostled by other students, (6) an aide who will tell the student in advance of any school bells being rung or who will hold her hand if there is an actual fire alarm, and (7) permission to opt out of art and cooking classes in which the odors cause her to be hyperactive.

M.B. v. Arlington Central School District et al. (2002)

For a sixth-grade student with specific learning disabilities with special challenges in reading, writing, organizational skills, and work habits, reasonable accommodations consist of (1) a consultant teacher to support the student academically, instead of placement in a resource room; and (2) a special class in study stills, based in large part on a specific methodology (Orto-Gillingham), instead of a remedial reading class based entirely and solely on that methodology.

DeBord v. Board of Education of the Ferguson-Florissant School District (1997)

For a student with attention-deficit/hyperactivity disorder for whom a dosage of medication was prescribed that exceeded the recommended dosage in the *Physicians' Desk Reference (PDR)*, a reasonable accommodation consists of administering only the *PDR* dosage, consistent with a local education agency's policies that, with respect to every student for whom medication is prescribed that must be administered at school, it will comply with *PDR* dosage-administration but not exceed it.

Other Reasonable Accommodations

A "reasonable accommodation" may include extra time to take a test, the assistance of a note-taker, excuse from mandatory physical education but participation in adapted physical education, or a reduction in homework assignments. As long as the accommodation does not substantially modify the general education program (essentially, the curriculum—what is taught and how—and extracurricular activities), the student has a right to the accommodation. If, however, the accommodation does substantially alter the curriculum or an extracurricular activity, the student will "need" special education and will qualify for IDEA benefits and protection.

The Principle of Dual Accommodations

As you have read about IDEA and Section 504 and ADA, you will have noted some similarities. All three laws offer a benefit to the student for the purpose of building the student's capacity. IDEA offers special education and related services. Section 504 and ADA offer reasonable accommodations. All three laws also protect the student against discrimination by requiring state and local education agencies to include students in school and to change the ways they educate the students.

These two different approaches to disability—build the student's capacities and change the agencies' behaviors and build their capacities, too—reflect an important principle of disability law: the principle of dual accommodations. Under that principle, the student receives a benefit and is expected to take advantage of the benefit. Remember IDEA's findings that "low expectations" have impeded the full implementation of the law? The opposite of "low expectations" is "great" or "high" expectations, as articulated in NCLB. So one aspect of the principle of dual accommodations is simply this: Laws require and make it possible for state and local education agencies to put resources into the student and thereby to build the student's capacities. In turn, the student is expected to use those inputs to fit into school and the other activities of American life.

The other aspect of the principle of dual accommodations is that the policies, programs, and activities of the education agencies and of other public- or private-sector entities must accommodate the student. IDEA authorizes special education and related services, which are accommodations to the student's disability. Section 504 and ADA offer reasonable accommodations to disability. Thus, the principle of dual accommodations holds that the student and society must "fit" each other, the student through education and society by accommodations to the student's disability.

The principle of dual accommodations justifies just a few more words of explanation. On the one hand, the principle explains why students with disabilities are worthy of special education (and why all people with disabilities are worthy of reasonable accommodations)—namely, that the impairment is real and is part of them that can be overcome to some extent, if not entirely. On the other hand, the principle explains why a society in which people with disabilities do not easily "fit" must change—namely, societal change itself reduces the effect of the impairment. Thus, the principle acknowledges both the personal attribute that we call impairment and the environmental–social effect on that impairment.

Part D of IDEA (20 U.S.C. Secs. 1451–1482): System Capacity Building

We just said that the principle of dual accommodations requires educational agencies—that is, public entities—to accommodate students with disabilities (the environmental–social part of the principle). They cannot do that, however, unless they have the capacity to do so. Accordingly, Part D authorizes three different programs to develop SEAs' and LEAs' capacities to educate students with disabilities appropriately and in an integrated (inclusive) setting (environment):

1. One program addresses the capacity of the teachers and other faculty in the schools. It makes grants available to SEAs and LEAs for retraining teachers already working in the schools ("personnel development") and to colleges and universities to train students who are preparing to work in the schools ("personnel preparation").

2. A second program makes grants available for a combination of activities—namely, technical assistance (expert advice on how to carry out IDEA), demonstration projects (models of how to implement IDEA), and dissemination activities (publicizing research, state-of-the-art and best practices so all state and local agencies and their employees will know what to do and how to do it when they educate students with disabilities).

3. The third program makes grants available to parent training and information centers and to community parent resource centers so parents and other family members will receive training and information, and referral and advocacy services, so they may participate in their children's education (consistent with the IDEA and NCLB principles of parent participation).

All three of these Part D authorizations create a capacity for education agencies and parents to work together, as partners, to implement IDEA on behalf of students with disabilities.

IDEA as a Grant-in-Aid Law

We have already said that IDEA is a grant-in-aid law. It authorizes activities (assistance to educate infants/toddlers under Part C and assistance to educate young children and students under Part B, and various capacity-building activities under Part D). It also makes the activities conditional: Any state or local education agency (under Parts B, C, and D) and any other entity (under Part D) that accepts any funds deriving from IDEA must comply with IDEA's provisions.

To "authorize" activities, however, is not the same as making the funds available to carry out the activities. "Authorize" simply means that Congress, through IDEA, approves various activities by various individuals (educators and parents) and entities (state and local education agencies and any individuals and entities carrying out Part D activities). To make the federal funds available so individuals and entities can act, Congress must "appropriate" funds. That is, it must pass a federal budget that contains money so the IDEA-authorized activities can occur. Thus, IDEA is an "authorizing" grant-in-aid program that depends on "appropriations." In Part Three, we will further explain the appropriations and how IDEA requires them to be allotted.

SUMMARY

In this chapter we provided a brief history of IDEA, focusing on its original purposes, the major findings of the President's Commission on Excellence in Special Education, the "dependency model" that special education allegedly advances, IDEA's key definitions (including the categorical and functional approaches), the subset of students (homeless and limited English proficient) within IDEA, and the "co-morbidity" and "new morbidity" theories. We described Part B (ages 3 through 21) and Part C (ages birth through 2, or "zero" to 3).

We then connected IDEA to the No Child Left Behind Act, incorporating IDEA's six principles and NCLB's six principles and describing how the two laws align with each other. Next, we explained two antidiscrimination laws (Section 504 and ADA) and their relationship to IDEA through the principle of dual accommodations. Finally, we described and then explained how the principle of dual accommodations becomes a reality—namely through IDEA's Part D capacity-building activities. In chapter 4, you will learn the details about IDEA, organized around its six principles.

Before launching into that enterprise, however, let's return to the Case on Point and the point it makes. Ryan White would not have had a right to go to school if Congress had not enacted IDEA. He would not have been protected against discrimination in education if Congress had not enacted Section 504 and ADA. And he would not have had any entitlement to medical services if Congress had not created that entitlement. His positive rights to education and entitlements and his negative right against discrimination protected him for as long as he lived. That's what law can and should do: protect the most vulnerable of our country's citizens.

Part Two

The Six Principles of IDEA

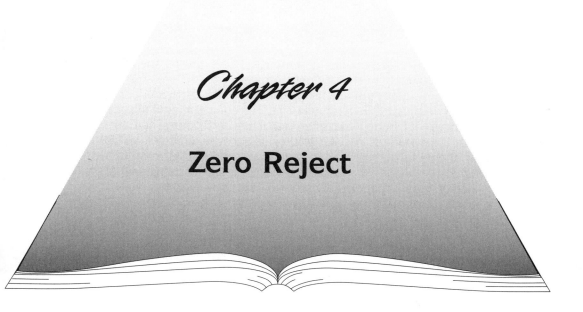

Chapter 4

Zero Reject

Case on Point: *Honig v. Doe*
484 U.S. 305, 108 S. Ct. 592 (1988)

Students don't always control themselves. They break rules, are disruptive, and occasionally harm their peers and instructors. Students who have emotional or behavioral disorders sometimes are prone to such behaviors because of their disabilities—particularly in environments that don't address their emotional and behavioral needs.

Indeed, in 1988 this was true of two students in the San Francisco school district. Both were classified into special education as having emotional–behavioral disorders, and both were receiving IDEA services. One of them, taunted and ridiculed by other students, choked one of his tormentors and kicked out a window at his school. The other made lewd sexual remarks to female classmates.

The LEA levied the most severe sentence it could against the students: expulsion for an indefinite time. In imposing that sentence, it had no way to know that it was setting out on a course that eventually would come to define the term *zero reject* and affect Congress as it reauthorized IDEA in 1997 (P.L. 105-17) and again in 2004 (P.L. 108-446).

The students challenged their expulsion. They argued that Congress's intent in enacting IDEA in 1975 (then called the Education for All Handicapped Children Act) was to prevent LEAs from indefinitely expelling IDEA-covered students, that Congress deliberately chose a zero reject policy, and that the LEA must amend its sentence, or if it refuses, the SEA must provide services directly to the students.

In due time, the U.S. Supreme Court took the students' case, and in 1988 held that IDEA prohibits an LEA from cutting off all special education services to a student classified into IDEA protection. The Court further held that IDEA requires the SEA to provide services directly if an LEA is unwilling or unable to do so. The Court, however, did not leave an LEA defenseless against students who violate school codes or endanger other students or faculty. It said that for dangerous or disruptive conduct growing out of students' disabilities, the LEA may

- suspend a student for up to 10 school days each year for the safety of others and to provide a "cooling off" period for the student;
- use disciplinary procedures that did not exclude or change the placement of the student (i.e., time-outs, detention, or the restriction of privileges); or
- secure parental consent or a court order to change the student's placement, but the student must "stay put" in his or her current placement pending a court or hearing officer's decision.

How did Congress respond to *Honig*? In addition to renewing the stay-put provision (already in IDEA in 1975), Congress based the 10-day rule, manifestation determination, and no-cessation provisions—incorporated into IDEA in 1997—on the Court's rationale. *Honig* also brought discipline to the front line of debates about IDEA reauthorization and the zero reject principle, a debate that continued through IDEA's reauthorization in 2004.

COMPREHENSIVE COVERAGE: ALL CHILDREN

The zero reject principle stands for the proposition that students with disabilities may not be excluded, either physically or functionally, from public education. Nothing is clearer in IDEA than Congress's intent to provide all children with disabilities with full educational opportunities. Thus, IDEA requires SEAs to follow a policy of zero reject and establish the goal of "providing full educational opportunities to all children with disabilities. ..." (20 U.S.C. Sec. 1412(a)(2)).

Congress found (as did the courts in *Mills v. District of Columbia Bd. of Ed.*, 1972, and *Pennsylvania Ass'n for Retarded Children (PARC) v. Commonwealth of Pennsylvania*, 1972) that children with disabilities were both totally excluded (completely kept out of school) and functionally excluded (physically present but without the means to benefit) from education (20 U.S.C. Secs. 1400(c)(2)(B) and (C)), and that it was in the national interest to provide programs to meet the needs of children with disabilities and thereby assure them equal protection of the law (20 U.S.C. Sec. 1400(c)(6)). Congress adopted a zero reject policy by declaring that the purpose of

IDEA is to ensure that all children with disabilities receive a free appropriate public education (20 U.S.C. Sec. 1400(d)(1)(A)).

Exclusion from educational opportunities can result from a variety of causes. Difficulties with identifying children as having disabilities, the variety of settings in which such children are educated, a lack of resources, questions of educability, and behavior-based challenges can all lead to exclusion. IDEA addresses each of these issues and the contexts and situations in which exclusion may occur.

Child Find

Before they can benefit from protections against exclusion, children must be found and identified. Accordingly, the zero reject policy requires a child identification program so SEAs and LEAs can plan, develop programs, and allocate money for special education. That is why IDEA requires each SEA to conduct an annual program to identify, locate, and evaluate all children with disabilities residing in their respective jurisdictions, including homeless children, wards of the state, and children attending private schools, regardless of the severity of their disabilities (20 U.S.C. Sec. 1412(a)(3)).

The child census also must locate two specific types of children (34 C.F.R. Sec. 300.111(c)):

1. Children *suspected* of having a disability, without regard to whether they are progressing from grade to grade
2. Highly mobile children with disabilities, including those of migrant workers

Child find has three purposes, the primary one of which is to ensure that no children with disabilities are denied a free appropriate education because they have not been located. The focus of the child census is to locate students with disabilities, so LEAs and the SEA may conduct a noncategorical child census, counting the students without labeling them with, or putting them into, one of IDEA's 10 disability categories. But the SEA must develop and implement a practical method to determine which of the children located are receiving special education and related services (20 U.S.C. Sec. 1412(a)(3)).

The other purposes of the child-find requirement are to

- ensure cooperation between the educational agencies and others (such as health, mental health, developmental disabilities, social services, corrections, private schools, and private agencies); and
- enable the SEA and LEA to appropriate funds, plan and deliver programs, and be held accountable to all children with disabilities.

Residence

IDEA always has apportioned responsibility for educating children with disabilities to each state; each is responsible for educating its children (20 U.S.C. Sec.

1412(a)(1)(A)). It also allots IDEA funds to each SEA and then to each LEA on the basis of student enrollment so the LEA serving the student receives appropriate levels of funding from the state. These provisions reflect the idea that states should be responsible for only their own residents and LEAs for only the children they actually serve.

The zero reject principle supports the education of all children with disabilities. Yet, whether a child qualifies for IDEA protections, and even the type of protection IDEA offers, can differ depending on which of five age categories a child fits:

> Ages 0–3 (early intervention)
> 3–5 years old (preschool)
> 6–9 (early school age)
> 9–17 years (school age)
> 18–21 (extended school age)

As we pointed out in chapter 3, the first age category (early intervention) is covered under Part C, and the last four age categories (preschool through extended school age) generally fall under Part B of IDEA. Because Part B covers most of the age groups, we will discuss its age and eligibility provision before we discuss Part C.

Part B: Required Coverage, Exceptions, and Options

Part B requires states to provide full educational opportunities to all children with disabilities between the ages of 3 and 21 (20 U.S.C. Sec. 1412(a)(1)(A)). IDEA defines "children with disabilities" as those who have a disability and because of that disability need special education. As we explain more fully below, each SEA and LEA has discretion to include children ages 3–9 or any subgroup therein (e.g., ages 3–5) who are experiencing developmental delays (20 U.S.C. Sec. 1401(3)(B)).

IDEA provides that a state need not serve children ages 3 to 5 or 18 to 21 if a state law, practice, or court order is inconsistent with these requirements (20 U.S.C. Sec. 1412(a)(1)(B)(i)). In a very real sense, this exception, as well as the optional expansion of eligibility for children ages 3–9, pays deference to the principle of federalism and the tradition of state and local autonomy over education. It recognizes that the states themselves should have some autonomy in educating their own citizens.

Ages 3 to 5: Preschool Grant Incentive

Because preschool is rarely a public entitlement provided to children without disabilities, equal opportunity arguments are not likely to apply to the option to serve preschool children with disabilities. But, unlike the option to serve ages 18 to 21, there is a federal financial incentive to serve children ages 3 to 5 under IDEA.

IDEA's preschool grant program (20 U.S.C. Sec. 1419) requires the secretary of education to issue grants to eligible states for special education for children with disabilities ages 3 to 5. The SEA has the option to make funds available to serve 2-year-old children who will turn 3 during the school year. But to be eligible for a preschool grant, states must make a free appropriate public education available to all children ages 3 to 5 and also must meet all other Part B eligibility requirements. Since 1993, all states have made a free appropriate public education available to children starting at age 3 or lower. (Some provide FAPE from birth.)

Part C: Early Intervention: Zero to Three

Another example of state autonomy under IDEA is the option for states to provide federally assisted services to infants and toddlers and their families. Allowing voluntary expansion of services to include children ages 0 to 3 further supports and advances the zero reject principle by expanding its application outside traditional school-age and preschool education to include early intervention and family support services. If a state chooses to opt-in to the program, it receives federal funds under Part C to provide services to children ages 0 to 3 and their families. Although states also may choose not to participate in the Part C program, all states currently are opting-in to early intervention.

History and Purposes of Early Intervention

In 1986, Congress, through the EHA amendments of P.L. 99–457, extended IDEA benefits to infants and toddlers, ages zero (birth) to 3. It did this by enacting what currently is known as Part C of IDEA (20 U.S.C. Secs. 1431-1445). Part C is a pro-family bill because it identifies the infant and toddler with a disability and his or her family as IDEA beneficiaries (20 U.S.C. Sec. 1431). Later in this chapter we will discuss in greater detail the difference between beneficiaries of Part C and Part B.

Moreover, Part C is motivated by concerns that are broader than those that persuaded Congress to enact Part B. For one thing, Congress understood that early intervention services were cost-effective and recognized the significant brain development that occurs during the first three years of life. Part C's five goals, which are different and more comprehensive than those of Part B, reflect this broader conception. Part C goals are

1. to enhance the development of infants and toddlers and minimize their potential for developmental delays, and to recognize the significant brain development that occurs during a child's first three years;
2. to reduce the educational costs to society, including the nation's schools, by minimizing the need for special education and related services after infants and toddlers reach school age;
3. to maximize the potential of individuals with disabilities to live independently;
4. to enhance families' capacities to meet the needs of their children with disabilities; and
5. to enhance the capacities of state and local agencies and service providers to identify, evaluate, and meet the needs of all children, particularly minority, low-income, inner-city, and rural children and infants and toddlers in foster care (20 U.S.C. Sec. 1431(a)).

Eligibility Under Part C

Part C provides separate funding for the education of infants and toddlers (ages zero to 3). Infants and toddlers who qualify for the services must need early intervention because they either

- experience developmental delays, or
- have diagnosed physical or mental conditions that carry a high probability of causing developmental delays (20 U.S.C. Sec. 1432(5)).

Each SEA and LEA also has the option of serving children "at risk"—those who would be at risk of experiencing substantial developmental delays if they do not receive early intervention (20 U.S.C. Sec. 1432(1)). The developmental delays must be in one or more of the following areas of development: cognitive, physical, communication, social or emotional, or adaptive. Although the states may otherwise define "developmental delay," they must include delays in the enumerated areas of development (20 U.S.C. Sec. 1432(3)).

It is important to contrast the broad eligibility provisions of Part C (zero to 3) with those of Part B (ages 3 through 21). Under Part B, only those children and youth age 6 or older who have disabilities that cause them to need special education are entitled to IDEA's benefits. By contrast, Part C eligibility is based on a need for early intervention because of the existence or likelihood of developmental delay. Developmental delay involves the five different categorical elements that we listed above; by contrast, Part B categorizes disabilities (as we pointed out in chapter 3).

Part B, however, does allow for an optional extension of services for children ages 3 to 9 who are experiencing developmental delays and, by reason thereof, need special education and related services (20 U.S.C. Sec. 1401(3)(B)). But Part B does not authorize a state to serve with IDEA funds those ages 3 to 9 who are at-risk students. Assuming that a state has decided to participate in Part C, eligibility is required for infants and toddlers *experiencing* developmental delay, or who are *likely to experience* serious developmental delay, and, at the state's discretion, may be extended to infants and toddlers who, without early intervention, are *at risk* for serious developmental delay. Figure 4.1 shows the tiered or nested levels of coverage related to developmental delay, and Table 4.1 contrasts the requirements of eligibility for Part B and Part C.

A final difference in eligibility for services between Part B and Part C involves services to the family. Although Part C eligibility depends entirely on whether the infant or toddler is experiencing, likely to experience, or is at risk for experiencing developmental delay, the child's family, as well as the child, becomes eligible to receive services if the threshold qualifications criteria are met (we discuss family services in chapter 6, "Individualized and Appropriate Education"). Many people consider this one of the main benefits of Part C services and one of the main reasons that the 2004 reauthorization included an option to extend Part C services into preschool.

Note the difference between Part C and Part B with respect to beneficiaries. Under Part B, services are provided primarily and directly to the child with

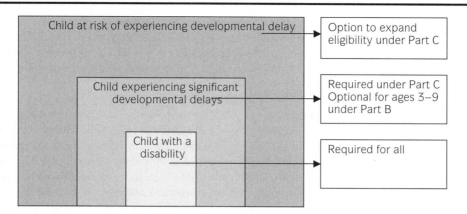

FIGURE 4.1
Tiered Eligibility

TABLE 4.1
Contrasting Program Eligibility

Eligibility Type	Optional	Categorical Disability Requirement	Functional Requirement
Part B			
Child with a disability	no	Child has a disability in one of 10 categories . . .	. . . and by reason thereof, needs special education
Child experiencing developmental delay	yes	Child experiences developmental delay in one of five categories . . .	. . . and by reason thereof, needs special education
Part C			
Child experiencing developmental delay	no	Child experiences developmental delay in one of five categories . . .	. . . and by reason thereof, needs early intervention
Child with high probability of developmental delay	no	Child has condition with high probability of causing developmental delays . . .	. . . and by reason thereof, needs early intervention
Child at risk of developmental delay	yes	None explicit.	. . . who would be at risk of experiencing substantial developmental delay without early intervention

a disability and the family benefits only through those services or, sometimes, because the family members themselves receive "related services" that are delivered directly to them. Under Part B, the primary beneficiaries are the students and the secondary beneficiaries are their families. Under Part C, by contrast, the primary beneficiaries are the infants and toddlers and their families, apparently in equal priority.

Early Intervention for Preschool-Age Children

Special education for preschool-age children historically has been problematic. Although Part B covers preschoolers generally, assuming that the coverage is not inconsistent with state law or practice, the needs of preschool children and the nature of the services they need arguably are more similar to those of infants and toddlers than school-age children. For instance, preschool children without disabilities are rarely entitled to a public education. As with infants and toddlers, preschool-age children without disabilities generally attend private child-care programs or remain at home with a parent. Further, services for preschool children are more likely to emphasize their developmental progress than their educational achievement. For these reasons, transition from preschool to more advanced education can be challenging.

To ameliorate the challenge, Part B requires a student's IEP team to consider the child's and family's Part C individualized family service plan (IFSP) as it develops the IEP (20 U.S.C. Sec. 1414(d)(2)(B)). Indeed, the team may elect to use the IFSP as the IEP for a preschool-age child with disabilities if

- consistent with state policy, and
- the school and parents agree.

It is unclear whether this option would substitute Part C provisions and protections for Part B's provisions and protections other than in the use of the IFSP. Arguably, in allowing the IFSP to serve as the IEP, IDEA extends Part C services into preschool but does not relieve the SEA and LEA of their duties under Part B.

SEAs also have the option of increasing the number of children with disabilities served under Part C by offering to extend Part C eligibility to preschool-age children (ages 3–5) who previously were served under Part C. This option, however, has several limitations and requirements:

- Only states that are recipients under the preschool grant program may extend Part C services under this option. All states currently are recipients.
- Only infants and toddlers previously served under Part C may take advantage of this option. Children who never were served under Part C as infants or toddlers are not eligible for Part C services in preschool.
- In addition to Part C services, the state must provide eligible children with educational services that "promote school readiness and that incorporate pre-literacy, language and numeracy skills."
- The state also must provide parents with a written notice that outlines their "rights and responsibilities" in determining whether their child will receive services under Part C or under the preschool programs.

Families of preschool children must consider carefully whether to adhere to Part C benefits when their children become eligible for Part B benefits. Although continuing to receive services under Part C provides many advantages, including continuation of family services and a smoother transition into preschool, there are trade-offs. The most significant one is that infants and toddlers served under Part C are not entitled to a free appropriate public education (by contrast, students under Part B do have the right to FAPE). Accordingly, a family that elects to continue to receive Part C rather than Part B services surrenders its child's right to FAPE.

Still, the advantages and consequences of electing Part C services include the following:

- Some fees may be charged for services under Part C, generally based on a sliding scale.
- Placement issues will be resolved using the natural environment mandate rather than the least restrictive environment rule (chapter 7, "Least Restrictive Environment").
- Students have more limited procedural due process protections available under Part C (chapter 8, "Procedural Due Process").
- Parents may accept some and reject other services in the child's individual plan under Part C; they do not have to accept or reject the plan in its entirety.

Refer to Figure 4.2 for a summary of the age-related coverage.

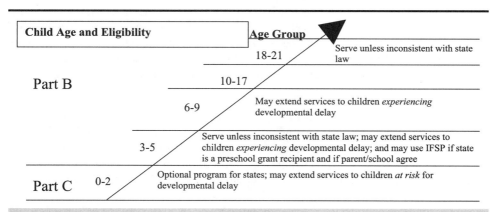

FIGURE 4.2
Summary of Age-Related Coverage

COMPREHENSIVE COVERAGE: ALL EDUCATIONAL ENTITIES

As we discussed above, the zero reject principle supports the identification and education of all students with disabilities regardless of age. Similarly, the zero reject principle supports educational opportunities for all students with disabilities regardless of educational setting. Students with disabilities, as residents of a state that receives IDEA funding, benefit from the law and federal aid wherever they are served or live within the state.

That is so because IDEA coverage encompasses public elementary and secondary LEAs and IEUs (intermediate educational units), publicly operated residential facilities that provide elementary or secondary education, and charter schools—in short, any "nonprofit institutional day or residential school, including a public ... charter school" (20 U.S.C. Sec. 1402(6) and (27)). IDEA even applies, in part, to private schools (20 U.S.C. Sec. 1412(a)(3) and (10)).

By providing for such comprehensive coverage, Congress obviously intended to prevent "service gaps" or "cracks." It wanted to reach all children without regard to the nature of the educational system by which they are, or should be, served.

State Custody

Children in the care and custody of the state itself often fall through the gaps of the service-provider system, yet they, too, are entitled to IDEA benefits if they have disabilities.

Incarceration and Juvenile Offenders

Incarcerated juveniles who qualify for special education can be especially vulnerable to policies that result in denial of a free appropriate education. This is so because they tend to be difficult to serve. They not only have disabilities but also are lawbreakers and are locked up in penal facilities. The growing trend of trying juveniles as adults is likely to further complicate the provision of special education and related services to juveniles with disabilities who are convicted as adults and incarcerated in adult correctional facilities.

IDEA and Incarcerated Youth   The 1997 amendments to IDEA first addressed the issue of providing special education to juveniles incarcerated in adult prisons, and the 2004 amendments leave those provisions substantially untouched. IDEA contains two provisions that limit its application to juveniles incarcerated in adult prisons. One provision excludes them entirely from IDEA benefits, and the other excludes them only partially.

Students ages 18 to 21 who are incarcerated in adult correctional facilities and who were not identified as having a disability or who did not have an IEP before they were incarcerated are not eligible for special education unless their education is required by state law (20 U.S.C. Sec. 1412(a)(1)(B)(ii)). This provision wholly prevents juveniles who are imprisoned in adult correctional facilities from attempting to alter the conditions of their confinement by claiming that they are eligible for special education.

But juveniles who have IEPs (and thus have been identified already as needing special education or related services) and are incarcerated in adult correctional facilities continue to have a right to a free appropriate public education, subject to some exceptions that take into account the fact that they are incarcerated. Indeed, the rights of students in adult prisons are limited in several ways:

- The state and the LEA are not required to include the student in general and statewide assessment programs.
- Juveniles who will become ineligible for special education during their incarceration because of their age (also known as *aging out* of eligibility for services) are not entitled to receive transition planning or transition services.
- If the state can demonstrate a "bona fide security or compelling penalogical interest that cannot otherwise be accommodated," juveniles incarcerated in adult facilities are not entitled to be served in the least restrictive environment; their program and/or placements may be modified. (20 U.S.C. Sec. 1414(d)(7)(B))

IDEA does not define a "bona fide security or compelling penalogical interest." The courts will have to determine the meaning of that phrase.

ADA and Section 504 Protections for Incarcerated Youth   Clearly, IDEA benefits incarcerated juvenile offenders. But may these student offenders also claim that the denial of educational opportunities in the facilities violates their Section 504 or ADA rights to be free of discrimination? The Supreme Court decided the issue in 1998. In *Pennsylvania Dept. of Corrections v. Yeskey*, the Court held that "the plain text of Title II of the ADA unambiguously extends to state prison inmates." The similarities between Section 504 and ADA suggest that the decision in *Yeskey* also would support application of Section 504 to prison inmates.

Administration of Special Education for Incarcerated Youth

The limitations on IDEA, ADA, and Section 504 rights for students with disabilities in prisons represent an attempt to strike a balance between the state's legitimate interests in prison management and criminal rehabilitation on the one hand, and the juvenile's interest in an education on the other hand. In addition to the limitations on rights extended to juveniles in adult prisons, IDEA provides flexibility to the state in administering IDEA services to such students. Which state agency is responsible for meeting IDEA requirements is subject to the discretion of the state for students in adult prisons. Governors may assign to any agency (most likely the state department of corrections) the duty to comply with IDEA with regard to students who are convicted as adults and incarcerated in adult prisons (20 U.S.C. Sec. 1412(a)(11)(C)).

Private-School Placements and Options

Because FAPE, the cornerstone of IDEA, provides for a free appropriate *public* education, you may assume that students in private schools are not affected by or covered under IDEA. But you would be wrong. It is not entirely correct that the word *public* in "free appropriate public education" means public schools. That is so because the term *public* refers to the responsibility to offer and pay for an appropriate education, not a specific placement or type of placement. In other words, the SEA and a state's public educational system must offer an appropriate education at no cost, whether the student attends public or private school.

This is the heart of zero reject: All means all. But, although IDEA requires the SEA to offer students in private school an opportunity for an appropriate education at public expense, IDEA does not require the SEA and LEAs to provide FAPE *in* the private setting. If the SEA and LEAs offer FAPE in the public school to all children, even those whose parents want them to remain in a private school, they have met their basic responsibility to offer FAPE. Of course, parents do not have to accept an LEA's offer of education in a public school, and some parents unilaterally place their child in private school, but in doing so, they may forego many IDEA rights and remedies.

Voluntary Placement in Private School by Parents

As a general rule, if a free appropriate public education is available to a child in an LEA or other public agency but the parent chooses to place the child in a private school, the LEA is not required to pay for the private-school education (20 U.S.C. Sec. 1412(a)(10)(C)(1)). This does not mean that the LEA has no responsibility for meeting the special education needs of private-school children with disabilities unilaterally placed there by their parents (without the agreement of the LEA or IEP team). Even in the case of children voluntarily enrolled by their parents in private school, the LEA must make special education and related services available to the child (Sec. 1212(a)(10)(A)(i)). The extent to which such services must be made available is determined according to this formula:

> Amounts to be expended for the provision of those services (including direct services to parentally placed private school children) by the local educational agency shall be equal to a proportionate amount of Federal funds made available under this part (20 U.S.C. Sec. 1412(a)(10)(A)(i)(I)).

Under this formula, the extent of services that students with disabilities in private-school settings must still receive is determined as a proportion of the federal funds available, as divided equally among all students with disabilities in private-school settings. The number of students with disabilities in private schools is determined by the child census. Thus, if the census finds that 100 children with disabilities are in private schools and $200,000 is available to provide them special education, the children share $200,000 worth of services.

But a child who has been placed in private school by his or her parent(s) has no individual right to receive all of the specific special education and related services that the child would receive if he or she were enrolled in a public school (20 U.S.C. Sec. 1412(a)(10)(A)). By electing to have their child attend private rather than public school, parents trade their child's right to individualized services offered by the public school district for the right to an amount of services that is proportionally distributed to all students with disabilities in private schools.

The types and extent of services, as well as how, where, and by whom services will be provided to a student with disabilities in a private school, are determined through a consultation process between the private school and the LEA (20 U.S.C. Sec. 1212(a)(10)(A)(iii)). Although the LEA has discretion in determining what services will be provided and can refuse to provide services in some situations, in those situations the LEA must provide a written explanation of why they will not provide such services (20 U.S.C. Sec. 1212(a)(10)(A)(iii)(V)).

Consistent with the rights of private-school students with disabilities to benefit from IDEA, an equitable proportion of services can be provided in one of two ways:

1. Direct provision of services by public employees
2. Through contracts with private providers

Under the 2004 reauthorization, LEAs may not adopt a policy that prohibits the use of either direct services or contracted services. But LEAs retain the discretion to decide in individual cases which of these mechanisms to use.

Private Placement by Parents Necessary to Obtain FAPE

As we stated above, the general rule is that an LEA is not obliged to pay for the cost of a private-school education, including tuition, fees, and/or special education and related services over and above those proportional to the number of students with disabilities enrolled in private schools. This rule, however, is subject to a major qualification: It applies only if the LEA has made a free appropriate public education available to the student and the parents nevertheless have elected to enroll their child in the private school or facility (20 U.S.C. Sec. 1412(a)(10)(C)(i)).

If the parents enroll their child in a private school or facility without the consent of, or a referral to, that school by the LEA, they may recover the cost of that enrollment only if a due process hearing officer or court finds that the LEA did not make a free appropriate public education available to the student in a timely manner before the parents enrolled their child in the private program (20 U.S.C. Sec. 1412(a)(10)(C)(ii)).

In part, the 2004 amendments codify the prior case law, which held that the parents may receive tuition reimbursement only if the LEA did not provide an appropriate education. They also limit tuition reimbursement to children who previously received special education from the LEA. This limitation prevents parents from avoiding the LEA's programs altogether and then seeking to charge private education to the LEA. A final limitation on private-school reimbursement is found in the case law—that the private-school placement provides an appropriate education.

In *Burlington Sch. Comm. v. Massachusetts Dept. of Education* (1985), the Supreme Court held that IDEA requires LEAs to reimburse parents for their expenditures for private placement if the LEA does not provide the student an educational benefit but the private-school placement does. *Burlington* held that not only must the public school have failed to offer FAPE, but the private-school placement also must have succeeded in providing an appropriate education. The Court did not consider it proper to reimburse parents for choosing a private-school placement that did not provide an appropriate education. Although the LEA violated its duty to provide FAPE, if the private school also failed, a private-school reimbursement is not the proper remedy.

Thus, parents' ability to recover private-school tuition from an LEA requires three evidentiary findings:

1. The child previously received special education from the LEA.
2. The LEA did not provide an appropriate education.
3. The private school did.

Private-School Placement by the LEA

Because LEAs are not always able to provide an appropriate education to every child, they sometimes contract with private schools to educate some children. These children, placed in private schools by LEA agreement between the private schools and parents, rather than unilaterally by their parents, become the beneficiaries of the contract between the LEA and the private school. Moreover, if an LEA places a child in a private school as its way of discharging its IDEA duties to that child, the child's IDEA rights follow him or her to the private placement.

Specific requirements apply to children placed in private schools by public agencies. These children must

- be provided with special education and related services,
- in conformance with their individualized education program, and
- at no cost to their parents (20 U.S.C. Secs. 1412(a)(10)(B)).

Moreover, when the LEA makes such a placement or referral, the SEA must have determined previously that the private school or facility meets the state standards and that the child retains all IDEA rights (20 U.S.C. Sec. 1412(a)(10)(B)(ii)).

If an LEA and the parents disagree about whether an appropriate program for the child is available or whether the agency is financially responsible for the private school fees, either may initiate a due process hearing (34 C.F.R. Sec. 300.148(b)). (See chapter 8 for discussion of due process.)

Clearly, Congress intended for zero reject to apply to all children, whether they are placed in private schools by school authorities or by their parents. Congress also intended that the state must remain responsible for educating them, thus attempting to respond to its findings (in 1975) that "because of the lack of adequate services within the public school system, families are often forced to find services outside the public school system, often at great distance from their residence and at their own expense" (20 U.S.C. Sec. 1400(c)(2)(E)).

Placement in Religious Schools

A new emphasis on value-based education has led many people to question why parents' right to choose private settings for their children seems to have been limited to non-religious schools. People ask, "Are not children with disabilities whose families prefer an education infused with their religious values entitled to services as much as children enrolled in non-religious schools? Why should they be excluded?" IDEA says that they should not be excluded, but its answer comes with limitations.

IDEA explicitly provides that special education and related services may be provided on the premises of religious schools, but it creates two interrelated exceptions to this rule:

1. Services may be provided on the premises of religious schools only "to the extent consistent with law" (20 U.S.C. Sec. 1412(a)(10)(A)(i)(III)).
2. The services, and any materials and equipment provided to the private school, must be "secular, neutral, and non-ideological" (20 U.S.C. Sec. 1412(a)(10)(A)(vi)(II)).

These exceptions reflect a limit that exists for all federal statutes: They always must bow to the mandates of the U.S. Constitution (chapter 1). The First Amendment right to free speech—specifically, the section referred to as the *establishment clause*—prevents a state from enacting laws that have the "purpose" or "effect" of advancing or inhibiting religion (*Agostini v. Felton,* 1997). That is why IDEA, while expressly allowing students in private religious schools to participate in the program, recognizes the constitutional limits on the manner in which they participate to ensure constitutional separation of church and state. The establishment clause (as the U.S. Supreme Court has interpreted it) guides how SEAs and LEAs apply limits to special education and related services at religious schools.

In *Lemon v. Kurtzman* (1973), the Supreme Court held that a federal or state government does not violate the establishment clause by providing government funds to students in a religious school if the government's programs

- have a secular purpose,
- do not have the primary effect of advancing religion, and
- do not create excessive entanglement between church and state.

The *Lemon* test for determining whether IDEA funds violate the establishment clause is one of "skewing" or "entanglement." Does the service or the public program tilt (skew) the public funding toward the religion? Stated alternatively, is the service or public program so entangled and intertwined with the school's religious mission that the service or public program advances or furthers the school's religious mission? Several cases have applied *Lemon*.

In *Zobrest v. Catalina Foothills Sch. Dist.* (1993), the issue was whether providing related services to a student claiming IDEA benefits at a private religious school violated the establishment clause. In *Zobrest*, a district court and the circuit court of appeals had held that the establishment clause is violated when a deaf student receives publicly paid day-long interpreter help and the parochial school that he attends inextricably intertwines its secular education and religious training.

The U.S. Supreme Court disagreed and reversed the decision. It ruled that students who are placed in parochial schools (even if placed by their parents) may receive special education or related services provided to them there by the parochial school and at public expense. The use of federal funds to pay for an interpreter for a deaf student does not entangle the government in the religious mission of the school; it does not skew, tilt, or favor the school's religion. The interpreter does not advance the school's religious mission deliberately, nor does the student's placement there, with a publicly paid interpreter, mean that the federal aid is assisting the school as it carries out its mission of religiously based education.

In *Agostini v. Felton* (1997), the Supreme Court reiterated the *Zobrest* criteria, allowing teachers whose salary is a federal–state package to teach at parochial schools when (a) the federal aid is allocated on the basis of neutral, secular criteria; (b) the criteria neither favor nor disfavor religion; and (c) the aid is made available to both religious and secular programs on a nondiscriminatory basis. The Court held that such aid does not result in governmental indoctrination of students or teachers into any religion; it does not define its recipients by reference to religion; and it does not create an excessive entanglement of government with a church.

Zobrest involved only one student and one school. What if a state legislature enacts a law that benefits many students and many schools and does so solely to accommodate their religion and to fund their special education in religious schools? That was the issue in *Bd. of Educ. of Kiryas Joel Village School Dist. v. Grumet* (1994). There, the state legislature re-drew school district lines to create a school district that was exactly contiguous with the boundaries of a separate religious community of Hasidic Jews. Under this redistricting, public money (including IDEA funds) would fund a district that was to educate only the children of that religious community.

Consistent with *Zobrest*, the New York State Court of Appeals held that state law created a distinct school district solely to accommodate a separatist, exclusionary religious community, had the inevitable effect of advancing a religious belief, and was deliberately and unconstitutionally skewed toward that belief. The U.S. Supreme Court agreed.

Finally, in its most recent decision, the Supreme Court held in *Zelman v. Simmons-Harris* (2002) that Ohio's Pilot Project Scholarship Program—a school voucher program in Cleveland—did not violate the establishment clause. In *Zelman*, the Court departed from the *Lemon* test by noting the distinction between (on the one hand) programs that impart aid directly to religious schools and (on the other hand) programs of private choice in which government aid reaches religious schools through the choices of private individuals. Citing *Zobrest*, the Court said:

> Where a government aid program is neutral with respect to religion, and provides assistance directly to a broad class of citizens who, in turn, direct government aid to religious schools wholly as a result of their own genuine and independent private choice, the program is not readily subject to challenge under the Establishment Clause.... The incidental advancement of a religious mission ... is reasonably attributable to the individual recipient, not to the government, whose role ends with the ... disbursement of benefits.

The Court determined the validity of the program based on three facts:

1. The program was neutral with regard to religion.
2. Money flowed to religious schools only through the decisions of parents.
3. The program offered genuine secular options to parents, which are unaffected by constitutional questions.

What is the upshot of *Zobrest, Agostini, Grumet*, and *Zelman*? Predictably (in an area of law as complex as the establishment clause and in a statute so expensive to the state to carry out as IDEA), there are three distinguishable lines of cases. One line holds that various types of instructional and related services may be provided to students in parochial schools without violating the establishment clause. The schools do not violate the establishment clause when they use IDEA money to provide the following services in parochial schools:

- Transportation between parochial and public schools (where the student receives services in both settings) (*Felter v. Cape Girardeau School Dist.*, 1993)
- Remedial classes delivered in a mobile unit located on the grounds of a parochial school involving only secular subjects (*Walker v. San Francisco Unified School Dist.*, 1995)
- A consulting teacher and teaching aide to a student enrolled in a parochial school (*Russman v. Sobol*, 1996)
- Occupational therapy for a student enrolled in a parochial school (*Natchez-Adams School Dist. v. Searing*, 1996)

These services are essentially neutral and do not entangle the public and IDEA money with a religion. Indeed, they are just the kind of services that were at issue in *Zobrest* and that the Supreme Court held to be religiously neutral. By contrast, they are quite unlike—in degree and purpose—the entanglement that was so evident in *Grumet*.

The second line of cases involves the withdrawal of services from children in parochial schools (as differentiated from the furnishing of services to them). For example, the court in *Natchez-Adams Sch. Dist. v. Searing* (1996) held that an LEA's blanket policy denying services to students in parochial schools violated its duty to provide a genuine opportunity for equitable participation for all children with disabilities in private schools. The LEA could not coerce parents into enrolling their child in public school or nonreligious private school by retracting an offer to provide related services based on the religious nature of the private school. That "take-it-or-leave-it" approach limits the child's education and impinges on the parents' right to practice their own religion freely.

The third line of cases involves applications of IDEA or special voucher programs that offer parents the option of using public funds for their child's private school education. These cases hinge on *Zelman*'s "true choice" rationale: Those programs are constitutional if they are neutral toward religion, provide money to parents rather than private schools, and offer parents real options for using the vouchers in non-religious schools.

These court decisions implicate, but do not expressly incorporate, a second constitutional guarantee: freedom of religion. Freedom of religion is the other side of the coin, so to speak, of the First Amendment prohibition against establishment of religion. Not only does the First Amendment prohibit Congress from making a law "respecting establishment of religion," but it also states that Congress may not make a law "prohibiting the free exercise thereof."

Proponents of school choice argue that restricting government funds to non-religious institutions restricts the ability of families to pass their religious values and teachings to their children. The wall between church and state, they argue, should not fall between parents and the religious upbringing of their children.

As evidenced by *Zobrest, Agostini*, and *Zelman*, the Supreme Court is increasingly tolerant of federal–state programs being delivered, and public funds being used, on parochial school premises. If anything, the 2004 reauthorization of IDEA became more supportive of the use of public money and service delivery in religious schools. It seems safe to assume that students with disabilities will continue to receive IDEA's benefits notwithstanding their enrollment in parochial schools.

Charter Schools

The school-choice movement reflects a desire to take more educational decision making out of the hands of the bureaucracies and empower families to make such choices. It is also fed by the perception that public schools are failing to provide an adequate education to students and that a differently organized and operated school system can do a better job. Many state legislatures have enacted laws providing for the creation of charter schools.

Although the state statutory schemes vary, basically these provisions allow qualified individuals or groups who meet criteria developed by the SEA to establish public educational programs (charter schools) that are independent from other school district programs. IDEA requires LEAs to serve children with disabilities in charter schools in the same manner that they serve children in other schools. Furthermore, LEAs must provide funds to charter schools in the same manner that they provide monies to other schools (20 U.S.C. Sec. 1413(a)(5)).

Direct Services by the State Education Agency

As stated previously, the purpose of the zero reject principle is to include every child in the educational process and ensure each student a free appropriate education. Thus, IDEA provides for services to be given to children in state custody, prisons or juvenile justice, private schools, and public charter schools in addition to regular public school placements.

Closing the Gap

In addition to providing this broad range of covered placements, IDEA (consistent with *Honig*) makes the state education agency ultimately responsible to ensure that children with disabilities receive FAPE. When the LEA fails or refuses to do its job, the SEA must remedy the problem. The SEA must use the federal funds otherwise available to an LEA to provide services directly to children with disabilities whenever it determines that an LEA is unable or unwilling to do so, is unwilling or unable to be consolidated with another LEA, or has students who can be served best in a state or regional center (20 U.S.C. Sec. 1413). The purpose of the direct-services provision is to ensure that all eligible students in a state receive a free appropriate public education; it is another one of the gap-closing provisions of the law.

Single-Agency Responsibility

The direct-services requirement is the practical manifestation of Congress's intent to make the zero reject principle effective by providing for one, and only one, ultimate point of responsibility and accountability. IDEA requires a single state agency, the SEA, to be responsible for assuring that IDEA's requirements are carried out. In addition, all special education programs within the state, including programs administered by another state or local agency (such as social welfare, mental health, mental retardation, human resources, public health, corrections, or juvenile services), are under the general supervision of the SEA, must be monitored by the SEA, and must meet the SEA's educational standards (20 U.S.C. Sec. 1412(a)(11)(A)).

To ensure that all children are provided a free appropriate public education, the SEA must develop interagency agreements or mechanisms for interagency coordination with other human services agencies (20 U.S.C. Sec. 1412(a)(12)). These interagency agreements or mechanisms must contain provisions that address the financial responsibilities of each agency for providing education or related services.

To buttress the single-agency device for zero reject, the SEA also may reallocate funds to other LEA programs in the state that are not adequately providing an appropriate education to students in those districts (20 U.S.C. Sec. 1411(g)(4)) and require LEAs to consolidate their services (20 U.S.C. Sec. 1413(e)(1)). There is no doubt that these provisions were designed to close the service gaps and prevent the buck passing and responsibility shuffling that resulted in some children being excluded from educational programs in the past.

EXCLUSION DUE TO INSUFFICIENT RESOURCES

By covering any and all students with disabilities no matter where they receive educational services, IDEA attempts to narrow the seams in the educational system so children with disabilities do not fall into gaps of eligibility or coverage. But creating a seamless system with regard to where services are provided does not guarantee that sufficient resources will be available to make the services effective and meaningful.

That is why Section 1400(c)(2)(D) notes that before IDEA was enacted, a lack of adequate resources within the public school system forced families to find services outside the public school system. Thus, IDEA also supports the zero reject principle with provisions designed to ensure the capacity of the system to meet the needs of all children in special education. Some of these provisions relate to cost shifting and personnel development.

Cost Shifting and Allocation of Funds

As states attempted to implement IDEA with limited federal and state dollars (IDEA never has been funded by Congress at the full limit it authorizes; see chapter 3 for a description of the authorization of federal funds), they faced huge expenses. States and LEAs increased their own appropriations, but still funds were not sufficient, particularly for students with severe disabilities.

A major funding stream, however, existed outside of IDEA: the Medicaid program of the Social Security Act. This program provides federal funds to pay for some of the medical or medically related expenses of people with severe disabilities (who usually are required to be poor to qualify for the medical assistance funds).

To tap into the Medicaid funding stream, some states created programs that combined the special education personnel and funds under IDEA with the medical personnel and funds under the Medicaid program. By taking this approach, they could ensure enough funds in the aggregate to pay for the education and related services (such as physical therapy, occupational therapy, and medical evaluations) required to provide an appropriate education to students with severe disabilities. In short, by using more than just IDEA funds, they sought to prevent either total exclusion or functional exclusion, either of which violates the zero reject principle.

The federal agency that administers Medicaid challenged this approach and refused to reimburse Massachusetts for Medicaid dollars that it had spent for meeting the education costs of students with severe disabilities who lived in a Medicaid-approved facility. Massachusetts sued the federal government for reimbursement, and the Supreme Court, in *Bowen v. Massachusetts* (1988), approved use of the Medicaid funds for students' education.

On July 1, 1988, the president signed into law the Medicare Catastrophic Coverage Act of 1988 (MCCA, P.L. 100-360). This law provided the most significant expansion of the Medicare program since its inception. The MCCA made numerous technical amendments to the Medicare and Medicaid programs and added three new Medicaid provisions. However, the following year, the president effectively repealed these major expansions of the Medicare program by signing into law the Medicare Catastrophic Coverage Repeal Act of 1989 (P.L. 101-234). This law (42 U.S.C. Sec. 1396b(c)) prohibits Medicaid agencies from refusing to pay for medical services that are (a) covered under a state's Medicaid or Medicare plans, (b) provided to children with disabilities, and (c) included in the students' individualized education programs. (We discuss IEPs and IFSPs in chapter 6, "Individualized and Appropriate Education.") Typically, the reimbursable services include speech pathology and audiology, psychological services, physical and occupational therapy, medical counseling, and services for diagnostic and evaluation purposes.

The effect of the *Bowen* case and the Medicare Catastrophic Coverage Act is that there is a new funding stream for related services and that states may combine educational programs (funded under IDEA) with medical programs (funded under the Medicaid program). This relieves the pressure on the state's educational dollars but increases the pressure on its health-care dollars. In the case of students who have medical complications or are primarily in health-care delivery systems (such as those in congregate-care facilities), the prospects are that they will receive jointly operated and jointly financed services.

This could have the ultimate effect of ensuring no violation of the zero reject rule through their total or functional exclusion from special education. At the same time, the federal and state governments are clearly concerned with the burgeoning costs of the Medicaid program and are trying to contain those costs. One of their strategies may be to restrict the Medicaid funds that go to special-education–related uses.

Since 1997, IDEA has clarified the issue of financial responsibility for public agency services by requiring that public agencies (including state Medicaid agencies), through interagency agreements, assume financial responsibility for services to children with disabilities before LEAs or SEAs must assume these obligations. Essentially, the interagency agreements must provide that the other public agencies are the first payors and the SEA is the payor of last resort.

Furthermore, public agencies that are legally obligated under state or federal law to provide or pay for educational or related services to children with disabilities must fulfill these obligations and responsibilities (20 U.S.C. Sec. 1412(a)(12)(A)(i) and (B)(i)). If public agencies fail to fulfill their responsibilities, IDEA authorizes LEAs or SEAs to claim reimbursement for services from the public agencies that fail to provide or pay for special education or related services (20 U.S.C. Sec. 1412(a)(12)(B)(ii)).

High-Risk Pools and Innovative Cost Sharing

The needs of students with disabilities vary greatly, and so can the costs for their education. Because services for a child with extensive educational needs may have a significant financial impact on the budget of the LEA in which the child is enrolled, IDEA provides states with the option of allocating 10% of funds designated to state-level activities to create a high-cost risk pool (20 U.S.C. Sec. 1411(e)(3)(G)). The risk pool allows states to disperse funds from the pool to assist LEAs in meeting the high cost of services for high-need students. Alternatively, states may use up to 5% of these same funds to support innovative and effective methods of sharing costs among LEAs.

The state must develop a plan for how the risk pool will work and ensure that disbursements are not used to pay costs associated with a legal cause of action or costs that are reimbursable under Medicaid. Furthermore, the fund cannot be used to limit the right of a child to FAPE.

Free Education; Use of Private Insurance

Although cost shifting and sharing are useful and equitable means to ensure that schools have the capacity to meet the needs of their students with disabilities, children with disabilities are still entitled to a *free* public education under IDEA. This means that schools are not allowed to involve these children in cost-sharing measures for special education services.

Prior to IDEA, schools traditionally excluded students with disabilities by charging them fees for special services—that is, for services that were based on disability only and therefore were not provided to nondisabled students. The fees often were high because (a) the services were expensive, or (b) the LEA wanted to discourage the enrollment of these students. Under IDEA, if an LEA charges any fees to all students, it may charge students with disabilities as well; uniformly assessed fees are permissible. But expenses for transportation may not be billed.

In addition, parents who have insurance policies that reimburse for medically related services may not be required to make a claim on their insurers if the services are provided to comply with IDEA and utilization of such insurance benefits would require them to incur a financial loss (*Raymond S. v. Ramirez,* 1995; *Seals v. Loftis,* 1985).

States may not charge for the living expenses of students they place in public or private residential programs to comply with IDEA. IDEA, however, does not relieve an insurer or similar third party from an otherwise valid obligation to provide or pay for services rendered to a student with a disability (34 C.F.R. Sec. 300.105(b)). Accordingly, a parent, at his or her option, may offer to have an insurer pay for services that an LEA otherwise must provide.

Comprehensive System of Personnel Development

The 2004 reauthorization included significant changes to the requirement for the state to have in place a comprehensive system of personnel development, but the purpose—to ensure an adequate number of trained professionals to meet the educational needs of children with disabilities—has not changed. The state is required to establish and maintain

> qualifications to ensure that personnel ... are appropriately and
> adequately prepared and trained, including that those personnel

have the content knowledge and skills to serve children with disabilities. (20 U.S.C. Sec. 1412(a)(14)(A))

Paraprofessionals and those providing related services are required to have approved licensing, certification, registration or otherwise meet state standards for their activities and must be "appropriately trained and supervised." The state licensing and certification requirement does not allow for waivers to be granted, even if temporary, provisional, or in emergencies (20 U.S.C. Sec. 1412(a)(14)(B)(ii)).

Under IDEA, special education teachers must be "highly qualified" by the same date as general education teachers under the Elementary and Secondary Education Act (ESEA, as amended by No Child Left Behind Act of 2001). Furthermore, the state must require LEAs in their jurisdiction to take measurable steps to recruit, hire, train, and retain highly qualified special education instructors (20 U.S.C. Sec. 1412(a)(14)(D)).

IDEA's requirements regarding staff qualifications and training are important. Without a sufficient number of adequately trained personnel, the zero reject principle (as well as the principles relating to appropriate education and least restrictive environment) could not be implemented. The "highly qualified" mandate attempts to ensure that an insufficient number of, or inadequately trained, special education teachers and service providers does not result in functional exclusion of children with disabilities from educational opportunities.

Meeting the "Highly Qualified" Standard

But what does highly qualified mean? NCLB defines the term, and IDEA retains the NCLB definition with some additions and alternative means for meeting the requirement. Under NCLB, "highly qualified" requires

- state licensing or certification that has not been waived (no matter whether the waiver is temporary, provisional, or emergency) and demonstrated competence in all academic subjects in which the teacher teaches, as measured by a uniform state standard for evaluation; or
- for new elementary school teachers, a bachelor's degree and demonstrated subject knowledge and teaching skills related to the basic elementary school curriculum, as measured by a rigorous test; or
- for new middle school or secondary teachers, a bachelor's degree, its equivalent, or demonstrated competency in the subjects that the teacher will teach, as measured by a rigorous test.

IDEA's "highly qualified" standards provide that for a special education teacher to be highly qualified, he or she has to meet the NCLB requirements and three additional requirements:

- Be certified or licensed for special education
- Not have such certification or licensing waived
- Hold at least a bachelor's degree

It is important to note that the NCLB requirements apply only to teachers who are providing instruction in core academic areas. Special education teachers who provide consulting services to general education teachers to help them adapt the curriculum and meet the needs of students with disabilities in general education classrooms have to meet only the special education certification and degree requirement.

IDEA also allows teachers to use alternative criteria in place of the NCLB's criteria for "highly qualified," but only in two circumstances:

1. *The special education teacher teaches exclusively to alternative achievement standards.* Special education teachers teaching to alternative achievement standards are those who teach students whose disabilities warrant an entirely different measure of their progress than typically is used to assess students without disabilities.
2. *The special education teacher teaches multiple subjects exclusively to students with disabilities.* Special education teachers who are teaching multiple subjects are those who teach two or more core academic subjects exclusively to children with disabilities.

A special education teacher who teaches exclusively to alternative standards must meet either the regular requirement under the NCLB (licensure, certification, etc. in general education and demonstrated competence) or the requirement for new teachers (degree and/or competence testing)—regardless of whether the teacher is actually new.

In addition, the subject knowledge and competence requirement just has to be "appropriate to the level of instruction being provided." Under IDEA, that level is presumed to be elementary school level or above and is determined by the state. Special education teachers teaching to alternative standards exclusively must still, of course, additionally meet the IDEA requirements for special education certification and a bachelor's degree.

Special education teachers who are teaching multiple subjects also may use an alternative standard for meeting the NCLB "highly qualified" criteria:

- If they are not new to the profession, they may meet the requirement by demonstrating competency in the subjects taught through the state uniform evaluation.
- If they are new to special education and are already highly qualified in math, language, or science, they may meet the NCLB requirement by demonstrating competency within 2 years in all subjects taught.

In any case, those special education teachers teaching multiple subjects also must meet the IDEA special requirements for "highly qualified": certification/licensing in special education and a bachelor's degree.

The maze of requirements and figuring out which "highly qualified" standard applies depends upon the specific circumstances and whether the special education teacher is new or old, provides direct instruction or consultation, teaches to alterna-tive standards exclusively, or teaches multiple subjects exclusively to students with disabilities. Further complicating the situation is that each state creates and imple-ments its own licensing/certification, core competency tests, and high objective uni-form state standards for evaluation (HOUSSE).

PREVENTING DISABILITY-BASED EXCLUSION

Physical barriers can cause some students with disabilities to be excluded from school. That is why IDEA authorizes the secretary of education to make grants and to enter into cooperative arrangements with SEAs to remove architectural barriers (20 U.S.C. Sec. 1404). For students to have educational opportunities, they first must have access to educational resources—have the door of the school open to them.

The zero reject principle is founded on the premise that individuals should not be excluded from educational opportunities because of their disability or a lack of services to accommodate their disability. Zero reject is about access and opening doors to education. Yet, even this basic principle of equality, echoed in both the Americans with Disabilities Act and Section 504 of the Rehabilitation Act, has not gone unchallenged. Arguments about the educability of some children with disabil-ities led some to challenge whether "all children" meant those who, in their estima-tion, could not benefit from education.

Educability

Are any children totally ineducable and therefore not entitled to IDEA's protection because, by definition, they inherently lack the ability to learn? Until 1988, the courts followed the finding in *PARC v. Commonwealth* (1971, 1972) that all—repeat, all—children are capable of learning. Earlier, however, *Levine v. New Jersey* (1980) put up the question for debate, and in 1988 a federal court of appeals answered the question conclusively.

State Law Basis for Exclusion

Timothy W. v. Rochester School Dist. (1988) involved a student who was denied admission to school because of his disability. He was 13 years old, was blind and deaf, had cerebral palsy, was spastic and subject to frequent convulsions, lacked carotid tissue, had profound retardation, had no communication skills, operated "at the brainstem level," and had acquired reflex behavior (some ability to respond to external stimuli—light and noise) but had made no developmental progress in about a year. Moreover, he seemed to be regressing, had not achieved a level of response to stimuli beyond his original baseline (first measured response), engaged in only passive and nonvolitional activities, and had to have his hands and feet manipulated completely to move them.

For all of these reasons, the trial court found that he was "not capable of ben-efiting from special education" at present, that there was no reason to include ineducable children in an education system, and that he should be provided "continuous, but periodic evaluations, intended to identify any development which illustrates a capability to benefit from special education."

The issue on appeal was whether public policy justifies exclusion from the educational system of this child and others with similarly extensive disabilities, on two grounds:

1. The system cannot benefit them.
2. The expenditure of funds cannot be defended.

The court of appeals reversed the trial court, holding that IDEA was enacted to ensure that all children with disabilities, even those who arguably are ineducable, are provided an appropriate public education. Indeed, "not only are severely handicapped children not excluded from the Act, but the most severely handicapped are actually given priority under the Act" (as it provided at that time; the priority for serving those with the greatest needs does not exist in the current or the 1997 version). Moreover, the court of appeals said, IDEA has no prerequisite that the student be able to benefit from education. Instead, IDEA speaks about the state's responsibility to the child.

In holding that ineducability could not be used to justify exclusion under IDEA, the court of appeals reasoned that Congress intended to include even children with the most profound disabilities in special education.

■ The Congressional history demonstrated that "educational benefit was neither guaranteed nor required as a prerequisite for a child to receive such an education."

■ Congress had amended the Act four times since it was enacted in 1975, and Congress not only had reaffirmed repeatedly the Act's original intent—to educate all children—but it also had expanded the provisions covering students with the most severe disabilities.

■ Congress relied on the *PARC* and *Mills* cases in creating IDEA and establishing the zero reject principle.

■ The Supreme Court's use of a benefit standard in *Rowley* was a "substantive limitation placed on the state's choice of an educational program; it was not a license for the state to exclude certain handicapped children." The court interpreted *Rowley* to support Congress's intent to ensure public education to all children with disabilities without regard to the level of achievement they might attain. *Rowley* recognized IDEA's intent to open the doors but not to guarantee any particular level of education once they are open. And Congress had not seen fit to change the Court's approach. (See chapter 6 on *Rowley*.)

In addition to refusing to allow the exclusion, the court of appeals may have established a duty that LEAs must use state-of-the-art procedures for educating children with severe disabilities. Indeed, Congress seems to have stated as much when it provided, in the 2004 reauthorization, that one of the ways by which students' education can be made more effective and the outcomes of education more accept-able is for educators to have the skills to use "scientifically based instructional prac-tices, to the maximum extent possible" (20 U.S.C. Sec. 1401(c)(5)(E)).

The education of students with severe disabilities is defined broadly and includes not only traditional academic skills but also basic functional life skills. The educational methodologies in these areas are not static but are constantly evolving and improving. Under *Timothy W.*'s dicta and under the "scientifically based instruc-tional practices" language now in IDEA, it seems that a case can be made that the LEA is responsible for availing itself of these new approaches in providing an edu-cation program geared to each child's individual needs. The only question for the LEA to determine, in conjunction with the child's parents, is what constitutes an appropriate education for the child.

The problems with concluding that some children are not educable are manifold:

- Few conclusive research data justify the conclusion that some children are not educable. Indeed, there is strong debate on both sides of the educability issue. A conclusion that some children are not educable, then, seems scientifically debatable.
- Where does one draw the line? Once a child is found "not educable," the ten-dency may be to open up the class of ineducable children to include some chil-dren who are simply difficult or expensive to educate but who can be educated or benefit from training.
- Special education and related professions would be relieved of the pressure to find ways to educate children with more profound disabilities, stifling the development of new knowledge that could benefit them.

It is significant that, for now, the debate about educability seems to have abated. *Tim-othy W.* and IDEA are the causes for the abatement, and the zero reject principle is the foundation on which they rest.

Contagious Disease

One other line of cases, like those involving educability, has tested the outer limits of the zero reject principle. These are cases involving the education of students with contagious diseases.

The Supreme Court's decision in *School Bd. of Nassau County v. Arline* (1987), involving a teacher who had tuberculosis, laid the foundation for interpreting Sec-tion 504 as it applies to students with contagious diseases. In that case, Jean Arline had experienced TB some 15-plus years before the disease recurred. When it returned, she suffered several relapses. After the third relapse, her LEA employer discharged her from all of her duties.

Claiming that Section 504 of the Rehabilitation Act protects her from discharge because of her disease, Arline sued to recover her job and damages. Her suit raised a critical question: Is a person with TB entitled to the protection of Section 504?

Alternatively and more broadly stated, the issue was whether a person with a contagious disease, such as AIDS, is "otherwise qualified" to participate in various activities—in Arline's case, to be a teacher. In the case of students with AIDS, the analogous issue is whether they are entitled, under Section 504 or IDEA, to be enrolled in school.

The Supreme Court held that Section 504 protects Arline and others with contagious diseases against discrimination based on their disabilities. In her case, Arline met all three criteria for protection under Section 504: She had a disability, had a record of one, and was regarded as having one. Moreover, her medical condition significantly affected her ability to work as a teacher (though, perhaps, not to work in other capacities in an LEA, where the risk of infection was not so great).

Having found Arline to be a person with a disability, the Court addressed the issue of whether she was "otherwise qualified" for employment. If so, she may not be discriminated against because of her disability. To determine whether Arline, or others with contagious diseases are "otherwise qualified," the Court laid down four standards to be applied in the context of employment of a person with a disability (these standards have been extended to education placement decisions):

1. What is the nature of the risk—how is the disease transmitted?
2. What is the duration of the risk—how long is the carrier infectious?
3. What is the severity of the risk—what is the potential harm to third persons of becoming infected?
4. What is the probability of transmitting the disease to others—what is the likelihood that the person will infect others and cause them various degrees of harm?

In all cases, the Court indicated that the answers to these issues must be determined on an individual basis and by appropriately qualified professionals (physicians or other public health officials). Individualized decision making, coupled with judicial or LEA deference to professional judgment, is the proper way to protect people with disabilities against "deprivations based on prejudice, stereotypes, or unfounded fear, while giving appropriate weight to such legitimate concerns … as avoiding exposing others to significant health and safety risks" (*Arline*, p. 288). The Supreme Court sent the case back to the lower courts to determine whether Arline was entitled to continue to teach (a matter not relevant to our discussion here).

AIDS, Eligibility, and the Bragdon Decision

Of the several diseases that implicate questions of contagion in a school setting (e.g., tuberculosis and some varieties of herpes), the issues are drawn most sharply when a student has AIDS. The Supreme Court in *Bragdon v. Abbott* (1998) addressed the question of whether ADA (1990) applied to persons infected with the human immunodeficiency virus (HIV). As with Section 504, ADA requires two elements to establish eligibility as a person with a disability. The person must

1. have an impairment, have a record, or be regarded as having a disability; and
2. the impairment must substantially affect a major life activity.

In holding that infection with HIV, and thus AIDS, satisfied the ADA definition of disability, the Court found that HIV infection was a covered impairment, that a positive HIV test provided an adequate record of the impairment, and that HIV affected the major life activity of reproduction (*Bragdon v. Abbott,* 1998).

Although *Arline* and *Bragdon* have settled the issue of whether a student with AIDS can claim protection under ADA, and by extension under Section 504, the rights of a child with AIDS to IDEA rights and services do not arise automatically upon the finding that the child has AIDS (*Dist. 27 Community School Bd. v. Bd. of Educ. of New York City,* 1986; *Doe v. Belleville Public Schools Dist. No. 118,* 1987). To be eligible for IDEA benefits, a child must qualify as "other health impaired" as a result of limited strength, vitality, or alertness that (a) are caused by chronic or acute health problems, and (b) adversely affect the student's educational performance (34 C.F.R. Sec. 300.8(c)(9)). The child's disability must meet the categorical requirement of IDEA eligibility.

Furthermore, even if the student qualifies as "other health impaired," unless the student also requires special education as a result of the disability, the student does not meet the standards for being classified as a "child with a disability" and is not entitled to IDEA rights (34 C.F.R. Sec. 300.7(a)). Some students with health conditions such as AIDS may not need special education and would not be IDEA-eligible, as we pointed out in chapter 3.

Exclusion, Placement, and Safety Issues

Assume that a student meets the definition of a person with a disability and is entitled to ADA and Section 504 protection and that the student also qualifies for IDEA. The question remains: Where does the student receive an education? Two additional issues must be addressed.

First, both ADA and Section 504 protections apply only to situations in which the person with a disability is "otherwise qualified" for participation in an activity. Does having a contagious disease undermine an individual's ability to be "otherwise qualified?" If so, the person could be legitimately excluded.

Second, a student with a contagious disease, particularly one that may be fatal, may pose a safety risk to other students and school personnel. Even if ADA, Section 504, or IDEA protections apply to a student with a contagious disease, how should educators balance that student's right to educational opportunity and the benefits of the zero reject principle against the risk that the student's participation may pose to others? Don't the other students and school personnel have a right to be free from any harm that the contagious student may present? May an LEA provide educational opportunities to the child in another venue? Under what circumstances? Again, the issues are sharpest with respect to students with AIDS.

The First Issue: May an AIDS-Affected Person Be Excluded?   In 1987, the New Jersey Supreme Court in *Bd. of Educ. of City of Plainfield v. Cooperman* (1987) approved regulations of the state commissioners of education and health that set forth the procedures by which children with AIDS may be placed in or out of general or special education programs (but not excluded wholly from some school services—typically, homebound or hospital-based special education). The state's regulations provide that, as a general rule, students with full-blown AIDS, AIDS-related complex (ARC), or seropositive diagnoses will be admitted into regular school. Three exceptions are

1. children who are not toilet-trained,
2. those who are unable to control their drooling, and
3. those who are unusually physically aggressive toward other students.

Presumably, the state adopted these exceptions to address the contagion issue with respect to HIV-transmission through exchange or contact with bodily fluids. For those students, other placements and programs must be developed.

A panel of medical experts must review all decisions in which an LEA decides to place a child on the basis of AIDS. The LEA bears the burden of proving that the child fits into one of the exceptions. And a full hearing must be held before the LEA and medical panel, with a right to appeal to the state commissioner of education. The New Jersey Supreme Court approved the following principles:

- The presumption is in favor of inclusion and against exclusion (zero reject principle).
- Medical judgment is controlling as long as it is reasonable.
- Individualized determinations must be made and may be appealed through a fair-hearing process.

The Second Issue: Where Must a Student With AIDS Be Educated?

Thomas v. Atascadero Unified School Dist. (1986) prohibited an LEA from excluding a student with AIDS who bit a classmate. Because no evidence showed that the student posed a significant risk of harm to his kindergarten classmates or teachers, and because the LEA failed to meet its burden to show that he was not otherwise qualified to attend a regular-school kindergarten class, the court ordered that he be retained in that class.

Although the decision did not involve an interpretation of IDEA, it does apply to IDEA. This is because the regulations under Section 504 are substantially the same as under IDEA. Thus, placement in the general class, in the absence of proof of dangerousness, is presumed to be correct.

Students who qualify for special education because they have a disability in addition to HIV and AIDS still are required to be educated in the least restrictive environment. In *Martinez v. School Bd. of Hillsborough County* (1988), the student, who was diagnosed as "trainable mentally handicapped" (TMH), began her fight to be educated in the regular TMH room although she was incontinent and sucked her thumb continually.

The Eleventh Circuit held that this student, like any other who is eligible for IDEA protection, has a right to be educated in the least restrictive environment.

Certain precautionary measures must be taken, and instruction must be provided so the student will learn to use the toilet and refrain from sucking her thumb. The LEA must educate the student in the regular TMH classroom behind a glass barrier until she has acquired these desirable behaviors. In addition, if a question arises as to the advisability of the student being in the classroom on a certain day, the school nurse should be consulted to evaluate the student or any other student to prevent infections. The court concluded that the appropriate placement for the student then was the regular TMH classroom.

Conclusion and Rationale

The AIDS cases demonstrate the following:

- Determinations regarding students with contagious diseases must be individualized (not a "meat-ax" approach that covers all students or persons affected by an AIDS condition).
- There must be a public health basis for exclusion (a close connection between the child's condition and behavior on the one hand, and the safety of students and teachers on the other hand).
- The exclusion must rest on defensible and reasonable medical testimony.
- The decision must be appealable through the fair-hearing process (for due process hearing, see chapter 8).

The reasons for these results are the following:

- People with AIDS are considered to have a disability under Section 504 and the ADA and may be considered eligible for IDEA benefits if the disability causes them to need special education.
- The zero reject principle and the equal protection doctrine prohibit discrimination and exclusion as long as the person is found to have a disability under Section 504, ADA, or IDEA.
- The doctrine of the least restrictive alternative/environment (see chapter 7) creates a presumption that students with AIDS should be educated in general education programs. Although the presumption may be overcome in the event of dangerousness to others, the LEA has the burden of proof in seeking to overcome the presumption.
- The due process clause of the Fourteenth Amendment (see chapter 8) requires not only individualized determinations but also opportunities for the student to protest any planned exclusion. The regulations implementing Section 504, as well as IDEA and its regulations, codify the principle of due process and procedural protection.
- The public's fear—"fear itself"—does not justify exclusion of the student any more than fear justified an exclusionary zoning ordinance that prohibited group homes for people with mental retardation (*Cleburne v. Cleburne Living Center, Inc.*, 1985) or permitted a person who is not dangerous to himself or others to be incarcerated involuntarily in a mental hospital (*O'Connor v. Donaldson*, 1975).

- Education is an especially valuable public service, and access should not be denied except for the most serious of reasons (*Brown v. Board of Education,* 1954, and *Plyler v. Doe,* 1982).
- Exclusion, coupled with identification of the student as having an AIDS condition, creates a special stigma and, in the words of the Supreme Court in *Plyler v. Doe* (1982), can cause "lifetime hardships on a discrete class of children not accountable for their disabling status."
- Homebound or hospital-based special education is an appropriate alternative to total exclusion for the student whose dangerousness has been proved and for whom the presumption of inclusion in general education programs has been overcome.

PREVENTING DISCIPLINE-BASED EXCLUSION

As the Supreme Court noted in *Honig* and as IDEA long has recognized, SEAs and LEAs have used disciplinary procedures such as suspension and expulsion to exclude or remove students with disabilities from public schools, both physically and functionally. That seems wrong and, under IDEA, is wrong. Yet, schools still must have the right to discipline students with disabilities. That is so for three reasons:

1. Discipline can be an effective teaching tool for students with disabilities.
2. It preserves a positive learning environment.
3. It safeguards children with and without disabilities and school personnel.

To resolve these tensions, IDEA prohibits exclusion, allows for discipline, addresses the disparate impact of exclusion on students with disabilities, and thereby carries out the zero reject principle. IDEA achieves all this by setting out standards and a process that SEAs and LEAs must follow when disciplining students with disabilities. As you soon will learn, IDEA has general rules, and then exceptions to them. Let's start with the most fundamental general rule: same discipline.

The Same-Discipline Rule and Its Exceptions

The general rule is that an LEA may discipline children with disabilities "in the same manner and for the same duration" that it disciplines children without disabilities (20 U.S.C. Sec. 1415(k)(1)). This is a rule against discrimination through discipline, such as by the application of more severe or longer terms of punishment. Stated alternatively, it is a rule of equal treatment: LEAs must apply the school discipline policies consistently to students with and without disabilities. But IDEA provides three exceptions to this rule so discipline does not prevent students with disabilities from receiving FAPE and so the zero reject principle persists, even in the face of discipline.

Three Substantive Exceptions

There are three basic substantive exceptions to the same-treatment rule:

1. An LEA may not deny FAPE to a student through suspension, expulsion, or other disciplinary action (20 U.S.C. Sec. 1412(a)(1)(A)). This exception, often referred to as "no-cessation," guarantees the rights of IDEA students and requires LEAs to provide them with services during some periods of suspension or expulsion (see below).
2. LEAs must, in some circumstances, address the behavior that led to disciplinary action. This exception can be referred to as "addressing-the-behavior." After all, behavioral needs are likely to interfere with the education of the child and thus warrant action on the part of the student's IEP team.
3. At times, the behavior that led to the discipline results from the child's disability. It would be both inequitable and futile to punish children with disabilities for behaviors not completely under their control. These exceptions are generally grouped under the term "manifestation."

Procedural Exception: Notice

IDEA also requires LEAs to take an additional procedural action when disciplining a child with a disability: The LEA must notify the student's parents about the discipline on the same date on which it decides to change the child's placement because of a violation of a code of conduct (34 C.F.R. 300.530(b)), and the LEA must provide information on the rights of the parents and student with respect to challenging a disciplinary decision. (The statute does not define "discipline," leaving it to the SEA and/or LEA to do so. Moreover, the statute does not limit the "notice" rule to only some cases of discipline; apparently, the LEA must give the notice in all cases of discipline.) Parents have the right to appeal disciplinary decisions, and, if they request a review, the LEA or SEA must arrange for an expedited hearing of the matter (34 C.F.R. 300.532(a) and (c)).

Quasi-Substantive and Quasi-Procedural Exception for Unique Circumstances and Student Placement

The LEA has some flexibility in considering whether and to what extent a child with a disability should be removed from his or her usual educational setting. Section 1415(k)(1)(A) and 34 C.F.R. 300.530(a) provide that an LEA may consider "any unique circumstances on a case-by-case basis when determining whether to order a change of placement for a child with a disability who violates a code of student conduct." It is not clear what "unique circumstances" are or when they will advantage or disadvantage the student. This is an area ripe for litigation and court interpretation.

Disciplinary Actions and IDEA

The general rule of same treatment is limited by the situations that trigger any of the above three substantive exceptions (no cessation, address-the-behavior, and manifestation). Two factors play into whether the exceptions are triggered.

The first factor relates to the student's behavior. IDEA addresses two categories of student behavior. The first category involves violations of the school code of conduct, and the second category involves incidents pertaining to weapons, drugs, and serious bodily injury.

The second factor involves the disciplinary action that the LEA proposes to take. The two categories of disciplinary actions are

1. those that result in removals of not more than 10 days (short-term), and
2. those that result in removals of more than 10 days (long-term).

We will describe how the two behavior categories and two disciplinary action categories work together with respect to the general rule and the exceptions. We also will describe how each exception is applied and what it requires as we identify what triggers each exception.

Discipline for Violating the School's Code of Conduct

Violations of school codes are, for students with and without disabilities alike, the most common causes of disciplinary action by the school. This category encompasses a wide range of behaviors and is easier to define by saying what it does not include than what it does. Put simply, violations of the school code include everything except conduct involving drugs, weapons, and serious bodily harm—the other category of disciplinary action under IDEA.

When a student with a disability violates the school code, the first question is: What action does the school propose to take to punish or otherwise address the behavior? Does it result in no removal or a removal that is not more than 10 days? If so, the requirements for a short-term removal apply.

Short-Term Removals—Not More Than 10 Days   IDEA bows to school-safety concerns and codifies *Honig*'s short-term 10-day suspension right by allowing school personnel to make a change in placement to an "appropriate interim alternative educational setting, another setting, or suspension, for not more than 10 school days (to the extent that such alternatives would be applied to children without disabilities)" (20 U.S.C. Sec. 1415(k)(1)(B); 34 C.F.R. 300.530(b)). The regulations protect the student by providing that the 10 "school days" mean 10 "consecutive" school days (34 C.F.R. 300.530(b)(1)), but the regulations also provide that the LEA may use the short-term (10 consecutive school days) removal for "separate incidents of misconduct." The exception to the LEA's power to use the 10-day plus 10-day approach is that the various 10-day removals may not constitute a "pattern" that results in a change of placement (34 C.F.R. 300.536(a)(2)).

Note that an LEA has three choices of placement:

- "An appropriate interim alternative educational setting" (IAES)
- "Another setting"—which apparently also must be appropriate but which is not an IAES (it is not clear what that would be, but homebound or other more restrictive settings may be permitted)

■ "Suspension"—apparently either from school altogether or by way of an "in-school" suspension, with the student allowed to have some partial participation in school activities (e.g., not permitted to attend school except to take mandatory examinations)

Although the LEA has the authority to initiate any number of these short-term removals, if any of the removals cumulatively result in more than 10 school days of removal and are found to constitute a pattern of related removals, the LEA's imposition of discipline may trigger the long-term removal requirements. The 1999 regulations (34 C.F.R. Secs. 300.519(b) and 300.520(a)(1)(1999)) specifically addressed the question of cumulative removals that add up to more than 10 school days, using this very test for a "pattern" of removals.

The regulations for IDEA 2004 continue this approach, but they significantly narrow the terms under which a pattern of removals exists compared to the 1999 regulations. The regulations now provide that a change of placement occurs when a child has been removed for more than 10 school days or when "the child has been subjected to a series of removals that constitute a pattern" (34 C.F.R. Sec. 300.536(b)). A pattern exists under the regulations when

■ a series of removals cumulate to (total) more than 10 school days in a school year (34 C.F.R. Sec. 300.536(a)(2)(i));
■ the child's behavior is substantially similar to the child's behavior in the previous incidents that resulted in the series of removals (34 C.F.R. Sec. 300.536(a)(2)(ii)); and
■ there are additional factors such as the length of each removal, the total amount of time the child has been removed, and the proximity of the removals to one another (34 C.F.R. Sec. 300.536(a)(2)(iii)).

Although this regulation is very much the same as the one adopted in 1999, subsection (a)(2)(ii) is new and adds the "substantially similar behavior" requirement.

The effect of this change is to connect the same-treatment rule to the finding of a pattern of behavior underlying the removal. In other words, in each case of removal the student's actions must be substantially related to all of the other behaviors involved in the series of removals.

If the behaviors involved in the series of removals are determined not to be substantially related, the series of removals does not constitute a pattern and is governed by the same-treatment rule, just like other removals that do not exceed 10 days.

To summarize—a series of removals constitutes a pattern of removals only if

■ they cumulatively exceed 10 days;
■ the behaviors resulting in the series of removals are substantially similar to each other;
■ additional factors, such as the length of each removal, the total amount of time the child has been removed, and the proximity of the removals, support the inference that the series constitutes a pattern of removals.

If, on the one hand, any one of these findings is absent, the series of removals does not constitute a pattern and the child may be disciplined under the same-treatment rule to the same extent and for the same duration that a child without a disability would be disciplined for similar conduct. The LEA is under no obligation in such circumstances to provide services, convene an IEP team meeting, or otherwise take action that they would not take if the child did not have a disability. If, on the other hand, all three findings support a pattern of removals, the proposed removal is considered a long-term removal (one for more than 10 school days).

Long-Term Removals or Change of Placement   If an LEA removes a child from his or her usual educational setting for more than 10 consecutive school days, or engages in a "pattern" of removals, IDEA treats that action as a long-term removal or disciplinary change of placement (34 C.F.R. Sec. 300.536). A long-term removal also triggers the no-cessation and address-the-behavior exceptions (20 U.S.C. Sec. 1415(k)(1)(D)) and may trigger the manifestation exception (20 U.S.C. Sec. 1415(k)(1)(E)).

The no-cessation exception requires the LEA to continue to provide special education services to students with disabilities who are suspended, expelled, or otherwise removed for more than 10 school days or as a result of a pattern. The services must allow the child to continue to participate in the general education curriculum and continue to progress toward meeting his or her IEP goals (20 U.S.C. Sec. 1415(k)(1)(D)(i); 34 C.F.R. 300.530(d)).

The address-the-behavior exception requires the LEA to provide, as appropriate and as related to the behavior that resulted in the removal,

- a functional behavior assessment, and
- behavioral intervention services and modifications designed to address the behavior violation so that it does not recur (20 U.S.C. Sec. 1415 (k)(1)(D)(ii); 34 C.F.R. 300.530(d)).

The no-cessation and address-the-behavior exceptions support the principle of zero reject by requiring continuation of those services without which the student will not be able to receive FAPE. By requiring the LEA to address the behavior that led to the expulsion, IDEA also helps prevent future removal of the student from educational opportunities because of similar issues. Finally, IDEA supports the principle of safe schools by reducing behavior that might result in harm to students with and without disabilities or school personnel.

Manifestation Determinations and More-Than-10-Day Removals   A removal for more than 10 days requires school personnel to answer yet another question: Was the behavior that led to the removal a manifestation of the student's disability? To answer this question, IDEA requires "the LEA, the parent and relevant members of the IEP team (as determined by the parent and the local educational agency)" to meet and conduct a manifestation determination (20 U.S.C. Sec. 1415(k)(1)(E); 34 C.F.R. 300.530(e)). IDEA does not specify whether individuals can participate on the manifestation team if the LEA and parent do not agree upon their relevance to the proceedings.

A manifestation determination proceeding inquires into the relationship of the behavior to the disability. IDEA requires that the manifestation team determine that the behavior was a manifestation of the student's disability if the behavior

- was caused by the student's disability and had a direct and substantial relationship to the student's disability, or
- was the direct result of the LEA's failure to implement the IEP (20 U.S.C. Sec. 1415(k)(1)(E); 34 C.F.R. 300.530(e)).

If either of these statements is true, the behavior is a manifestation of the student's disability. If neither of these statements is true, the behavior is not a manifestation of the student's disability (34 C.F.R. 300.530(e)).

If the manifestation-determination team concludes that the child's behavior is the direct result of the LEA's failure to implement the child's IEP, the LEA must take "immediate steps to remedy those deficiencies" (in failure to implement). It seems, then, that the LEA, perhaps together with the manifestation-determination team, must also reach judgments about cause and correction: Why was the child's IEP not implemented and what corrective action must the LEA take to remove the cause(s)?

In making a manifestation determination, the team members must consider evidence that has a tendency to show the truth or falsehood of the behavior as a manifestation of the student's disability. Apparently they also may consider any "unique circumstances" on a case-by-case basis, even for the same student, because the result of the manifestation determination will determine the student's placement (34 C.F.R. 300.530(a)); indeed, even for the same student, the circumstances of behavior and discipline may vary on a case-by-case basis.

It is important to point out that two defenses to a finding of no manifestation, previously available under the 1997 amendments to IDEA, are no longer available under the 2004 amendments. Under the 1997 amendments, parents could assert, first, that the child's disability impaired his or her ability to understand the impact and consequences of the behavior and, second, that the child's ability to control the behavior was impaired.

Neither of these defenses is part of the manifestation determination process under the 2004 law. Nevertheless, the question of whether they might still be relevant to the finding of a manifestation, and thus admissible and carrying some weight, is yet to be determined by the courts. And it does not seem that the "unique circumstances" clause and "case-by-case" approach bar the manifestation-determination team members from taking these "old" defenses into account.

The new requirements for a finding that a behavior is a manifestation of a child's disability tighten the defense loopholes that the 1997 amendments arguably created. Consider the language of the 2004 amendments: "Caused by," "direct relationship," and "direct result" are significantly more stringent than the heretofore relaxed mere "relationship."

Coupled with the loss of the "understanding" and "control" defenses, IDEA 2004 significantly reduces protections for students with disabilities whose behavior may well result in exclusion from school. Why? Because one principle of the No Child Left Behind Act is school safety (see chapter 3); because equal treatment of students with and without disabilities is allowable under IDEA, subject to the limitations we have just discussed; and because, if the behavior is not a manifestation of the child's disability, a student may and arguably should be disciplined just as any nondisabled student may be disciplined. That discipline can include a long-term expulsion from school (although a long-term expulsion may not entail a total cessation of services).

Let's consider the 2004 discipline provisions from a bit of distance. Bear in mind that IDEA's roots are in the school desegregation case *Brown v. Board of Education* and include a ban on disability-based discrimination. If, however, there is no manifestation of disability in the student's behavior, it is not defensible to argue that the student is experiencing discrimination on account of disability. That is why equal or same treatment, the general rule for discipline under IDEA, applies.

But if the behavior is a manifestation of disability, the LEA may not treat the student the same as one who does not have a disability. To do so would be the same as punishing the child for having a disability. That clearly constitutes discrimination, violates the zero reject rule, and is appropriately prohibited under IDEA.

Now, having reminded ourselves that the discipline and manifestation provisions rest on theories of discrimination, let's return to IDEA's provisions. We find that IDEA is highly specific as to the actions an IEP team must make in the event that it determines that the behavior is a manifestation of the child's disabilities.

First, the IEP team must return the student to his or her current placement unless and until the student's parents and the LEA agree to an alternative setting as part of the student's behavior intervention plan (BIP) (20 U.S.C. Sec. 1415(k)(1)(F)(iii); 34 C.F.R. 300.533).

Second, the IEP team must conduct a functional behavioral assessment (which is also part of the address-the-behavior exception and is required regardless of manifestation) and implement or modify the child's behavioral intervention plan (20 U.S.C. Sec. 1415(k)(1)(F)(i) and (ii)). Note that this is a more stringent requirement than the requirement for behavioral interventions "as appropriate" under the address-the-behavior exception. When the team determines that behavior is a manifestation of disability, it must develop a plan to address the behavior so that it will not recur (34 C.F.R. 300.530(d)(1)(ii)).

In addition to supporting zero reject and the antidiscriminatory purpose of IDEA, the provisions for a functional behavior assessment and behavioral plan echo the principles of nondiscriminatory evaluation and appropriate education. When a behavior results from a disability, that behavior represents a need of the student and, according to IDEA, should be addressed through the process of individualized assessment and services. It also preserves the principle of the least restrictive environment both by guaranteeing the child's return to the more inclusive setting and by providing services to prevent future removal.

Weapons, Drugs, and Serious Bodily Injury

The principle of zero reject—as well as those of nondiscriminatory evaluation, appropriate education, and least restrictive environment—all support and are supported by the exceptions to the same-treatment rule under IDEA. But those principles are not the only ones at work in the 2004 amendments, and when exceptions conflict with the principle of school safety, school safety comes first.

That is so because school safety issues not only implicate the physical well-being of students and school personnel, but they also involve the negative effect that dangerous behaviors can have on the environment of teaching and learning in the school. This explains the provisions of the No Child Left Behind Act (related to school choice) that are activated by harm to a student, and why IDEA provides LEAs additional discretion in applying more stringent disciplinary procedures when the behavior threatens the safety of the students or school personnel.

In three "special circumstances" (34 C.F.R. 300.530(g)), school safety warrants disciplinary actions outside of the framework for violation of a school code (20 U.S.C. Sec. 1415 (k)(1)(G)). These circumstances allow an LEA to remove the child from his or her usual educational setting whether the behavior was or was not a manifestation of the child's disability:

1. If the student carries a weapon to or possesses a weapon at school, on school premises, or at school functions under the jurisdiction of an SEA or LEA (20 U.S.C. Sec. 1415(k)(1)(G)(i); 34 C.F.R. 300.530(g)(1))
2. If the student knowingly possesses or uses illegal drugs or sells or solicits the sale of a controlled substance while at school, on school grounds, or at school functions under the jurisdiction of an SEA or LEA (20 U.S.C. Sec. 1415(k)(1)(G)(ii); 34 C.F.R. 300.530(g)(2))
3. If the student has inflicted serious bodily injury on another person at school, on school grounds, or at school functions under the jurisdiction of an SEA or LEA (20 U.S.C. Sec. 1415(k)(1)(G)(iii); 34 C.F.R. 300.530(g)(3))

IDEA defines a weapon consistently with the federal criminal code's definition of "dangerous weapon"—namely, "a weapon, device, instrument, material, or substance, animate or inanimate, that is used for, or is readily capable of causing, death or serious bodily injury" (20 U.S.C. Sec. 1415(k)(10)(D); 18 U.S.C. Sec. 930 (g)(2)).

"Illegal" drugs under IDEA refer to those that are never legal under any circumstances (except that some state laws, such as Oregon's, allow marijuana to be used for medicinal purposes). Doctors may not prescribe these drugs, and it is never legal to possess them. Among the drugs are amphetamines, anabolic steroids, heroin, marijuana, mescaline, methadone, opium, peyote, and phenobarbital (21 U.S.C. Sec. 812(c)).

Unlike drugs that are always illegal, controlled substances may be prescribed for some legitimate uses. Thus, IDEA does not allow an LEA to discipline a student if the student legally possesses or uses drugs under the supervision of a licensed health-care professional or under any other federal law (20 U.S.C. Secs. 1415(k)(10)(A) and (B); 34 C.F.R. 300.530(i)(1) and (2)). It allows discipline only if the student sells or solicits the sale of these controlled substances.

Previously under IDEA, students could be disciplined for dangerous behavior only if a court or hearing officer found that there was substantial evidence showing that maintaining the student's current placement was substantially likely to result in injury to the student or other students or staff, even considering the appropriateness of the student's placement and whether the LEA had or had not made reasonable efforts to minimize the risk of harm. Furthermore, the hearing officer had been required to determine that the IAES proposed would allow the student to continue to participate in the general curriculum and meet IEP goals.

Under the 2004 amendments, the LEA does not have to even consult a hearing officer—let alone provide evidence of dangerousness, appropriateness, minimized risk, and continued educational opportunity—if the behavior resulted in serious bodily injury; the LEA may act immediately and unilaterally (34 C.F.R. 300.530(g)(3) and (i)(3)). "Serious bodily injury," as defined in the U.S. Criminal Code, means

> bodily injury which involves a substantial risk of death, extreme physical pain, protracted and obvious disfigurement, or protracted loss or impairment of the function of a bodily member, organ, or mental faculty. (18 U.S.C. Sec. 1365(h)(3))

Interim Alternative Educational Setting (IAES)

As with long-term removals for violations of the school code, safety-based removals are subject to both the no-cessation and the address-the-behavior exceptions to same treatment. Because LEAs are required to continue to provide services for students who are subject to long-term removals and those who are disciplined because of weapons, drugs, or serious bodily injury, the IEP team must identify the IAES in which it will provide those services. If any of the above three conditions is met—drugs, weapons, or serious bodily injury—the LEA may remove a student with a disability to an IAES for not more than 45 school days, which is the equivalent of nine weeks of school (20 U.S.C. Sec. 1415(k)(1)(G)).

The power to remove students with disabilities from the school when their behavior poses a safety risk is intended to give broad and swift powers to the school to ensure a safe learning environment, but it still does not allow discriminatory application of discipline. Schools may not provide for stiffer or more punitive disciplinary actions for students with disabilities than they do for students without disabilities. Policies and the actions taken by school districts involving removal or expulsion must be applied equally to students with and without disabilities.

Appeal of Discipline or Manifestation Determination

As part of the procedural due process rights afforded children with disabilities and their parents (see chapter 8), IDEA grants parents the right to challenge the school's application of discipline or finding under the manifestation determination rule. IDEA does not limit the right to appeal a decision to the parents. LEAs also may challenge disciplinary placement or manifestation determination under certain conditions.

When a parent disagrees with any decision regarding placement or manifestation, the parent may request a hearing on the matter. Similarly, an LEA may ask a hearing officer to order that the alternative educational setting be used even if the behavior is found to be a manifestation of the student's disability. The hearing officer may continue the student's placement in the IAES if the officer determines that restoring the student's current placement is "substantially likely to result in injury to the child or to others" (20 U.S.C. Sec. 1415(k)(3)(A)).

The appeal in either case must be expedited so it occurs within 20 school days of the request for a hearing. The determination by the hearing officer must come within 10 school days after completion of the hearing.

Disciplinary Stay-Put

Under the basic stay-put requirement (see chapter 8, "Procedural Due Process," for more details), the general rule is that a student remains in his or her then-current placement while a due process hearing is pending. The LEA may not change a student's placement while waiting for a hearing officer to rule on whether the change in placement is allowable under IDEA. This general rule has two discipline-related exceptions:

1. If a hearing officer already has ordered or allowed a change of placement, that new placement continues during any appeal of the hearing officer's decision. In other words, the hearing officer's authorization of the change of placement goes into effect and that new placement becomes the stay-put placement during hearings for subsequent litigation or hearings. The parents and LEA may agree that the child need not stay placed in the IAES while the hearing is underway and pending the decision of the hearing officer (20 U.S.C. Sec. 1415(k)(4)(A); 34 C.F.R. 300.533)).

2. Whenever a removal or change of placement resulting from a disciplinary action by the school is at issue, the disciplinary placement ordered by the LEA is considered to be the stay-put placement for the student during the hearing officer's review of the LEA decision and the student must stay there—unless the parents and LEA agree otherwise (34 C.F.R. 300.533). This is a new provision under IDEA and supports the school-safety focus of reauthorization in 2004. The disciplinary setting remains the stay-put placement until the hearing officer determines the appropriate placement or until the timeline for an expedited hearing and decision under IDEA expires.

If the LEA believes that returning the student to the original placement from a disciplinary placement is "substantially likely to result in injury to the child or to others," the hearing officer may, during an appeal by the parent concerning a placement or manifestation determination or by an LEA concerning substantial likelihood of injury to the child or to others, repeat the process of returning the child to the original placement or to the IAES (34 C.F.R. 300.530(b)(3)).

Prior to the 2004 amendments, the exception to the general stay-put rule applied only to discipline involving guns, drugs, and serious injury. Under the 2004 amendments, it applies to all disciplinary actions by the LEA, whether for violations of the school code or for weapons, drugs, or serious bodily injury. The exception, in effect, has become the rule for disciplinary placements while the due process hearings are pending. The stay-put rule no longer has any real application with regard to discipline—at least not until the hearing officer rules on the matter.

We summarize the complicated discipline provisions in Figure 4.3.

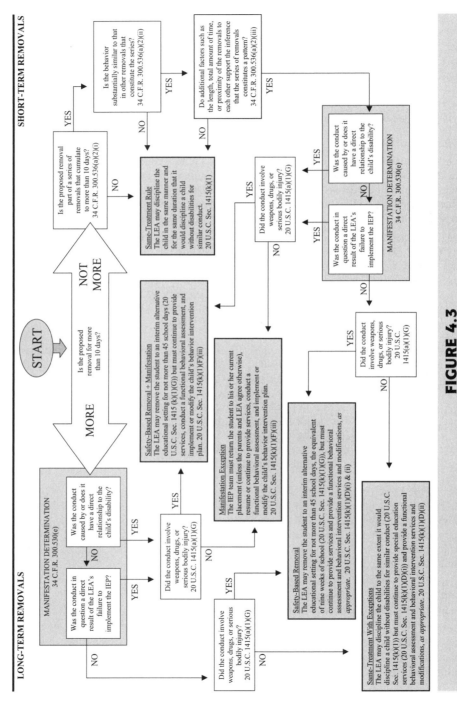

FIGURE 4.3

Summary of Discipline Provisions in Decision Tree Structure

Figure 4.3 maps IDEA's discipline process when an LEA proposes to remove a student from a current placement. Figure 4.3 reinforces these key points:

1. An LEA may discipline children with disabilities by using short-term removals in the same manner and to the same extent that the LEA may discipline students without disabilities for the same behavior.
2. If the proposed removal is more than 10 *consecutive* days, it is a long-term removal.
3. A removal of not more than 10 days may still be a long-term removal if the following is true:
   a. The removal is part of a series of removals that cumulate to more than 10 days.
   b. The removals in the series involve substantially similar behavior.
   c. Other factors, such as proximity of removals, suggest a "pattern" of removals.
4. All long-term removals trigger (a) the address-the-behavior exception and (b) the no-cessation exception.
5. All long-term removals require the LEA to conduct a manifestation determination.
6. A manifestation team includes the parents, LEA representative, and any other relevant members of the IEP team.
7. A behavior is a manifestation if
   a. the disability directly caused the behavior, OR
   b. the LEA's failure to implement the IEP caused the behavior.
8. If a behavior is a manifestation, the child must be returned to his or her previous placement (unless weapons, drugs, or serious bodily injury were involved, or the LEA appeals the decision) and the LEA must create or amend the IEP and behavior intervention plan (BIP).
9. If a behavior involved weapons, drugs, or serious bodily injury, the LEA may remove the student for up to 45 days to an interim alternative educational setting (IAES), regardless of manifestation.

Figure 4.3 also raises two important questions:

1. What about disciplinary actions that don't involve removal?

   All disciplinary actions that do not involve removal are subject to the "same-treatment rule." An LEA may discipline a student with a disability in the same manner and to the same extent that it may discipline a student without a disability for the same conduct. Therefore, the only IDEA issue with regard to a disciplinary action that does not involve removal is whether the discipline is discriminatory: Is the LEA disciplining the student with a disability in a different way and applying different sanctions because the student has a disability? If so, the LEA violates IDEA and arguably the Americans with Disabilities Act and Sec. 504 of the Rehabilitation Act.

2. What about placement when a disciplinary removal is challenged in due process or on appeal?

   The usual "stay-put" rule is that a child with a disability remains in his or her then current placement while awaiting a decision on a challenge to the change of placement. But IDEA 2004 changes this result when changes of placement are made for disciplinary reasons.

   For disciplinary removals, the basic stay-put rule is that the child must remain in the IAES while awaiting a decision on a challenge to the removal. There are two exceptions to this rule:

   1. The stay-put placement can be other than the IAES if the parent and school agree on another stay-put placement.
   2. A prior hearing officer or manifestation team overturned the proposed change of placement AND dangerousness is not at issue on appeal (such as if weapons, drugs, or serious bodily injury were involved).

FIGURE 4.3
(continued)

EFFECTS OF THE ZERO REJECT RULE

Having reviewed developments that led to adoption of the zero reject rule by the courts and later by Congress, and having examined provisions of IDEA and their interpretation by the courts, let's consider briefly the major effects of the zero reject principle.

New Definitions for Equality

Students with disabilities owe an enormous debt to the civil rights movement. Without doubt, the Supreme Court's decision in *Brown* (the 1954 school desegregation case) is the most important case ever decided by any court insofar as the education of students with disabilities is concerned. At the very least, it established the doctrine of equal educational opportunity, attacked the dual system of education and law that had relegated Blacks, students with disabilities, and other minority children to second-class status, and laid a foundation in the Constitution's Fourteenth Amendment (the equal protection clause) for *PARC*, *Mills*, and the other early special education cases.

The Effects of the Early Cases and IDEA

The early cases and IDEA began to fulfill *Brown's* promise that no school or other government agency may lawfully condone the second-class citizenship of any child. Extension of the civil rights movement from one discrete minority (Blacks) to another (children and adults with disabilities) was the fulfillment of the Supreme Court's principle of equality under the eyes of the law.

The right-to-education cases following *Brown* deliberately and creatively expanded *Brown's* doctrine of equal opportunity by establishing that the exclusion of children with disabilities from any opportunity to learn—much less from any reasonably beneficial opportunity—is unconstitutional under the equal protection clause. More than that, those cases, together with IDEA and other laws, established a new equal access (or equal opportunity) doctrine. They articulated the proposition that children with disabilities require access to the same or different types of resources as their nondisabled peers for the same, not necessarily different, purposes.

When it comes to disability, our understanding of "equality" must change; it cannot continue to be our customary one. The usual meaning of equality is (per *Brown*) equal access to the same resources for the same purposes. In disabilities law, the new meaning is access to the same resources (general education) or different resources (special education) for the same, not always different, purposes and outcomes. For an important reason, equality means something different for children with disabilities than it does for children without disabilities: The child's disability is a distinction that usually justifies a different approach. Let's consider, then, the meaning of equality when it applies to students and other people who have disabilities.

The Meaning of Equal Treatment

Equal treatment arguably includes exactly equal treatment. Under that understanding of equal treatment, a person without a disability and a person with a disability are treated exactly alike. Of course, that may discriminate by producing unequal opportunity; alternatively, it may not. Why? Because in some contexts some disabilities do not impair or impede a person's participation.

For example, a student in a wheelchair can learn Latin as easily as one who walks, assuming that both have somewhat the same cognitive capacities. In other contexts, however, exactly equal treatment will result in discrimination. For example, a deaf student who is not provided an interpreter or other accommodations certainly will not benefit from the same Latin class as a hearing student who has comparable cognitive abilities.

In the first scenario (a Latin student in a wheelchair), exactly equal treatment produces equal opportunity. In the second (a deaf student without an interpreter), exactly equal treatment produces discrimination (denial to benefit because of disability), but equal treatment plus an accommodation—that is, admission to the Latin class with an interpreter or other appropriate accommodation—produces equal opportunity to benefit.

Finally, some people have such extensive disabilities that they will not experience equal opportunity to benefit unless they are treated quite differently from those who have no disabilities or have less challenging disabilities. For example, a person who uses a wheelchair, a joystick to operate a computer, and augmentative communication will not be able to hold down a desk job unless he or she is provided with an ergonomically suitable desk, a computer that responds to the commands of a joy stick (instead of a mouse), and allowances to "speak" face to face or on the telephone by using the augmentative communication device. Here, unequal but noninvidious treatment produces equal opportunities to work.

These three tiers of equality—exactly equal treatment, equal treatment plus accommodations, and unequal but noninvidious accommodation—are manifestations of disability-specific approaches to equality. The distinction between these tiers and how they are carried out is important to policy makers (and their constituents) who want (or do not want) to attack discrimination in an effort to afford people with disabilities opportunities to participate in the nondisabled world. Unless policy makers, their constituents, disability advocates, and those who oppose "special (i.e., unequal) treatment" understand the distinction, discrimination will be the bill of fare on the table of many people with disabilities and their families.

Redefinitions of Equal Opportunity and Equal Access

One important effect of the zero reject rule is to redefine the doctrine of equal educational opportunity as it applies to children with disabilities and to establish different meanings of equality as it applies to people with and without disabilities. These fundamental redefinitions—based on the fact of the disability, which is the distinction that makes a difference—remain apparent in IDEA and various other laws.

IDEA makes it clear (through the principles of appropriate education and least restrictive environments—see chapters 6 and 7—and through the transition provisions) that employment, full participation in community life, and integration into the general curriculum are critical national priorities for students with disabilities. Likewise, the 1988 Technology-Related Assistance for Individuals with Disabilities Act funds statewide assistive technology programs to increase the independence, productivity, and integration of individuals with disabilities.

The 1986 amendments to the Rehabilitation Act created the supported-employment initiative. The 1986, 1990, and 2000 amendments to the Developmental Disabilities Assistance and Bill of Rights Act clarified that the purpose of the law is to help individuals with disabilities become independent, productive, and integrated into society. Finally, the 1990 Americans with Disabilities Act prohibited discrimination solely on the basis of disability in state and local government services, transportation, privately owned public accommodations, communications, and employment.

We already have argued that these laws reflect a major change in the concept of equality, and we have analyzed "equality" in the disability-policy context. So you can fully grasp these important concepts, let's return to one of our original points—which is that "equal access" means something different in 2006 than it did in 1975.

When IDEA was first enacted in 1975, the equal access doctrine required that students with disabilities have equal access to different resources (special education, primarily) but for different purposes (traditional outcomes generally included placement in group homes or sheltered workshops). The original doctrine assumed that, as a rule, individuals with disabilities would not be able to do what people without disabilities can do, even with support. Thus, although they should have equal access to the different resources of special education (to take into account their needs), they should have these resources to produce different results—a life different from that of individuals without disabilities.

Today, the equal access doctrine means something radically different. It means that, as a general rule, individuals with disabilities should have equal access to the same resources for the same results. This doctrine assumes that individuals with disabilities will have the same or a somewhat different kind of life as individuals without disabilities, depending on the extent of their disabilities, the extent to which society accommodates to their disabilities, their choices, and the availability of support to meet their needs. The key, of course, is the assumption of "sameness." No longer is "different" assumed; now, "same" is assumed.

The doctrine thus assumes that equal access to the same resources—that is, access to general education services and to other public and private services and networks—will occur, with support. It also assumes that access to different resources—that is, special education, vocational rehabilitation, assistive technology, and special support systems—will occur, but for the purpose of enabling those with disabilities to have access to the nondisabled or generic world, as well as to a world that is primarily disability-oriented.

Thus, federal law no longer assumes a limited life for individuals with disabilities, lived separate and apart from people without disabilities. Instead, it assumes that individuals with disabilities will have opportunities to live in the "regular" world and be educated in regular programs, work in regular jobs, live in regular housing, and otherwise be more like than different from people without disabilities.

Change of Locus of Control of Education

By attacking school conduct that went to the very heart of education—exclusion from educational opportunity and improper educational assessment and place-ment—the early cases (*PARC* and *Mills*) and, later, the Congress in IDEA and the courts that interpreted IDEA have brought the conduct of schools, traditionally a matter of state and local control, under significant federal oversight. Frequently that oversight has been by federal judges' supervising the actions of state and local elected or appointed officials.

For example, *Brown* established federal control over where general education students were to be educated; Black and White students were to be educated together because school segregation was unconstitutional under the equal protection doctrine. *PARC, Mills*, and the other early right-to-education cases established federal control over which students are to be educated ("All children can learn … all children shall be educated") and the terms on which they are to be educated (the new equal access doctrine). IDEA also affects what the students will be taught and where they will be taught; it affects the nature of the curriculum (appropriate education, chapter 6) and the place it is delivered (LRE, chapter 7).

Like *Brown*, the special education cases and IDEA together have had an enor-mous impact on state and local education budgets. State and local legislators and school administrators have had to redirect the flow of funds within education to ben-efit students with disabilities. The special education cases and IDEA also caused those same officials to seek new money for the education of students with disabilities.

In large part because of the large fiscal impact of IDEA on state and local budg-ets, and also in part because school reform efforts involve students with disabilities as well as those without disabilities, IDEA allows state and local education agencies some flexibility in how they use the federal and state funds. This flexibility includes the optional eligibility and service provisions for ages 0–2 and 3–5, discussed ear-lier. But while this flexibility may mitigate, to some extent, the federal impact on education, it by no means signals a reversal of the *Brown*-originated, IDEA-solidi-fied federal presence in education.

Law-and-Order Issues

As noted earlier in this chapter, the most controversial issue involving the zero reject principle—and, to some, the most controversial issue involving all of IDEA—has been that of school discipline. The public's legitimate desire for safety in school, a desire shared by those involved in special education, arguably has come into conflict with IDEA's policy to provide federal funds so that all (repeat: all) students with disabilities, whether they are or are not lawbreakers, shall receive an appropriate education.

In reconciling this conflict, the Supreme Court's decision in *Honig* created the "causal connection" or "manifestation" doctrine, enforced IDEA's "stay-put" rule, but created a "safety valve" (access to courts for an order allowing the schools to remove a dangerous student) so a hard-and-fast rule of "all" would not collide with a valid need for school safety. The 2004 amendments, while continuing to balance the zero reject principle with school safety concerns, shift the balance toward school safety.

At the same time, IDEA addresses the difficult task of educating individuals with disabilities who, convicted as adults and imprisoned in adult correctional facilities, have, or may have, disabilities and thus a claim to special education. Again, there is a delicate balance between extending to these individuals, many of whom are from minority populations, the full rights of IDEA and at the same time assuring that the punitive and corrective/rehabilitative aspects of conviction and imprisonment can be carried out.

Behavioral Assessments, Modifications, and Interventions

Ever since the mid-1980s, professionals in disciplines relating to individuals with disabilities and family members have been greatly divided over another critical issue: Is it ever appropriate, as a matter of effective intervention, good law, and consensus-based ethics, to use aversive interventions to change the behavior of students with disabilities? Those interventions—sometimes called negative consequences or punishments—have included the use of electric shock, noxious substances, and extensive bodily restraints.

Reauthorization of IDEA has always drawn into conflict (a) those who believe that the students' rights to an education and to treatment justify, even demand, the use of aversive interventions; and (b) those who believe that there is a better way—one that is more humane and also just as effective in overcoming the challenging behaviors that impede students' learning and disrupt the lives of others. IDEA's provisions do not settle the matter entirely. Nevertheless, by requiring LEAs to use FBAs and to consider using positive behavioral interventions and supports, and other strategies, when developing or revising an IEP for a student whose behavior impedes the student's learning or the learning of other students (20 U.S.C. Sec. 1414(d)(3)(B)), and by requiring LEAs to conduct an FBA and implement a BIP for a student whose behavior (a) is the subject of school discipline, and (b) is a manifestation of the student's disability, IDEA goes a long way toward settling the issue about the use of positive or other interventions. Granted, IDEA allows an LEA to consider using interventions other than positive ones in developing an IEP, but it clearly gives a preference to the positive ones. And, when a student has been disciplined, the LEA must conduct an FBA and develop a BIP; even though IDEA does not require the LEA to consider positive interventions as components of that plan, it does seem to lean heavily in that direction. A BIP should be part of the student's IEP; when a student's behavior impedes learning, as is most likely the case in all discipline matters, the LEA would be remiss not to consider positive interventions as part of the BIP for the disciplined student.

So, even though IDEA does not absolutely prohibit state and local education agencies from using aversive or negative interventions, it does create a strong presumption in favor of positive behavioral supports, which are, needless to say, non-aversive and non-negative. Given IDEA's provisions for the use of evidence-based interventions and its reference to state-of-the-art positive behavioral interventions and supports, LEAs will be hard-pressed not to use positive interventions.

A consequence of the zero reject rule, then, is to merge state-of-the-art research on behavior and interventions with the law and public policy, and to create, through that merger, a humane and effective environment—the school. After all, one of the barriers to effective special education has been the schools' failure to replicate research on effective learning (20 U.S.C. Sec. 1400(c)(4)); and one of the solutions to that problem is, at last, a requirement for FBAs and BIPs, and a legal presumption in favor of positive behavioral interventions and supports—a thoroughly researched and effective method of intervention.

Expanded Practices and Individualization

The court cases and IDEA have pushed hard at the limits of public education systems. They have demonstrated the plasticity of the system, that seemingly intransigent systems can change (albeit slowly—never underestimate the power of inertia), and that a (sometimes fragile) consensus exists about the inherent rightness of special education. The early cases, coupled with IDEA, thus have had the effect of both commanding and enabling change and of requiring and facilitating expansion of the educational system so it can provide equal educational opportunities to children with disabilities.

One of the most significant changes in school practices has been in the methods of instruction. The zero reject principle has individualized educational services for children with disabilities. More than that, it has caused educators to extend the individualization practice to children who are gifted and talented (and enact special education laws that grant to those children substantially the same rights as are granted to children with disabilities). It also has caused educators and policy makers to be particularly aware of the benefits of educating at-risk students (children who are not classified formally as disabled under IDEA but who still require special attention). The metapolitics of the zero reject doctrine, then, have been to extend to others the benefits (individualized education) that children with disabilities have as a matter of right. (The incidental benefit rule, discussed in chapter 6, underscores this conclusion.)

The Integration Impetus

On still another level, the cases and IDEA have begun to integrate children with disabilities into the mainstream of American life. The courts and the Congress both asserted the value of inclusion in requiring that, to the maximum extent appropriate, children with and without disabilities be educated together. (See chapter 7 for a detailed discussion of this principle.)

The integration–inclusion principle also has had an important effect on state mental retardation centers, psychiatric hospitals for children, and schools for deaf or blind children. The children in those institutions have been given an opportunity to be deinstitutionalized. They have been given a right to education in the public school system. The result is that, in many cases, they have not been placed in the institutions to begin with, have been discharged from institutions, or have been kept in the institutions but given more adequate and effective educational services there or in cooperating local school districts.

The integration–inclusion principle in education was developing at the same time that the institutions (psychiatric hospitals and mental retardation facilities) were admitting fewer children. This reduction was caused by several related and important factors:

1. State legislatures were tightening up the procedures by which people could be committed to the state institutions. They were requiring much more due process and thereby discouraging commitment. Similarly, legislatures were enacting stricter criteria for commitment, requiring that the usual standard of "dangerousness" be met more clearly and indisputably.
2. The U.S. Supreme Court ruled in *Addington v. Texas* (1979) and in *Parham v. J.R.* (1979), respectively, that states must prove dangerousness by fairly strict procedures, and that states must provide for neutral review of admission decisions when children are candidates for institutionalization. Both cases had the effect of putting real clamps on institutionalization.
3. The states (with federal assistance under the home-and-community-based authority in Title XIX, the Medicaid program of the Social Security Act) were developing more community-based treatment programs for children and using institutional placements less and less often.

The cumulative effect of these three developments was to accelerate the impetus for integration. In conjunction with IDEA provisions for zero reject and least-restrictive placement, these developments changed the character of the public schools significantly.

New Norms and Pluralism

The norms of schools themselves have changed in important ways. The norm now is not nearly as nondisabled. The presence of children with disabilities in school has changed the composition of the schools. In a real sense, their presence has augmented the schools' cultural diversity and pluralism.

This enrichment undoubtedly will have important effects on the lives of adults. A result of the integration impetus is greater diversity in society. And professionals who once regarded some children as unworthy of an education or unable to benefit from training now are engaged in educating and training those same children. Just as systems changed, so have people.

Lifetime Service

The court cases and IDEA also have forced health, mental health, social services/welfare, and educational systems to begin serious efforts, separately or cooperatively and jointly, to provide community-based services. These include child-find, educational placement, cost-sharing, facility-sharing, and family-support services. These efforts represent the first long-range efforts, on a large scale, to secure community integration and at-home placement of children with disabilities. They also represent the beginnings of a lifetime service system for people with disabilities.

Given the early childhood initiative, the requirement for related services, and the transition or aging-out initiative, IDEA set into motion a link between schools and other agencies. During the school years of individuals with disabilities, the schools are the primary service providers and other agencies are secondary providers. Upon the person's exit from school, the agencies take over the principal-provider role. Accordingly, the change wrought in schools also effected a change in adult service systems (regulated by Section 504 and ADA, just as the schools are).

"Defective" Newborns

At the same time that *Brown* and the zero reject rule were being applied to students with disabilities, an awareness developed in the public, and especially among the professionals dealing with people with disabilities, that gross discrimination was being practiced against newborns with birth defects. Withholding or withdrawing medically appropriate treatment from "defective" newborns has been, and continues to be, at the center of a major policy and legal debate.

On the one hand, the policy issue is whether families, physicians, and the public should condone the withholding or withdrawing of treatment (or engaging in other practices that jeopardize the child's life). The legal issues, on the other hand, center on newborns' constitutional rights to be treated in the same way as nondisabled newborns are treated (equal protection in medical care), the enforcement of state and federal child abuse and neglect laws, and the tolerable zones of privacy that families and physicians may establish to fend off external review of their treatment/nontreatment decisions.

In a very real sense, the constitutional doctrines of *Brown* and the special education cases are applicable by analogy to the *Baby Doe* cases (so-called because of the name given to unidentified newborns in lawsuits involving their treatment). If equality before the law means anything, these newborns are entitled to appropriate medical treatment. And if that treatment is given and is lifesaving, the medical and other interventions must be forthcoming: A society that compels a life to be saved is one that also must compel services to the person. Thus, special education is involved in the *Baby Doe* cases in two ways:

1. By extension of the equal protection doctrine
2. By providing early intervention and education

Dignity at the End of Life

Even more controversial nowadays than the issues surrounding the first stages of life are the issues related to disability in our final moments. Here, the issue is not only the opportunity to have a life worth living but also how people are treated as their life ends or even at what point and by what measures we should determine when a life has ended.

Although the questions may be somewhat different, the principles remain similar. The concept of equality demands that persons who have disabilities, even those with disabilities so severe that they are unable to communicate and require assistance for meeting the most basic of human needs (such as food and water), should have the same rights as people without disabilities to interventions that will treat their condition, prolong their life when possible, and mitigate their pain.

Yet, part of the right to consent to treatment afforded individuals without disabilities includes the right to refuse treatment. But what if the person with a disability cannot communicate his or her consent or refusal? And what if the treatment at issue is life-sustaining but cannot improve the person's health or condition? How can policy support the rights of individuals with profound disabilities to consent or refuse services?

These questions arose most recently when an undiagnosed cardiac condition resulted in Terri Schiavo's near total disability (the courts ruled that she was in a "persistent vegetative state"). Terri's husband sought to refuse, on her behalf, all medical and nonmedical interventions (food and water). Other members of her family—namely, her parents and siblings—intervened. They rejected the diagnosis and the assertion that her spouse had the authority to refuse food and water on her behalf, and argued that she had a right to medical and rehabilitation services.

Ultimately, in a drawn-out public battle between Terri's spouse and her other relatives—one that involved the legislative and executive as well as the judicial branches of the Florida and federal governments—the issue was whether Terri had indicated previously that she would want all medical and nonmedical interventions to cease if such an event (one that resulted in her being in a persistent vegetative state) were to occur. The courts ruled that she had given sufficient indication of what she would want should such a situation occur and that her prior indication reasonably supported her spouse's decision to terminate treatment, and so the courts authorized the doctors and hospital to remove her feeding tube.

Terri Schiavo's life and death provoked profound questions that remain unanswered. While the public debate often focuses on who should make life or death decisions for those who cannot make them for themselves, a more fundamental question, which goes to the root of disability discrimination, remains: To what extent can people predict what they would want or how they would feel if they suddenly were to have a disability? Doesn't the pervasive nature of stereotypes and prejudices against disability make such future decision making questionable at best? Don't they also undermine substitute decision making? The history of special education, and disability generally, suggests that such beliefs and prejudices have a considerable effect on our decisions and actions.

Given that some children who are served under IDEA have life-threatening health conditions and that their parents have directed educators with respect to how to respond, or not respond, if the child's life is in danger while the child is in school, state laws, SEA policies, and even LEA policies guide what educators will do. But educators and parents do not need to rely solely on those laws and policies to guide them. They also may want to be guided by the accompanying statement. This statement was developed after the Schiavo court decisions were announced, she had died, and the U.S. Senate and House of Representatives had conducted hearings on end-of-life decision-making policy. (For the Senate testimony of the first author of this book, see H. R. Turnbull, 2005. Note that he was among those who drafted the statement.)

A Statement of Common Principles on Life-Sustaining Care and Treatment for People With Disabilities

WHEREAS:

- All people have fundamental human, civil, and constitutional rights.
- Among these fundamental rights are the rights to life-sustaining care and treatment *and* to self-determination and autonomy.
- These rights must not be sacrificed because a person has a cognitive, psychiatric, emotional, developmental, intellectual, sensory, or physical disability.
- People acting as surrogates for persons who are limited in their ability to exercise self-determination and autonomy must never sacrifice the fundamental rights of those persons and must always act in accord with the rights and best interests of those with limited ability.

AND WHEREAS:

- Disability is a natural part of the human condition.
- Historically, people with disabilities have been subjected to prejudice and discrimination.
- Disability has been used as a justification for depriving people of their fundamental rights.
- Children and adults with significant disabilities have been especially vulnerable to violations of their fundamental rights, including the

denial of access to life-sustaining care and treatment, such as routine medical treatment and food and fluids.

- People may be capable of exercising their right to self-determination and autonomy in some situations and not in others.
- People who do not have disabilities may not be able to anticipate what their wishes would be if and when they become disabled.
- When people are capable of making decisions regarding life-sustaining care and treatment, their informed decisions must be respected.
- For people who are limited in their ability to exercise their right to self-determination and autonomy with respect to life-sustaining care and treatment, family members, friends, or legally authorized surrogates can help them to make informed decisions about such matters as long as these decisions do not threaten their lives.

THEREFORE:

In fulfillment of fundamental rights and in recognition of the historical treatment of people with disabilities in society:

- People with disabilities are entitled to exercise their rights to life-sustaining care and treatment *and* to self-determination and autonomy.
- Absent clear and convincing evidence of the desires of people with disabilities to decline life-sustaining care or treatment, such care and treatment should not be withheld or withdrawn unless death is genuinely imminent and the care or treatment is objectively futile and would only prolong the dying process.
- For the limited number of people who have lifelong cognitive disabilities and who have never had the ability to exercise self-determination regarding life-sustaining care and treatment, such care and treatment should not be withheld or withdrawn unless death is genuinely imminent and the care or treatment is objectively futile and would only prolong the dying process.
- When doubt exists as to whether to provide life-sustaining care and treatment a presumption must always be made in favor of providing such care and treatment.

Source: "A Statement of Common Principles on Life-Sustaining Care and Treatment of People With Disabilities" by Center on Human Policy. Retrieved on April 3, 2006, from http://thechp.syr.edu/endorse/index.htm

Cost-Effective Education

People have always argued—and probably always will—that spending public money to fund the education of students with disabilities is not a wise expenditure.

Nonetheless, early intervention for infants and toddlers with disabilities or at risk of having disabilities is clearly cost-effective. That is an undergirding premise of Part C (zero to 3). Moreover, it has become clear that special education at the elementary, middle, and secondary school levels is cost-effective. It reduces the number of persons classified as having a disability, prevents or reduces grade retention, enables some people with disabilities to acquire skills that make them less dependent on others, and allows many to become wage earners.

The fiscal contribution of zero reject and the equality doctrine is important not only for persons with disabilities but also for the larger public. More than that, the naysayers of equality have been answered with doctrine and dollars. The response is, indeed, powerful.

In its 2004 version, IDEA recognizes that special education has been effective, though not as effective as it could have been (20 U.S.C. Secs. 1400(c)(3) and (4)). To have improved the educational results for students with disabilities is itself a cost-effective accomplishment. Yet, the 2004 amendments also recognize that state and local education agencies have been limited in what they may do with federal funds. Accordingly, IDEA creates new flexibility for those agencies in the hope that general and special education, together, will become more effective (20 U.S.C. Sec. 1400(c)(5)).

IDEA also clarifies that, when a student is eligible for federal or state benefits (in addition to special education), the agencies that provide those benefits must put up their funds first and in advance of the state and local education agencies. Only after the "payors of first resort" have done so and the student has exhausted his or her claim to those benefits may a state or local education agency be required to contribute to the student's education.

These provisions have a significant cost-effectiveness aspect. They marshal the entire range of federal–state funds for which the student is eligible, thereby assuring access to a wider and deeper pool of money for the student's education. That in itself is cost-effective for the student. More than that, they shift some of the costs of the student's education from the state and local education agencies to other agencies, thereby relieving the education agencies' budgets of the cost of educating that student (and others similarly eligible for other funding sources). At the same time, these provisions enlarge the agencies' ability to serve other students. In short, cost spreading and cost sharing are strategies for cost-effective special education.

Private Schools and Parent Choice

Two themes underlie IDEA's provisions and the Supreme Court's decisions about the education of students with disabilities in private schools. One theme is pro-family: The family should have the opportunity, even a right, to choose where to educate its child, and if that choice is in favor of a private school, the choice should not be discouraged by denying the student access to special education. Accordingly, IDEA provides for a student in a private school, enrolled there by the parents, to benefit from IDEA.

IDEA also recognizes that charter schools are still relatively new and, in some parts of the country, popular alternatives to the longstanding, traditional public schools. IDEA extends to the charter schools the same duties that the usual public schools have, recognizing that parents who enroll their children in charter schools should not lose the right to IDEA benefits as a consequence of that choice.

A second theme, originating in the Constitution's First Amendment requirement of separation between church and state, is more ephemeral and nebulous but nonetheless very real. It is that moral education is a valid dimension of public education and public policy. The Supreme Court's decisions (*Zobrest, Kiryas Joel Village School, Agostini,* and *Zelman v. Simmons-Harris*) can be read fairly as acknowledging that, though there must be a wall between church and state and that entanglement of those two entities of American life should be minimized, schools themselves are in the business of providing a moral basis for a student's life; indeed, that is an express purpose of religion-based schools and it arguably is a purpose of many private, non-religion-based schools, too.

By extending IDEA's benefits to students enrolled in private, religion-based schools, Congress declared that, like the Supreme Court, it will support some enmeshment of church and state so moral education may be made available to those who seek it. Note, however, that children who are placed in private schools by their parents have no individual right to receive some or all of the special education and related services that the child would receive if enrolled in a public school and no claim to a free appropriate public education (20 U.S.C. Sec. 1412(a)(10)(A); 34 C.F.R. Sec. 300.137(a)).

Hiring People With Disabilities

For a child's education to be meaningful after he or she leaves school, SEAs and LEAs must make positive efforts to hire and promote qualified persons with disabilities in programs receiving IDEA funds (20 U.S.C. Sec. 1405). All of the education and training the schools provide to students is meaningless unless the students have a realistic opportunity to make use of it later. Zero reject in special education should not be an empty promise. And, of course, economic benefits will accrue to the public if individuals with disabilities are hired. The employment provisions in Section 1405 of IDEA dovetail with Section 504 of the Rehabilitation Act and ADA to prohibit discrimination in employment and to require reasonable accommodations in the school system so that people with disabilities can be employed.

SUMMARY

When Congress first enacted IDEA in 1975, it intended the law to benefit all students with disabilities. Despite some modifications in the extent of students' rights, the 2004 amendments adhere to the original intent.

Although certain aspects of the *Honig* decision, as implemented by the 1997 amendments, have been limited by the 2004 amendments, the case still illustrates the basic rule of IDEA—that all students with disabilities must be given equal educational opportunities and may not be physically or functionally excluded from participation in public education, even those who have been suspended or expelled.

All means all, and zero reject means zero. More than just benefiting all students with disabilities, IDEA benefits all students, including those without disabilities. Its impact on schools extends to other domains of society as well: IDEA has justified Congress in declaring that disability is a "natural part of the human experience," leading us all to accommodate, even to welcome, those whom so many had rejected. Today, it is correct to declare that, in part because of the zero reject principle, "disabled" does not mean unworthy.

Chapter 5

Nondiscriminatory Evaluation

Case on Point: *Larry P. v. Riles*
793 F. Supp. 969, 1984 U.S. App. LEXIS 26195 (1984)

The decade of the 1960s shaped us all in ways that we are still coming to understand. Civil rights. Wars and protests. New laws. Among these new laws was the Civil Rights Act of 1964 (P.L. 88-352), which prohibited public and private entities from discriminating against individuals on the basis of their race.

Only a decade before, the Supreme Court had declared in *Brown v. Board of Education* (1954) that schools must not segregate by race and that they must desegregate with all due deliberate speed. The Civil Rights Act sought to facilitate desegregation, not just in schools but elsewhere. Little did anyone suspect, however, that the act also would profoundly affect special and general education.

It would not have done so had it not been for six Black schoolchildren in San Francisco who filed a lawsuit against the city and state superintendents, the state Board of Public Instruction, and the city Board of Education, alleging that their placement into special education violated the Civil Rights Act and the Fourteenth Amendment.

In *Larry P. v. Riles*, these students, on behalf of themselves and other Black students placed into special classes for the "educable mentally retarded" (EMR), alleged that the state's use of IQ tests was discriminatory and directly caused them to be placed erroneously into the EMR classes. They further alleged that their placement stigmatized them permanently, was itself an irreversible commitment to inadequate education, and was educationally inadequate.

The courts agreed and, in effect, ordered the state and local educational authorities not to place any Black students into an EMR class on the basis of criteria that relied solely on the results of an IQ test.

Civil rights, race, special education, and the means for determining who is placed into special education, then, were embedded in *Larry P.* In a sense, *Larry P.* was all about fairness—and the courts responded by requiring school districts to include in their assessments diagnostic tests designed to reveal specific learning needs, adaptive behavior observations, and even the child's developmental and health histories.

Larry P. became the basis for the IDEA (20 U.S.C. 1400 *et seq.*) concepts of fairness and how evaluations have to take into account the whole child. It also foretold IDEA's nondiscriminatory evaluation provisions. As we said, we are still coming to understand how the decade of the 1960s has affected us all, but we know this much: *Larry P.*, the Civil Rights Act, and race discrimination have profoundly affected special education and IDEA.

MAJOR CRITICISMS OF SCHOOL EVALUATIONS

The purpose of the zero reject principle is to assure that each student with a disability has access to education. Zero reject is the door-opener—a rule against exclusion and a rule in favor of school enrollment and participation. The zero reject principle, however, does not assure that, once the student is admitted to the school system, the student will receive an appropriate education in the least restrictive environment. Much more is required than simply opening the doors. That "more" begins with an evaluation of the student's strengths and needs.

Criticisms of Pre-IDEA Evaluations

There are many major criticisms of evaluation. We summarize them below, but before we do, let's remember that evaluation is absolutely necessary in order to determine whether a child is eligible for special education and to allow SEAs and LEAs to plan, appropriate, and program for educating the eligible children.

Intellectual Ability Alone as a Necessary but Insufficient Determinant

A legally sufficient evaluation accurately identifies the student's abilities (strengths) and disabilities (needs) and thereby lays the foundation for subsequent interventions, including those in general and special education. That has not always been the case. Indeed, before Congress enacted the predecessor to today's IDEA, school evaluations were criticized because they relied extensively—some would say exclusively—on tests of intellectual ability.

Evaluations largely focused on either intellect or physical/sensory capacity/incapacity and did not take into account the "whole person." Each student is the sum of various traits, not just those related to intellect or physical and sensory capacities.

Racial Bias in Testing

Another criticism was that IQ tests had been used to determine the intelligence of children who are unfamiliar with the English language or with the White middle-class culture that underlies the test questions. In short, it had been argued that tests based on a White middle-class socioeconomic group should not be used with individuals who are not of that group. Those tests put students who were not members of that socioeconomic group at an initial disadvantage and almost always caused them to be classified mistakenly as having a disability. This was especially true when the tests were not administered in the child's native language (e.g., Spanish) or when they did not also measure the child's adaptive behavior—the ability to cope and get along in his or her own cultural environment.

Stigma and Expectations

Yet another criticism was that misclassification resulting from inappropriate testing stigmatized the students by labeling them as having a disability. Misclassification tells a child that he or she is deficient, and the injury to the child's self-esteem is incalculable. It also can isolate the child from normal school experiences and induce other students and adults to exclude the child from any of those experiences.

Further, a perceived disability can create stereotypical expectations of behavior and can lead to a self-fulfilling prophecy—namely, that the student, being perceived as different, will begin to act in conformity to the perception—all to the student's irreparable harm. Finally, misclassified students might be placed in special education programs whether they do or do not need those placements, or they might be placed in inappropriate special education programs or be institutionalized inappropriately.

Once In, Never Out

Evaluations also were criticized because a disability label usually was permanent and could not be escaped, outgrown, or rebutted. Thus, being assigned to a special education program could become permanent, despite an original intention to make it temporary. The label could limit (or increase) the resources available to the student because public and private agencies tended to serve only persons identified as belonging within their categorical clientele. Ironically, being placed in a special education program did not necessarily ensure that the student would receive effective training in overcoming the disadvantages of being classified as having a disability.

Disproportional Representation

Minority students are represented disproportionately in special education. This has been a problem ever since Congress enacted IDEA (then, EHA) in 1975, and it continues to be a problem even now. Indeed, in the 2004 reauthorization of IDEA, Congress found as a matter of fact that

- the U.S. population is increasingly diverse, and its racial profile is rapidly changing;
- minority students comprise an ever larger percentage of public school students;
- the limited-English-proficiency population is the fastest-growing population;
- greater efforts are needed to prevent problems associated with mislabeling and high dropout rates among minority students with disabilities; and
- there is a need to bring more minority individuals into the professions that serve students with disabilities (20 U.S.C. Sec. 1400(c)(10)–(13)).

The Meat-Ax Approach and No Individualized Testing

As a final criticism, no individualized decision making was involved in choosing the tests for an individual evaluation or even how the results were used. This criticism—namely, that the testing was more like a meat ax that cut indiscriminately instead of like a scalpel that cut carefully and finely—was at the heart of what was to become the nondiscriminatory evaluation (NDE) process: For an evaluation to be successful, the evaluation must take the whole child into account. The evaluation then must be tailored individually to provide accurate and unbiased information that is useful for developing an individually appropriate educational plan.

As you read about IDEA's procedural safeguards for NDE, keep these criticisms in mind. Keep in mind, too, the two cases that responded most directly to the criticisms. If you keep the criticisms and the two cases in mind, you will note how well IDEA responds to each criticism and why we are justified in concluding what we have observed about classification.

Two Courts' Responses to the Criticisms

Reflecting the previous criticisms and hoping to persuade courts to require SEAs and LEAs to evaluate students more fairly, advocates for students with disabilities began, in the 1970s, to sue SEAs and LEAs. Two decisions exemplify the cases and the issues underlying them, and both also help explain IDEA's provisions related to procedural safeguards in evaluation.

Larry P. v. Riles

In *Larry P. v. Riles*, advocates for Black students who were classified into special education in California sued to prevent the SEA and LEAs from relying on tests of the students' intelligence as the basis for classifying them into special education. The federal district (trial) court agreed, holding that the SEA and LEAs should no longer use standardized IQ tests as the sole means for identifying and placing Black children into segregated special education classes for students classified as educable mentally retarded. The district court found that the tests

- were racially and culturally biased and had a discriminatory impact on Black children;

- were not validated for the purpose of essentially permanent placements into "educationally dead-end, isolated, and stigmatizing classes for students regarded as educable mentally retarded";
- were evidence of the schools' discriminatory intentions (in violation of equal protection); and
- could not be justified under the "compelling interest" standard applicable to racial discrimination cases.

Accordingly, the court ruled that schools using such tests violated Title VI of the Civil Rights Act of 1964, Section 504 of the Rehabilitation Act of 1973 (29 U.S.C. 794), IDEA, and the equal protection clause of the Fourteenth Amendment.

The Ninth Circuit Court of Appeals rejected an appeal by the SEA and LEAs and affirmed the district court's conclusions and remedies. Specifically, the Court of Appeals

- rejected the state's argument that tests that are valid predictors of future performance can be used even if they have a discriminatory impact;
- found that the state could not sustain the burden of showing that the tests predict specifically that Black elementary school children who score an IQ of 70 or below have mental retardation and are incapable of learning in the general school curriculum;
- found that the state was not using other measures or criteria—such as the child's educational history, adaptive behavior, social and cultural background, or health history—for determining special education placement;
- noted that improper placement in those classes was having a demonstrable and negative impact, putting children into dead-end classes that did not teach academic skills but was stigmatizing them, and that no nondiscriminatory factors, only the tests, were the cause of the adverse impact; and
- upheld the district court's remedy of suspending the use of the tests and requiring school districts with disproportionate racial balance in special education to devise 3-year remedial plans and to report racial disparities to the district court.

Larry P. was a race discrimination case coupled with a disability-discrimination case that put the court in the unenviable position of choosing among three possible explanations for the overrepresentation of minority children in special education:

1. The tests and their invalidity
2. The "gene pool" argument that minority children are inherently less intelligent than nonminority children
3. The socioeconomic explanation of low performance on standardized tests

Given that the court in *Larry P.* found minority overrepresentation in special education, the tests were the most likely candidates for the courts' remedy. Although the courts could hold the tests invalid and impose a remedy (no more testing under most conditions, or different evaluations under other conditions), they would have been at a loss to impose a remedy that would speak to the politically charged gene pool or socioeconomic arguments. The students' rights extended only as far as the courts' ability to order remedies.

Thus, the courts themselves ducked the highly politically charged issues about gene pool and socioeconomic status as causes of poor test performance. Those two issues, along with the issues about the tests' inherent bias, surfaced a few years later in *Parents in Action on Special Education (PASE) v. Hannon* (1980).

Parents in Action on Special Education (PASE) v. Hannon

Relying on the precedent in *Larry P.,* advocates for students in another racially segregated school system, Chicago, sued to prevent the LEA from using the tests to classify students with disabilities. On the surface, the facts in *PASE* appeared much like those in *Larry P.* The result, however, was quite different. In *PASE*, the court interpreted and applied IDEA (then, EHA), which had not been enacted when *Larry P.* was first decided. Thus, it avoided deciding the case on the basis of a constitutional right or a right under Section 504 or other federal statutes.

Relying on IDEA (after *Larry P.*) and holding that the tests were, on the whole, not discriminatory and that the LEA's placement decisions did not discriminate on the basis of race, the court reasoned that

- because the tests were not the sole basis for classification, the LEA was complying with IDEA, which requires multifaceted testing; and
- the IQ tests were only minimally discriminatory, and even that slight discrimination was offset by the LEA's careful adherence to other classification safeguards.

In reaching this result, the court addressed four major controversies surrounding classification, testing, race, and special education.

The Gene Pool Argument   The court concluded that IQ tests measure a human capacity (intelligence as evidenced by test performance) that is changeable rather than fixed for all time, and that can be increased and improved. No evidence was presented, the court noted, to support the hypothesis that Blacks have less innate mental capacity than Whites. Accordingly, the court rejected the gene pool argument as an explanation for the disproportionate representation of Blacks in special education.

The Racial/Cultural Bias Argument   The court also rejected the argument that the disproportionate placement was caused by Blacks' use of nonstandard English. The 96 vocabulary words that the students' lawyers alleged were discriminatory were, the court said, of "ordinary, common usage." Accordingly, the court also discounted the argument that the tests were "Anglocentric" rather than "Afrocentric" and, therefore, necessarily biased against Blacks. Instead, the court found—after 35 pages of its opinion—that only eight items on the tests (the WISC-R and the WISC) were "either racially biased or so subject to suspicion of bias that they should not be used," and that only one item on the Stanford-Binet fell into the same category.

Moreover, the court noted, a student's IQ score was "not the sole determinant" of whether a child was classified as having mental retardation; "clinical judgment plays a large role in the interpretation of IQ test results." Indeed, "the examiner who knows the milieu of the child can correct for cultural bias by asking the questions in a sensitive and intelligent way."

Finally, the court noted that the likelihood of a Black child being placed in a class for students labeled (in those days) as being educable mentally retarded (EMR) without at least one Black professional having participated in the evaluation is "very slight." The court thus concluded that "the possibility of the few biased items on these tests causing an [EMR] placement that would not otherwise occur is practically nonexistent."

The Socioeconomic Argument   The court addressed the socioeconomic explanation for special education placement by acknowledging that, "(E)arly intellectual stimulation is essential.... Lack of opportunity for cognitive development is ... often due to factors associated with economic poverty in the home." Moreover, it was "uncontradicted that most of the children in the [EMR] classes do in fact come from the poverty pockets" of Chicago. "This tends to suggest that what is involved is not simply race but something associated with poverty."

The Assessment Process   The court then addressed the assessment process, finding that it involved several levels of investigation (IQ testing, observation in the classroom, screening conferences by educators, individualized examinations by professionals, multidisciplinary staff conferences, and a potential veto of special education placement by the psychologist who evaluated the child). That process, the court observed, substantially mitigates any "hypnotic effect" that an IQ score might have. Indeed, later reevaluation of the students involved in the case indicated that they did not have mental retardation and had normal intelligence but "suffer from learning disabilities which make it difficult for them to perform well in certain kinds of learning situations."

Distinguishing and Disagreeing With *Larry P.*   Finally, the court distinguished its holding from that of the court in *Larry P.* The *PASE* court noted that the court in *Larry P.* devoted its lengthy and scholarly opinion "largely" to the question of legal consequences resulting from a finding of racial bias in the tests. The court, however, engaged in "relatively little analysis of the threshold question of whether test bias in fact exists" and even noted that the cultural bias of the tests "is hardly disputed." Indeed, the *Larry P.* court referenced only one specific test item. The *PASE* court noted that this inference of bias from only one item was not persuasive and that a more detailed examination of the test items was necessary.

Moving Forward From Larry P. *and* PASE *to* IDEA

Larry P. and *PASE* demonstrate the transition from a time without IDEA procedural safeguards to a time when, under IDEA, the evaluation procedures guard against racial, cultural, or linguistic bias. Now it is appropriate to describe IDEA's nondiscriminatory procedural and substantive safeguards and to consider them in light of the various criticisms that have been raised regarding evaluation and special education placement.

IDEA

Both *Larry P.* and *PASE* agree that procedures should be established to protect students from improper evaluation, misclassification, and inappropriate placement, and thus to avoid the criticisms of testing outlined above. Evaluations should accurately describe students' strengths and disabilities so the evaluation results can be used to develop an appropriate educational program. Accordingly, IDEA addresses both the techniques for classification and the action founded on the classification, which requires both procedural safeguards and substantive protection.

No Placement Without Evaluation

IDEA requires a multidisciplinary, multifaceted, nonbiased evaluation of a child before classifying and providing special education for that child. The requirement of fair evaluation as a prerequisite to classification also is a requirement of individualization. Due process mandates nothing less. If a student is not assessed individually when the result of that assessment could be a benefit (e.g., special education if needed) or a special burden (e.g., assignment to special education if the child does not have a disability), the student's constitutional rights to due process—enjoyment of life, liberty, and property—may be violated. In this regard, the law has erected substantive protection.

These safeguards also reflect sound professional practice, assuring that service providers will deal appropriately with students they are trained to serve. This result inures to the benefit of the student and the professional alike.

Standards: The But–For (or Causal) Factor

A student may not be classified under IDEA unless he or she has one or more of the disabilities listed in the statute (see chapter 3) and "by reason thereof require(s) special education and related services" (20 U.S.C. Sec. 1401(3)(A)(i)–(ii)). Similarly, a student does not qualify for a related service unless it is "required to assist the student to benefit from special education" (20 U.S.C. Sec. 1401(26)(A)).

In both cases, classification (as disabled or as qualifying for related services) has a but–for functional element. A causal relationship between the service, the classification, and the student's functioning (needs) must be present. Thus, IDEA insists that the techniques and effects of evaluation be connected.

Team Evaluation

The individuals responsible for organizing and interpreting a child's evaluation are part of a team consisting of the student's parents and other qualified professionals

(20 U.S.C. Sec. 1414(b)(4)(A)). The evaluation team is described as the "IEP team and other qualified professionals" (20 U.S.C. Sec. 1414(c)(1)), so one must refer to the requirements for the team that develops the student's individual education program known as the IEP (see chapter 6) (20 U.S.C. Sec. 1414(d)(1)(B)).

Briefly, the team must be composed of parents, special education teachers, general education teachers, an LEA representative with knowledge of special education and available resources, and professionals who are qualified to interpret the evaluations and their results. Both the parents and the LEAs have the option to invite other individuals with specialized knowledge, such as related services personnel. Even the student may participate.

As a rule of practice, then, the members of the student's IEP team also may serve on the nondiscriminatory evaluation team, thereby ensuring links among the evaluation process, program, and placement. Overlapping of the teams is clearly validated in IDEA, which now allows an LEA to consolidate reevaluation meetings and other IEP meetings for the child (20 U.S.C. Sec. 1414(d)(3)(E)).

Evaluation Standards

For IDEA to simply designate the membership on the evaluation team is not sufficient. To respond to the risks that a student may be misclassified or not evaluated properly, IDEA specifies the standards the evaluation team must adhere to and the procedures it must follow.

Standards Relating to the Student: Cultural Bias

The team must assess the student in all areas of suspected disability and ensure that

- tests and other evaluation materials are selected and administered so as not to be discriminatory on a racial or cultural basis (20 U.S.C. Sec. 1414(b)(3)(A)(i)); and
- tests and other evaluation materials are provided and administered in the language and form most likely to show what the child knows and can do academically, developmentally, and functionally, unless it is not feasible to do so (20 U.S.C. Sec. 1414(b)(3)(A)(ii)). The regulations still state that the tests must be provided in the child's native language or other mode of communication (34 C.F.R. 300.304(c)(1)(i)–(ii)).

Standards Relating to the Tests' Validity and Administration

The team must ensure that all standardized tests (20 U.S.C. Sec. 1414(b)(3)(A))

- have been validated for the specific purpose for which they are used (20 U.S.C. Sec. 1414(b)(3)(A)(iii));
- are administered by trained and knowledgeable personnel (20 U.S.C. Sec. 1414(b)(3)(A)(iv)); and
- are administered in accordance with any instructions provided by the test's producers (20 U.S.C. Sec. 1414(b)(3)(A)(v)).

Additional Evaluation Standards: Exclusionary Criteria

To further ensure that students, especially minority students, are not classified into special education unless they truly have a disability, and to address the criticism of disproportionate representation, IDEA creates an exclusionary rule that the evaluation team must follow. The team may not determine that the student has a disability

> if the determinant factor for such determination is lack of appropriate instruction in reading, including in the essential components of reading instruction (as defined in section 1208(3) of the Elementary and Secondary Education Act of 1965, now 20 U.S.C. 7801); lack of instruction in math; or limited English proficiency. (20 U.S.C. Sec. 1414(b)(5)(A)–(C))

(The No Child Left Behind Act, P.L. 107-110, amended the ESEA of 1965 so the reference in IDEA to that law is really to the reading components referred to in NCLB.)

This section does not prevent the evaluation team from making students eligible for special education even though the students may have experienced no or poor instruction in reading or math or have limited English proficiency. It does, however, prevent the team from making any of those three shortcomings the "determinant factor"—the one factor on which the team's decision turns.

Thus, this section assures that children from language-minority groups or from educationally impoverished programs will not be made eligible for IDEA solely because of those factors. The 2004 amendments, then, still reflect the continuing concerns that minority students continue to be overrepresented in special education, so additional criteria are in place to reduce their representation in special education.

Additional Evaluation Standards: Specific Learning Disabilities

Congress carefully defined children with "specific learning disabilities" so children who do not satisfy the definition will not be classified as having a disability (20 U.S.C. Sec. 1401(30)). IDEA continues to define "specific learning disability" by way of inclusionary and exclusionary criteria. The inclusionary criteria (20 U.S.C. Sec. 1401(30)(A)–(B) and 34 C.F.R. 300.8(c)(10)(i)) provide that

- a specific learning disability is a disorder in one or more of the basic psychological processes involved in understanding or using written or spoken language;
- the disorder may manifest itself in the imperfect ability to listen, think, speak, read, write, spell, or do mathematical calculations; and
- such disorders may include perceptual disabilities, brain injury, minimal brain dysfunction, dyslexia, and developmental aphasia.

The exclusionary criteria (20 U.S.C. Sec. 1401(30)(C) and 34 C.F.R. 300.8(c) (10)(ii)) provide that the term "specific learning disability" does not include a learning problem that is primarily the result of

- visual, hearing, or motor disabilities;
- mental retardation;
- emotional disturbance; or
- environmental, cultural, or economic disadvantage.

IDEA has substantially altered the procedure for identifying specific learning disabilities by adding a provision stating that an LEA may but is not required to take into account whether the student has a "severe discrepancy between achievement and intellectual disability in oral expression, listening comprehension, written expression, basic reading skill, reading comprehension, mathematical calculation, or mathematical reasoning."

Further, the LEA may but is not required to use a "process that determines if the child responds to scientific, research-based intervention" (20 U.S.C. Sec. 1414(b) (6)). The significance is that these changes encourage the use of the scientifically based intervention standard, further aligning IDEA with NCLB.

Accordingly, the U.S. Department of Education regulations (2006) dramatically revise Secs. 300.541–543 of the 1999 regulations by listing additional procedures for evaluating students with specific learning disabilities.

- States must not require the use of a severe discrepancy between intellectual ability and achievement for determining whether a student has a specific learning disability (34 C.F.R. 300.307(a)(1)).
- States must permit the use of a process that determines if the student responds to scientific, research-based intervention (34 C.F.R. 300.307(a)(2)).
- States may permit the use of other alternative research-based procedures for determining whether a child has a specific learning disability (34 C.F.R. 300.307(a)(3)).
- The general requirements of nondiscriminatory evaluation must be followed (34 C.F.R. 300.122, 300.304). These are the same requirements that apply to all children who are thought to have a disability. If the child is thought to have a specific learning disability, additional evaluations must be made (34 C.F.R. 300.307).
- The evaluation team must consist of the child's regular teacher (if the child does not have a regular teacher, a regular classroom teacher qualified to teach a child of the child's age) and other professionals, if appropriate, who are qualified to conduct individual diagnostic evaluations of the child, such as a school psychologist, speech–language pathologist, or remedial reading teacher (34 C.F.R. 300.308(a)–(b)).
- The regulations allow the evaluation team to determine that a child has a specific learning disability if the child does not achieve adequately with the

child's age or does not meet state-approved grade-level standards in one or more of the following areas when provided with learning experiences and instruction appropriate for the child's age or state-approved grade-level standards (34 C.F.R. 300.309(a)(1)):

□ Oral expression
□ Listening comprehension
□ Written expression
□ Basic reading skill
□ Reading fluency skills
□ Reading comprehension
□ Mathematics calculation
□ Mathematics problem solving

■ A student also may be found to have a severe learning disability if (1) the child does not make sufficient progress to meet age or state-approved grade-level standards in one or more of the areas above when using a process based on the child's response to scientific, research-based intervention; or (2) the child exhibits a pattern of strengths and weaknesses in performance, achievement, or both, relative to age, state-approved grade-level standards, or intellectual development, that the team determines is relevant to identification of a specific learning disability, using appropriate assessments consistent with Secs. 300.304 and 300.305 (34 C.F.R. 300.309(a)(2)).

■ Finally, the team must determine that its findings (that the child does not achieve adequately with the child's age or that the child is not learning at a sufficient rate) are not primarily the result of

□ a visual, hearing, or motor disability;
□ mental retardation;
□ emotional disturbance;
□ cultural factors;
□ environmental or economic disadvantage; or
□ limited English proficiency (34 C.F.R. 300.309(a)(3)(i)–(vi)).

■ If the team suspects that the child has a specific learning disability, the team also must review, as part of the evaluation process described above, data demonstrating that

□ prior to, or as a part of the referral process, the child was provided appropriate instruction in regular education settings, delivered by qualified personnel; and
□ the student's parents regularly received data-based documentation of repeated assessments of achievement at reasonable intervals, reflecting formal assessment of student progress during instruction (34 C.F.R. 300.309(b)(1)–(2)).

- If the child has not made adequate progress during an appropriate period of time during which the child is provided appropriate research-based instruction and the parents are given documentation, the child may be referred to special education and all of the appropriate timelines established in 34 C.F.R. 300.301 and 300.303 must be adhered to unless extended by mutual written agreement of the child's parents and the group described in 34 C.F.R. 300.306(a)(1) (34 C.F.R. 300.309(c)).

Clearly, then, IDEA continues to respond to the concerns of overrepresentation of children in special education, the growing costs of special education, and the resulting stigma of having those children so categorized.

- IDEA narrowly defines the category of specific learning disability and erects additional procedural hurdles for that classification, thereby potentially reducing the number of students classified.
- IDEA recognizes that a large number of children simply do not perform as well as others but do not have other obvious disabilities. Their lack of performance could result in a large number of these children being classified as having learning disabilities and the costs of educating them appropriately would be enormous. IDEA thus requires that the child suspected as having a severe learning disability receive appropriate research-based instruction for a period of time before classification.

The general and additional evaluation requirements recognize that a stigma is attached to any disability. Accordingly, they seek to disallow that classification to prevent the child from being stigmatized. Yet, the general and special evaluation requirements for learning disabilities convey a strange message: to have the stigma of sensory, physical, mental, or emotional disability is worse than to have the stigma of learning disability. This message is inherent in the definition of learning disability.

Evaluation Procedures

IDEA also clearly establishes procedures for evaluations, and these procedures are another safeguard for preventing the misclassification of students into special education. For an evaluation to be nondiscriminatory and comprehensive, the team must do the following:

- Use a variety of assessment tools and strategies to gather relevant functional, developmental, and academic information, including information provided by the parent, to determine whether the student has a disability, and, if so, the content of the student's IEP so the student can progress in the general education curriculum, or for preschoolers, appropriate activities (20 U.S.C. Sec. 1414(b)(2)(A) and 34 C.F.R. 300.304(b)).

■ Not use any single measure or assessment as the sole criterion to determine whether the student has a disability and, if so, the student's appropriate educational program (20 U.S.C. Sec. 1414(b)(2)(B)).

■ Use technically sound instruments to assess the student across four domains: cognitive, behavioral, physical, and developmental (20 U.S.C. Sec. 1414(b)(2)(C)). Note that this requirement reflects the NCLB emphasis on using scientifically based interventions.

■ Use evaluation methods that are sufficiently comprehensive to identify all of the child's special education and related service needs, whether or not linked to one of the disability categories in which the child has been classified (34 C.F.R. 300.304(c)(6)).

■ Use assessment tools and strategies that assist the team directly in determining that the student's educational needs are satisfied (20 U.S.C. Sec. 1414(b)(3)(C)).

■ Review existing evaluation data, including evaluations and information from parents, current classroom-based, local or state assessments, classroom-based observations, and observations by teachers and related services providers (20 U.S.C. Sec. 1414(c)(1)(A)). In reviewing existing data, identify what additional data the team needs to determine the following (20 U.S.C. Sec. 1414(c)(1)(B)):

  □ Does the student have a specific disability, and does the student continue to have that disability?
  □ What are the student's present levels of performance and educational needs?
  □ Does the student need (or continue to need) special education and related services?
  □ What, if any, additions or modifications to the student's special education and related services are needed to enable the student to meet the measurable annual goals of his or her IEP and to participate as appropriate in the general curriculum?

Intent of Standards and Procedures, Responses to Criticisms

Taken together, these standards and procedures help to minimize the various criticisms, such as the stigma of being inappropriately classified, the use of only intellectual or physical/sensory criteria, and the lack of individualized testing. The intent of IDEA's nondiscriminatory evaluation process is to ensure that students are evaluated properly so fair and accurate information is available. This information then can be used to determine what, if any, disability the student has and to develop an appropriate individualized education program for the student in the least restrictive environment. This is done through several means:

■ Essentially the same people serve on the evaluation and on the IEP/placement teams, thereby creating a link between evaluations and the development of educational programs.

- The statute requires that assessments be properly validated and administered according to strict standards. As such, tests cannot be racially or culturally discriminatory.
- The school district is required to use multiple assessments that comprehensively test all four areas of development: cognitive, behavioral, physical, and developmental.
- The team must consider input from parents and an assortment of school assessments and personnel.

The function of IDEA evaluations is to determine how a particular disability affects a student's educational needs, not the student's or family's other needs. Thus, those needs will not be considered no matter how much they may affect the student's education.

Initial Evaluation, Process, and Timing

IDEA has expanded the list of individuals or entities who may request an initial evaluation. Now, a parent, an SEA, other state agency, or an LEA may initiate a request for an initial evaluation to determine if the child has a disability. Because IDEA does not define "other state agency," this potentially could include child welfare and protective services agencies serving "wards of the state" in foster care or even agencies holding children in custody within the juvenile justice system (20 U.S.C. Sec. 1414(a)(1)). IDEA requires LEAs to obtain parental consent before conducting an initial evaluation (20 U.S.C. Sec. 1414(a)(1)(D)).

The 2004 amendments also establish a timeline for evaluations. The initial evaluation must be done within 60 days after the agency receives parental consent for the evaluation or, if the state establishes a different time frame (longer or shorter than 60 days), within that time frame (20 U.S.C. Sec. 1414(a)(1)(C)(i)(I)). The only exceptions are if a student transfers mid-evaluation before a result can be reached and the receiving LEA demonstrates sufficient progress toward completion or if the parents refuse to produce the student for the evaluation (20 U.S.C. Sec. 1414(a)(1)(C)(i)(II)).

Reevaluations, Process, and Timing

Although an LEA initially may evaluate a student as having a disability and then provide an IEP and least restrictive placement for the student on the basis of the initial evaluation, IDEA recognizes that reevaluation is desirable. Disabilities are not constant. They change over time, especially as a student develops and if special and general education interventions are effective in ameliorating the effect of the disability.

Moreover, the change in the student's disability (it may become more or less severe) may be accompanied by changes in the student's life that affect how the student learns. Often, the student's home and family life affects the student's learning capacities, especially in light of life changes such as divorce, death, marriage, moving out of or into the family, the birth of siblings, and other events. Accordingly, IDEA provides for reevaluation of the student.

IDEA clarifies the reevaluation process by removing the former (1997) language "if conditions warrant" and stating that the team must conduct a reevaluation if

- the LEA determines that the educational or related-services needs, including improved academic achievement and functional performance, of the child warrant a reevaluation; or
- the parents or a teacher request a reevaluation because they may have or need new information about the student to make the student's special education more effective (20 U.S.C. Sec. 1414(a)(2)).

If a reevaluation is to be conducted, IDEA also specifies several limitations as to how often. These limitations highlight how the 2004 amendments seek to reduce the "paperwork burden" that reevaluations allegedly have caused. A reevaluation

- may not occur more frequently than once a year, unless the parent and the local LEA agree otherwise;
- must occur at least once every 3 years, unless the parent and the LEA agree that a reevaluation is unnecessary and jointly waive the 3-year reevaluation requirement (20 U.S.C. Sec. 1414(a)(2)); and
- is no longer required under the 2004 amendments when a student is graduating with a "regular diploma" or "is exceeding the age eligibility" for IDEA benefits under state law. Instead, the LEA has to provide nothing more than a summary of the student's academic achievement and functional performance that also contains recommendations on how to assist the student with his/her postsecondary goals (20 U.S.C. Sec. 1414(c)(5)(B)). This provision also furthers the aim of reducing paperwork but still provides for educational data to be used for transition and the four IDEA outcomes.

IDEA further requires LEAs to obtain parental consent prior to conducting a reevaluation. An LEA is exempt from this requirement only if it can demonstrate through documentation that it took reasonable measures to obtain parental consent and the parent did not respond (20 U.S.C. Sec. 1414(c)(3); 34 C.F.R. 300.300).

Whenever it conducts a reevaluation, the evaluation team must comply with all of the standards and procedures governing the initial evaluation. These standards and procedures also apply to an evaluation that is done before a change in eligibility—

the one conducted for the purpose of determining whether the student should be removed from special education and placed into general education (20 U.S.C. Sec. 1414(c)(5)).

When doing a reevaluation, the team (including the parents and other qualified personnel as appropriate) also must do the following (20 U.S.C. Sec. 1414(c)):

- Review existing evaluation data, including current local or state classroom-based assessments, classroom-based observations, and teachers' and related service providers' observations
- Identify what additional data they need to determine four facts:

   □ Does the child have a particular category of disability, does the student continue to have that disability, and what are the educational needs?
   □ What are the student's present levels of performance and related developmental needs?
   □ Does the student need (or continue to need) special education and related services?
   □ What, if any, additions or modifications to the student's special education and related services are needed to enable the student to meet the measurable annual goals of his or her IEP and to participate as appropriate in the general education curriculum?

When conducting a reevaluation, the evaluation team has two sources of data:

1. It has, and must consider, all of the data from the preceding evaluation.
2. It must administer tests and other evaluation materials as may be needed to determine whether the student still has a disability and, if so, the student's present levels of academic achievement, educational needs, and related developmental needs (20 U.S.C. Secs. 1414(a)(2), (c)(1)–(2)).

If the evaluation team determines that it does not need any new data to complete its duties, the team must (20 U.S.C. Sec. 1414(c)(4))

- notify the parents that no additional data are needed to determine if the student remains eligible for special education and give reasons for reaching that decision; and
- notify parents that they have a right to request an assessment to determine whether the child continues to have a disability and to determine the child's educational needs, and that they also can appeal the conclusion via mediation or due process.

This is a significant provision in that it relieves the team, the student, and the parents from having to undergo a complete reevaluation if current information is sufficient for the team to develop an appropriate educational plan. For example, there may well be no need to retest the student; retesting might not be productive or might, in fact, be counterproductive. Moreover, it is cost conscious not to retest unnecessarily; resources should be spent only on necessary evaluation and services. Note, however, that the parents may require the team to conduct any assessment that it has proposed to omit; the parents essentially may veto the "no new tests/assessments" decision (20 U.S.C. Sec. 1414(c)(4)(B)).

The reevaluations are meant to determine the student's educational needs only, not the student's or family's other needs. Practically speaking, a student can have disability-related needs that are not connected to the student's education, and those needs do not interfere with the student's ability to learn in the general education setting. That student would not require special education.

Regardless, IDEA's mechanism for reevaluation helps ensure that a student's diagnosis as having a disability is not permanent and can be escaped, resulting in the student's no longer needing special education. This acknowledges that students and circumstances can change and that education has to be capable of changing fluidly with the student.

PARENTS' ROLE

Because IDEA always has been concerned about protecting the rights of students and their parents, it has abided by yet another major principle: parent participation (see chapter 9 for a detailed discussion of this principle). Parents have access to unique information about the child, such as medical history and current treatment. Parents also have an opportunity to observe the child in a variety of settings other than school.

Thus, nowhere is parent participation more important than in the critical issues of identifying whether a student has a disability and, if so, what the student needs in general and special education, including what individualized program and placement are appropriate. The links among evaluation, program, and placement is explicit in IDEA (20 U.S.C. Sec. 1414). Participation of the student's parents in decisions that affect each element of that link is, therefore, essential.

With at least one parent as a member of the team and various requirements for parental consent, the evaluation process can focus on each area of the child's educational needs and each area of concern for the parents. But, under IDEA, the contrary also is true: The uninvolved or uninformed parent causes the student to pay the price of the parent's inaction or ignorance. That fact alone significantly increases parent participation by adding parents' responsibility for choosing wisely, for accepting the consequences of their choices, and for involving themselves in the entire evaluation process.

Participation

As stated, IDEA continues to require that the student's parents must be members of the evaluation and IEP teams (20 U.S.C. Sec. 1414(d)(1)(B)), and it specifies that parents

- must be afforded an opportunity to participate in any group meeting in which decisions may be made with respect to the identification, evaluation, placement, or provision of FAPE to the child (34 C.F.R. 300.501);
- must be given a copy of the evaluation report and documentation concerning their child's eligibility (or lack of eligibility) for special education;
- may submit to the team and require it to consider evaluations and information that they (the parents) initiate or provide;
- have a right to be notified that the team has determined it does not need any additional data or what, if any, additional data are needed for purposes of deciding whether their child is or remains eligible for special education (still has a disability) (34 C.F.R. 300.305); and
- have a right to request an assessment to determine whether their child continues to be eligible for special education (the team does not have to conduct the assessment unless the parents request one) (34 C.F.R. 300.305).

To challenge the discriminatory effect or intent of classification, students also may need an advocate. Thus, IDEA requires SEAs to appoint surrogate guardians for children who have no parents or are wards of the state.

Consent

Another way of ensuring parental participation is to give parents extensive consent rights. With participation, however, comes responsibility, and the 2004 amendments clearly put parents in charge of critical decisions during the special education process.

- Before any agency conducts an initial evaluation or any subsequent reevaluation, the agency must obtain the informed consent of the child's parents. The parents' informed consent applies *only* to that specific evaluation and "shall not be construed as consent for placement for receipt of special education and related services" (20 U.S.C. Sec. 1414(a)(1)(D)).
- If the parents do not respond or refuse to consent to an initial evaluation, the LEA may, but is not required to, use mediation or due process procedures to secure approval for an evaluation. (We explain those procedures later in this section and in chapter 8, "Procedural Due Process.") If the LEA does not utilize these methods, the LEA can legally claim that it does not have any responsibility to provide IDEA benefits to the student. The LEA then may proceed with discipline and other general education consequences. The LEA must have made a reasonable effort to obtain consent and documented its efforts (34 C.F.R. 300.300).
- If the LEA cannot secure parental consent prior to a reevaluation, the LEA may proceed with the evaluation if it can "demonstrate that it had taken reasonable measures to obtain such consent and the child's parent has failed to respond" (20 U.S.C. Sec. 1414(c)(3)).
- If a parent refuses to consent to special education and related services, the 2004 amendments make clear that "no means no." The LEA may not put the

child into special education or provide any special education services to the student under IDEA.

- A parent's refusal to consent to special education services essentially frees the LEA from any obligations to provide the student with either special education or related services (20 U.S.C. Sec. 1414(a)(1)(D)(ii)). Specifically,

  □ the LEA shall not be considered to be in violation of the requirement to make available a free appropriate public education to the student because it has not provided the student with the special education and related services for which the LEA has requested the parents' consent; and

  □ the LEA shall not be required to convene an IEP meeting or develop an IEP for the student to provide the special education services for which the LEA has requested but not received the parent's consent.

If a parent does not want his or her child categorized as needing "special education," one other route can be attempted to ensure that the student receives some benefit in school: A parent could attempt to assert that the student has a disability under Section 504 of the Rehabilitation Act and the ADA. Proving through evaluations, however, that the student meets the definition of having a "disability" under those laws may be difficult, given the parent's choice not to have the student qualify under IDEA. If the student qualifies under either law, the LEA must offer "reasonable accommodations" to the student.

The purpose of these provisions is to emphasize how parent participation in the evaluation process is critical. Parental consent throughout the special education process ensures

- collaborative decision making;
- parents' involvement in the child's education, including program and placement;
- parents' responsibility for their child's educational programming;
- parents' information that aids the other members of the team; and
- parents' knowledge about whether the child has a disability.

Substitute Consent

As a general rule of law, a person may not legally consent or withhold consent to educational, health, or mental health services if he or she is not mentally competent (unable to engage in a rational process of decision making). Mental capacity is an indispensable element of consent.

Moreover, children generally are presumed to be incompetent, because of their age, to act for themselves, especially in regard to special education services. And some children with disabilities have no parents alive or available and are wards of the state. Those children usually are subject to judicial proceedings that result in the appointment of a legal guardian who has power to consent to services on their behalf. In addition, IDEA requires states to continue to rely on parental consent for an adult child who has not been adjudicated as incompetent but who nevertheless may be unable to give legally effective consent (see chapter 8).

Independent Evaluations

A parent who disagrees with the findings of an LEA's initial evaluation or reevaluation has the right to obtain an independent evaluation of the child (20 U.S.C. Sec. 1415(b)(1)). Also, parents have the right to obtain independent evaluations and to submit them as additional information for the team to consider (20 U.S.C. Secs. 1414 (b)(2), (c)(1), and 1415 (b)(1)).

Although a parent has a right to request an independent evaluation, IDEA is not definitive as to whether the LEA or the parent should bear the cost of the independent evaluation. According to IDEA's regulations, parents have a right to charge the cost of independent evaluation to LEAs under certain circumstances—namely, if the LEA's evaluation was inappropriate or the LEA was under an order by a due process hearing officer or court to pay for an independent evaluation (34 C.F.R. 300.502). The regulations also state that the school may avail itself of due process procedures to show that its evaluations were appropriate and valid and that it, therefore, is not required to pay for independent evaluations requested by the parents. Parents are entitled to only one independent evaluation at public expense for each evaluation conducted by the LEA (34 C.F.R. 300.502).

Due Process and Procedural Safeguards

Due process safeguards also tend to minimize the risk that the child's parents will dispute, or find error in, the evaluation; they are means for holding an LEA accountable for its actions in evaluating and classifying a student into or out of special education. Thus, the student's parents are entitled to notice of the action the school proposes to take, a hearing before an impartial trier of fact and law, an opportunity to present and rebut evidence, and the right to appeal an adverse decision (see chapter 8).

Access to Records

Another technique of accountability is to grant affected persons or their representatives the right to have access to the professional records concerning them. Thus, IDEA allows a student's parents to see the school records or records of the school system's special education programs (20 U.S.C. Sec. 1415(b)(1)) (see chapter 8).

In granting access, IDEA relies on the principal federal law governing school records. That law is the Family Educational Rights and Privacy Act (FERPA) (20 U.S.C. 1232g). Under FERPA, parents have the right to "inspect and review" records within 45 days of providing the LEA with the request (FERPA Regulations, 34 C.F.R. Part 99). We discuss FERPA in detail in chapter 8, "Procedural Due Process."

There are other avenues for accountability through access to records. Some states have enacted statutes that allow people with disabilities or their representatives access to social work, health, or mental health records. Further, people with disabilities or their representatives normally can access court and quasi-judicial proceedings or records related to them (such as the impartial hearing guaranteed under IDEA—see chapter 8).

Advocacy

To ensure that students and their parents have access to assistance in knowing and enforcing their rights, IDEA authorizes the establishment of parent training and information centers (also known as PTI centers or PTC) (20 U.S.C Sec. 1471). These centers are designed to help parents understand the nature of their child's disability and their educational, developmental, and transitional needs. They also help with how to communicate with schools and other professionals and assist parents in resolving disputes.

There is another law that authorizes access to advocates to students and parents. Under the Developmental Disabilities Assistance and Bill of Rights Act of 1975 (42 U.S.C. Secs. 1500 *et seq.*), states that receive federal funds for use in serving people with disabilities must create a protection and advocacy system to advocate for them against state and local governmental agencies. Federally financed P&A offices have been involved extensively in special education lawsuits involving the classification and education of children with developmental disabilities.

Part C

IDEA, Part C, provides that a state's system of early intervention must include a component for a timely, comprehensive, multidisciplinary evaluation of the functioning of each infant or toddler and a family-directed identification of the needs of each such family. Both the evaluation of the infant/toddler and identification of family needs must assist appropriately in the infant's/toddler's development (20 U.S.C. Sec. 1435(a)(3)).

The remainder of the nondiscriminatory evaluation safeguards for an infant/toddler and the family are set out in the regulations implementing Part C. In a nutshell, these regulations require that tests be administered by appropriately qualified personnel (who are entitled to apply their clinical opinion to reach an evaluation result) and be in the parent's native language or other mode of communication, that they not be racially or culturally discriminatory, that no single procedure be used, and that qualified personnel administer the tests (34 C.F.R. Sec. 300.304). Evaluation is done for the purpose of determining a child's eligibility for Part C and identifying the child's needs, the family's strengths and needs, and the services necessary to meet the child's and family's needs (34 C.F.R. 303.322).

The purpose of the family assessment is to determine the family's strengths and needs related to enhancing the child's development. The family assessment must be voluntary on the family's part. It must be based on information the family provides through a personal interview and must incorporate the family's description of its strengths and needs with respect to enhancing their child's development (34 C.F.R. 303.322(d)).

As a general rule, child and family evaluations and assessments must be completed within 45 days after the state lead agency (the agency designated by a governor to oversee Part C; it can be the SEA) is notified of the family's application for service (34 C.F.R. 303.322(e)).

SIGNIFICANCE OF IDEA SAFEGUARDS

The 2004 amendments have simplified and expanded many of the provisions of IDEA 1997 (P.L. 105-17) by

- maintaining that an evaluation team include the members of the IEP team (parents, student, and school personnel), thereby linking the evaluation to IEP development and programming and also encouraging consolidation of reevaluation meetings and other IEP meetings;
- expanding the list of individuals or entities that may request an initial evaluation to include other state agencies;
- establishing a timeframe for evaluations that can be modified only upon special circumstances or by agreement between the schools and the parents;
- increasing parent participation by creating new and detailed requirements for consent, not just for initial evaluations and reevaluations but also for special education and related services;
- establishing that if a parent does not consent, the LEA is absolved from any further responsibility and obligations to provide special education and related services;
- clarifying that a reevaluation may not be done more than twice a year unless the school and the parents consent, and allowing for the LEA and parents to waive the requirement for a reevaluation at least every 3 years;
- removing the requirement that an LEA complete an evaluation on a student who is either graduating with a general education diploma or is aging out of IDEA eligibility and instead providing for a comprehensive summary of the student's present levels of performance and transition and other goals;
- continuing to emphasize that an evaluation must focus on a student's participation in the general education curriculum (a pro-LRE) provision;
- continuing to require that classroom-based data be generated and considered, and thus target not only the student's behavior but also the staff's capacity to deliver effective general and special education services;
- continuing to focus equally on four student domains—cognitive, behavioral, physical, and developmental—and thereby provide data that can be used to develop effective interventions (including those that prevent suspension and expulsion) and that incidentally assess the effectiveness of the services the student receives;
- still requiring the team to use "tools and strategies" that indicate whether the school is meeting the student's educational needs, thereby adding yet another

accountability provision in favor of the student and linking evaluation and intervention to general school-improvement initiatives;

- making certain that an evaluation is meant to determine how a disability affects a student's educational needs, thereby confining the overall function of IDEA to education of the student, not other student or family needs; and
- changing the eligibility requirements for the category of "specific learning disability" by making it optional for schools to use the discrepancy standard in favor of the scientifically based interventions of NCLB.

Another way to appreciate the significance of the IDEA evaluation safeguards is to ask whether they sufficiently answer the criticisms of classification and evaluation that opened this chapter: reliance on only the intellectual evaluations, racial bias, stigma and expectations, permanent placement, disproportionate representation, limited focus, and no individual testing. Do they sufficiently answer the criticisms? Generally speaking, the answer is "yes." What justifies that answer?

First, IDEA requires holistic and fair evaluations. They are holistic because they require the evaluation team to

- assess the student's strengths and needs in four domains: cognitive, behavioral, physical, and developmental;
- link all assessments to the student's IEP, and especially to the student's participation in the curriculum;
- decide what the student needs to be able to meet the student's annual goals (including participation in the general curriculum);
- determine how to increase teachers' capacity to deliver an appropriate education; and
- identify the tools and strategies the evaluation/IEP team will use to decide whether the school and its teachers are meeting the student's educational needs.

Next, IDEA evaluations are fair because the team must

- use instruments that are "validated" for the purposes for which they are used;
- use instruments that are "technically sound" for evaluating the student in each of the four domains, thereby reflecting NCLB's and IDEA's emphasis on scientifically based interventions, including those used for qualifying students for special education;
- take into account specific exclusionary criteria by incorporating the reading instruction definition from NCLB, thereby helping to assure that children from language-minority groups or from educationally impoverished programs will not be made eligible for IDEA solely because of these factors.

The concept of fair and holistic evaluations, then, is IDEA's answer to the criticisms found in *Larry P.* and the basis for the finding that the evaluations in *PASE* were nondiscriminatory. The court in *Larry P.* clearly sought to prevent the schools from misclassifying a student as having a disability based solely on findings of an IQ test. Although the test itself was found to be discriminatory, the court also stressed that no single instrument should be used to determine a child's educational future. This ruling led to development of IDEA evaluation provisions that outline in great detail not only those individuals responsible for doing the evaluation but also the process by which those evaluations have to be done.

By establishing a procedure for schools to follow and parents to participate in, IDEA established the presumption followed in *PASE* that, even if a few questions on an IQ test could be termed discriminatory, any discriminatory impact is lessened if the test is only one component of a comprehensive evaluation.

SECTION 504

Like IDEA regulations, the regulations implementing Section 504 (34 C.F.R. 104.1–104.61) acknowledge that failure to provide students with an appropriate education can result from misclassification. Accordingly, Section 104.35(a) requires an evaluation of any person who needs or is believed to need special education or related services because of a disability. The evaluation must be completed before a school takes any action (including denial of placement) with respect to initial placement in a general or special education program or any subsequent significant change in placement. But a full reevaluation is not obligatory every time a lesser adjustment in the child's placement is made.

Evaluation and Placement

Sections 104.35(b) and (c) set out procedures to ensure that children are not misclassified, unnecessarily labeled as having a disability, or placed incorrectly because of inappropriate selection, administration, or interpretation of evaluation materials. Section 104.35(b) requires schools to establish standards and procedures for evaluation and placement to ensure that tests and other evaluation materials are validated for the specific purpose for which they are used and are administered by trained personnel in conformance with the instructions of their producer. Tests and other evaluation materials are to include those tailored to assess specific areas of educational need and not merely those designed to provide a single general intelligence quotient.

In addition, tests are to be selected and administered to students with impaired sensory, manual, or speaking skills so the test results accurately reflect the student's aptitude or achievement level—or whatever other factor the test purports to measure—rather than the student's impaired skills, except when those skills are the factors the test seeks to measure. Section 104.35(b) drives home the point that tests should not be misinterpreted, that undue reliance on general intelligence tests is undesirable, and that tests should be administered in such a way that their results will not be distorted because of the student's disability.

Section 104.35(c) requires that schools, when evaluating and placing students, draw upon information from a variety of sources, including aptitude and achievement tests, teacher recommendations, physical conditions, social or cultural background, and adaptive behavior. Schools must establish procedures to ensure that information obtained from all such sources is documented and considered carefully. The placement decision is to be made by a group of people including those who are knowledgeable about the child. The meaning of the evaluation data and the placement options must be made clear to all concerned. Placement decisions are to conform to the doctrine of least restrictive (most integrated) setting.

Reevaluation

Section 104.35(d) requires periodic (though not necessarily annual) reevaluation. It makes clear that reevaluation procedures consistent with IDEA (which allows reevaluation at 3-year intervals unless more frequent reevaluations are requested) are a means of meeting the reevaluation requirement.

Section 104.36 requires schools to provide for due process in evaluation procedures. This includes notice, right of access to records, impartial hearing, right to counsel, and appeal procedures. Chapter 8 focuses on due process in detail.

OBSERVATIONS ABOUT CLASSIFICATION

As *Larry P.* and many other early cases on nondiscriminatory evaluation recognized and as Congress acknowledged in IDEA, classification of a person as having a disability, through evaluation in school, can have important educational and adult life consequences. At the worst, it can relegate the person to second-class citizenship and, as such, subject the individual to a dual system of law. That dual system allows those without disabilities to treat those with disabilities as less worthy because of their disabilities. It now is appropriate to explain how a dual system occurs by making several observations about classification and evaluation.

We begin by arguing that classification through evaluation involves the exercise of power. We follow that argument by explaining how classification can be both helpful and harmful (power as beneficent or maleficent).

We then examine the concept of disability itself, explaining that it is not just a trait that is inherent in a person but often can be the consequence of the interaction between the person and society and that the interaction is affected by a "fix-the-person" approach (a focus on the person's pathology, the disability). We move from that perspective to one that asks how various models of thinking about disability affect the person, and we explain how disability policy has moved from, but not abandoned, the *medical model* in favor of a *social model* of disability and how the social model takes into account the "new morbidity" (the correlation of disability with social disadvantages).

Having asked you to take such a broad view about classification and evaluation, we bring you back to our original thesis that classification is an exercise in power, and we ask who classifies, how they classify, and why they classify. We then explain that the who-how-why of classification gives great power to professionals, and we describe the consequences of this deference to professional judgment: namely, that it takes policy leaders and others off the hook for deciding who has a disability and what society, including the law, owes to that person.

Finally, having advanced arguments about power and explanations of why and how power is exercised, we return to IDEA and show how its use of substantive standards and procedural safeguards attempt to minimize the negative effects of classification.

The Dominance Theory: Classification as the Exercise of Power

Special education originated, in part, from the efforts of various scientists to document human development and to develop interventions that assist a person to overcome various limitations.

It also, however, originated as a response to the inability of the schools to accommodate the wave of immigration that began in the middle of the nineteenth century. As non-English-speaking immigrants came to the East Coast of the United States and as Asian immigrants came to the West Coast, they often were classified as "special" and segregated in their education from well-established, earlier-arrived, English-speaking Americans. (The fact that this classification had religious undertones and was done on the basis of native language, country of origin, or ethnicity should not go unnoticed.)

In one of the most insightful books about special education, Sarason and Doris (1975) argued that classification occurred to

- preserve the social status quo and prevent disruption of the social structure,
- put distance between people so that those who are different (subject to a negative stigma) are not in the presence of others, and
- altruistically justify some ameliorative (special education) interventions.

Classification, then, is an exercise in political, social, and economic control. It is a means for securing the supremacy of some at the expense of others. For that reason alone, classification and the methods and instruments (evaluation and assessment tests) that facilitate classification must be specially scrutinized so that they will be fair and the results used for good, not ill.

Classification and Theories of Beneficence and Maleficence

The individuals who developed intelligence tests in the early years of the twentieth century intended to use them for entirely beneficent purposes—that is, to benefit individuals and society alike. But the tests—which is to say, science itself and the systems and methods of classification that derived from the science—had the potential for being used for malevolent purposes.

That, almost certainly, is what happened with respect to the intelligence tests. They originated in beneficence and descended into malfeasance, not because they themselves were inherently oppressive but because some people used them for oppressive purposes. That fact of history explains not just the criticisms of testing and classification but also IDEA's procedural safeguards related to evaluation. Moreover, the intelligence tests did not sufficiently explain why some people function well in society despite their cognitive impairments while others do not. In a word, they did not explain how impairment and society interact with each other. That explanation comes by looking at the transactions of people with each other.

Disability as a Transactional Phenomenon

Sarason and Doris (1975) directed their attention to a single disability, mental retardation, and argued that classification of a person as having mental retardation reflects social policy; thus, the disability itself is a social invention. To make this point, they argued that disability—unlike genetic makeup—is a characteristic that is not necessarily inherent in a person. Rather, disability is a consequence of how a person functions within a social context. It is a transactional phenomenon, something that results from the way a person relates to and transacts social relations with others. If the person functions differently than others, the person is said to have a disability. And, thus, the person is said to be at fault; the disability is part and parcel of the person (it is inherent in the person).

Yet it is clear, as (for example) the American Association on Mental Retardation (AAMR, 2002) acknowledges, that disability—functioning differently from others—is also a consequence of how the person's environment does or does not accommodate to the person. The less the accommodation, the greater is the likelihood that the person will be functionally different from others and thus be regarded as having a disability. We develop that point immediately below, bringing you back to the principle of dual accommodations that you learned about in chapter 3 and asking you to think about how special education and other related rehabilitative services focus on the disability of a person and seek to remediate it and then about the consequences of an intervention, both for the person and for society.

The Dual Accommodations Model

Under the dual accommodations model, special interventions—special education, for example—are warranted to "fix" the person's disability and often to separate that person from those who do not have a disability. That is so because, in special education and other related rehabilitative services, the traditional thinking has been that a disability reflects a broken aspect of the person and justifies professionals in offering services (such as special education) that attempt to "repair" or "fix" the disability. Likewise, a disability justifies the separation of those who are different or broken from those who are not; thus, special education has been organized and operated separately and differently from general education for so many years (although IDEA and NCLB bring the systems more into line with each other). Intervention and separation rest on a pathologically focused view of the person: the disability is the pathology, and a proper response to it is to "fix" the person.

What that approach fails to acknowledge, however, is that changing the person is only one part of the solution to the "misfit" of the person in society, only one way of accommodating to the fact of difference. The other part of the solution, of course, is to change the society itself. Accommodation, after all, should be a two-way street and must require antidiscrimination laws such as ADA and Section 504. This two-part approach to the transactions between the person and society is called the principle of dual accommodations. It involves rights and duties: The individual has a right to interventions and a duty to take advantage of education to accommodate to the demands and expectations of society, but society itself must not discriminate on the basis of the disability and indeed must change by offering reasonable accommodations to the individual's differences and disabilities.

The Medical Model and the Social Model

Underlying the "intervene and separate" approach is a certain way of thinking about disability, often called the *medical model*. That model regards the person as having an inherent impairment that the professional (physician, special educator, or other specialists) must remediate.

There is a different and more recent model for thinking about disability and the interactions and transactions that those with a disability make with those who do not have a disability. That model is known as the *social model*. Sometimes it is called the "new paradigm" of disability. As you read the definition of the new paradigm, you will note how it explicitly references the interactions and transactions that we have discussed and that reveal the shortcomings in the medical model and fix-it approach. The new paradigm maintains that

> disability is a product of the interaction between characteristics of the individual (e.g., conditions or impairments, functional status, or personal and social qualities) and the characteristics of the natural, built, cultural, and social environments. (NIDRR, 2002)

The Medical Model, the Old Paradigm

Note the profound shift in paradigms. The old paradigm rested on a medical model and held that the person owned the impairment in the sense that the impairment was inherent in the person; that is what made the person "disabled." In that view, the "fault" lay within the person. As we explained, that view held that the proper focus of interventions such as special education is the person, not the environment or contexts within which the person exists.

The Social Model, the New Paradigm

By contrast, the new paradigm holds that the person has an impairment but becomes disabled not by reason of the impairment but, rather, by reason of the fact that the person's environment does not accommodate to the person and the impairment. That is why the principle of dual accommodations is part of disability policy: Both the individual and society accommodate to each other.

The principle of dual accommodations reflects the social model of disability by declaring that the proper focus of interventions such as special education is not just the person but also and equally the environment *or contexts within which the person exists.*

Harkening back to the Sarason and Doris (1975) argument that classification is a method of control and reflecting the new paradigm, the AAMR (2002) has adopted the position that educators and other professionals must focus their attention on three areas related to the person and society:

1. The person's capabilities
2. The environments and contexts (such as schools) in which the person functions
3. The types and intensity of formal (i.e., professional) and informal (i.e., family, friends, and community) supports that the person receives to function more effectively in each of the person's environments

What contributes to the person's capabilities or lack of capabilities? Is it only the inherent limitations of the person, consistent with a strict reading of the medical model? No, but not entirely. Is it only the environments and contexts in which the person lives, consistent with the social model/new paradigm? Yes, but not entirely. In fact, capabilities and environment relate to each other in a particularly distressing way, one that IDEA mentions when (in Section 1401) it notes the persistent presence in special education of students from minority backgrounds and one that the courts in *Larry P.* and *PASE* addressed.

The Theory of New Morbidity and the Fact of Co-morbidity

There is clear evidence that disability is positively correlated with a person's family structure (single-parent families); racial, ethnic, or linguistic backgrounds (non-Anglo, non-English-speaking); socioeconomic status (poverty and poor education); and place of residence (urban or rural) (National Research Council, 2002). The positive correlation between disability and any one or more of these four other factors is known as the *theory of the new morbidity*: Disability will exist in tandem with other disadvantaging factors. That fact is called co-morbidity, the simultaneous existence of more than one disadvantaging factor.

IDEA responds to the theory and the fact by providing for inclusionary and exclusionary criteria for evaluating a student into or out of special education. You may recall that a student may be classified into special education only if the student has one or more of the listed categories of disability and functions in such a way as to need special education. You also may recall that the student may not be classified into special education if the determinant factor in the student's limitations is a lack of appropriate instruction in reading or math or the student's limited English proficiency.

The exclusionary criteria reflect the new morbidity and co-morbidity by specifically acknowledging that the student's socioeconomic status ("lack of appropriate instruction" is a proxy for that status) and native language may make it seem that the student has a disability when in fact the student does not. The role of special education, IDEA makes clear, is to serve those who have a disability, not those who are disadvantaged by reason of other factors in their lives.

Classification, Perceptions, Discrimination, and Domination

In chapter 4, we argued that educability (more precisely, the argument that some students are simply not educable), contagious disease, and behavior that warrants discipline are three of the major areas that the zero reject principle addresses. There, and in the previous section, we have been making an even more significant point. It is that the characteristic of the person on which intervention usually has been, and often still is, predicated is "disability," not "person." The person is seen to be qualitatively different from other people in this important and debilitating sense: The person is "deviant."

For example, we noted in chapter 4 that the newborn with an observable anomaly has been deemed a defective child and is called *Baby Doe* because giving the baby a real name makes the baby all the more human and all the less disposable. Because the child's defect is seen to inhere in the child rather than in the society into which the child is born, the defect, and indeed the child, must be "treated" in the sense of being subjected to diagnosis, prescription, regimen, and cure, or, in the case of Baby Doe or those with disabilities who are older but also at the edge of life ("Granny Doe"), to the withholding or withdrawing of treatment. The treatment is rendered by many helping professionals, not just physicians (Gliedman & Roth, 1980); it also is denied sometimes simply because of the child's disability—that is, it is denied on the discriminatory basis of disability alone.

Beyond discrimination, however, lies another and often more subtle but equally disabling result for Baby Doe or Granny Doe, or anyone between those two edges of life. The result is that the person often is regarded as a perpetual patient. Those so classified are defined by what they are not, instead of what they are or may become.

Regarded as "sick" (i.e., disabled) and not responsible for their own condition because the disability is inherent in them, they often are obliged to play the role of an obedient patient (Gliedman & Roth, 1980). In this role they learn to be helpless and inferior and to accept professionals' control over their lives. Infrequent rebellion against professional dominance itself is treated as a symptom of sickness, and the person's parents or family who resist professionals' dominance also become "patients" (Turnbull & Turnbull, 1985).

Obedience of the person and family to professional dominance simply reinforces the original perception that the person is incapable and possibly incurable. This stereotypified regardedness reflects the prevailing social mores. Classifying a person as having a disability enables us—who are "able" and not "disabled"—to use a convenient concept, one ostensibly rooted in science: We must do unto others (the disabled/special education student) what we would abhor having done to us, all in the name of altruism and intervention to "fix" the person. Inaccurately regarding persons with disabilities as sick, we easily can conclude, as the law traditionally did, that they are not responsible (competent) and must be dealt with in unusual ways (Morse, 1978).

Thus it is that able-bodied and mentally competent people—those who fit a norm—come to regard the incapacity of the person with a disability as a kind of failure of the person. The next "regarded as" step is to build on the assumption that the person is a failure and to conclude that the professions and society as a whole have a reduced duty, if any, to act on the person's behalf. "We" are off the hook for any responsibility to "them." We ultimately have no responsibility for their exclusion from the normal patterns of life and, with a relatively clean conscience and legal impunity, we can assign them to lower echelons of life, to second-class citizenship at law.

Thus does classification enable discrimination and domination. That, however, is a conclusion that begs even more questions: Who is involved, how, and why in the use of classification as a technique for discrimination and domination?

The answers are uncomfortable but informative. They suggest that, in the typology proposed by Alan Stone (1976), there are four types of people: the good, the bad, the mad, and the sad. The good classify and serve; they are, by and large, professionals. The bad are the lawbreakers; the mad are those affected by emotional, behavioral, or mental disorders; and the sad are those affected by other disabilities (developmental, physical, or sensory).

Who Classifies

Every society needs professionals who will bring their expertise to bear on difficult situations and resolve those difficulties through the use of special training, talents, and status. These professionals include the following:

- *Physicians.* Physicians' curative abilities (to prevent a disability, to intervene early so as to minimize its effects, and to be a sustaining force throughout a person's life) make them important resources for saying who has a disability. They do this through developmental testing of newborns, infants, children, and youth. Once they diagnose or classify, they treat. It is little wonder that physicians have become agents for deciding what to do about disabilities.
- *Educators.* Arguably, schools label more children as having a disability than does any other governmental or social entity. This classification has massive

consequences—both positive and negative—for the children, as we noted previously.

- *Other professionals and agencies.* Any profession having contact with people classifies, however tangential the contact may be. Social workers, psychologists, and rehabilitation specialists classify. Institutions of higher education classify by limiting whom they admit and how much they accommodate those admitted. Law enforcement and criminal justice agencies classify. Courts accept classification arguments to assess whether and, if so, to what extent persons are criminally or civilly liable for their actions or failures to act. The armed forces classify.
- *Professional organizations.* The AAMR, for example, classifies by changing its concept and definition of mental retardation. The American Psychiatric Association classifies when it changes the standards and definitions in its *Diagnostic and Statistical Manual* (APA, 1994). Professional societies classify by defining the condition that they address (for example, specific learning disabilities or autism and its related spectrums).
- *Families.* It is not so much that families say that their child, brother, sister, or other relative has a disability; others do that for them. It is more that they classify by determining how they react to what others say. The decision to keep a child in their own home or to secure placement in special education or an institution, or to try an inclusive education instead of a more separate one, is in the first (and sometimes the last) place a family decision. Among other things, it reflects a decision to classify a person more or less into or out of a disabled status.
- *Everyone.* Everyone classifies. We all make choices to associate or not to associate with certain other people. Human beings are discriminating in the neutral sense of the word. We make discriminations about ourselves and others. We also discriminate in a different sense: We discriminate for invidious as well as altruistic purposes. Some of us let defective newborns die because their existence horrifies us, but we say we do it because we are concerned about the quality of their and others' lives. Others of us withhold or withdraw medical treatment and food and water from older people, also out of concern for their quality of life. Classification is not inherently wrong, merely natural.

How We Classify

We classify in several ways, as we describe below.

- *By resorting to science.* The concept of science has some magical quality. Call something scientific, and it becomes less assailable. The presumption is that science and its products are researched, reliable, validated, evaluated, and unbiased. But what we do—our policies—are not always based on good science, or defensible science. It is little wonder, then, that our policies are not always good.

The fallibility of the medical model is well known (Blatt & Kaplan, 1974). After all, science taught that people with mental retardation were a menace, so the eugenics movement spawned legalized compulsory institutionalization and sterilization (Wald, 1976). Science teaches that intelligence can be measured, so classification as having a cognitive impairment, with consequent categorization into special education, receives the blessings of the law.

It is no great matter that some bases for scientific "facts" are open to doubt as long as they are not clearly erroneous. Yet, decisions by physicians, other service providers, and families, made on the basis of relatively acceptable assessment techniques, still can be highly debatable. Thus, we sometimes classify by using relatively fallible science or by acting in someone's interests on the basis of what that science tells us or on the basis of how we would not want to live like that/him/her. That is one reason why IDEA and NCLB require evaluations to use evidence-based, scientifically valid approaches.

- *By social vulnerability.* Classification is affected by nonscientific means as well. Educators, for example, too often identify students who make life difficult for the educators as having disabilities. Boys seem to be more subject to special education classification than girls are, aggressive students more than acquiescent ones, and racial, cultural, linguistic and ethnic minority students more than White students. The "science" of these classifications is highly doubtful. Instead, some students' differential vulnerability to special education classification seems to be an artifact of their racial, cultural, linguistic and ethnic traits and of their social or economic differentness, not a consequence of a documented and fairly determined (evaluated) disability.
- *By legal proceedings.* Likewise, classification as having a disability occurs in a host of legal proceedings, often without a sufficient scientific basis. For example, if persons are aggressive, unable to care for themselves, or, because of mental/behavioral/emotional disability, in need of treatment, family members, mental health, public health, or social services agencies may choose to intervene by asking a court or other public entity to

- ☐ commit them involuntarily,
- ☐ adjudicate them to be incompetent so third-party consent to treatment or placement can be obtained,
- ☐ order temporary social service custody for treatment of neglect or abuse, or
- ☐ obtain criminal prosecution for alleged violation of a crime.

Any of those four responses is legally sanctioned and may be effective as a way of intervening appropriately. So, too, is doing nothing; inaction is a form of action. Whatever the choice—whether to intervene and, if so, how—classification is the result. In Stone's (1976) typology, the classified person becomes mad, sad, or bad: mad if committed involuntarily; sad if referred to special education, social services, mental retardation, or developmental disabilities agencies; or bad if convicted of a crime. The classifier, of course, is good.

- *By reason of serendipity.* There is, moreover, no clear reason why a specific intervention prevails. So much depends on serendipity. Is the school's staff overloaded with students who have disabilities? Is the state psychiatric hospital full? Does a developmental center or community-based service have enough beds, or are all of its slots full and it has a waiting list of people wanting to receive service? What agency does the person's family have the most contact with? Are private or third-party funds available to pay for services? Is the person an "interesting case" for the professional staff? How effectively does a lawyer represent the parties? Have political, economic, or social influences been brought to bear on the agencies or courts? Have community resources been tried unsuccessfully?

  These are some of the factors—all of them far removed from the allegedly precise scientific basis for classification that is supposed to be obtained in special education or mental health intervention, for example—that affect whether a person is classified and, if so, how, why, and with what effect.

- *By reason of our language.* Language has the power to describe and, by describing, to value or devalue. To say that a person is "worth her weight in gold" or that "he's a big-hitter" (in business or sport) is to ascribe value to the person and thereby to elevate him or her in society's hierarchy. Conversely, to say that a person is an idiot, moron, feeble-minded, imbecile, cretin, mentally defective, mentally deficient, crazy, mad, nuts, or insane is to devalue that person.

  By changing the terms for describing people with disabilities, we can change how others regard disability and those affected by it. Thus, for example, the pejorative words "crazy," "mad," "nuts," and "insane" and even the more recent terms "mentally ill" or "seriously emotionally disturbed" have yielded to the less devaluing phrase (in IDEA) of "emotional disturbance" (20 U.S.C. Sec. 1401(3)). Similarly, but not yet in IDEA, the term "mental retardation" is being replaced with "intellectual disability."

  To change our common usage and our legal language, then, is to revalue the described person, change the person's perceived value in society, and thereby increase the likelihood that their status in schools and communities will improve.

Why We Classify

Classification may be impossible to avoid. We are, after all, discriminating, choosy, selective, and exclusive in almost every facet of our lives, whether the issue is so trivial as the choice of food at a carry-out restaurant or so momentous as the choice of a partner for life. In addition to our natural restrictions or traits (age, gender, race, and ability), we restrict and classify ourselves voluntarily, such as by the jobs we choose. And in most cases the law recognizes our rights to be selective in the important matters of speech, religion, and personhood (the privacy rights to secure or refuse various types of professional interventions), as well as in less significant matters such as the types of clothes we wear (symbolic speech).

Yet, our natural instincts and legal rights to be selective, to classify ourselves and others, are not unbridled. Our rights of free speech do not extend to some aspects of pornography or harassment based on another's traits (hate crimes). Some consensual conduct is regulated (e.g., the use of controlled substances) and, of course, so is nonconsensual conduct (e.g., crimes against persons or property).

One reason for regulation is that the effects of absolute liberty for everyone are bound to be unacceptable to others. Thus, the possession of pornography may be protected but its sale or distribution may not be. Similarly, the free exercise of one's religion does not give a person the right to impose his/her religion and its doctrine and practices on another person. The reasons for governmental classification must be examined; the due process and equal protection clauses of the Constitution forbid invidious, irrational, indefensible classifications (such as those made on the basis of race or, in some instances, disability). To inquire into why people classify others as having a disability, therefore, is legally relevant. Other reasons that we classify are explored below.

Altruism

Sometimes classification is done for the most altruistic of purposes. When someone is classified as having a disability, it enables that person to be the recipient of services that the classifier (schools), and sometimes the classified, thinks will be helpful (special education). Classification also may prevent the person from being subject to disadvantaging conditions. Some people believe that classification and segregation of students by reason of disability will protect those students from nondisabled students and the ordinary conditions of schools.

Classification that is motivated by social beneficence, however, has negative results. Lionel Trilling (1980) made the point that people who are the objects of our pity soon become the objects of our study and then the objects of our coercion. And Kai Erickson (1966) highlighted the paradox that deviance—differentness on account of disability—is nourished by the agencies that were designed to inhibit it, in proportion to society's ability to control it.

Thus, the conditions of education, including special education, have been disadvantageous to children in some instances (Sarason & Doris, 1975). But special education is not the only service system that, in the name of doing good, does not always do so. Blatt and Kaplan (1974) have documented the horrible conditions to which people with disabilities were subjected in institutions originally predicated on a medical model. And Gliedman and Roth (1980) have produced strong evidence of the shortcomings of the medical model in a host of "helping" professions.

Negative Reactions

We also classify for reasons having to do with our instinctive negative reaction to disabilities. After all, the grossly macrocephalic child may not be easily or immediately lovable to some people. Fecal smearers can be unpleasant to live or work with.

Some children are aggressive, and some are slow to show affection. Many aspects of disabilities, such as severe self-injurious behavior, are not only especially intractable but also deeply disturbing to families and caregivers alike. Thus, when the decision is made to place a child in special education, to institutionalize a child or, more seriously, to withhold or withdraw medical treatment of a "defective" newborn or an aged person, it seems inevitable that, for some people, the instincts for being with pleasant, attractive, able, and promising people are at work.

By the same token, one's ability to succeed with a person who has a disability—if we are a physician, to cure, or an educator, to teach—is threatened by some people with disabilities. Surely the emotional reactions of parents are not the only ones operating in a classification decision. Physicians know firsthand the terribly difficult task of telling parents that their child has a disability. To place a child in an institution—to put him or her out of sight and sometimes out of mind—is partly a human condition. And the human condition is an imperfect one.

Riddance Motive

We also classify because some of us at times actively and admittedly wish to rid ourselves of the person who has a disability. The decision to abort a "defective" fetus, while protected constitutionally, may reflect the mother's wish to avoid life with a child with a disability. Decisions to withhold or withdraw life-sustaining medical treatment or to institutionalize a child or elderly disabled person may reflect similar reactions of parents not to be disabled themselves by reason of having a child with a disability.

Parents are not alone in their reaction to disabilities. Educators who refer a child to a special education program, community agency social workers who counsel for institutionalization, and institutional psychologists who recommend deinstitutionalization may all be motivated by a desire to rid themselves of a "problem" person.

Agency Self-Interest

Another motive that explains classification is related more to agency interests than to personal interests. Educators and others test and thereby engage in classification decisions to absolve themselves of moral responsibility for decisions about what happens to people with disabilities, taking refuge in science. By resorting to science, they also gain credibility with parents.

Finally, agencies serve their own interests through classification standards and procedures. A well-organized school system has to have students so programs can be planned, financed, operated, and perpetuated. By the same token, social services, health, and mental health agencies sometimes classify a person as having a disability, or as having a certain degree of disability, for self-serving purposes. They may want to include or exclude a person from a service category because it will increase their head count (number of people served) and thereby their budget or constituency base, or decease it and thereby enable them to serve someone else. Resource allocation is a powerful motive.

Classification, Professionals, and Policy Consequences

As we have pointed out in this chapter (and as we will continue to point out in chapters 6 and 7, relating to appropriate education and least restrictive placements, respectively), Congress (in IDEA) and the courts (in classification, appropriate education, and least restrictive placement cases) rely heavily on professionals to say who has a disability and needs special education. By turning to the professionals to help determine who is disabled enough to be treated differently, Congress and the courts can avoid coming to grips directly with the social, political, and moral dilemmas posed by disability.

Thus, for example, decisions about institutionalization are characterized as "medical" just as other types of decisions (eligibility for special education) are called "educational." The consequence is that the true nature of the decisions—what shall be done about disabilities, people with disabilities, and schools—is answered by letting professionals decide.

By the fiction that all people with disabilities really are different and should be treated differently, largely by professionals, the law has avoided the ultimate questions: Who should decide who should care for them, where, how, at whose expense, and why? Even more fundamentally, who is different enough to be treated differently? And who has the sagacity to tell us the answer? These are the issues of classification.

The traditional answer to these questions has been: the professionals. Once policy makers know that professionals can give the answers, they tend to ask professionals to answer other questions. For example, is this psychological examination valid for the purpose it is used? Has the evaluation followed the procedures and standards that IDEA prescribes? Is the student's resulting IEP appropriate? Thus, our responsibility (or lack of it) for other people, for people with disabilities, is made manifest to us: Do as the professionals say.

By deferring to professional judgment, IDEA, which is to say, the law itself as a tool for regulating society, takes nonprofessionals (judges, other policy leaders, and the citizenry at large) off the hook, relieving them of the responsibility to make decisions that are educational as well as moral, legal, and economic in nature.

The rule of deference to expert judgment is well-settled law. (It is also called the doctrine of presumptive validity: the professional's judgment is presumed to be valid.) IDEA simply reflects it in the nondiscriminatory evaluation safeguards that we just explained, as well as in the appropriate education and LRE placement provisions that we will explain in the next two chapters. Inherently, nothing is wrong with relying on professional judgment; each of us does this in our lives, so it is legitimate for all of us to do it collectively through the law. What is important to bear in mind, however, is that a trade-off is involved in the rule of deference: Professionals secure power, and others cede power.

Procedural and Substantive Law Reform Techniques

By avoiding some of the difficult policy questions and by allowing people to be classified and sorted, the law can do an injustice not only to them but to itself as well. It condones a double standard, a dual system. But when courts and legislatures insist on procedural and substantive approaches in dealing with people who have disabilities, the law reshapes not only itself but also, it is hoped, our culture itself. That is the ultimate purpose of IDEA's nondiscriminatory evaluation rules. These two approaches—procedural law reform techniques and substantive law reform techniques—warrant some discussion.

1. Procedures are *rules of conduct*. They tell certain individuals how they must proceed in making or carrying out decisions. IDEA follows the procedural approach; it specifies the membership of a nondiscriminatory evaluation team and how the team members must go about making decisions, such as by using only certain evaluation instruments. The shortcoming of the procedural approach is that it does not tell the decision-makers the basis on which they must make a decision. It tells them how but not why or what they must do.
2. To compensate for that shortcoming, the law resorts to *substantive approaches*. A substantive approach identifies for decision-makers the criteria on which they must rely. IDEA adheres to the substantive approach by setting out the inclusionary and the exclusionary criteria by which the student's nondiscriminatory evaluation team members will determine whether the student has a disability and, if so, whether the student may be classified into special education.

Thus does IDEA use both procedural and substantive approaches to reforming the law by attempting to respond to the criticisms of classification and by attempting to turn classification into a beneficial, not a malevolent, consequence for students.

SUMMARY

Let's return to the very beginning of this chapter and to *Larry P. v. Riles,* the Case on Point. We have said throughout this chapter that the point of that case is that classification can be tainted by discrimination and the desire to dominate. Because classification entails that power, fairness in classification is essential. What we did not say at the outset of this chapter is that IDEA's procedural and substantive safeguards related to nondiscriminatory evaluation attempt to ensure fairness so that the result of classifying or not classifying a student into special education is based solely on the professionally defensible conclusion that the student does (or does not) have a disability and does (or does not) need special education. Evaluation and classification are not ends in and of themselves; they are simply the means by which educators and IDEA try to achieve a beneficial outcome for the student and for society—namely, an opportunity for an appropriate education. That opportunity—indeed, under IDEA, that right—is the topic of chapter 6.

Chapter 6

Individualized and Appropriate Education

Case on Point: *Board of Education v. Rowley*
458 U.S. 176; 102 S. Ct. 3034 (1982)

Assume that you are the parent of an elementary school student who has significant hearing impairments. She is progressing from grade to grade because she is working hard and because she is receiving a large number of related services. Assume also that you and your spouse are yourselves deaf, and that your own life experiences convince you that your daughter will benefit even more if she has an interpreter in addition to the other services the school is offering. Finally, assume that your daughter clearly is highly intelligent and, indeed, may be academically gifted, and that an interpreter would enable her to fulfill her academic capacities.

Would you demand that your daughter's school provide her with an interpreter as part of "related services," and if it did not, would you take your grievance all the way to the U.S. Supreme Court? If you were the parents of Amy Rowley, the answer in both cases would be "yes." But the result of your lawsuit would not be what you want, even though it benefits her somewhat and many other students with disabilities quite substantially.

In *Rowley*, the Supreme Court had to decide whether IDEA required an LEA to provide an interpreter for Amy Rowley. The Court answered "no," reasoning that, although IDEA places an affirmative duty on the LEA and SEA to ensure that FAPE is provided to all students with disabilities, the LEA "satisfies this requirement by providing personalized instruction with sufficient support services to permit the child to benefit educationally from that instruction."

The Court framed its inquiry guided by two questions:

1 Has the state complied with the procedures set forth in the act?
2. Was the IEP developed through the act's procedures reasonably calculated to enable the child to receive educational benefits?

The Court thus outlined two statutory requirements for an appropriate education: meeting the procedural criteria and meeting the benefit criteria.

Noting the extensive procedural requirements of IDEA, the Court held that Congress intended procedural compliance to help ensure that FAPE was provided to each child with a disability. Thus, the definition of FAPE includes providing special education and related services "in conformity with the individualized education program." Special education, in turn, is defined as "specially designed instruction ... to meet the unique needs of a handicapped child."

IDEA clearly demonstrates the "legislative conviction that adequate compliance with the procedures prescribed would in most cases assure much, if not all, of what Congress wished in the way of substantive content in an IEP." In the case of Amy Rowley's educational program, the Court found that the LEA met all these procedural requirements.

In contrast to the procedural requirements of IDEA, the Court noted that a "substantive standard prescribing the level of education to be accorded handicapped children" was "noticeably absent from the language of the statute." The Court held that Congress did not intend to guarantee any particular level of educational benefit to students with disabilities but, rather, to provide a basic floor of opportunity and require only that the personalized instruction provided to the student be "sufficient to confer *some educational benefit*" (emphasis ours). The Court declined to adopt any single test for substantive benefit under IDEA and instead applied a fact-specific, "situational" analysis.

The Court concluded that the "evidence firmly establishes that Amy is receiving an 'adequate' education, since she performs better than the average child in her class and is advancing easily from grade to grade." Having provided Amy with an opportunity to benefit, as proved by her progress, the school has discharged its IDEA obligations to her. She gets nothing more, certainly not an interpreter, but other students with disabilities now know that they have, at the least, an IDEA-based right to an opportunity to benefit from being in school.

BACKGROUND

When the federal courts decided *PARC* and *Mills* in 1972, they held that a student is entitled to individually tailored special education. The purpose of their decisions was to assure that the schools provide some educational benefit to the student—a goal best accomplished by individualizing the student's education. A few years later, Congress incorporated into IDEA the concept of appropriateness as an educational benefit achieved through individualized education.

This chapter addresses five aspects of an appropriate education:

1. IDEA's process and outcome definitions of an appropriate education
2. The different types of individualized plans for implementing an appropriate education
3. Special education, related services, and other services necessary for FAPE
4. Evidence of appropriateness
5. Government functions relating to children with disabilities and how these functions affect a student's right and receipt of an appropriate education

DEFINING "APPROPRIATE"

IDEA and its regulations define an "appropriate education" by two criteria: standards and individualization (20 U.S.C. Sec. 1401(9)). Let's consider each, in turn.

First, under the "standards" criterion, an appropriate education is one that consists of special education and related services that

- are provided at public expense and without charge;
- are provided under public direction and supervision;,
- meet the standards of the state education agency; and
- include appropriate preschool, elementary school, and secondary school education.

Second, under the "individualized" criterion, each student must have an individualized education program (IEP) tailored to fit his or her educational needs, and each infant/toddler and family must have an individualized family service plan (IFSP) tailored to fit their needs. As the Court observed in *Rowley,* an appropriate education must be provided "in conformity with the individualized education program."

The four standards criteria and the one individualized criterion are not especially clear if read in isolation from their history and from the rest of IDEA. They provide only the foundation for the inquiry into what is and is not an appropriate education, and even then they are limited in that they speak only to the procedural or process definition of appropriateness. So let's now consider those two definitions.

The Process Definition

The two statutory definitions of appropriate education—the standards criteria and the individualized criterion—are best understood together and in the overall context of IDEA and its approach to special education. IDEA's approach is highly procedural and accordingly defines appropriate education by a process.

As the Court noted in *Rowley,* Congress clearly intended to require the states "to adopt procedures which would result in individualized consideration of and instruction for each child." Among these procedures are those related to individualized consideration (nondiscriminatory evaluation) and individualized instruction (the IEP).

Likewise, the Court identified procedural requirements, especially (a) notification of the student's parents whenever an LEA proposes or refuses to change the student's identification, evaluation, educational placement, or the provision of a free appropriate public education to the student (chapter 9, "Parent Participation"); and (b) an opportunity to protest the decision (chapter 8, "Procedural Due Process").

Accordingly, an appropriate education is one that conforms to IDEA's process. For example, assume that LEA personnel are concerned about what kind of education and placement are appropriate for a 9-year-old child who has a disability. How do they answer this question? They do it by following these steps, in order:

1. Conduct a nondiscriminatory evaluation (chapter 5).
2. Develop an IEP to meet the child's needs (this chapter).
3. Place the child in the least restrictive program appropriate for the child (chapter 7).

Throughout this three-step process, the LEA ensures that the parents are given meaningful opportunities to participate in the educational planning process (chapter 9) and have access to due process procedures (chapter 8) if and when the parents wish to protest the placement or any other action related to the child's right to a free appropriate education.

One of IDEA's techniques for defining "appropriate," then, is to require that a process be followed, in the belief that a fair process will produce fair and acceptable results. As *Rowley* noted, however, that is not the end of the inquiry into what an appropriate education is for any IDEA-covered student.

The Benefit Definition

As the Court in *Rowley* also pointed out, "Implicit in the congressional purpose of providing access to a 'free appropriate public education' is the requirement that the education to which access is provided be sufficient to confer some educational benefit." Congress would not have provided for access without any requirement that such access be meaningful. Yet, the extent to which a student is entitled to benefit is minimal.

The Court in *Rowley* specifically declined to create a single test for determining whether a student has benefited so sufficiently from her IEP that the student has received an appropriate education. Instead, the Court adopted a case-by-case approach and stated only that the standard for benefit in any student's case is that the student's IEP be "reasonably calculated to enable the child to receive educational benefits."

Note that IDEA does not require maximum benefit, or even substantial benefit. It requires only that the student receive a level of benefit such that her access to educational services is meaningful. That is what Amy Rowley received, as evidenced by her progress from grade to grade, and thus she was not entitled to an interpreter to further enhance or even maximize her education.

Process and "Some Benefit" in the Age of Accountability

As you learned in chapter 2, the No Child Left Behind Act ushered in a new age in school reform by emphasizing assessment and outcomes, not process, as indicators of student success. IDEA's 2004 amendments extend the NCLB accountability approach to special education. That is not surprising, because the report of the President's Commission on Excellence in Special Education (2002) called for increased accountability for outcomes in IDEA and less attention to procedure. Indeed, Rod Paige, then secretary of the Department of Education, made it crystal clear that the reauthorized IDEA explicitly adopted this approach:

> IDEA should ensure that students with disabilities have access to and make progress in the general curriculum, and are appropriately included in state accountability systems. IDEA must move from a culture of compliance with process to a culture of accountability for results. (U.S. Department of Education, 2003)

And, at the signing of the 2004 IDEA amendments into law, President Bush said that, through the amendments, "We're applying the reforms of the No Child Left Behind Act to the Individuals with Disabilities Education Improvement Act so schools are accountable for teaching every single child."

But how does this shift from process compliance to outcome-based accountability affect the process and benefit standards for appropriateness (as laid out in *Rowley*)? To answer that question, we must pay close attention to IDEA's language.

In terms of the process definition of appropriateness, IDEA (20 U.S.C. 1415(f)(1)(E)) codifies the change from process to outcomes by providing as follows:

- A decision made by a hearing officer must be made on substantive grounds based on a determination of whether the child received a free appropriate public education.
- With respect to allegations that procedural violations deprived a student of an appropriate education, a due process hearing officer (and thus a court) may find that a student did not receive a free appropriate public education only if the procedural inadequacies
  - impeded the student's right to a free appropriate public education,
  - significantly impeded the parents' opportunity to participate in the decision-making process regarding the provision of a free appropriate public education to the student, or
  - caused a deprivation of educational benefits with respect to the student.

Clearly, IDEA now is no longer hospitable to process as a standard for appropriateness and no longer favors—and indeed arguably disfavors—complaints based on procedural violations. Thus, an LEA's failure to follow IDEA's process and procedures generally will rise to the level of failing to provide an appropriate education only if it directly and significantly negatively affects the student's ability to benefit or the parents' right to participate in the process.

But what about the "some benefit" standard? The Court's ruling in *Rowley* was based largely on the history of IDEA in the congressional record. The Court determined that Congress intended to base appropriateness on process compliance, on the theory that fair procedures (complying with IDEA's processes) usually will result in substantive benefits. Because the 2004 reauthorization arguably changes that focus by emphasizing outcomes, should not the benefit standard be similarly affected?

Let's put that question in a somewhat different way: Because Congress has clearly voiced its intention to turn away from the "fair process–fair results" approach to accountability in favor of more direct measures of outcomes and progress, has it now raised the bar for determining benefit? Is the "some benefit" rule still an adequate measure of an appropriate education?

Although the courts have yet to interpret the 2004 amendments in light of *Rowley,* it seems clear that the new emphasis on outcomes is likely to affect the application, if not the actual holding, of *Rowley's* benefit standard. The 2004 amendments provide no more guidance to define the level of benefit required, but they do place much greater emphasis on the measurement of outcomes. That is so now for two reasons, each grounded in IDEA's language:

1. A student's IEP must contain a description "of how the child's progress toward meeting the annual goals will be measured" and a statement of "appropriate accommodations that are necessary to measure the academic achievement and functional performance of the child" on state or district assessments (20 U.S.C. Secs. 1414(d)(1)(A)(i)(III) and (IV)).

2. The LEA also must provide a timeline "when periodic reports on the progress the child is making toward meeting the annual goals (such as through the use of quarterly or other periodic reports, concurrent with the issuance of report cards) will be provided" (20 U.S.C. Sec. 1414(d)(1)(A)(i)(III)).

These two new provisions for measuring and reporting progress are all the more telling in light of the emphasis that IDEA now puts on the use of research-based and scientifically valid methods (20 U.S.C. Secs. 1400(c)(4) and (5)).

Congress's intent in the reauthorization is clear (both with respect to the substantive definition of appropriateness and, as we pointed out above, with respect to the process definition of appropriateness):

- Accountability under IDEA depends on whether students with disabilities have received a substantive benefit from special education as measured by the student's progress in school (as determined by the student's grades, on state or local assessments, and other measurements of progress toward IEP goals).

- Procedural violations can impair a student's right to an appropriate education only under stringently defined circumstances—namely, when they can be shown to have affected the student's progress (e.g., such as when scientifically valid and reliable methods of instruction are available but not used).

So, although the "some benefit" standard of *Rowley* may be unchanged by the exact language in the reauthorized IDEA, the statute itself may require an LEA to provide measurable evidence of that benefit to show that the child has indeed been provided with an appropriate education. But the extent to which this result creates an increased need for LEAs to document a student's progress in due process is limited by the Court's 2005 decision in *Schaffer v. Weast* (see chapter 8), which puts the burden of proof on a student's parents to show that the LEA did not do enough to enable the student to benefit. Less arguable is the increased responsibility of the school to provide parents with reports that (a) clearly demonstrate the child's progress or lack thereof; and (b) the parents can use to call for changes in the IEP, whether in an IEP meeting or in due process.

Part C and Appropriate Services

Unlike students served under Part B, infants and toddlers in the Part C early intervention program are not entitled to a free appropriate public education (20 U.S.C. Sec. 1435(b)(4)). Nor does *Rowley* apply to Part C, because *Rowley* relied heavily on the definition of FAPE and special education as principal tools for defining *appropriate* under Part B. Further, with respect to FAPE, the term *special education* applies only to students in Part B. In lieu of an entitlement to special education and related services, those children qualifying under Part C have a right to early intervention services, not special education.

Despite the fact that *Rowley* does not apply to Part C and that children served under Part C are not entitled to FAPE, Part C's own procedural and substantive requirements are similar to those of Part B in many ways. Let's consider those ways.

Part C (20 U.S.C. Secs. 1431(4)(A), (B), and (D)) defines early intervention services as developmental services that

- are provided under public supervision and at no cost except where federal or state law provides for a system of payments by families, including a schedule of sliding fees;
- meet the standards of the state in which the services are provided; and
- include designated services provided by qualified personnel.

These standards criteria are only slightly different from the four standards criteria of Part B. Each addresses parental expense, public agency oversight, and state standards. The only substantial difference is that Part C is not completely without cost for parents. Parents whose children receive services under Part C may be required to pay some amount for services based on a sliding scale (i.e., lower income pays less).

The individualized criteria under Part C also are nearly identical to those in Part B. They require that early intervention services must be

- designed to meet the developmental needs of an infant or toddler with a disability, as identified by the individualized family service plan (IFSP) team (20 U.S.C. Sec. 1432(4)(C)); and
- provided in conformity with an IFSP adopted in accordance with the procedures outlined in the law (20 U.S.C. Sec. 1432(4)(H)).

Part C's individualization requirement is almost exactly the same as under Part B: Services must be designed to meet the needs of the child through the usual evaluation and planning process—the IEP under Part B and the IFSP under Part C. The only substantial differences relate to the role of the family as a recipient of services under Part C and specific procedural differences between the two individual service plans. These similarities suggest that infants and toddlers served under Part C have much the same right to a fair process as do students with disabilities under Part B.

The similarity between appropriateness under Part B and Part C does not end with the process definition. Although *Rowley* does not apply directly to early intervention and although children served under Part C are not entitled to an "appropriate education," the rationale of *Rowley* applies equally well to establish a "some benefit" requirement for the entitlement to "appropriate early intervention services." That is so because *Rowley* reasoned that Congress could not have intended to guarantee access to an education without requiring the services to be meaningful by providing some level of benefit. Similar logic can apply to Part C. The requirement for appropriate early intervention services would be meaningless unless some level of substantive benefit were required.

Therefore, despite the absence of a right to FAPE, infants and toddlers served under Part C arguably are entitled to a similar level of both procedural compliance and substantive benefit as students served under Part B—a level of compliance that (a) does not deny them individualized services designed to meet their needs or deny the right of their parents to participate, and (b) provides them some nontrivial benefit.

INDIVIDUALIZED PLANS

IDEA and *Rowley* make clear that the linchpin of a student's education is the individualized plan. The "I-plans"—IEP and IFSP—form the basis for both procedural and substantive appropriateness by outlining the individualized services that will be provided to the child to address the needs identified in the child's nondiscriminatory evaluation. The two I-plans each cover a different period of the student's life. For students in the Part B preschool programs (ages 3 through 5) and Part B's subsequent special education programs (ages 6 through 21), the plan is called the IEP. The IFSP in Part C covers infant–toddler programs and sometimes can be extended for use with preschool-age children (ages 3 through 5) who have an IFSP prior to turning 3 (see chapter 4 for details).

Part B and the IEP

IDEA and good practice dictate that, for a student's education to be appropriate, it must be individually tailored to fit that student. The policy of providing an appropriate education is achieved principally by the ways in which LEAs develop and then implement a student's IEP (20 U.S.C. Secs. 1401(9), (14), and 1414(d)). Let's discuss the development aspects, which derive from IDEA, and not the implementation aspects, which relate to how LEAs and their professional staff put IDEA into practice.

Membership on the IEP Team

An IEP is a written statement for each student developed by a team whose membership is similar to that of the evaluation team (20 U.S.C. Sec. 1414(d)(1)(B)). As we stated in chapter 5, LEAs and parents may agree to combine the teams. The IEP team consists of

- the student's parents;
- at least one regular education teacher of the student, if the student is or may be participating in the general education environment;
- at least one special education teacher or (where appropriate) a provider of special education to the student;
- a representative of the local agency who is qualified to provide or supervise specially designed instruction to meet the unique needs of students with disabilities and is knowledgeable about general curriculum and the availability of local agency resources;
- an individual who can interpret the instructional implications of evaluation results (who may be a member of the team already);
- at the parents' or agency's discretion, other individuals who have knowledge or special expertise (including related services personnel, if appropriate); and
- the student (when appropriate).

The Regular Educator's Role

IDEA requires a regular education teacher (now often termed *general educator*) to be a member of the IEP team and specifies that the person's duties are, to the extent appropriate for the teacher and the student, to assist in

- developing the IEP; and
- determining in particular what, if any, appropriate positive behavioral interventions and strategies should be provided to the student, and what, if any, supplementary aids and services for the student, program modifications, and support for school personnel are appropriate (20 U.S.C. 1414(d)(3)(C)).

To the extent appropriate, the regular education teacher also must participate in reviewing and revising the student's IEP. The regular education teacher's role also relates to the discipline and expulsion issues (see chapter 3).

Parent Participation

Because parent participation is one of IDEA's six principles, the LEA must take specified steps to ensure that one or both of the student's parents are members of any group (including the IEP team) that makes decisions regarding the educational placement of their child (20 U.S.C. Secs. 1414(e)–(f)). These steps include advance notice of the meeting, mutually agreed upon scheduling of the meeting, and arranging for interpreters for deaf or non-English-speaking parents. If parents cannot attend the meeting, they still may participate through individual or conference telephone calls.

The LEA may have an IEP meeting without parent participation only when it can document that it was unsuccessful in convincing the parents to attend. The LEA should document its efforts by maintaining detailed records of telephone calls, copies of letters to and from the parents, and the results of visits to the parents' homes or places of work. Also, the LEA must give the parents a free copy of the IEP (34 C.F.R. 300.322(d)).

The requirement that parents must be members of the IEP team assures that they will participate in placement decisions. Most of those decisions will be made by the IEP team, but when a placement is not made by the team, the parents still must be involved in the group that makes the decision (20 U.S.C. Sec. 1414(e)).

Significance of Membership Requirements

What is significant about the membership of the IEP team? The answer is a single word: *consistency*—consistency in evaluation and programmatic intervention across all aspects of the student's life. Why is consistency the significant aspect of the membership rule, and why is consistency important? There are three answers.

First, the student's parents are members of the team. Their ability to inform their child's educators thus increases, as does their ability to hold the team's professional members accountable for developing and implementing an individualized program.

More than this, the parents' participation may ensure that the parents will help the LEA carry out the student's IEP when the student is at home or in the community. A disability, after all, is not a 6-hour condition but, rather, a 24-hour condition. Carrying out the student's IEP in school, in the home, and in the community helps the student's skills develop in all the environments in which they are needed. Parent participation advances the principle of generalization of skills across environments, and that outcome in turn supports the IDEA's postsecondary goals.

Second, the team may, and usually will, consist of the individuals—professionals and parents alike—who were members of the nondiscriminatory evaluation team. The linkage between evaluation and program, and between program and placement, is strengthened when the evaluators also are the developers and implementers of the student's IEP. This is true especially when related services personnel are team members; they should be on the team when the student's parents or school personnel request that the team discuss a certain related service. Among the team members may be a school nurse, whose presence is desirable whenever the team has to make decisions about how to safely address a student's educationally related health needs. A stable team membership assures consistency in evaluation findings and recommendations on the one hand, and in the student's program and placement on the other hand.

Third, the team includes a regular educator. That person's presence on the team ensures that the regular educators will participate in the student's IEP development, be more able and willing to carry it out, will suggest what school personnel need by way of supplementary aids and services to accommodate the student in the general curriculum, and assist in developing and carrying out behavioral interventions.

Attendance at an IEP Meeting

Because developing an IEP takes LEA professionals away from their classroom and other duties that benefit the student (the so-called paperwork burden problem), IDEA provides that members of the IEP team are not required to attend if the student's parents and the LEA agree in writing that their attendance is not necessary because their area of expertise is not being discussed or modified at the meeting. Even if the meeting does involve modification or discussion of the member's area of curriculum or related service, that member still may be excused if, in addition to parent and LEA agreement, the member submits written input on the development of the IEP prior to the meeting (20 U.S.C. 1414(d)(1)(C)).

Further, although IEP meetings are key to the development and implementation of a child's educational program, specific day-to-day adjustments in instructional methods normally do not require IEP team action. But the team must reconvene to address any significant changes that educators or others contemplate in the student's measurable annual goals, benchmarks, or short-term objectives, or in any of the services, program modifications, or other content of the IEP (20 U.S.C. 1414(d)(4)).

Components of an IEP

Having specified the membership on the IEP team, IDEA also specifies what each student's IEP must contain. The IEP must include the following (20 U.S.C. Sec. 1414(d)(1)(A)):

- A statement of the student's present levels of educational performance, including how the disability affects the child's involvement and progress in the general curriculum, and for preschool children, as appropriate, how the disability affects the child's participation in appropriate activities
- A statement of measurable annual goals, including academic and functional goals, and, for children who take alternate assessments aligned to alternate

achievement standards, a description of benchmarks or short-term objectives, designed to

- □ meet the child's needs that result from the child's disability to enable the child to be involved in and make progress in the general education curriculum; and
- □ meet each of the child's other educational needs that result from the child's disability

■ A description of how the child's progress toward meeting the annual goals described will be measured and when periodic reports on the progress the child is making toward meeting the annual goals (such as through the use of quarterly or other periodic reports, concurrent with the issuance of report cards) will be provided

■ A statement of the (a) special education and related services and (b) supplementary aids and services, based on peer-reviewed research to the extent practicable, to be provided to the child, or on behalf of the child, and (c) a statement of the program modifications or supports for school personnel that will be provided for the child

- □ to advance appropriately toward attaining the annual goals,
- □ to be involved in and make progress in the general education curriculum and to participate in extracurricular and other nonacademic activities, and
- □ to be educated and participate with other children with disabilities and nondisabled children in the activities described in this subparagraph

■ An explanation of the extent, if any, to which the child will not participate with nondisabled children in general education and other general curriculum activities

■ A statement of any individual appropriate accommodations that are necessary to measure the academic achievement and functional performance of the child on state and districtwide assessments, or

■ If the IEP team determines that the child shall take an alternate assessment on a particular state or districtwide assessment of student achievement, a statement of why the child cannot participate in the regular assessment and why the particular alternate assessment selected is appropriate for the child

■ The projected dates for beginning the listed services and modifications and the anticipated frequency, location, and duration of those services and modifications

Beginning not later than the first IEP to be in effect when the child is 16, and updated annually thereafter, the child's IEP must contain

■ appropriate measurable postsecondary goals based upon age-appropriate transition assessments related to training, education, employment, and, where appropriate, independent living skills;

■ the transition services (including courses of study) needed to assist the child in reaching those goals; and

- beginning not later than 1 year before the child reaches the age of majority under state law, a statement that the child has been informed of the child's rights under this title, if any, that will transfer to the child on reaching the age of majority.

To ensure that the team develops an IEP that contains these required elements and also to ensure that the team addresses matters that sometimes might be overlooked, IDEA requires the team to separately consider additional matters, student strengths, and other special factors (which we describe in the following sections).

Student Strengths

When developing the IEP, the team must consider the student's strengths, the parents' concerns, and the results of all evaluations (20 U.S.C. Sec. 1414(d)(3)(A)). This requirement is notable because it changes the focus of special education. For many years, special education has been both applauded and criticized for concentrating so much on a student's disability and related needs. The "fix-it" approach (which we reviewed in chapter 5) has been useful in that it has had the purpose, and often the effect, of ameliorating the effects of a disability. But it also has been limiting in that it often has overlooked a student's natural strengths and has sent a message of a pathological nature, emphasizing only that the student is "broken" and needs to be "fixed"—a message that can be discouraging as well as inaccurate. Given that Congress found that low expectations often impeded students' progress (20 U.S.C. Sec. 1400(c)(4)—see chapter 3), it makes sense for the IEP to focus on strengths and not to pathologize a student.

Special Factors

The IEP team must consider other special factors (20 U.S.C. Sec. 1414(d)(3)(B)):

1. For a student whose behavior impedes his or her or others' learning, the IEP team must consider the use of positive behavioral interventions and supports, and other strategies, to address that behavior (see chapter 4, "Zero Reject," to review the discipline provisions).
2. For a student with limited English proficiency, the team must consider the student's language needs.
3. For a student who is blind or visually impaired, the team must provide for the use of Braille or other appropriate reading and writing media.
4. The IEP team must consider the communication needs of any child, and for a student who is deaf or hard of hearing, the team must consider the student's language and communication needs, opportunities for direct communications with peers and professionals in the student's language and communication mode, academic level, and full range of needs.
5. For all students, the team must consider whether the child needs assistive technology devices and services (which are "related services").

The IEP team must consider these five special factors as appropriate for the individual student. Some students may need interventions to address their behavior, and indeed they also may need assistance with learning English, using Braille, communicating with peers and others who have hearing impairments or are deaf, or acquiring or using assistive technology. Other students may need only one of these five types of assistance. Whatever the student's special education and related services needs are, the IEP team, because it is required to consider these five factors, is more likely to address them by taking the mandatory, broad-based view that these five factors command.

Considering Positive Behavioral Supports (PBS)

As we noted above, one of the special factors that the IEP team must consider involves positive behavioral interventions and supports and other strategies in the case of a child "whose behavior impedes his or her learning or that of others." Note that the word *consider* simply means that: The team members must think about whether to use positive behavioral interventions and supports. They are not required to use positive behavioral interventions and supports, only to think about—to consider—whether to use them or other interventions or no interventions at all. But "consideration" itself implies that certain steps be taken, even though IDEA does not specify these steps. And "impede" certainly almost always involves behavior for which a student may be disciplined (see chapter 4). We think that the following are good steps for assuring that *consider* takes on its fullest meaning—to consider in order to benefit the student.

- To be able to truly consider the use of PBS, team members must have adequate information about PBS.
- For a team to consider anything requires discussion among the team members. Otherwise, the consideration is being given only by individual members of the team and not the team as a whole. IDEA requires that the IEP be developed by a team, and that means discussion.
- If the LEA has adequately considered PBS, it will have one or more reasons for electing or not electing to use it as a strategy to address the child's behavior. Consideration of PBS requires the IEP team to make a decision based on knowledge and discussion of PBS by the team.

IDEA also requires the IEP to consider other strategies. Whether this implies comparative analysis of the options available or not is a debatable point. Not debatable is that it requires, at a minimum, that IEP teams evaluate more than one strategy for addressing the behavior.

Defining Impeding Behavior

IDEA does not define the concept of *impeding behavior*, but the term most likely means behaviors that

- are aggressive, self-injurious, or destructive of property, or are manifestations of depression, passivity, or social isolation, or are manifestations of obsessions, compulsions, stereotypes, or irresistible impulses, or are annoying, confrontational, defiant, taunting, or disruptive;

- could cause the student to be disciplined, including being suspended or expelled from school, pursuant to any applicable state or federal law or regulation, or could cause any consideration of a change of educational placement; and
- are recurring and therefore require a systematic and frequent application of positive behavioral interventions and positive behavioral support (Turnbull, Wilcox, Turnbull, Sailor, & Wickham, 2001).

It is important to repeat that, despite these criteria as offered by professionals in the field of PBS and public policy, IDEA and its regulations do not define *impeding behavior*. That is why a professionally developed definition is so useful in interpreting IDEA. The definition set out above

- is based on research;
- includes students who have been the most usual subjects of research—namely, those with challenging behaviors that derive from mental retardation or autism or a combination of those or other developmental disabilities;
- includes students who have serious emotional disabilities;
- includes students who have learning disabilities, attention-deficit/hyperactivity disability, or comparable impairments; and
- includes students whose behaviors derive from one or more movement disorders.

Because this definition encompasses many types of behaviors, it is atheoretical and pragmatic. It is atheoretical in that it does not rest on any single theory or explanation of impeding behaviors. It is pragmatic in that it recognizes that many types of behaviors impede the learning of the student with a disability and of other students, too. Accordingly, it encompasses those behaviors. Moreover, the definition encompasses the identified behaviors in part because

- IDEA does not exclude them;
- students with those behaviors have been subjected to discipline in school and discipline may trigger a functional behavioral assessment (FBA) (20 U.S.C. Sec. 1415(k)(1));
- the research into positive behavioral interventions and supports is beginning to address impeding behaviors in students who do not have developmental disabilities; and
- students with impeding behaviors, whatever the etiology of those behaviors and however those students may be classified (labeled) by school systems, deserve the benefits of positive behavioral interventions and supports.

Two key possibilities arise because of a student's impeding behaviors. One relates to discipline, a matter covered by IDEA (20 U.S.C. Sec. 1415(k)(1)). If a student's behavior could result in discipline, the student has an interest in receiving an intervention such as PBS to change the behavior.

The other possibility relates to behavior that could cause the IEP team to consider a change in educational placement. Any change must be addressed through the IEP process and by the student's IEP team (20 U.S.C. Sec. 1414(d)) and could result in the student being placed in a more restrictive program, possibly to the detriment of the student's right to receive an appropriate education. Whatever the consequences of the behavior, the behavior impedes and should result in a plan for evaluation (FBA) and intervention (a BIP that is incorporated into the student's IEP and employs positive behavioral interventions and supports).

IDEA and its regulations do not specify the level of impeding behavior that triggers an FBA and a BIP based on positive behavioral interventions and supports, so a state or local education agency may or may not set a level. The benefit of setting no level is that any impeding behavior arguably should justify an FBA and positive intervention because proactive intervention can prevent possible subsequent, and sometimes less easily remediable, behavior.

Another approach, however, sets a level by requiring the behaviors to be recurring and therefore to require a systematic and frequent application of positive behavioral interventions and supports. Setting a level requiring recurrence balances the present limitations of school systems and the claims of students with durable and chronic behaviors against the interests of students who have less durable and chronic behaviors by excluding the latter from the definition of students with impeding behaviors.

This approach recognizes that educators face various constraints when it comes to their use of positive behavioral interventions and supports. It also acknowledges that some students could benefit from PBS even though their behaviors are not durable and chronic—that is, not a regular part of their behavioral repertoire—but that students who have recurring behaviors are needier than those with nonrecurring behaviors. The downside of the recurring approach is that it postpones an intervention and thereby may not prevent the impeding behaviors. Of course, if an LEA decides to provide PBS to students with nondurable, nonchronic impeding behaviors, that would be consistent with a schoolwide approach to improving all students' behaviors via the use of positive interventions and supports.

Linking PBS to the Evaluation and the IEP

Regarding the requirement that the IEP team consider PBS, note the following:

- The IEP team must consider PBS, but membership on the IEP team is fundamentally the same as that of the team that completes the student's nondiscriminatory evaluation, the consequence being that the evaluation data are known to the IEP team and must be taken into account when the team decides whether to consider PBS.
- The team must consider PBS "when appropriate"—namely, when the student's behavior impedes learning (that is, the student's progress toward IEP goals and objectives or others' learning, as most certainly will be the case in nearly all discipline situations).

- The team must consider various other strategies in addition to positive behavioral interventions and supports but may decide to use strategies other than, or in addition to, PBS, or to use no interventions at all.
- The strategies (whatever they may be) must address the student's behavior—that is, they must be targeted at preventing, reducing, replacing, or otherwise appropriately addressing the behavior (or behaviors).

In addition, the new requirements related to PBS are consistent with, and should be part of, the IEP for such students. The student's BIP (the positive behavioral intervention and support plan and the plan for other interventions as well) is part and parcel of the student's IDEA rights and should be part of the IEP, which itself is the linchpin to an appropriate education.

Private-School Students and IEPs

If an SEA or an LEA places a student in a private program as a means of ensuring FAPE, the student remains entitled to an IEP in the private school (20 U.S.C. Sec. 1412(a)(10)(B)(i); 34 C.F.R. 300.146). The SEA must assume responsibility for implementing the student's IEP in the private school. This responsibility may include initiating a meeting to develop an IEP before the student is placed in the private school and monitoring compliance with IDEA through written reports, on-site visits, and parent questionnaires (34 C.F.R. 300.147(a)).

Students with disabilities placed by public agencies in private school retain all of the rights of a child with a disability in public school. Thus, the SEA also is required to disseminate copies of applicable standards for special education to each private school or private facility to which an LEA has referred or placed a student with a disability (34 C.F.R. Sec. 300.147(b)). (Review chapter 4, "Zero Reject," for an in-depth discussion of issues regarding placement in private schools.)

Timing of IEPs

Each LEA must establish or revise, if appropriate, and have in effect an IEP for each student at the beginning of each school year (20 U.S.C. Sec. 1414(d)(2)(A)). The LEA must review and revise the IEP at regular intervals, but not less than annually (20 U.S.C. Sec. 1414(d)(4)(A)(i)).

Amendments to IEPs

If the parents and the LEA want to make changes to an IEP after the annual IEP meeting, the LEA and the parents may agree not to convene an additional IEP meeting for the purpose of making any change (20 U.S.C. Sec. 1414(d)(3)(D)). Instead, they may amend or modify the IEP by a written document (20 U.S.C. Sec. 1414(d)(3)(D)). The parents are entitled to a copy of the amended IEP upon request (20 U.S.C. Sec. 1414(d)(3)(F)). The LEA is responsible for ensuring that the IEP team is informed of any changes made to a child's IEP outside of an IEP meeting (34 C.F.R. 300.324(a)(4) and (6)).

Review of IEPs

The purpose of the review is to determine whether the student's annual IEP goals are being achieved (20 U.S.C. Sec. 1414(d)(4)(A)(i)). If they are not being achieved, a revision of the IEP is warranted, because the team must revise it to address the following (20 U.S.C. Sec. 1414(d)(4)(A)(ii)):

- Any lack of expected progress by the student toward the annual goals, and in the general curriculum, where appropriate
- The results of any nondiscriminatory reevaluation
- Information about the child provided to or by the parents
- The student's anticipated future needs
- Any other matters

IEP conferences for a student who already is receiving special education and related services must be conducted early enough to ensure that the student's IEP is revised and in effect by the beginning of the next school year (20 U.S.C. Sec. 1414 (d)(2)(A)). To meet this provision, the LEA may conduct the meeting at the end of the prior school year or during the summer. If a student is not receiving special education, the LEA must convene an IEP meeting within 30 days of the determination that the student needs special education and related services (34 C.F.R. 300.323(c)(1)).

Part C and the IFSP

Family members play a variety of roles in enhancing the child's development. Throughout the process of developing and implementing IFSPs, it is important for LEAs to recognize these roles as well as the needs of the family (34 C.F.R. 303.343). Accordingly, participants in the initial and each annual IFSP meeting thereafter must include

- the child's parent or parents;
- other family members as requested by the parent(s) if it is feasible to include them;
- an advocate or person outside the family, if the parent requests that the person participate;
- the service coordinator for the child and family;
- a person or persons directly involved in conducting the child and family evaluations and assessments; and
- as appropriate, persons who will provide services to the child or family (34 C.F.R. 303.343).

If a required person is not available to attend the meeting, other means for securing that person's participation must be used, such as telephone conference calls, attendance by a knowledgeable representative, or making pertinent records available at the meeting (34 C.F.R. 303.343).

Development of the IFSP

Part C (20 U.S.C. Sec. 1436) is specific about the development of the IFSP. It must

- be based on a multidisciplinary assessment of the unique strengths and needs of the infant or toddler and identify the appropriate services to meet those needs (20 U.S.C. Sec. 1436(a)(1)), and

- be developed in writing by a multidisciplinary team that includes the infant's or toddler's parents (20 U.S.C. Sec. 1436(a)(3)).

Components of the IFSP

Part C is equally specific about the content of the IFSP. The IFSP must include

- a statement of the child's present levels of physical, cognitive, communication, social or emotional, and adaptive development, based upon objective criteria (20 U.S.C. Sec. 1436(d)(1));
- a family-directed assessment of the resources, priorities, and concerns of the family and identification of the supports and services necessary to enhance the family's capacity to meet the developmental needs of the infant or toddler (20 U.S.C. Sec. 1436(a)(2));
- a statement of the family's resources, priorities, and concerns relative to enhancing the development of the family's infant or toddler (20 U.S.C. Sec. 1436(d)(2));
- a statement of the measurable results or outcomes expected to be achieved for the infant or toddler and the family, including preliteracy and language skills as developmentally appropriate for the child, and the criteria, procedures, and timelines used to determine the extent to which the child is progressing toward achieving the results or outcomes and whether modifications or revisions of the results or outcomes of services are necessary (20 U.S.C. Sec. 1436(d)(3));
- a statement of specific early intervention services, based on peer-reviewed research, to the extent practicable, that are necessary to meet the unique needs of the infant or toddler and the family, including the frequency, intensity, and method of delivering services (20 U.S.C. Sec. 1436(d)(4));
- a statement of the natural environments in which early intervention services shall appropriately be provided, including justification of the extent, if any, to which services will not be provided in a natural environment (20 U.S.C. Sec. 1436(d)(5));
- the projected dates for initiation of services and the anticipated duration of services (20 U.S.C. Sec. 1436(d)(6));
- identification of the service coordinator who will be responsible for implementing the plan and coordinating with other agencies and persons (20 U.S.C. Sec. 1436(d)(7)); and
- the steps to be taken to support the toddler's transition to preschool or other appropriate services (20 U.S.C. Sec. 1436(d)(8)).

Timing

The initial meeting for developing the IFSP must be held within 45 days after the child or family is referred to the state's lead agency (34 C.F.R. 303.342(a)). The IFSP must be developed within a reasonable period after assessment is completed (20 U.S.C. Sec. 1436(c)).

The IFSP must be evaluated once a year, but the family must be provided a review (not an evaluation of the IFSP but, rather, a review of it) at 6-month intervals, or more often if appropriate, to address the infant/toddler or family needs. Thereafter, periodic review is available in two ways:

1. By a meeting or other agreeable means every 6 months to review the child's progress and provide appropriate revision (20 U.S.C. Sec. 1436(b))
2. By the aforementioned annual meeting to review its appropriateness (20 U.S.C. Sec. 1436(b))

The meetings must be at times and places convenient to the family and must be scheduled so the family can plan to attend. Also, the meetings must be conducted in the family's native language or other mode of communication (34 C.F.R. 303.342(d)).

Special rules apply to providing services before the evaluation and assessment of the child and family are completed. Services may begin prior to evaluation and assessment if the parents agree (20 U.S.C. Sec. 1436(c)). An interim IFSP names the service coordinator and demonstrates that the child and family need the services immediately, and the evaluation and assessment must be completed within the allotted 45-day period (34 C.F.R. 303.345).

Accountability and Potential Impact of IFSP

Earlier in this chapter we characterized the 2004 reauthorization, as applied to students in Part B, as grounded in accountability. A logical question is whether Part C is just as accountability grounded as Part B. Let's think about that issue by first considering the IDEA regulations and by then considering how the IFSP and Part C are intended to work.

The current regulations implementing Part C state that every agency or person having a direct role in providing early intervention services is responsible for making a good-faith effort to assist the child in achieving his or her IFSP outcomes but that no agency or person may be held accountable if the child does not achieve the growth projected by the IFSP (34 C.F.R. 303.346).

Further, the IFSP and Part C generally have potential for strengthening families by helping them

- develop high expectations for their infant/toddler and themselves;
- see the positive contributions the infant/toddler can make to the family, its friends, and society;
- make choices about how they want to be involved in their infant's/toddler's life;
- create relationships with professionals and with others who are not in the business of providing disability services;
- learn what their infant's/toddler's strengths and needs are;
- learn what new strengths can be developed;
- determine how the family can cope with difficulties and learn new coping skills;

- improve or develop new techniques for communicating within the family and with professionals;
- see the possibilities for integration and independence of the infant/toddler and, indeed, of the whole family;
- secure and coordinate services from a variety of disciplines, service providers, and funding streams;
- learn how to take charge of their situation and become their own case manager if they wish to do so; and
- be launched successfully as families affected by a disability.

Moreover, the IFSP recognizes that families play a crucial role in the infant's/toddler's development and always will play an important role in child development. The IFSP extends the notion of "parent participation" to that of "family participation," subject to the final decision by the parent(s). It recognizes that families are systems and that no one member of the family (the infant/toddler) can be helped unless all members of the family are strengthened and the whole family comes from a position of strength (Turnbull & Turnbull, 1997; Turnbull, Turnbull, Erwin, & Soodak, 2006).

Having said this much, let's return to the issue of Part C and accountability. Just how accountable does Part C make a public agency, and just how large and effective is a parent's claim that the child is entitled to accountable outcomes? It seems clear that, at the most, the parent can hold an agency or specific practitioner accountable only if that agency or individual did not engage in a good-faith attempt to comply with the process and outcome expectations under Part C. Arguably, that is not a great deal of accountability, and the means for achieving it, through due process, probably will not be terribly effective because Part C does not specifically address the issues of bad-faith compliance.

SERVICES

Let's return now to Part B, and recall that one of the mandatory elements of each student's IEP (20 U.S.C. Sec. 1414(d)(1)(A)(i)(IV)) is a statement of

- special education and related services;
- supplementary aids and services; and
- program modifications or supports for school personnel to be provided to the child, or on behalf of the child.

These components—related services, supplementary aids and services, and program modifications and personnel support—have three purposes. They are to benefit the student so that he or she may

1. advance appropriately toward attaining the annual goals,
2. be involved in and make progress in the general education curriculum and participate in extracurricular and other nonacademic activities, and

3. be educated and participate with other children with disabilities and nondisabled children in school activities.

Part B: Related Services

Under Part B of IDEA, the related services to which a student is entitled to accomplish these three results include those listed here. This listing of related services in the statute and regulations of IDEA is not exhaustive.

Part B: Related Services (20 U.S.C. Sec. 1402(26))

- "Audiology" includes identifying children with hearing loss; determining the range, nature, and degree of hearing loss; providing habilitative activities; creating and administering programs for treatment and prevention of hearing loss; counseling and guidance of children, parents, and teachers regarding hearing loss; and determining a student's amplification needs (34 C.F.R. 300.34(c)(1)).

- "Counseling services" include rehabilitation counseling and services provided by qualified social workers, psychologists, guidance counselors, or other qualified personnel (34 C.F.R. 300.34(c)(2)).

- "Early identification and assessment of disabilities in children" mean implementing a formal plan for identifying a disability as early as possible in a child's life (34 C.F.R. 300.34(c)(3)).

- "Interpreting services," as used with respect to children who are deaf or hard of hearing, include oral transliteration services, cued language transliteration services, sign language, and transcription services (34 C.F.R. 300.34(c)(4)).

- "Medical services" are those provided by a licensed physician to determine a child's medically related disability that results in the child's need for special education and related services (34 C.F.R. 300.34(c)(5)). The term does not include a medical device that is surgically implanted, or the replacement of such device (20 U.S.C. Sec. 1401(26)(B)).

- "Occupational therapy" means services provided by a qualified occupational therapist and includes improving, developing, or restoring functions impaired or lost through illness, injury, or deprivation (34 C.F.R. 300.34(c)(6)).

- "Orientation and mobility services" mean services provided to blind or visually impaired students by qualified personnel to enable attainment of systematic orientation to and safe movement in school, home, and community environments (34 C.F.R. 300.34(c)(7)).

- "Parent counseling and training" mean assisting parents in understanding the special needs of their child, providing parents with information about child development, and helping parents acquire necessary skills that will allow them to support the implementation of their child's IEP (or IFSP for Part C) (34 C.F.R. 300.34(c)(8)).

- "Physical therapy" refers to services provided by a qualified physical therapist (34 C.F.R. 300.34(c)(9)).

- "Psychological services" include administering psychological and educational tests and other assessment procedures; interpreting assessment results; obtaining, integrating, and interpreting information about the child's behavior and conditions relating to learning; consulting with other staff members in planning school programs to meet the special needs of children as indicated by psychological tests, interviews, and behavioral evaluations; planning and managing a program of psychological services, including psychological counseling for children and parents; and assisting in developing positive behavioral intervention strategies (34 C.F.R. 300.34(c)(10)).

- "Recreation" includes assessing leisure function, therapeutic recreation services, recreation programs in schools and community agencies, and leisure education (34 C.F.R. 300.34(c)(11)).

- "Rehabilitation counseling services" mean services provided by qualified personnel that focus specifically on career development, employment preparation, achieving independence, and integrating a student with a disability in the workplace and community. This term also includes vocational rehabilitation services provided under the Rehabilitation Act (34 C.F.R. 300.34(c)(12)).

- "School nurse services" are services provided by a qualified school nurse, designed to enable a child with a disability to receive FAPE as described in the child's IEP (34 C.F.R. 300.34(c)(13)).

- "Social work services in schools" include preparing a social or developmental history on a child with a disability; group and individual counseling with the child and family; working with those problems in a child's living situation (home, school, and community) that affect the child's adjustment in school; mobilizing school and community resources to enable the child to learn as effectively as possible in his or her educational program; and assisting in developing positive behavioral intervention strategies (34 C.F.R. 300.34(c)(14)).

- "Speech pathology" and "speech/language pathology" include identification, diagnosis, and appraisal of specific speech or language impairments; referral to or provision of speech and language, medical, or other services; and counseling and guidance of parents, children, and teachers regarding speech and language impairments (34 C.F.R. 300.34(c)(15)).

- "Transportation" and "related costs" cover travel to and from early intervention services, school, and between schools; travel in and around school buildings; and specialized equipment (such as special or adapted buses, lifts, and ramps), if required to provide special transportation for a child with a disability (34 C.F.R. 300.34(c)(16)).

Part C: Early Intervention Services

Under Part C, many of the early intervention services to which the child is entitled are the same as, or similar to, the related services provided under Part B. Nevertheless, there are a few differences, as you can detect by comparing the B and C services. (At the time this book went to press, the U.S. Department of Education had not issued proposed regulations for Part C in the 2004 version of IDEA. Accordingly, the regulations related to Part C are those that were issued after Congress enacted the IDEA amendments of 1997.)

Part C Services

- "Assistive technology device" means any item, piece of equipment, or product system, whether acquired commercially off the shelf, modified, or customized, that is used to increase, maintain, or improve a student's functional capacities (20 U.S.C. Secs. 1401(1) and (2)).

- "Assistive technology service" means service that directly assists a child with a disability in the selection, acquisition, or use of an assistive technology device. These services include (1) the evaluation (including a functional evaluation of the child in the child's customary environment) of the needs of the child; (2) purchasing, leasing, or otherwise providing for the acquisition of assistive technology devices by children with disabilities; (3) selecting, designing, fitting, customizing, adapting, applying, maintaining, repairing, or replacing assistive technology devices; (4) coordinating and using other therapies, interventions, or services with assistive technology devices, such as those associated with existing education and rehabilitation plans and programs; (5) training or technical assistance for a child with disabilities or, if appropriate, that child's family; and (6) training or technical assistance for professionals (including those providing early intervention services) or other individuals who provide services to or are otherwise substantially involved in the major life functions of individuals with disabilities (pre-2004 regulations 34 C.F.R. 303.12(d)(1).).

- "Audiology" includes identification of children with auditory impairment; determination of the range, nature, and degree of hearing loss and communication functions; referral for medical and other services necessary for habilitation or rehabilitation; provision of auditory training, aural rehabilitation, speech reading and listening device orientation and training, and other services; provision of services for hearing-loss prevention; and determination of the child's need for individual amplification, including selecting, fitting, and dispensing appropriate listening and vibrotactile devices, and evaluating their effectiveness (pre-2004 regulations 34 C.F.R. 303.12(d)(2)).

- "Family training, counseling, and home visits" refer to services provided, as appropriate, by social workers, psychologists, and other qualified personnel to assist the child's family to understand the child's special needs and to enhance the child's development (pre-2004 regulations 34 C.F.R. 303.12(d)(3)).

- "Health services" are services necessary to enable a child to benefit from the other early intervention services during the time the child is receiving the other early intervention services (pre-2004 regulations 34 C.F.R. 303.12(d)(4) and 303.13).

- "Medical services," allowed for diagnostic or evaluation purposes only, are services provided by a licensed physician to determine a child's developmental status and need for early intervention services (pre-2004 regulations 34 C.F.R. 303.12(d)(5)).

- "Nursing services" include (pre-2004 regulations 34 C.F.R. 303.12(d)(6)) the assessment of health status for the purpose of providing nursing care, including identification of patterns of human response to actual or potential health problems; provision of nursing care to prevent health problems, restore or improve functioning, and promote optimal health and development; and administration of medications, treatments, and regimens prescribed by a licensed physician.

- "Nutrition services" include (pre-2004 regulations 34 C.F.R. 303.12(d)(7)) conducting individual assessments in

  □ nutritional history and dietary intake;
  □ anthropometric, biochemical, and clinical variables;
  □ feeding skills and feeding problems;
  □ food habits and food preferences;

❑ developing and monitoring appropriate plans to address the nutritional needs of children; and

❑ making referrals to appropriate community resources to carry out nutrition goals.

■ "Occupational therapy" includes services to address the functional needs of a child related to adaptive development, adaptive behavior and play, and sensory, motor, and postural development. These services are designed to improve the child's functional ability to perform tasks in home, school and community settings, and include (1) identification, assessment, and intervention; (2) adaptation of the environment, and selection, design, and fabrication of assistive and orthotic devices to facilitate development and promote the acquisition of functional skills; and (3) prevention or minimization of the impact of initial or future impairment, delay in development, or loss of functional ability (pre-2004 regulations 34 C.F.R. 303.12(d)(8)).

■ "Physical therapy" includes services to address the promotion of sensorimotor function through enhancement of musculoskeletal status, neurobehavioral organization, perceptual and motor development, cardiopulmonary status, and effective environmental adaptation. These services include (1) screening, evaluation, and assessment of infants and toddlers to identify movement dysfunction; (2) obtaining, interpreting, and integrating information appropriate to program planning to prevent, alleviate, or compensate for movement dysfunction and related functional problems; and (3) providing individual and group services or treatment to prevent, alleviate, or compensate for movement dysfunction and related functional problems (pre-2004 regulations 34 C.F.R. 303.12(d)(9)).

■ "Psychological services" are defined as they are in Part B, except these do not include assisting other staff members in developing school planning or to assist in the development of positive behavioral interventions (pre-2004 regulations 34 C.F.R. 303.12(d)(10)).

■ "Service coordination services" are assistance and services provided by a service coordinator (case manager) to a child and the child's family (pre-2004 regulations 34 C.F.R. 303.12(d)(11)).

■ "Social work services" include (1) making home visits to evaluate a child's living conditions and patterns of parent–child interaction; (2) preparing a social or emotional developmental assessment of the child within the family context; (3) providing individual and family group counseling with parents and other family members, and appropriate social skill–building activities with the child and parents; (4) working with those problems in a child's and family's living situation that affect the child's maximum utilization of early intervention services; and (5) identifying, mobilizing, and coordinating community resources and services to enable the child and family to receive maximum benefit from early intervention services (pre-2004 regulations 34 C.F.R. 303.12(d)(12)).

- "Special instruction" includes (1) the design of learning environments and activities that promote the child's acquisition of skills in a variety of developmental areas, including cognitive processes and social inter- action; (2) curriculum planning, including the planned interaction of personnel, materials, and time and space, that leads to achieving the outcomes in the child's IFSP; (3) providing families with information, skills, and support related to enhancing the skill development of the child; and (4) working with the child to enhance the child's develop- ment (pre-2004 regulations 34 C.F.R. 303.12(d)(13)).

- "Speech/language pathology" is defined in essentially the same manner as in Part B (pre-2004 regulations 34 C.F.R. 303.12(d)(14)). IDEA 2004 added sign language and cued language services to the definition;

- "Transportation and related costs" are defined in essentially the same manner as in Part B (pre-2004 regulations 34 C.F.R. 303.12(d)(15)).

- "Vision services" include (1) evaluation and assessment of visual func- tioning, including the diagnosis and appraisal of specific visual disorders, delays, and abilities; (2) referral for medical or other professional serv- ices necessary for the habilitation or rehabilitation of visual functioning disorders, or both; and (3) communication skills training, orientation and mobility training for all environments, visual training, independent living skills training, and additional training necessary to activate visual motor abilities (pre-2004 regulations 34 C.F.R. 303.12(d)(16)).

Medical Services and Other Health-Care Services

If a student has a tracheostomy (a hole and a tube in the throat to assist with breath- ing and speaking), must the LEA require its staff to suction mucus and other imped- ing matter from the student's throat? What if the student depends on a breathing machine? Must the LEA maintain the machine and provide staff to operate it? In a word, is a specific service such as these two a related service that the LEA must pro- vide and pay for, or is it a medical service that the LEA is exempt from providing (so long as the service is not for diagnosis- and evaluation-related special education placement and services)? The courts have addressed these questions in cases where the student has needed catheterization, nursing services, and mental health services.

Catheterization

In *Irving Indep. School Dist. v. Tatro* (1984), the Supreme Court clarified the defini- tion of a related service. *Tatro* involved the meaning of a related service as applied to clean intermittent catheterization (CIC). CIC is a procedure in which a catheter tube is inserted into the urethra and the bladder to drain urine from the kidneys. The Court held, in a unanimous opinion, that CIC is a related service that schools must provide. The Court found, as a matter of fact, that CIC is a "simple procedure … that may be performed in a few minutes by a layperson with less than an hour's training." Indeed, the student herself soon would be able to perform the service, as her parents, babysitters, and teenage brother had been doing all along.

To conclude that CIC is a related service under IDEA, the Court had to determine the answers to these questions:

- Is CIC a supportive service that enables students to benefit from special education?
- Is CIC excluded from the supportive service definition because it is a medical service serving purposes other than diagnosis or evaluation?

The Court held that CIC is a supportive service because, without it, the student could not attend school and thereby benefit from special education. Relying on its earlier decision in *Rowley,* the Court stated that Congress's intent was to make public education available to students with disabilities and to make their access to school meaningful. A service that allows the student to "remain at school during the day is an important means of providing the child with the meaningful access to education that Congress envisioned." The Court was not about to allow any violation of the zero reject principle by permitting schools to escape their obligation of providing such a beneficial service.

Next, the Court found that CIC is not a medical service needed for purposes other than diagnosis and evaluation. First, the Court deferred to the U.S. Department of Education regulations, which defined CIC to be a related school health service, not a medical service. Second, the Court found that Congress plainly required schools to hire various specially trained personnel, such as school nurses. Because nurses long have been a part of educational systems and perform duties such as dispensing oral medication and administering emergency injections, which are difficult to distinguish from CIC, it follows that CIC is a service that school nurses (among others) are qualified to provide.

Tatro held that the term "medical services" referred only to services that must be performed by a physician, and not to school health services. This is the "bright-line" rule: The definition is the bright line that separates health-care services that are provided as a related service (health services not provided by a physician or that are provided by a physician but are evaluative or diagnostic in nature) and those that do not qualify as a related service (medical services [physician-provided] that are not evaluative or diagnostic in nature). No other factors may be considered—only the precise language of the definition. The Supreme Court restated and reinforced the approach in *Cedar Rapids Community School District v. Garrett F.* (1999).

Full-Time Nursing Services

In *Garrett F.,* the Court held that the related-services provision of IDEA requires a public school district to provide nursing services to a child with a disability during school hours if those services are required to assist the student to benefit from special education. In that case, the student, Garrett F., required nursing services that included urinary bladder catheterization, suctioning of a tracheostomy, ventilator setting checks, ambubag administrations as a back-up to the ventilator, blood-pressure monitoring, observations to determine if he was in respiratory distress (autonomic hyperreflexia), and disimipation in the event of autonomic hyperreflexia. Because these services were necessary if Garrett were to remain in school, the school district must fund these services, the Court held, to guarantee the meaningful access to education and integration that IDEA requires.

Until the *Garrett F.* decision, not all medically associated services were so easily included as a related service. This was true particularly for services provided by full-time nurses or similar health-care providers and technicians. Not surprisingly, a number of cases focused on nursing services. The leading case prior to *Garrett F.* was *Detsel v. Bd. of Educ. of the Auburn Enlarged City School Dist.* (1987), which involved a student who was oxygen-dependent, requiring a constant supply of oxygen administered through a respirator. The respirator was operated by a nurse or other qualified professional who was required to be in attendance with the student and monitor the respirator on a constant basis.

The issue in *Detsel* was whether the LEA must pay for the nurse to constantly monitor and provide necessary respirator support and oxygen. The federal Court of Appeals held that the district does not have to provide the nurse and that the service is not a school-health or related service. The court examined the following factors, which focus on the nature of the service and its relationship to the child's education, to arrive at its decision:

- The person who must provide the service must be professionally licensed, such as a registered nurse or a licensed practical nurse; and an aide for the principal professional usually is required.
- Traditionally, a school nurse's duties have not included this service.
- The procedure itself is complex, consisting of many separate but interrelated steps.
- The expense of providing the service is great.
- The service is life-sustaining, and the risk of a malfunction in the service—that the student would experience respiratory distress and, if not rescued, might die—is great.
- Provision of the service is supervised and prescribed by a physician.
- The student, although clearly benefiting from the service, is not using the service directly to benefit from special education.

Detsel had a prolonged impact. After the court's ruling, Congress amended the Medicaid law in 1986 to allow Medicaid funds to be used for health-related services of a student whose IEP calls for those services, as long as a state's Medicaid plan permits the funds to be used for those services and the child is Medicaid-eligible (P.L. 99–272, 42 U.S.C. Sec. 1396n(g)). (See chapter 4, "Zero Reject," for a discussion of the Medicaid Catastrophic Coverage Act and its impact on special education funding.)

After Congress amended the Medicaid law, Detsel's parents sued to require the Department of Health and Human Services (HHS), which administers the Medicaid program, to provide a private-duty nurse to the student during her time in school. The secretary of HHS declined to authorize payment for the private-duty nurse. A federal appeals court ruled that the secretary's regulations (prohibiting payment) were unreasonable because they contravened congressional intent (*Detsel v. Sullivan,* 1990).

As a result of the court's decision, in 1991 HHS announced a new policy concerning private-duty nursing services. Consistent with the *Detsel* decision, the Health Care Financing Administration (HCFA, which administers Medicaid under the auspices of the HHS, has a new name: Center for Medicaid and Medical Services—CMS) began paying for private-duty nursing services (via the Medicaid program) for eligible recipients when those services were provided during the hours when a student is outside his or her home engaging in normal life activities such as attending school (*Pullen v. Cuomo,* 1991). Thus, a student whose IEP called for private-duty nursing services during school hours and who was entitled to Medicaid benefits could charge the private-duty nursing costs to Medicaid for the time the student was receiving those services in school, and the LEA would escape having to pay for them.

This result encouraged schools to help students qualify for Medicaid services, write IEPs calling for private-duty nursing services, and charge the costs of those services to Medicaid. Simply because a student could obtain Medicaid-financed services, however, did not mean that schools were off the hook. Not all students qualified for Medicaid, and those who did not qualify continued to want the schools to provide health-related services.

Generally, LEAs remained unwilling to pay for full-time nursing services when a student did not qualify for Medicaid assistance, and some courts agreed with that position. For example, *Neely v. Rutherford County School* (1995) found that a student with congenital central hypoventilation syndrome was not entitled to receive full-time nursing services at the school's expense. The LEA offered to provide a nursing assistant but rejected the parents' wish for a registered nurse or respiratory assistant.

Because the student required almost constant care due to the life-threatening nature of her disease, the Court determined that the burden on the LEA of providing such services was too great. The Court held that in such a case, monitoring and suctioning the student's feeding tube was a medical service not provided for in the act. Moreover, because the care required for these students was varied, intensive, provided by a nurse under a physician's supervision and prescription, time consuming, expensive, and, perhaps most important, involved life-threatening situations that required the constant vigilance of a professional, the Court remained reluctant to require a full-time nurse as a related service.

Garrett F., however, restated the *Tatro* bright-line standard and disagreed with the *Detsel/Neely* line of cases, stating that their decisions, which relied on the nature and extent of services performed, hinged erroneously on dicta articulated in *Tatro. Garrett F.* explicitly rejected the *Detsel* arguments regarding costs of providing such services as well. The Court made it clear that the related-services provision was broad enough to encompass those services that would be required to assist a child with a disability to benefit from special education *without regard to cost.*

Applying *Tatro's* two-prong test, the Supreme Court in *Garrett F.* found that the services were supportive services the student must be provided so he could benefit from special education, as he could not attend school without those services. Furthermore, the Court found that the services were not medical services for purposes beyond diagnosis and evaluation because such services could be administered by a nurse or layperson and were not required to be administered by a physician. This determination of who administers the service—namely, that the administrator is not a physician—is *Tatro's,* and now *Garrett F.'s,* bright-line rule.

Mental Health Services

Although the *Tatro* and *Garrett F.* decisions clarified the issues surrounding related services that are targeted on students' physical health, they did not address—and thus left unresolved—the issues around related services and students' mental health. Fundamentally, the question is whether an LEA is required to pay for services that are associated with a student's mental health needs. It is helpful to frame the issue by developing some factual scenarios.

Assume, for example, that an LEA has formally classified a student as one who has emotional disturbance (one of IDEA's disability categories, 20 U.S.C. Sec. 1401 (3)(A)(i)). Or assume that an LEA has classified a student as one who has other disabilities and who also has some mental health issues—the so-called dual diagnosis classification in which a student is classified as having more than one disability.

Assume further that the LEA, the student's parents, or both, believe that the student could benefit educationally from receiving mental health services. Now assume that the LEA and the student's parents disagree about whether IDEA requires the LEA to pay for these services. Both the LEA and the parents say they are not required to pay for them; there is a stand-off between these two potential sources of payment.

Finally, assume that both the LEA and the parents seek to place the student into a residential facility and to charge the cost of the services that the facility provides to the facility and its funding source. Then assume that one available facility is privately operated, in which case it wants to look to the LEA and the parents' private health insurance for payment, and that another available facility is publicly funded, in which case it wants to avoid its budget from becoming the sole, or even principal, source of funding. There is a stand-off between the three parties—the LEA, the parents, and the facility—with each attempting to shift the costs to one or both of the others.

How have the courts responded to this kind of conflict? Predictably, they have not responded with a single voice, but there are several trends and multiple factors that they take into account. Here, the law is by no means as well settled as it is in the conflict regarding health services that are both educationally beneficial and that address the student's physical health. In that area of the law, the *Tatro–Garrett F.* bright-line test prevails. In the mental health services area of the law, considerable confusion reigns. All courts, however, begin by looking to the language of IDEA and its regulations.

Here, they find scant help. What is clear is that the costs of medical services that are for diagnostic and evaluation purposes only are IDEA-covered costs; an LEA must pay them (20 U.S.C. Sec. 1401(26)). This is the clear language of IDEA's definition of related services. Thus, if the mental health services are provided solely for the purposes of determining whether the student has a disability and, if so, the educational implications of that finding, the services are chargeable against the LEA.

Beyond that, the courts look to the definition of the related services, turning to the IDEA regulations. They look principally at the regulations' definition of psychological services. Under this definition, the term *psychological services* includes "planning and managing a program of psychological services, including psychological counseling for children and parents" (34 C.F.R. 300.34(c)(10)(v)). The common assumption is that psychological counseling includes one-on-one or group therapy through traditional psychotherapeutic means—namely, traditional psychotherapy.

A dictionary definition of *psychotherapy* is "treatment of mental or emotional disorders or of related bodily ills by psychological means" (*Merriam-Webster's Collegiate Dictionary,* 10th edition, 1996). Arguably, psychological services (the related services in question) include psychotherapy, and thus psychotherapy should be classified as a related service. Lay definitions, however, are both circular (as in "psychotherapy") and are not controlling when courts interpret IDEA.

Failing to receive much, if any, guidance from the available definitions, the courts conduct a "functional analysis." They ask: Who does what to whom, under what circumstances, where, why (for what purposes and outcomes), and with what connections between the student's educational program as it would be in the absence of the convoluted issues about mental health services? Using this method of analysis, the cases tend to yield two results.

Service Benefit Standard   The first result is that mental health services and psychotherapy or psychological counseling are related services because a student often cannot actualize his or her educational abilities—cannot effectively learn—without them. A student who has emotional challenges (without regard to whether the student is classified as primarily having an emotional disturbance or as having another disability with emotional/mental health needs associated with it) therefore needs mental health services to obtain an educational benefit; accordingly, the LEA is required to pay for the services.

This is a "service benefit" standard: The service confers a benefit that is primarily educational. The services, though they respond to the student's mental and emotional needs, allow the student to benefit academically. The ultimate benefit is educational though the means may seem to be medical.

Two early but still relied-on cases illustrating this approach are *Papacoda v. Connecticut* (1981) and *Vander Malle v. Ambach* (1987). In *Papacoda*, the court held that an LEA must pay tuition, board, and psychotherapy for a student's placement at a residential facility. The purpose of that placement was to provide educational services in a therapeutic environment. Further, because of the intimate relationship between the student's need for psychotherapy and his ability to learn, and in light of the federal regulations' definition of related services, psychotherapy was considered a related service.

The court in *Vander Malle* followed this line of reasoning as well. *Vander Malle* involved a student with schizophrenia who required a residential placement that provided treatment in an extremely structured environment, the use of antipsychotic medication, and a behavior reinforcement plan to educate the student. This program, designed by the psychiatric staff, enabled the student to gain control of his emotions and improve his interpersonal relationships so he could learn. The court held that states may not escape their responsibility to pay for such treatment solely because the treatment program addresses a student's psychological needs.

In addition, the court followed *Papacoda* and agreed that the regulations and the plain meaning of the statute required the conclusion that psychotherapy is a related service. The court held that the service benefit standard involves evaluating two criteria: (1) whether the program is designed to improve the student's educational performance, and (2) whether the program is based on the student's classification as having a serious emotional disturbance.

Benefit as a Byproduct   The second line of cases regards mental health services fundamentally as ends for relief of mental or emotional problems in and of themselves. These services also may be a means for assisting the student to benefit from special education, but that benefit is a byproduct, not their primary purpose.

Under this approach, some courts refuse to hold LEAs responsible for the financial burden of providing mental health services to a student. For example, *Clovis Unified School Dist. v. California Office of Admin. Hearings* (1990) held that an LEA may not be charged with costs of placement and therapy at a psychiatric hospital. The court declared that the service benefit standard for determining whether psychotherapy is a related service was overly broad and inordinately encompassing.

The court compared a student who needed psychotherapy to benefit educationally with a visually impaired student who needed surgery to see better and thus benefit educationally. Because the public school was not required to pay for the student's eye surgery, it should not be required to pay for the student's psychotherapy. An interpretation requiring such a result would tremendously strain the fiscal resources of the public school system. In addition, the court found that, because the facility did not operate a full-time school and because physicians, not educators, determined which services the student would receive, the treatment could not qualify as a related service to enable the student to meet his or her educational needs.

Basically, *Clovis* applied a medical-model analysis to mental health services, regarding these services essentially as medical and not educational, and thus as excluded from the meaning of related services. The services are fundamentally medical because their basic purpose and effect is to address and benefit the student's mental health. The student's educational benefit is secondary to the overarching medical model.

In determining whether mental health services are related services, other courts agree with *Clovis* in its medical-purpose approach, taking into account the type of facility, nature of services provided, existence of an educational component in addition to a medical component, and discipline of the providers. *Burke County Bd. of Educ. v. Denton* (1990) held that a 24-hour, in-home, behavior-management training program for the student and family was a medical service. *Field v. Haddonfield Bd. of Educ.* (1991) held that drug treatment programs are essentially medical, not educational, interventions. The type of placement is not always decisive, though. *River Forest School Dist. #90 v. Laurel D.* (1996) held that a nontraditional academic environment does not, per se, create a medical placement and relieve the school of paying for it.

Time of Day and Place   One factor in these two lines of cases has to do with the portion of the day when the services are provided. In both *Tatro* and *Garrett F.*, the services were provided during the school day. That suggests that the services were more educationally related than not: They were for the purpose of assisting the student to benefit from special education.

A second factor has to do with the place where the services are provided. Again, in both *Tatro* and *Garrett F.*, the services were provided at the school itself. That, too, tends to suggest that the services were more educationally related than not. They, too, were for the purposes of assisting the student to benefit from special education.

Tatro and *Garrett F.* involved students who were receiving services in an LEA during school hours. What about students who receive services outside of an LEA and not only during school hours but also thereafter? After all, that was the situation in *Papacoda*, *Vander Malle*, and *Clovis*. What happens when the student is placed into a residential program? Who pays? The answer depends on two factors:

1. *LEA-appropriate placement.* Did the LEA provide a valid alternative setting (other than the residential placement) in which the student could benefit and progress because he or she received a free appropriate public education there? If the LEA provided such a placement, it seems that the cost of the residential placement should not be charged against the LEA. After all, it fulfilled its duty to the student (the duty to provide benefit, under *Rowley*), and it did so in a

setting that was the more typical, least restrictive one (see chapter 7 for the requirements of least restrictive settings).

2. *Residential placement and educational program.* Did the residential setting itself have an educational component? If so and if the student was participating "in school" or receiving any traditional educational services (howsoever they may be linked to the mental health therapeutic services), it seems that the cost of the residential placement should be charged against the LEA. After all, the LEA was fulfilling its duty with the assistance of the residential facility. Here, if the SEA accredited the residential facility as an educational institution, the LEA should pay. The function of the facility was education; that's why it was accredited, and that was the defining characteristic of the services it provided.

In this line of analysis, two factors stand out:

1. *The student:* Does, or can, the student benefit from the nonresidential services the LEA offers? If so, the LEA is exonerated from the costs of the residential facility. Why should it carry those extraordinary costs when, for (usually) fewer funds, it can provide a benefit in its other, community-based programs? Here, three factors converge: (a) the student benefits (per *Rowley*); (b) the services are in the LEA's community-based programs (*Tatro, Garrett F.,* and the IDEA requirements for least restrictive environment—see chapter 7); and (c) the LEA can hold down its costs by providing community-based services, not residential-based services.

2. *Place.* Does the residential facility seem to be more educational or therapeutic? If educational, the LEA is charged with the cost of placement; if therapeutic, the LEA escapes the cost of placement.

To have said this much raises the question: What are the differences between "educational" and "therapeutic"? Three criteria come into play. The first two have to do with standards and programs.

1. *The "standards" standard.* Is the facility accredited by the state as a school or by the state or other accreditation or licensing bodies as a hospital (psychiatric hospital)? If as a school, the LEA is more apt to have to pay; if as a hospital, the LEA is less apt to have to pay.

2. *The "student standard."* Does the student receive traditional educational services during what normally would be school hours (say, 8 a.m.–3 p.m.) and then receive other services, or does the student receive both educational and therapeutic services during the regular school day? If the answer to either question, or to both, is "yes," the facility probably will be regarded as educational.

In trying to answer the student standard, courts are justified in asking about the nature of the staff that provides services to the student. Does the staff consist primarily of educators and related services personnel (psychologists, school social workers, or others)? Or does it consist primarily of health-care providers (physicians, especially psychiatrists, or nurses and other individuals licensed, trained, or paid/reimbursed for delivering health services)?

The reason for both results (having to do with accreditation/licensure and with program) is that the function and purpose of the facility is more educational than therapeutic.

3. *Initiative for placement.* If the LEA places the student into the facility or recommends that the student be placed there, and if in its recommendation are found reasons related to the student's education (such as the continuation of the student's IEP), the placement seems to be more educational than therapeutic. This is so simply because the LEA itself says so: It declares an educational purpose and assures an educational program. By contrast, if a parent initiates the placement and then seeks to charge the cost to the LEA, some courts may be disinclined to hold the LEA responsible for the costs and to regard the placement more as a therapeutic one—for the student or the parents or both.

In sum, it seems that courts will enter into a rather complex, fact-driven calculus: Is there a nexus—a solid connection—between the placement and the education the student receives? Is the placement itself one that provides education as a principal or important function, or is it one that provides therapy that involves some, but not a dominant, educational component? Is the purpose for educational reasons, with therapeutic benefits secondary? Or is it one that addresses primarily the student's mental health needs, with educational benefits secondary? Finally, is the place itself—the facility—accredited by the state as a school, or is it accredited or licensed by the state or other entities as a hospital? And, without regard to the nature of the place itself, does the LEA provide an appropriate education on its own, or is it necessary for the student to be placed into a facility to receive an education?

This is a confusing area of the law, so let's summarize what the cases seem to teach us:

- If the service is provided by a doctor, it is a related medical service and may be provided for diagnostic and evaluation purposes only.
- If the service is provided by anyone else, fits within the categorical definition of 20 U.S.C. Sec. 1401(26), and is necessary for the child to receive a benefit from special education, it is a related service.
- If a student is enabled to attend a general school program as a result of the service (*Tatro, Garrett F.*), it is apt to be a related service.
- If the service is a traditional function of a school nurse or a modest extension of the nurse's function (in *Tatro* and *Garrett F.*, the services were not unlike other school nurse functions, whereas in *Detsel* and *Bevin H.* the services were far more like a hospital-based service), and it is provided during school hours, it is apt to be a related service. If a court determines that the service is being provided for other than educational reasons, as in *Clovis* (the mental health medical-model case), courts are less likely to find that the service qualifies as a related service under IDEA.

Governmental Problems Arising From the Related Services Requirements

Those who propose providing related services as a solution to total and functional exclusion must be cognizant of the barriers to these services. Besides the difficulties in interpreting which services shall be provided, the practicalities of actually providing these services are problems in and of themselves. Essentially, these problems are intergovernmental; they go to the heart of the functions of governmental agencies involved with children with disabilities.

One major problem is intergovernmental coordination. The immediate task has been to assure that the federal, state, and local agencies that can offer special education and related services will provide those services in the least restrictive setting. Because there are so many service providers and because they often are operated by separate federal agencies (each with its own state and local counterpart), it is important, though difficult, to coordinate these agencies' activities and thereby assure through a "memorandum of understanding" (MOU) that their collective resources can be brought to bear on the educational problems of students with disabilities.

But federal interagency MOUs are not always translated into action at the point where federal services are delivered, and state and local counterparts do not necessarily enter into interagency agreements or carry out these agreements. When these fairly typical bureaucratic problems are added to the interpretation problems, the results are either a failure to deliver services or its opposite—duplication of services (with a resulting competition for funding and a waste of professional time and effort and increased cost of service).

Other Services Necessary for FAPE

Other services are necessary for ensuring that students receive a free and appropriate public education under Part B. These include the following:

- *Assistive technology.* Under IDEA, if a student with a disability needs technology-related assistance and the student's IEP calls for such assistance (either devices or services [note that these are defined in the same manner as they are in Part C]), the student may obtain them from the student's LEA or any existing statewide system for delivering assistive technology (34 C.F.R. 300.324(a)(2)(v)). These services or devices may be included in the IEP as a part of the child's special education, as a related service, or as supplementary aids and services. Thus, assistive technology services or devices should be part of the student's educational program where appropriate, and a student's IEP should call for these services and devices to be regarded as legally sufficient.

  As we noted in describing the components of an IEP and the special factors the IEP team must consider, the team is required to consider whether the student needs assistive technology (20 U.S.C. Sec. 1414(d)(3)(v)). Under the federal Technology-Related Assistance for Individuals with Disabilities Act of

1988 as amended (P.L. 105–394), each state receives federal funds to enable it to create a statewide system for delivering assistive technology. IDEA requires local education agencies to maximize collaboration with the state agency responsible for assistive technology programs. This system can be accessed through a student's IEP and the related services of IDEA.

- *Nonacademic services.* Each LEA must take steps to provide nonacademic and extracurricular services and activities in a way that affords children with disabilities an equal opportunity to participate in those services and activities. These may include counseling services, athletics, transportation, health services, recreation, special interest groups or clubs, referrals to agencies to provide relevant assistance, and employment-related activities (34 C.F.R. 300.107(b)).

- *Physical education.* These services must be available to every child receiving FAPE. Further, each child with a disability must be allowed to participate in the regular physical education program unless the child is enrolled full time at a separate facility, or the child needs specially designed physical education, and that is described in the IEP (34 C.F.R. 300.108).

- *Residential placement.* If placement in a public or private residential program is necessary to ensure that FAPE is provided for the child, the program, including nonmedical care and room and board, must be at no cost to the child's parents (34 C.F.R. 300.104).

- *Proper functioning of hearing aids.* Each public agency must ensure that the hearing aids worn in school by children with hearing impairments (including deafness) are functioning properly (34 C.F.R. 300.113(a)). An LEA must also ensure that the external components of surgically implanted medical devices (e.g., cochlear implants) are functioning properly (34 C.F.R. 300.113(b)(1)).

- *Extended school year (ESY) services.* These are services provided to a child with a disability (1) beyond the normal school year of the public agency, (2) in accordance with the child's IEP, (3) at no cost to the parents of the child, and (4) that meet standards set by the SEA. If ESY services are necessary to ensure FAPE, the LEA/SEA is required to provide them (34 C.F.R. 300.106).

Supplementary Aids and Services

Supplementary aids and services are those aids, services, and other supports provided in general education classes or other education-related settings so the student can be educated with nondisabled students to the maximum extent appropriate (20 U.S.C. Sec. 1401(33)). Note that the focus of these services is not on the provision of FAPE but is, instead, on making accommodations to allow education to occur in the least restrictive environment. Undoubtedly, the services that promote these separate but equally important goals overlap.

Postschool Transition Services

IDEA's findings state that "as the graduation rates for children with disabilities continue to climb, providing effective transition services to promote successful postschool employment or education is an important measure of accountability for children with disabilities" (20 U.S.C. Sec. 1400(c)(14)). Similarly, IDEA states that transition is a results-oriented process "focused on improving the academic and functional achievement of the child with a disability to facilitate the child's" movement to postschool activities including postsecondary education, vocational education, integrated employment (including supported employment), continuing and adult education, adult services, independent living, or community participation (20 U.S.C. Sec. 1402(34)).

Furthermore, transition services must be based on the child's individual needs and "take into account the child's strengths, preferences, and interests." Transition services can include "instruction, related services, community experiences, the development of employment and other postschool adult living objectives, and when appropriate, acquisition of daily living skills and a functional vocational evaluation."

IDEA (20 U.S.C. Sec. 1414(d)(1)(A)(i)(VIII)(bb)) provides that, beginning not later than the first IEP in effect when the child is 16 and annually thereafter, the child's IEP must include

- appropriate measurable postsecondary goals based upon age-appropriate transition assessments related to training, education, employment, and, where appropriate, independent living skills;
- the transition services (including courses of study) needed to assist the child in reaching those goals; and
- beginning not later than 1 year before the child reaches the age of majority under state law, a statement that the child has been informed of any rights that will transfer to the child on reaching the age of majority.

By requiring that transition services are to begin at age 16, Congress recognized that transition is a process. It also limited the scope of services; they must be needed, as determined in the context of appropriate education. Thus, any transition service that is necessary to ensure an appropriate education must be provided. Specifically, transition services (as defined in Sec. 1402(34)) include the following:

- A "coordinated set of activities" for the student. This language means that the student must have more than one transition activity and that the activities must be rationally related to each other and be able to operate in sync with each other. This set of activities must be "designed within a results-oriented process" and be focused on "improving the academic and functional achievement" in order to "facilitate ... movement from school to postschool activities," including postsecondary education, vocational education, integrated employment (including supported employment), continuing and adult education, adult services, independent living, or community participation. Note that the word *facilitate* implies the concept of *benefit*. If the transition services are not effective, in the sense of promoting movement to the specified outcomes, the services do not confer any benefit on the student. Thus, if a student's transition goals are not being met, the student likely can successfully claim a violation of the benefit test and a denial of appropriate education based on *Rowley.*

- It must be based on the student's strengths, preferences, and interests. This is an explicit affirmation that student participation in the IEP process is appropriate when the transition process begins. It also is an implicit recognition that a student's curriculum should include decision-making and choice-making skills as part of the student's progress toward independence, which is an outcome of special education.
- It must include instruction, related services, community experiences, the development of employment and other postschool adult living objectives, and, when appropriate, acquisition of daily living skills and functional vocational evaluation.
- In addition, the IEP of a student who is 16 years old or older must contain "appropriate measurable postsecondary goals based upon age-appropriate assessments related to training, education, employment, and, where appropriate, independent living skills" (20 U.S.C. Sec. 1414(d)(1(a)(VIII)(aa)). In addition, the student's IEP must include "the transition services (including the courses of study) needed to assist the child in reaching those goals."

With respect to transition issues generally, 20 U.S.C. Sec. 1436 (which provides for an IFSP), Sec. 1412(a)(9) (which addresses the transition from Part C to preschool programs), Sec. 1414(d)(1)(A)(i)(VIII) (which relates to transition planning for adolescents), and Part D (which relates to grants, contracts, and cooperative agreements awarded by the Department of Education) acknowledge that transition planning is a generic skill that is appropriate at various life stages of the student and family.

Because IDEA requires the student's transition plan to target how the student will move from school to adult activities and agencies, an LEA almost always will involve other agencies in developing the student's plan. The LEA is the sending agency and the other agencies are the receiving agencies. Although no longer required, the IEP may include a statement of the interagency responsibilities or linkages (or both) that the student needs before he or she leaves school. That is why Sec. 1414(d)(6) requires the LEA to reconvene the IEP team when other agencies do not carry out their agreement to provide transition services.

These transition provisions supply three directives for LEAs to follow (20 U.S.C. Sec. 1401(34)):

1. LEAs must use specified means to achieve the outcomes the transition provisions specify. Thus, the law sets out both the ends and the means.
2. LEAs are on notice that "acquisition of daily living skills and functional vocational evaluation" is appropriate in transition plans for some, but not all, students. Therefore, the law sets a general rule in favor of employment or other postschool adult living objectives for most students. Note that Congress put parentheses around the phrase "including supported employment," showing that it intended supported employment (work with a job coach) to be one work-related outcome, but not the only one (20 U.S.C. Sec. 1401(34)(A)). Indeed, Congress intended regular employment to be preferred over supported employment.

3. LEAs should use community-referenced, community-based, and community-delivered instruction. This ensures that the student will learn the skills in the place the student will have to use them. As a result, it acknowledges the principles of *generalization* and *durability* (students learn best and retain information when they actually must use their skills in the settings where the skills are required) and skill development in the least restrictive setting of the community.

Schools are sending agencies in that they prepare a student for the adult world and send the student off to that world, presumably prepared for it. Today, however, the receiving agencies—those to which schools send students—are much different than they were when the transition amendments were first adopted in 1990. Before the 1990 amendments, the receiving agencies too often were disability-provider agencies such as local mental health or mental retardation/developmental disability centers, independent living centers for people with physical disabilities, vocational rehabilitation agencies, group homes, or sheltered workshops.

Since the 1990 amendments, the receiving agencies include not only these traditional agencies but also programs of postsecondary education, continuing and adult education, adult services, and integrated employment. Given these expected outcomes, schools as sending agencies must include nondisability "generic" agencies in transition planning. Because schools must associate with generic as well as specialized receiving agencies, the principle of least restrictive environment (chapter 7) affords an opportunity for more integration and greater power.

The transition amendments represent a significant change in IDEA. Until they were enacted, IDEA generally was process oriented; it told the LEAs and SEAs what processes to follow to educate students with disabilities. Now IDEA is outcome oriented as well, stating explicitly that results-oriented education shall be provided through both the transition provisions and through the measurement of the student's progress and achievement in various assessments. Given that IDEA is now far more outcome/result oriented than process based, the question is this: How should educators and parents determine and prove that the student has received an appropriate education?

DETERMINATION AND EVIDENCE OF APPROPRIATENESS

Appropriateness, as we have said and as *Rowley* taught, involves both procedural compliance and substantive benefit. But what indicates that an IEP is appropriate and appropriately created and implemented?

With regard to procedural compliance, the issue is clear: an IEP is appropriate when the LEA complies with the required procedures for creating, revising, and implementing the IEP. Evidence of procedural compliance thus includes meeting minutes, parental consent, evidence of proper notice, and actual delivery of services in the manner and to the extent prescribed by the child's IEP. The ease with which evidence can be produced to demonstrate that the school has followed IDEA's process to a large extent underlies the reasoning in *Rowley*. Congress created the extensive procedural requirements to provide a means for parents and LEAs to effectively demonstrate when a child has or has not received an appropriate education.

Because IDEA now shifts the accountability emphasis from procedural compliance to substantive benefit, schools and parents must focus their efforts on identifying how to demonstrate substantive benefit or the lack thereof. The 2004 amendments provide some guidance to meeting this new evidentiary requirement by including new provisions about

- measures and outcomes,
- scientifically based interventions, and
- highly qualified instructors.

SEAs and LEAs are required to measure outcomes, use scientifically based interventions, and employ highly qualified teachers. The presumption behind these three standards is that an appropriate education will occur if each standard is met. Accordingly, advocates will examine whether the student makes progress on the assessments (or at least does not regress), whether the educators use scientifically based instruction, and whether they are highly qualified. In addition, the courts are also likely to rely on traditional means and doctrines related to determining benefit, including by considering expert testimony and giving due deference to professionals' judgment.

Evaluations and Appropriateness

As we have said, IDEA considers special education as involving a process. Like other approaches to the law, IDEA rests on the theory that fair procedures tend to produce fair results. Accordingly, IDEA ensures that sufficient information is available to parents, the LEA, and the IEP team to allow them to determine whether the student is receiving an appropriate education—namely, as in *Rowley* and the 2004 reauthorization, a real benefit, one that can be measured either by the student's scores on state and district assessments or by some other reasonably objective means.

Let's review how process and substantive benefit go hand-in-hand with each other. As we have pointed out in this chapter and in chapter 5, "Nondiscriminatory Evaluation," IDEA requires the LEA to provide a nondiscriminatory evaluation of the student and then to base the student's IEP on that evaluation.

As we also noted, the evaluation data provide evidence of the child's strengths and needs. To the extent the services outlined in the IEP relate to addressing the student's needs as evaluated, they support a conclusion that the student's IEP is appropriate and, if implemented effectively, will yield a substantive benefit for the student—namely, an appropriate education. To the extent that evaluation data are not reflected in the student's IEP, that fact supports an argument that the student's IEP is not appropriate and that, if the LEA is implementing the student's insufficient IEP, the LEA is failing to offer the substantive benefit of an appropriate education.

Both of these conclusions are the natural results of the required connection between the nondiscriminatory evaluation and development of the IEP. The content of the IEP and its implementation are the intended outcomes of the evaluation and, thus, the evaluation results provide evidence related to the substantive appropriateness of the IEP.

For example, the evaluation of a first-grade student (let's call her Eve) identifies three characteristics of her speech impairment:

1. It significantly impairs her ability to communicate effectively, participate in class, and interact with her peers. This limitation on her interaction with others aggravates the existing delay in her development of age-appropriate social skills.
2. Eve has become self-conscious about speaking, particularly with adults and people she is meeting for the first time. Her shyness limits the effectiveness of past speech/language pathology services.
3. Eve's impairment has not, however, had any effect on her participation (which includes singing) in music class. Her parents report that singing is one of her favorite activities because she isn't being asked, "What did you say?" and has received compliments on her voice.

Taking these findings, assume that the LEA offers low-intensity speech/language pathology services to Eve in a one-on-one setting. Would this offer of services be appropriate? Arguably not, for three reasons:

1. The LEA has failed to connect the intervention proposed in the IEP with the evaluations. The significance of the effect of the impairment on her school performance suggests that intensive services are required and that speech/language pathology services may not provide a significant benefit, at least not by themselves.
2. Services that remove Eve from opportunities to interact with other children may aggravate her existing social development problems.
3. Although the evaluation highlighted Eve's strength with regard to music, the IEP completely ignores that strength.

Thus, even before implementing the offered services and measuring progress, we can safely predict that these services will not provide Eve a meaningful benefit. That conclusion requires us to reach yet another conclusion: The proposed IEP is inappropriate because it does not adequately address the three findings in the evaluation.

Although there is no single way to appropriately address the findings in an evaluation, one possible approach would be to offer Eve music therapy as a related service and to integrate that service with more traditional speech/language pathology services. Furthermore, the IEP might include both efforts to increase Eve's opportunities to participate in extracurricular activities that involve music and also training for the general education teacher in how to integrate music into her assignments (for example, homework requiring Eve to sing a written song to her parents rather than to read a book). These services address all three findings in the evaluation and, building on Eve's love of music, provide increased opportunities for her to interact with peers, ways to adapt the curriculum to accommodate her impairment, and a more effective means of delivering speech and language pathology services.

Evidence-Based Interventions and Scientifically Based Research

Although the connection between a student's evaluation and proposed IEP services is an important factor in determining the appropriateness of an IEP, the IEP must do more than merely include a service to address each need identified in the evaluation. It also must, to the extent practical, provide for services that are based on peer-reviewed research (20 U.S.C. Sec. 1414(d)(1)(A)(i)(IV)). Thus, another source for assuring a substantive benefit—the student's appropriate education—is research that demonstrates the efficacy of the curriculum and methods of instruction that the LEA uses to meet the child's specific disability-related needs.

Indeed, IDEA's findings specifically recognize that special education can be made more effective by ensuring that

> all personnel who work with children with disabilities ... have the skills and knowledge necessary to improve the academic achievement and functional performance of children with disabilities, including the use of scientifically based instructional practices, to the maximum extent possible.
> (20 U.S.C. 1400(c)(5)(E))

New to IDEA in 2004, this evidence-based instruction provision suggests that IEP teams (or the experts on the team for each area) should select and administer services in a manner that reflects best practices (or at least acceptable practices) as tested through scientific studies and documented in peer-reviewed research articles. To the extent the research base justifies a specific IEP service to meet a student's needs, the LEA may argue that its selection and implementation of the service complies with the appropriate-education principle. "We followed the process in the evaluation, we used the evaluation data in the IEP, and we chose evidence-based curricula and instruction techniques," the LEA would say, "so we offered the student a genuine opportunity to learn and benefit from going to school."

By contrast, the student's parents must argue that the LEA failed to comply with the evaluation process and the student's IEP thus is flawed, and that the LEA's failure to use evidence-based instruction simply exacerbates the LEA's failure to provide an appropriate education. "If," the parent would argue, "the research does not support the use of the service to meet one of my child's particular needs, the LEA's selection and implementation of the service are inappropriate."

But what are peer-reviewed, evidence-based, or scientifically based practices? The NCLB provides some guidance here by providing a definition of scientifically based research, as follows (20 U.S.C. 6368(6)):

- Rigorous data analyses that are adequate to test the hypotheses and justify the conclusions
- Measurement or observational methods that provide reliable and valid data across evaluators, observers, multiple measurements, and studies by the same or different investigators
- Evaluation using experimental or quasi-experimental designs in which individuals, entities, programs, or activities are assigned different conditions with appropriate controls, with a preference for random-assignment experiments or other methods that contain within or across-condition controls
- Presentation of studies in sufficient detail to allow for replication or to build systematically on the findings
- Accepted by a peer-reviewed journal or approved by a panel of independent experts through a comparably rigorous, objective, and scientific review

The regulations have added a definition for "scientifically based research" that incorporates, by reference, the definition from NCLB (34 C.F.R. 300.35). It is important to note that the IEP provision in IDEA requires only "peer-reviewed" research—rather than scientifically based research—and even then, only to the "extent practical" (20 U.S.C. Sec. 1414(d)(1)(A)(i)(IV)). Although the courts have not yet interpreted the difference between peer reviewed and scientifically based, it seems likely that Congress intended (and the courts defensibly could rule) that peer review sets a lower standard than scientifically based.

But why the difference in terms? IDEA uses the term scientifically based in its findings of fact section (20 U.S.C. Sec. 1400(c)(5)(E)), but it then chose the term peer reviewed for the IEP requirements (20 U.S.C. Sec. 1414(d)(1)(A)(i)(IV)). One possible explanation lies in the nature and extent of current research in special education. Congress may have concluded that, to satisfy the many needs of students with disabilities, there was not sufficient research to support the higher standard represented by the term scientifically based. Accordingly, it may have settled on peer review as sufficiently requiring best practices without holding school districts to a standard that would be, in some situations, impossible to meet.

This approach would also explain the "to the extent practical" language. If it is not practicable to do so, in the sense that there is no or very little peer-reviewed research relevant to the student's needs (as identified in the evaluation) and program (as identified in the IEP), then the absence of evidence-based approaches is not fatal and does not tend to prove that the student is not receiving an appropriate education (a benefit). That proof of appropriateness must then come from other sources, such as the "progress toward annual goals" and "assessments progress" provisions.

Highly Qualified Personnel

It is also worth noting that IDEA (aligning with NCLB) now requires special education teachers and paraprofessionals to be highly qualified (20 U.S.C. Sec. 1401(10)). Although IDEA specifically denies a parent or student a right to sue based on the fact that any teacher or other professional involved with the student does not meet the "highly qualified" standard, that fact alone does not prevent a parent from discussing teacher qualifications at the meeting of the evaluation and IEP teams.

That discussion might take several forms:

- The parent might say: "Get me a highly qualified professional instead of one who is not qualified." That would force the LEA to comply or to assure the student's evaluation and IEP, and thus the student's appropriate education benefit, through other means.
- The evaluation and IEP teams and especially the parent are more likely to defer to the judgments of highly qualified professionals than to the judgments of professionals who are not so qualified.
- Even more significantly, a parent might be able to convince a court that it should not defer to the LEA simply because the LEA's evaluation and IEP teams did not consist of professionals who are highly qualified. Judicial deference to professional decision making is a well-established approach to adjudicating the "rights" and "wrongs" in relationships between laymen (parents) and professionals (educators). But it is hard to justify that approach when, in fact, the so-called professionals are not qualified and therefore arguably are not really professional.

Measurable Annual Goals

Even if the IEP services are based on the evaluation and peer-reviewed research and are provided by highly qualified personnel, an IEP and special education services are appropriate only if they actually provide a benefit. If a service is not working—it is not providing the student with an educational benefit—it should not be continued. But how can the parent or an LEA determine whether an IEP or specific services on an IEP are effective?

To ensure accountability for results, IDEA employs a process of goal setting and measurement of service results. Although we have already discussed IDEA's requirements related to each of these steps in this chapter, it is appropriate to put them into context and show how together they form a system of accountability for results.

Goal Setting

IDEA requires that each student's IEP include a statement of measurable annual goals, including both academic and functional goals related to the child's needs and progress in the general education curriculum (20 U.S.C. Sec. 1414(c)(1)(B)). If the child is 16 years old, is going to turn 16 during the current IEP, or is over 16, the IEP also must include appropriate "measurable postsecondary goals based upon age-appropriate transition assessments related to training, education, employment, and, where appropriate, independent living skills" (20 U.S.C. Sec. 1414(d)(1)(A)(i) (VIII)(aa)), and the transition services necessary for the child to reach those goals (20 U.S.C. Sec. 1414(d)(1)(A)(i)(VIII)(bb)). If the child will participate in NCLB accountability through use of an alternate assessment, the IEP also must include benchmarks and short-term goals (20 U.S.C. Sec. 1414(d)(1)(A)(i)(I)(cc)).

Goal setting also is related to the IDEA requirement for the IEP to contain a statement of the student's present level of performance (20 U.S.C. Sec. 1414(d)(1) (A)(i)(I)). Obviously, an LEA cannot justify goals until it has determined the student's present level of performance. Goals are objectives for the future and thus relate directly to increasing the student's current performance in each area of need identified in his or her IEP. The selected services then must be aimed at improvement of the student's abilities, with the goals serving as the predicted or desired level of improvement when compared to measures of the student's present performance.

Measuring Results

In addition to requiring the IEP team to set the goals and select services, IDEA requires the IEP team to specify how the child's progress toward meeting these annual goals will be measured and when periodic reports on the child's progress will be provided to the parents (20 U.S.C. Sec. 1414(d)(1)(A)(i)(III)). Periodic reports of the student's progress must be provided at least as often as the LEA provides reports (for example, midterm progress reports or grade cards) to the parents of children without disabilities (20 U.S.C. Sec. 1414(d)(1)(A)(i)(III)). The IEP team then must revise the IEP to address any lack of expected progress toward these annual goals and, if appropriate, in the general education curriculum (20 U.S.C. Sec. 1414(d)(4)(A)(ii)(I)).

But what is a measurable goal? The term *measurable* implies that goals must be chosen that, when met, can be reasonably proven or demonstrated. As we discussed previously, one aspect of this requirement involves using the student's present level of performance as a baseline from which to determine how much progress has been made toward each of the child's IEP goals. Without such a baseline, actual progress would be difficult to ascertain. After all, in the absence of data to show otherwise, it might reasonably be assumed that the student already had met the performance level reflected in the goal before any services were provided.

A similar difficulty arises if the IEP does not contain, or other records do not reveal, dates memorializing when a child achieved the IEP goals. A district court in Alabama summarized the problem with such goals:

> Needless to say, it would be extraordinarily difficult for meaningful programs to be fashioned prospectively . . . without reasonable records to demonstrate where he had been and what he previously had and had not been able to achieve. (*Escambia County Bd. of Educ. v. Benton*, 2005)

The term *measurable* also suggests that an objective means should be used to determine whether the student has made progress toward goals, such as by using tests, assessments, or evaluations. To be measurable suggests that results are not susceptible to subjective interpretation and would be roughly equivalent regardless of who does the measuring. Subjective means, such as assurances from LEA staff, teachers, or even parents, of a child's progress, do not seem to provide the measurable criteria required in the statute.

One potential source of objective criteria is the student's performance on state and district assessments. IDEA provides that the student's IEP must describe how the student will participate in state and district assessments (20 U.S.C. Sec. 1414(d)(1)(A)(i)(VI)(bb)). That provision clearly relates to how the student's progress is to be measured and reported—another required component of the IEP (20 U.S.C. Sec. 1414(d)(1)(A)(i)(III)). To the extent that a student's IEP goals are related to his or her progress in the general curriculum, standardized tests (designed to assess progress of students with and without disabilities in core subject learning) provide a means to identify whether IEP goals are being met—assuming that the IEP team has access to the student's individual scores on the standardized tests.

The academic literature on IEP goal development also provides some guidance. The clever acronym SMART—invented by Pam and Peter Wright—highlights the characteristics of good annual goals and how to write them (Wright & Wright, 2003). SMART stands for specific, measurable, action words, realistic and relevant, and time-limited. Thus, the IEP goals for SMART are those that

- precisely define the skills or knowledge that is to be learned (*specific*);
- provide a method for clearly determining when a goal has been reached and a skill learned (*measurable*);
- employ words that denote the action of proving the skill, such as "Eve *will read* at the fourth-grade level as measured by the Grey Oral Reading Test" (*action words*);
- reflect the student's individual needs and potential so that high, but not impossible, expectations can be set (*realistic and relevant*); and
- create expectations of continual progress and allow regular monitoring to support meaningful periodic reports of progress (*time-limited*).

Of course, SMART is only one method for implementing best practices in creating IEP goals and does not have any direct legal effect. But the extent to which the best practices are required most likely will depend upon the extent to which courts believe they represent a minimum standard of practice in the field of special education.

It also will depend upon the research base behind such methods, because, as we discussed, LEAs must utilize peer-reviewed methods to the extent practicable. In other words, if there is a consensus in the field of special education based on research that a goal must have certain characteristics (for example, specific, time-limited) to be measurable, the courts are likely to defer to that professional consensus and rule that goals without those characteristics—and IEPs that include such empty goals—are inappropriate.

APPROPRIATE EDUCATION AND CHANGES IN SEA AND LEA FUNCTIONS

Notwithstanding the progress made at federal, state, and local levels of government to comply with IDEA's appropriate education command and to overcome intergovernmental problems by adopting interagency agreements, fundamental problems remain. These problems stem from disagreements about the nature of public education for students with disabilities.

Traditional Roles of Education

Traditionally, public education has involved mass education of the masses. The purpose and techniques of public education were remarkably stable until a little more than 50 years ago. Ever since *Brown* (1954) ordered school desegregation by race, the schools have become the battleground for beginning and carrying forward substantial changes in American life: racial desegregation, extension of public services into historically private areas of family life (health and sex education, mental health services, social services, and other activities that tend to supplement or even supplant, in the eyes of some, the family's role), integration of persons with disabilities into the mainstream of life, and individualized services for those who have disabilities (not the provision of mass-produced and mass-consumed services).

This change in education—its centrality in debates about the role of government and its functioning as an agent of social change or stability—are easy to explain. Simply put, universal education is nearly as inevitable as death and taxes. Second only to the tax collector, schools cast the largest net thrown by government. Thus, schools have been asked to bear the brunt of social reform. In making schools the focal point of social reform and new government services for children with disabilities, however, policy makers have undertaken to transform the school and change its function from one of education alone to one of education plus physical health, mental health, and social services.

Can the schools carry this burden? Should they be asked to? If so, how can they be helped? If not, what agencies should be active in this area? These are the questions that thoughtful observers raise. But they are ones that the 2004 reauthorization of IDEA makes necessary and answers: IDEA and special education cover a broad range of services, because students with disabilities have a broad range of needs. So, yes, IDEA changes the traditional functions of schools as they serve students with disabilities.

New Functions of Education

Students with disabilities have a very real and defensible interest in obtaining an appropriate education and related services. The schools have an equally real and defensible interest and responsibility to satisfy those needs. In light of the present difficulties in providing related services, however, some people think it is only proper to ask whether schools alone should be required to meet every educational need of a student with a disability and, if so, how they best can carry out this responsibility and with what funds (federal, state, or local).

In this matter, the function of one agency of government (schools) is being balanced against the functions of other agencies (health, mental health, and social services) and against the interests of students with disabilities. It is increasingly clear that the decisions about governmental functions, and whether the school alone should bear the brunt of efforts to educate (in its fullest sense, by providing related services) students with disabilities, have not been addressed adequately in the context not only of students with disabilities but also of education as a whole.

In their original form (and as amended), Part C (P.L. 99–457), the Medicaid amendments (P.L. 100–350), and the Technology-Related Assistance for Individuals with Disabilities Act of 1988 (P.L. 105-394) prove this point: Schools are asked to do more nontraditional functions. Fortunately, IDEA clarifies the first/last payor issues; it does not, however, remove from the schools the ultimate responsibility for providing a free appropriate public education that addresses the student's "academic and functional performance"—the words in the definition of "individualized education program" (20 U.S.C. Sec. 1414(d)(1)(A)(i)(I)).

Regardless of whether a need can be considered educational or otherwise impacts a child's education, the LEAs must assess the child in "all areas related to the suspected disability, including, if appropriate, health, vision, hearing, social and emotional status, general intelligence, academic performance, communicative status, and motor abilities" (34 C.F.R. 300.304(c)(4)). The LEA also must use technically sound instruments to assess the child in cognitive, behavioral, physical, and developmental domains (20 U.S.C. Sec. 1414(b)(2)). Even medical services provided by licensed physicians—generally not considered valid related services under the act—are required if related to assessment of the child's needs or disability (20 U.S.C. Sec. 1401(26)).

Values and Principles

The Supreme Court's *Tatro* and *Garrett F.* decisions (concerning catheterization and nursing services) were decided correctly, and their principles are sound, both with regard to the behavior and the functions of schools and with regard to values and principles of IDEA, ADA, and Section 504—namely, inclusion and dual accommodations. The same is true of *Rowley*.

All of these cases seem to emphasize the need for integrating students into programs with their nondisabled peers. *Tatro* required catheterization and *Garrett F.* required nursing services so the students could continue to be educated at school (instead of at home). The 12-month-school-year cases indicate that the extended school year is required so students who require extended services to prevent regression can continue to receive such services. And *Rowley* made much of the fact that the student was integrated with nondisabled students and passing from grade to grade.

SUMMARY

In this chapter we emphasized the process definition of appropriate education, the outcome-/result-oriented one, and the decreasing importance of the former and the increasing importance of the latter. We described the two "I" plans (IEP and IFSP) and how, when, and by whom they are developed and what they must contain. And we described the relationship of traditional school functions to those that IDEA now sponsors.

By way of further summary, let's return to the case Case on Point, *Rowley,* and state the point of that case. In it and in the other cases we have reviewed and certainly under the 2004 amendments, an appropriate education (a) depends on the provision of special education (that is, individually tailored education, memorialized in the two "I-plans"), related services, and supplementary aids and services; and (b) consists of a benefit for each student that can, and indeed must, be measured. The purpose of the benefit standard is to comply with IDEA (per *Rowley*) and also to secure the outcomes that IDEA proclaims (see chapter 3).

But documenting benefit is more important now than ever before. That is the point of NCLB and the 2004 amendments to IDEA. Documenting benefits occurs through the standards-based assessments that state and local agencies administer and through the student's participation in them, consistent with the student's IEP. Benefit and its documentation make the schools accountable, and accountability for outcomes (which is to say for benefit) is a major theme in the principle of an appropriate education.

Another theme is at work, too, as *Rowley* and the subsequent cases and the 2004 amendments make clear. That theme relates to where the student must be educated and to the value of integration. The required content of the nondiscriminatory evaluation (chapter 5) and IEP and IFSP (this chapter) make it clear that IDEA seeks the education of each student with a disability in inclusive, nonsegregated settings. The objective is to advance integration and to prevent exclusion and segregation.

Just how far the courts will pursue these behavior-shaping and function-changing principles and values remains to be seen. The decisive tests in the past have been in *Tatro, Garrett F.,* and *Detsel,* involving related services for technology-supported students, the mental health service cases, and *Timothy W. v. Rochester,* involving the issue of educability (see chapter 4). These cases pushed to, and arguably beyond, the then-existing outer limits of schools' capacities and functions, and challenged traditional concepts about the fundamental roles of schools and the wisdom of requiring LEAs to do much for so few.

In these cases and in others where tradition, capacity, and roles were challenged so frontally, some courts decided that the integration principle should yield to practical considerations of cost, time, and professionalism, especially because the students could receive more effective individualized services in other service systems. The *Garrett F.* decision, however, seems to have rejected the cost concerns and to have held IDEA's goals of inclusion to be of much greater importance.

Apparently, the struggle for integration has gained new ground, and courts undoubtedly will go further to promote that goal than they have in the past. Certainly, the 2004 amendments to IDEA strengthen the students' claims for inclusion in the general education programs (integration) and for accountability for educationally related outcomes (where the related services cases give a broad definition to "educationally related" and cover not only academic but other domains of a student's development as well).

Nevertheless, there will continue to be cases of students for whom inclusion is impracticable. In those cases, the student arguably would not be denied an appropriate education (because health, psychiatric, and educational services still would be provided by other agencies) but would receive them in a less integrated setting (e.g., in an interim alternative educational setting or in a general or psychiatric hospital). Indeed, that result—exclusion from school-based services and inclusion in other service providers' systems for receipt of special education and related services—is a major issue of IDEA's requirements for student placement into the least restrictive environment (LRE). Therefore, it is timely to consider the LRE principle next, in chapter 7.

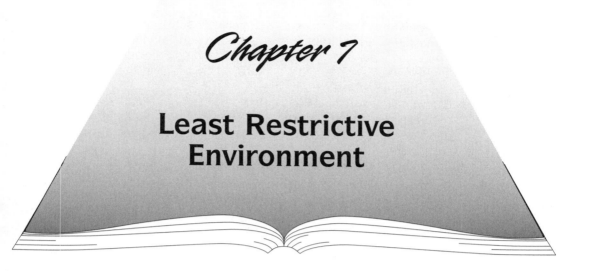

Chapter 7

Least Restrictive Environment

Case on Point: *Sacramento City School District v. Rachel H.*
14 F.3d 1398 (9th Cir. 1994)

Inevitably, parents and professionals will have their conflicts, often about inclusion, or, in IDEA's terms, the "least restrictive environment" for a student. What do these words mean? "Environment" has to be understood in light of the appropriate-education principle (chapter 6). But what does "restrictive" mean, and when is restriction more or less, or most or least restrictive?

The parents of Rachel Holland, a primary school student with mental retardation, tested the meaning of these words when they requested that the Sacramento LEA place their daughter full time into a regular classroom. The LEA refused but offered to have Rachel attend a special education class for academic subjects and a regular class for nonacademic activities such as art, music, lunch, and recess. Considering this placement inappropriate, the Hollands enrolled Rachel in the Shalom School, a private school where she attended school in a regular education classroom. The Hollands then initiated due process proceedings against the Sacramento City School District, maintaining that Rachel best learned social and academic skills in a regular classroom and would not benefit from being in a special education class. To determine whether a regular classroom placement did or did not meet the "least restrictive environment" rule, a federal court of appeals adopted four equally weighted criteria, as follows:

- *Educational benefit*. Rachel could receive a substantial benefit and all of her IEP goals could be met in a regular education classroom.
- *Noneducational benefit*. Rachel's social and communication skills and her self-confidence would be improved by being in the regular class with students without disabilities.
- *Effect on others*. Rachel was neither disruptive nor required so much of the instructor's time that the educational opportunities of other students would be affected by her placement in the general education curriculum.
- *Cost*. Rachel required only a part-time aide, but the district had "not offered any persuasive or credible evidence to support its claim that educating Rachel in a regular classroom with appropriate services would be significantly more expensive than educating her in the District's proposed setting."

After weighing these criteria, the court held that the least restrictive environment for Rachel was a full-time regular education classroom with services and supports. Do these four criteria survive in IDEA's 2004 reauthorization? The Hollands (whose last name is often used to cite this case) probably would be pleased to know that they do.

STATEMENT OF PRINCIPLE: INCLUSION AND THE LRE

No requirement of the right-to-education movement—both before Congress enacted P.L. 94-142 in 1975 and after—was as likely at the outset to generate such controversy as the requirement that students with disabilities be educated in the least restrictive environment (LRE). Originally called "mainstreaming," this requirement had the potential for encountering the same levels of opposition, misunderstanding, and ill will as the earlier requirements for racial desegregation of the public schools. But this requirement also had the potential for significantly improving the education of students with disabilities, redressing some of the wrongs that schools had imposed on them and their families, and contributing to the education of all pupils, the training of all educators, and enlightenment of the public at large. Why the controversy? And how does IDEA respond to it through the 2004 reauthorization?

LRE and the Equality of Integration

The LRE provisions in IDEA stand as the disability community's version of *Brown v. Board of Education*. Although *Brown* was a judicial decision rather than a legislative mandate, the LRE provision in IDEA is similar to *Brown* in that it ended the prior systematic segregation of students. In *Brown* the segregation involved Blacks; in IDEA the segregation involved children with disabilities.

In prohibiting unjustified segregation of children with disabilities in schools, the LRE mandate extends the zero reject principle, which rests on the legal theory of equal protection under the Fourteenth Amendment (see chapter 4). The LRE principle does so by emphatically denying that mere access to schools is legally sufficient.

The LRE principle owes a lot to the civil rights movement generally, and to *Brown* specifically. With respect to racial discrimination, the era of segregation and "separate but equal" education immediately followed an era of widespread exclusion of non-Whites from public education with their White peers or even from schooling generally. Before ratification of the Fourteenth Amendment, the education of Blacks was actually illegal in some states (*Brown*). But even after Blacks succeeded in securing the equal right to a public education, they still had to fight to ensure that they actually were provided equal educational opportunities—a fight that culminated in *Brown* (see chapter 4) and that continues even in 2006.

Congress learned from these past battles over educational equality and, recognizing the importance of ensuring that the access guaranteed by the Constitution and the zero reject principle was genuine, enacted the LRE provisions to prevent a similar segregation from undermining IDEA's equal opportunity goals. The LRE provisions thus ensure that the barriers to access addressed by the zero reject provisions—guaranteeing entry into the public school system—are not replaced by barriers to *equal* access. To be equal, access must involve participation in the settings, programs, and curricula alongside children without disabilities. Otherwise, "equal" opportunity still means "less than equal" opportunity. Students with disabilities will have access to the school but not on the same terms or for the same outcomes as for students without disabilities, and accordingly their opportunities to learn will be less than equal. As the Court stated in *Brown,* "Separate educational facilities are inherently unequal" and deprive students of "the benefits they would receive in a(n) ... integrated school system" (*Brown*, p. 484). So, in IDEA, separate educational facilities and curricula are inherently unequal when applied across the board and without regard to individualized decision making for students with disabilities. The matter of individualized decision making is important and justifies a few more comments (see chapter 4 and our discussion of equality in the section on the effects of the zero reject principle).

LRE as an Educational Approach

In extending the constitutional principle of integration to students with disabilities, Congress had to come to terms with an important difference between racial integration and disability integration. That difference lies in this fact (which we discussed in chapter 4): Disability is a difference that makes a difference. Unlike race or ethnicity, the presence of a disability unarguably has a direct effect on the education of students with disabilities. Therefore, those opposed to integrating students with and without disabilities have argued that it would be harmful, useless, or even cruel to put children with disabilities in schools with children who do not have disabilities. Although this argument may appeal to some more paternalistic instincts, Congress has concluded that, as a general rule, the research justifies a finding that the opposite is true. As the findings of IDEA make clear,

> almost 30 years of research and experience has demonstrated that the education of children with disabilities can be made more effective by ... having high expectations for such children and ensuring their access to the general education curriculum in the regular classroom, to the maximum extent possible. (20 U.S.C. Sec. 1400(c)(5))

The LRE principle is inexorably linked with the principle of individualized and appropriate services, both in practice and in the law. Appropriateness—that is, a benefit to the student (Congress uses the language "education ... can be made more effective") —is the purpose and limiting factor in the application of the LRE principle.

Let's consider LRE's purpose. IDEA's requirement to maximize inclusion and participation of students with disabilities is based on the academic and social benefits that inclusion brings. Inclusion is an outcome-focused approach that questions the ability of segregated settings to prepare students with disabilities, living in a non-segregated world, to achieve equal opportunity, full participation, economic self-sufficiency, and independent living (the four IDEA outcomes stated as the nation's disability policy goals (20 U.S.C. Secs. 1400(d)(1)–(4)). If students with disabilities are not integrated into classrooms and childhood activities to the maximum extent appropriate for each of them (that is, individualized decision making about placement for each student), how will they learn the skills necessary for them to integrate successfully into the workplace and community? As a general rule, they will not.

Congress's findings of fact reflect a judgment (broadly stated) that segregated settings historically have supported isolation from "normal" children, fostered low expectations for achievement in integrated settings, and promoted paternalistic attitudes and approaches to the education of students with disabilities—all of which, in turn, have impeded development of social skills, taught and excused failure (even failure to try), and institutionalized dependence. The LRE requirement addresses these issues by recognizing the benefits that children with disabilities receive from associating with their peers without disabilities and from being held to high expectations in order to achieve the four IDEA outcomes in real-world settings. The purpose of LRE is to include and thereby benefit the student, and its limitation is that, if the inclusion does not yield a benefit, it is not required.

Now let's consider LRE as a limiting rule. Inclusion is not a "silver bullet," and full inclusion is not appropriate for all students with disabilities. As we noted before, appropriateness is also the factor that limits inclusion. The principle of individualized and appropriate education requires the LEA to examine the specific needs of each student with a disability and, for some, be obliged to determine that full inclusion is simply unjustifiable because no level of modification or accommodation will allow them to benefit in a regular education environment.

That is why IDEA allows a continuum of services, including a resource room or other supplementary services in a segregated setting as may be necessary, either temporarily or throughout some students' academic careers, to allow them to receive an educational benefit (20 U.S.C. Sec. 1402(26)). That is also why the LRE principle does not require full inclusion for all students. It simply requires *maximizing* inclusion to the extent appropriate for the individual student.

Fallacies of Mainstreaming and Benefits of Inclusion

Neither the LRE requirements nor the research on the benefits of inclusion for students with disabilities have been completely successful in preventing several eras of segregation from occurring. Originally described as "mainstreaming," the principle of the least restrictive environment was, at first, misunderstood by many to be merely a flip-side of zero reject and to demand only access to general education classrooms. By adopting the term *inclusion* in response to this access approach to the LRE principle, individuals with disabilities, their families, and advocates clarified that elbow-to-elbow mainstreaming did not provide the arm-in-arm inclusion envisioned in the least restrictive principle. The LRE principle supports students with disabilities both being included in, and as part of, general education, not merely in general education classrooms. Note the distinction: General education involves more than just the classrooms. It involves the extracurricular and other school activities, too.

The misrepresentation of the LRE principle as limited to access alone fails to encompass, or even to consider, the broader implications of the right of individuals with disabilities to associate and participate in education and other activities with those who do not have disabilities. Inclusion is not only about academics; it is also about acceptance. As the Court found in *Brown*, there is a stigma (a socially created negative connotation) to segregation that attaches to persons in the societally defined "lesser" program and that undermines their acceptance and opportunities as individuals everywhere they go, live, learn, work, or play. Stigma is the root from which discrimination grows, and the LRE principle provides support for the only truly effective method of addressing stigma for persons with disabilities: familiarity.

If disability is to be regarded as a "natural part of the human experience," as the Americans with Disabilities Act explicitly proclaims and as IDEA echoes, schools could not continue to educate students with disabilities in trailers behind the school or otherwise provide them services in isolation from their peers without disabilities. To do so would be to continue to support the ignorance and perceptions of pity and fear of disability that fuel discriminatory attitudes and activities.

All of this becomes clear if we analyze the LRE requirement along four dimensions: the constitutional basis (foundations) for the requirement, the requirements of IDEA and other statutes, the nature of the LRE principle as a rebuttable presumption in IEP decision making, and the public policy values that the LRE principle seeks to achieve.

CONSTITUTIONAL FOUNDATIONS

The LRE education of students with disabilities originates in the constitutionally based doctrine called "the least restrictive alternative." This doctrine states that even if the legislative purpose of a government action is legitimate (e.g., promoting public health, regulating commerce, or providing education), the purpose may not be pursued by means that broadly stifle personal liberties if it can be achieved by less oppressive or restrictive means. Thus, legislative and administrative action must take the form of the least drastic means for achieving a valid governmental purpose.

In Chambers's (1972) memorable metaphor, the LRE doctrine forbids a state from using a bazooka to kill a fly on a person's back if a fly swatter would do as well. LRE, then, is a constitutional principle that accommodates individual and state interests to each other. It enables government to act but does not permit it to take action that intrudes unjustifiably into a person's liberty.

The LRE principle generally has been applied in areas affecting state regulations of interstate commerce and personal liberties. The LRE doctrine also has been applied in cases involving persons with disabilities in public institutions. A long line of cases addresses this issue. In one notable case, *Wyatt v. Stickney* (1972), a federal court stated that residents of Partlow State School and Hospital, an Alabama state institution for persons with developmental disabilities, have a right to the least restrictive conditions necessary to achieve the purpose of habilitation. This phraseology is significant because it highlights the point that the primary purpose of commitment is treatment; elimination of infringement on rights (in this case, deprivation of liberty) is secondary.

In legal terminology, this means that the LRE doctrine is a rebuttable presumption. That is to say, when it is not possible to grant liberty and at the same time provide effective treatment, the doctrine allows the state to deprive the person of his or her liberty but only to the extent necessary to provide the treatment. Members of an IEP team arguing for a more restrictive setting must overcome this presumption in favor of liberty (that is, the student's inclusion in the general curriculum) by demonstrating that a student's segregation (exclusion from the general education curriculum) is a necessary means for achieving an appropriate education. Treatment (intervention and education) is the trade-off for the loss of liberty. The right to placement in a general education environment is not an absolute right but is secondary to the primary purpose of an appropriate public education.

It is important here to note that when we refer to the LRE as creating a rebuttable presumption, we are not talking about the burden of proof in due process hearings or court. As we discuss in chapter 8, the burden of proof in a due process hearing or court is on the party who brings the complaint (plaintiff or appellant). The presumption created by the LRE provisions applies to IEP team decision making and the creation or modification of the IEP. If parents challenge LEA action—the offered IEP—as violating the LRE requirement, they have the burden of demonstrating that a more inclusive or more atypical placement or program would benefit their child.

LRE also is related to three other important constitutional principles: procedural due process, substantive due process, and equal protection.

1. *Procedural due process* (chapter 8) requires that a state must grant residents access to procedures that allow them to challenge a government action before the government may infringe adversely upon their individual rights. The state must prove that the proposed action is warranted, and the individual is given the opportunity to point out less restrictive or less drastic means of accomplishing the state's goal. As we point out in chapter 8, IDEA itself guarantees a hearing at which the student's parents or the LEA can try to show why the rebuttable presumption against placement in a special education program should be overcome, or they may challenge a proposed placement as being too restrictive.

2. *Substantive due process* places an outer limit on what a state may do, independent of the level of procedural protections provided. It protects certain individual rights from government intrusion and requires that the government, when intruding on a person's rights, must use the least intrusive means to accomplish its goals. LRE is related to substantive due process in that it prohibits the state from using more restrictive means than are necessary to accomplish its purpose. LRE, then, acts as an outer limit on permissible government action. In special education, LRE and substantive due process regard unwarranted, inappropriate special education classification and placement as too restrictive.

3. *Equal protection*, the third and last principle, requires that a state deal with similarly situated individuals in an evenhanded manner. The equal protection doctrine places the burden of proof on the state to show a compelling, important, or rational reason for its unequal treatment of similarly situated individuals. The level of required justification depends in part on the nature of the rights being limited. The person who alleges a violation of equal protection must prove that the state's conduct is not rationally related to a legitimate government purpose. That is why, under IDEA, the IEP team must justify a student's exclusion from the general curriculum by explaining the extent, if any, to which the student will not participate with nondisabled students in the regular class and other components of the general curriculum (20 U.S.C. Sec. 1414(d)(1)(A)(i)(V)).

As we pointed out in chapter 4 and again at the beginning of this chapter, equal protection was the basis for the right-to-education cases that challenged exclusion of students with disabilities from public schools in the early 1970s. The courts' attitude toward educational segregation can be summarized in the following comment from *PARC v. Commonwealth* (1972) (see chapter 4 for our discussion of that case):

> (A)mong the alternative programs of education and training required by statute to be available, placement in a regular public school class is preferable to placement in ... any other type of education and training.

In summary, the LRE doctrine is a constitutionally derived way of balancing the values surrounding provision of an appropriate education (the student's right to and need for an appropriate education) with the values associated with the individual's right to associate with nondisabled peers. It is supported by, and implemented through, the constitutional principles of procedural due process, substantive due process, and equal protection. As we will discuss next, LRE has been a powerful doctrine for accommodating legitimate state interests (educating all students appropriately, not just those with disabilities) and individual interests (the interests of all students in receiving an appropriate education in settings that promote association between students with and students without disabilities).

INDIVIDUALS WITH DISABILITIES EDUCATION ACT

It is not surprising that many of Congress's findings of fact in IDEA reflect the constitutional principle of LRE and are identical to the conclusions of the courts in pre-IDEA cases and the reasons those courts required students with disabilities to be placed in the least restrictive school environments. In 1975, Congress found as a matter of fact (when it enacted P.L. 94-142, the law that is now IDEA) that

- students with disabilities had been educated inappropriately (20 U.S.C. Sec. 1400(c)(2)(B)(1997));
- students with disabilities had been denied the opportunity "to go through the educational process with their peers" (20 U.S.C. Sec. 1400(c)(2)(C)(1997));
- students had been having unsuccessful educational experiences because their disabilities had been undetected (20 U.S.C. Sec. 1400(c)(2)(D)(1997)); and
- adequate services to students with disabilities within the schools had been lacking (20 U.S.C. Sec. 1400(c)(2)(E)(1997)).

Those findings of fact were the foundation for the 1975 law. In 2004, they remain a basis for IDEA, but they are not the only ones. Indeed, the new congressional findings of fact go much further than the old ones in propelling students with disabilities into the center of American life; the pro-inclusion basis of IDEA centers on these findings, making them important to recite.

Findings Supporting Inclusion in IDEA 2004

- One of the purposes of IDEA is to improve students' educational results so they can participate fully in American life (20 U.S.C. Sec. 1400(c)(1)). The goal of full participation is linked to the principle of the least restrictive environment because education in the LRE is a form of full participation in the life of the school and a technique for full participation in other domains of life.

- A technique for improving educational results for students with disabilities is to ensure their access to the general curriculum to the maximum extent possible (20 U.S.C. Sec. 1400(c)(5)(A)).
- Special education no longer should be a place to which students are sent but, instead, a service for the students, one requiring the coordination of educational and other services (20 U.S.C. Sec. 1400(c)(5) (C)).
- Special education, related services, and other (supplementary) aids and services should be provided to students in the general classroom, whenever appropriate (20 U.S.C. Sec. 1400(c)(5)(D)).
- Professionals should be able to provide services that assure the outcomes of productivity and independence (20 U.S.C. Sec. 1400(c)(5) (E)), and the purpose of IDEA is in fact to ensure that the students' education will prepare them for employment and independent living (20 U.S.C. Sec. 1400(d)(1)(A)).

The findings and purposes of IDEA apply to both Part B and Part C of IDEA and demonstrate the intention of each to promote the concepts of integration and normalization—inclusion of children with disabilities in typical settings and typical activities in which children without disabilities participate. But Part B and Part C use different requirements and procedures to support integration and normalization.

PART B REQUIREMENTS

Once an LEA determines that a student is eligible for special education and related services, the LEA must build the connections between the evaluation results and the child's opportunity to benefit from access to the general education classroom and the general education curriculum. Because the majority of students with disabilities are capable of participating in the general curriculum to varying degrees and with some adaptations and modifications (Turnbull, Turnbull, & Wehmeyer, 2006), the LEA must ensure that the student's special education, related services, and supplementary aids and services are additions to the general curriculum, not separate from it. Special education is, after all, a service, not a place to which students are sent (20 U.S.C. Sec. 1400(c)(5)(C)). Furthermore, if services are intended to promote postsecondary-school independence and productivity, students must be accepted into and learn to work with others in typical settings, and their development of knowledge and skills—their progress in the general education curriculum—must be recognized as necessary components of an appropriate education.

For these reasons, the focus of IDEA is on the accommodations and adjustments necessary for the students to have access to general education and on the related services and supplementary aids and services that are necessary for them to participate appropriately and to benefit from specific areas of the general curriculum (academic, extracurricular, and other nonacademic activities) (20 U.S.C. Sec. 1414 (d)(1)(A)(i)(IV)).

As the following discussion points out, Part B carries out this congressional intent by connecting a large number of discrete provisions to the general curriculum. It is fair to say—and to applaud the fact—that Congress has put a great deal of strength behind the LRE principle. No longer is there room for debate about the wisdom of the principle; there is room only for determining how to carry it out in the case of each student.

General Rule

Given the findings about the deleterious effects of segregation, the benefits of integration, and the fact that special education is a service, not a place, and given also that LRE rests on a constitutional foundation, Congress properly requires SEAs (20 U.S.C. Sec. 1412(a)(5)) and LEAs (20 U.S.C. Sec. 1413(a)(1)) to follow a policy of least restrictive placement. They must develop procedures to assure that, to the maximum extent appropriate for each student, students (ages 3 through 21) with disabilities—including those educated in public agencies, private institutions, or other facilities—will be educated with students who are not disabled (34 C.F.R. 300.114(a) and 300.116(a)(2)).

IDEA's emphasis on maximizing participation alongside students without disabilities stands in sharp contrast to the individualized, but low, threshold for academic benefit (the *Rowley* and now-IDEA standard; see chapter 6). If the student can be provided with additional opportunities to be educated in integrated learning environments, the student has a right to that opportunity. Although the LEA does not have to maximize the student's opportunity to learn and benefit from a curriculum, it must maximize a student's inclusion as long as the student can receive some benefit from it (as the *Holland* case pointed out). Thus, an appropriate education is a lower threshold than integration to the maximum extent appropriate for a given student.

Further, special classes, separate schooling, or other removal of students with disabilities from the general education environment may occur only when the nature or severity of a student's disability is such that education in general classes with the use of supplementary aids and services cannot be achieved satisfactorily for that student (20 U.S.C. Sec. 1412(a)(5)(A) and 34 C.F.R. 300.114(a)(2)). Note that the word "only" qualifies the provision about removing a student from the general education environment. Accordingly, a placement decision must focus most on the severity of the student's disability (and less on the type of disability) and thus is linked inexorably to the concept of student-centered appropriate education, not system-centered, convenience-based placements. Placements must be made with consideration of the student's needs as identified in the nondiscriminatory evaluation and the services identified in the student's IEP, not on what is administratively or academically more convenient for the LEA.

Inclusion: the Mix-and-Match Approach

As we noted, IDEA defines the term *general curriculum* as consisting of three components, so it accordingly requires integration/inclusion in each of the three:

1. The general (academic) curriculum
2. Extracurricular activities (school-sponsored clubs and sports)
3. Other nonacademic activities (such as recess, mealtimes, transportation, dances, and the like) (20 U.S.C. Sec. 1414(d)(1)(A)(i)(IV))

Thus, a student's IEP must include an explanation of the extent, if any, to which the student will not participate (with students who do not have disabilities) in the general class and in extracurricular and other nonacademic activities (20 U.S.C. Sec. 1414(d)(1)(A)(i)(V)).

The word "only" and the phrase "extent, if any" are highly significant provisions. Singly and jointly, they put the burden on the IEP team to justify why a student's program and placement will not be within each of these three components of the general education environment. As much as any other provision of IDEA, these two provisions make it clear that IDEA creates a presumption in favor of inclusion. There is no other explanation for requiring the IEP team to justify any separation from the general education environment.

These two provisions are significant for yet another reason. Singly and jointly, they say that the IEP team must explain "the extent, if any," to which the student will be separated from the general education environment. By requiring the LEA to justify the extent of separation, this provision allows for partial inclusion and partial separation from the general education environment. No longer is LRE an either–or proposition. Partial inclusion is contemplated, and indeed preferred, if total inclusion is not appropriate. The word "only" fortifies this conclusion.

Also, by listing the three components of the general education environment, IDEA instructs an IEP team to consider each of them separately and to consider and then justify the extent to which a student must be removed from each to secure an appropriate education. So IDEA now codifies a mix-and-match approach: The IEP team must include the student into each of the three components as is appropriate (beneficial to the student), given the match between his or her needs and the capacity of the LEA to respond to them in each component. The student is "mixed" into the general environment and "matched" to its three components.

Finally, IDEA (Secs. 1414(d)(1)(A)(i)(IV) and (V)) clarifies that students with disabilities must be given a chance to participate in nonacademic and extracurricular services and activities (34 C.F.R. 300.117 and 300.107) as well as academic ones. They are to have access to meals, recess periods, counseling services, athletics, transportation, health services, recreational activities, special-interest groups, clubs, referrals to agencies providing assistance to those with disabilities, and employment of students by the school or other employers. Further, in giving personal, academic, or vocational counseling and placement services to students with disabilities, a school may not discriminate because of disability and must make sure that those students are not counseled toward more restrictive career objectives than nondisabled students who have similar interests and abilities.

Figure 7.1 is a matrix that guides the members of a student's nondiscriminatory evaluation team and the members of the student's IEP team in implementing IDEA's mix-and-match provisions. Note that the matrix consists of two inclusion possibilities (on the horizontal axis): full inclusion or partial inclusion. The teams must prefer the full over the partial, consistent with IDEA's "only" and "if any" provisions. If they determine that full participation is not appropriate, even with related services and supplementary aids and services, they may consider partial. And, of course, they do that in each of the several domains of the general curriculum—academic, extracurricular, and other school activities.

Note that the matrix consists of three domains of the general curriculum as IDEA defines it (20 U.S.C. Sec. 1414(d)(1)(A)(i)(IV)) and that these are on the vertical axis: the academic curriculum, the extracurricular activities, and the other school activities. Accordingly, the teams must determine just how full or partial the student's participation will be in each of these three domains.

Finally, bear in mind that the matrix is useful for the IEP team, but the IEP team's decisions will have to rest on the data from the student's nondiscriminatory

Degree of Participation

Three Domains of General Curriculum		Full	Partial
	Academic Programs		
	Extracurricular Programs		
	Other School Activities		

FIGURE 7.1
The Mix-and-Match Matrix

evaluation. Thus, members of the evaluation team must, themselves, evaluate the student with respect to the student's strengths (that is, present abilities to be included fully or partially in each of the three domains) and the student's needs (that is, present needs for an appropriate education with related services and supplementary aids and services) to be included fully or partially in each of these three domains with related services and supplementary aids and services. As we have said many times, the nondiscriminatory evaluation is the basis for the IEP, so the evaluation team must evaluate the student in such as way as to provide evidence that the IEP team will rely on to implement the mix-and-match approach. Where an IEP team does not have evidence from the student's evaluation on which to make a decision about full or partial inclusion in each of the three domains of the general curriculum, it must prefer more integration over less, and it probably should (and most certainly is entitled to) ask for more evaluations to produce more evidence on which to make a placement fully or partially in those three domains.

Other LRE Considerations

The mix-and-match approach is the core of the LRE mandate, but the least restrictive environment principle is not limited to issues of place, or even participation with children who do not have disabilities. The LRE principle includes several other factors related to where, with whom, and what children with disabilities are taught.

Setting and General Curriculum

You might be inclined to think of LRE as related solely to the placement of students with disabilities and their opportunities to interact with children who do not have disabilities, that is, to the social aspects of integration and the places where that occurs. But IDEA is not solely about location or even the right to associate. It is about education. Thus, IDEA's mandate entitling students with disabilities to receive the same educational opportunities as children without disabilities means providing them the opportunity to learn the same things that students without disabilities are taught.

As we pointed out earlier in this chapter, Congress (in the 2004 reauthorization) found as a matter of fact that 30 years of research have shown that the education of children with disabilities can be made better by "ensuring their access to the general education curriculum in the regular classroom, to the maximum extent possible." In other words, children with disabilities must, to the maximum extent appropriate, be provided opportunities to progress in the subjects and acquire the knowledge and skills included in the curriculum for students without disabilities. IDEA makes this requirement clear at every stage.

- Nondiscriminatory evaluations must provide "information related to enabling the child to be involved in and progress in the general education curriculum, or, for preschool children, to participate in appropriate activities" (20 U.S.C. Sec. 1414(b)(2)(A)(ii)) (see also chapter 5).

- Reevaluations must identify any "additions or modifications to the special education and related services needed to enable the child to meet the measurable annual goals set out in the child's individualized education program and to participate, as appropriate, in the general education curriculum" (20 U.S.C. Sec. 1414(c)(1)(B)(iv)) (see also chapter 5).
- Each student's IEP must include, as part of the statement of the student's present levels of performance, "how the child's disability affects the child's involvement and progress in the general education curriculum" (20 U.S.C. Sec. 1414(d)(1)(A)(i)(I)(aa)) (see also chapter 6).
- IEPs also must include goals related to services that enable the child to be involved in and make progress in the general education curriculum (20 U.S.C. Sec. 1414(d)(1)(A)(i)(II)).
- IEPs must identify special education and related services that will be provided to allow the child to be involved in, and make progress in, the general education curriculum (20 U.S.C. Sec. 1414(d)(1)(A)(i)(II)(aa)).
- IEPs must be revised, at least annually, to address "any lack of expected progress toward the annual goals, and in the general education curriculum" (20 U.S.C. Sec. 1414(d)(4)(A)(ii)(I)).

Appropriateness and Supplementary Aids and Services

The requirement for children with disabilities to participate in the general education curriculum responds to the now-outdated but still unfortunately widespread and mistaken interpretation of the LRE as mainstreaming. Mainstreaming focused solely on placing children with disabilities into general education classrooms on an "as is" basis—that is, taking the general classrooms as they were at the time and simply placing students with disabilities into them without doing anything more for those students. (When we discuss the court cases that have interpreted the LRE provision, we will point out how the "take as is" approach was typical of the earliest cases and how it no longer is the preferred interpretation.)

Because mainstreaming also supported the perception of special education as a location rather than individualized education services, it often resulted in placing children in general education classrooms without adequate support to enable them to succeed there. Their subsequent failure justified a condemnation of the LRE principle. This outdated approach is flawed in three ways:

1. IDEA does not envision this limited version of access to general education. The purpose of the LRE, after all, is to extend the benefits of participation in general education to students with disabilities. IDEA therefore requires that separate services be provided "only when the nature or severity of the disability of a child is such that education in regular classes with the use of supplementary aids and services cannot be achieved satisfactorily" (20 U.S.C. Sec. 1412(a)(5)). So the appropriateness of a placement within general education classrooms or participation in the general curriculum is limited under IDEA

solely by the ability of the student to receive a benefit but only after consideration or provision of supplementary aids and services.

2. Rather than adopting the "as is" approach of mainstreaming, IDEA requires the nondiscriminatory evaluation and IEP teams to identify and provide the supplementary aids and services that will maximize meaningful access to the general education classroom and curriculum. The requirement for supplementary aids and services includes the "use of technology, including technology with universal design principles and assistive technology devices, to maximize accessibility to the general education curriculum for children with disabilities." If an IEP team fails to consider such aids and services or determines placement without regard to the possibilities that such supplementary supports may provide, the team will have failed in its duty to provide special education in the least restrictive environment.

3. Congress has found that students with disabilities can be more appropriately educated if they are included in the general curriculum than if they are not (20 U.S.C. Secs. 1401(c)(5)(A), (C), and (D)).

Continuum of Alternate Placements

In furtherance of the LRE mandate, particularly the mix-and-match approach, IDEA also requires that each LEA provide a continuum of possible placements, including instruction in general classes, special classes, special schools, home instruction, and instruction in hospitals and institutions (20 U.S.C. Sec. 1412(a)(5) and 34 C.F.R. 300.115).

The statute and the regulations constitute a policy judgment favoring a continuum of services in which each placement represents increasing degrees of separation from the general education curriculum. The concept of a "continuum of services" is, in many respects, an escape clause. It allows a student to escape the hard-and-fast interpretation of LRE that would place the student in general classrooms, general extracurricular activities, and general other nonacademic activities—all without regard to the student's unique needs for appropriate (that is, beneficial) special education and related services. Thus, the LRE provisions create a presumption in favor of inclusion, but the continuum of services and the "if any" language permit the presumption to be rebutted (set aside in favor of a less inclusive but appropriate program and placement).

How does an LEA go about rebutting the presumption? First, it reviews a student's placement on at least an annual basis and reviews and revises the student's IEP accordingly (change placement or services or both, as warranted to provide a benefit, still adhering to the mix-and-match approach).

Second, the IEP team, in selecting the least restrictive environment, must take into account any potentially harmful effect on the student or on the quality of services received (34 C.F.R. 300.116(d)), consistent with the *Holland* decision. This is a focus on the student's needs for an appropriate education. When those needs cannot be met in a general education program, the student's placement there will be inappropriate and restrictive of his or her rights to an appropriate education.

Third, if the student disrupts the education of nondisabled students in the general classroom to the extent that their education is significantly impaired, the student's needs cannot be met in that classroom and placement there is inappropriate, as the court made clear in *Holland*. (Recall that this also is the approach used in expulsion cases and those involving students with AIDS, as we pointed out in chapter 4.) These considerations, related to the student's needs and the needs of other students, figure prominently in judicial decisions regarding the LRE.

Thus, each LEA must provide the complete continuum of settings (34 C.F.R. 300.115) so children whose education cannot be achieved successfully in the general education classroom are provided educational opportunities in settings where they can succeed while still being included in general education settings, activities, and curriculum to the maximum extent appropriate.

Charter schools are public schools and are explicitly covered under the act (34 C.F.R. 300.209), so they, too, must provide the entire continuum of placements. Charter schools formed as a new educational option within an existing LEA do not have to meet the continuum requirement as long as all of the placements on the continuum are made available within their LEA (34 C.F.R. 300.209(b)).

Neighborhood Schools and Age-Appropriate Placements

Two other factors in the calculation of the LRE for each student appear in the regulations. First, the regulations provide that the child's placement is to be "as close as possible to the child's home" (34 C.F.R. 300.116(b)(3)). Unless the child's IEP requires some other arrangement, "the child is (to be) educated in the school that he or she would attend if nondisabled" (34 C.F.R. 300.116(c)). In other words, the IEP team should generally not consider placement outside the neighborhood school unless some aspect of the IEP indicates a need to consider distant placements.

The neighborhood school provision works as a stopgap measure to prevent students with disabilities from being bused out of their neighborhood schools. At the same time, it recognizes that not every school will have the capacity to meet the needs of all students. It also reflects the fact that it is the duty of the LEA, rather than each school, to provide the continuum of placement options.

It seems, then, that the neighborhood school preference may be overcome only in cases in which the student cannot receive a benefit in the regular education classroom or in the other placement options provided at his or her neighborhood school, even after the provision of supplementary aids and services. Like the LRE principle generally, the neighborhood school provision creates a presumption: Given two otherwise equally inclusive programs, the one closest to the child's home is presumed to be correct.

The second factor involves age-appropriate classrooms. The regulations provide that children with disabilities may not be removed from age-appropriate regular education classrooms unless they cannot benefit from those placements. But what is age appropriate? Does it refer to chronological age or to developmental level? The regulation refers to classrooms attended by children without disabilities of the same chronological age as the student with a disability (34 C.F.R. 300.116(e)).

This is another gap-closing provision addressing the now-rejected argument that inclusion is achieved when a child is placed with children of the same developmental age, the age level at which they are performing academically (e.g., third-grade reading level for a student who is chronologically at sixth-grade level), rather than chronological or actual age. The distinction is an important one. If the LRE provision could be read to require placement with developmental peers, children with disabilities would be forced into classrooms with children much younger than they are, and many of the benefits of inclusion (peer modeling, reduction of stigma, friendships, inclusion in the general curriculum, etc.) would be lost. Thus, the regulations clarify that the term "age appropriate" means appropriate for students without disabilities of the same chronological age.

Nondiscriminatory Evaluation and IEP Provisions That Advance LRE

As we discussed in detail in chapters 5 and 6, each student has a right to a nondiscriminatory evaluation (NDE) and an IEP. In creating those rights, IDEA linked them to the student's placement in the general education environment. Taken together, each of the NDE/IEP-linked rights confirm and strengthen the LRE presumption by commanding educators to (a) deliberately evaluate and plan for the student's participation and progress in the general curriculum, and (b) consider how the general curriculum itself can be modified to accommodate the student.

- In conducting the evaluation, the NDE/IEP team must use assessment tools and strategies that determine the content of the student's IEP, including information related to enabling the student to be involved in and progress in the general curriculum (or, for preschool students, to participate in appropriate activities) (20 U.S.C. Sec. 1414(b)(2)(A)). This is a command to evaluate the student with a view toward placement in the general curriculum.

- There is a special rule that excludes students from being classified into special education if the determinant factor for the student's classification is the student's lack of appropriate instruction in reading or math or limited English proficiency. This provision prevents overclassification of students as needing special education simply because they have had an inadequate education in the past or do not speak English as their native language. The rule requires these students to be retained in the general curriculum and excluded from the special curriculum unless they also have a disability and need special education (20 U.S.C. Sec. 1414(b)(5)).

- When conducting a reevaluation, the NDE/IEP team must determine whether the student needs additions or modifications to the existing IEP so the student may participate, as appropriate, in the general curriculum (20 U.S.C. Sec. 1414(c)(1)(B)(iv)). This provision keeps continuous pressure on the team to evaluate not just what the student's strengths and needs are and how they relate to the general curriculum but also to take into account what the general curriculum is and how it should be modified to accommodate the student.

- The IEP itself must contain a statement of how the student's disability affects involvement and progress in the general curriculum (or, for preschoolers, in appropriate activities) (20 U.S.C. Sec. 1414(d)(1)(A)(i)(I)). This provision places the disability into the context of the general curriculum and enables the NDE/IEP team to specify interventions for the student and modifications in the curriculum—a "dual accommodation" approach, changing both the student and the context in which the student is educated.

- The IEP must contain annual goals, including short-term goals or benchmarks for students taking the alternate assessment, related to meeting the student's needs and the effect of the disability on the student's participation in the general curriculum (20 U.S.C. Sec. 1414(d)(1)(A)(i)(I)). This provision, like the others listed here, give a context for intervention—the context being the general curriculum.

- The IEP must state what services the student will receive and what program modifications will be made so the student can be involved in and progress in the general curriculum, including extracurricular and other nonacademic activities (20 U.S.C. Sec. 1414(d)(1)(A)(i)(IV)). This is another contextual provision, calling for the team to propose modifications in the general curriculum—a context- or system-centered focus, not a student-focused one. The context must change to fit the student; the education and interventions the student receives changes the student so he or she will fit the context better.

- The IEP team must include a general educator, if the child is, will be, or may be participating in a general education classroom (20 U.S.C. Sec. 1414 (d)(1)(B)(ii)), and that educator has specific duties related to the student's appropriate positive behavioral interventions and supports, supplementary aids and services, program modifications, and support for school personnel (20 U.S.C. Sec. 1414(d)(1)(C)). The purpose for including the general educator is to assure that the context changes by having a context leader (the general educator) involved in the student's education.

- The IEP team also must include an LEA representative who is knowledgeable about the general curriculum and LEA resources that advance IEP goals (including general curriculum goals) (20 U.S.C. Sec. 1414(d)(1)(B)(iv)). This provision assures that a person who is able to shape a school system's resources to fit the student's needs is involved on the team and in the student's education.

Together these provisions require NDE/IEP team members, with knowledge and expertise related to meeting the LRE requirement, to

- assess the student's ability to participate in the general curriculum;
- select services to increase inclusion in the three domains (full or partial inclusion in the general curriculum, extracurricular, and nonacademic activities);
- set goals related to increasing inclusion;
- reassess to determine progress in achieving goals and current ability to participate in the general curriculum (and other activities); and, finally,
- add to or modify the child's IEP so the student may progress in the general curriculum to the maximum extent appropriate given the child's current needs.

As evidenced by these requirements, the LRE provision in IDEA involves, in addition to determining the present LRE for a child with a disability, an ongoing process for setting goals, providing services, reassessing, and modifying the student's IEP in an effort to increase inclusion over time. IDEA envisions an increasingly integrated education for each child as progress is made on the inclusion goals for that child.

Assessments as an LRE Technique

IDEA focuses on students' full participation and integration/inclusion rights in two other ways. These relate to the students' participation in statewide and district assessments of all students. NCLB and IDEA require that all students with disabilities participate in standardized assessments. This reflects two concerns:

1. Excluding students with disabilities from assessments will undermine school accountability under NCLB.
2. Excluding the student from participation can severely limit the student's postschool activities (including those that are typical for nondisabled individuals, such as postsecondary education and independent living).

IDEA further requires that each student's IEP contain a statement of the modifications in state or district assessments that the LEA will make so the student can participate in those assessments and, if the IEP team determines that the student should take the alternate assessment, an explanation of why the regular assessment is not appropriate and the alternate methods of assessment that will be used (20 U.S.C. Sec. 1414(d)(1)(A)(i)(IV) and (V)).

These provisions mirror the LRE requirement in that they create a presumption for participation in the regular assessment, but they also provide a continuum of options that includes the regular assessment with accommodations, an alternate assessment that tests the student with regard to the same standards, or an alternate assessment that tests to alternate standards (20 U.S.C. Secs. 1414(d)(1)(A)(i)(I)(cc) and 1414(c)). No matter which form of assessment is found to be the least restrictive and most appropriate option, IDEA requires the IEP to include an explanation of why a student cannot participate in the regular assessment, as well as a statement indicating how the student will participate in the assessment (20 U.S.C. Secs. 1414(d)(1)(A)(i)(VI)(bb)(AA) and (BB)). Simply put, inclusion in education includes involvement in school accountability, and schools must attempt to maximize participation of students with disabilities in the assessments upon which such systems are based.

Transition and LRE

The student's rights to transition planning and transition services (which we explained in detail in chapter 6) also advance and are advanced by the LRE principle. Transition supports inclusion by specifying that the outcomes of transition and the methods used to secure those outcomes are targeted on full participation in American life. Inclusion supports transition by requiring students to participate in integrated activities and environments so they are prepared for full participation, including doing tasks in integrated work environments, living independently, or postsecondary education. By contrast, segregated educational services basically prepare the student to live and work in similarly isolated postsecondary settings, that is, in segregated environments.

The outcomes of transition are those that many students without disabilities take for granted and will attain, including postsecondary education, vocational training, integrated employment, and continuing and adult education, so the student's transition program should consist of a process that leads to these kinds of full participation outcomes (20 U.S.C. Sec. 1401(34)(A)). Thus, the process by which transition services are provided includes inclusive methods such as community service and the development of employment and other postschool objectives (20 U.S.C. Sec. 1401(34)(C)).

Discipline and LRE

As we pointed out in chapter 4, students who are subject to discipline nevertheless retain important LRE rights (which are not always available to students in adult correction facilities). Even when a student is subject to discipline—and, some would say, *especially* when a student is subject to discipline—there are compelling reasons to continue to link that student's program and placement to the full participation outcomes that underlie IDEA. With respect to postsecondary settings, behavior and discipline problems can impede each and every goal of IDEA and foreclose employment and economic self-sufficiency, independent living, full participation, and continued equal educational opportunities for the student.

LRE and School Financing Mechanisms

Focusing on a student's rights is one thing, but if an entire school system is financed so it has no incentive to place students in the LRE, individual rights can be swallowed up by system financing and organizational considerations. In the past,

SEA and LEA financing and organizational practices often provided extra funds—a financial incentive—to programs that placed students into the less typical, more separate and specialized, more restrictive programs.

In reauthorizing IDEA in 2004, Congress acted to discourage the continued use of such incentives, stating in the *Conference Report* accompanying the 2004 reauthorization that

> some states continue to use funding mechanisms that provide financial incentives for, and disincentives against, certain placements. It is the intent of the changes to Section 612(a)(5)(B) to prevent State funding mechanisms from affecting appropriate placement decisions for students with disabilities. (U.S. Congress, 2004)

Eliminating Fiscal Incentives for Segregation

Recognizing the importance of overcoming the financial incentive for more restrictive placements, Congress amended IDEA in 2004 to provide that "a state shall not use a funding mechanism by which the state distributes funds on the basis of the type of setting in which a child is served that will result in the failure to provide a child with a disability a free appropriate public education according to the unique needs of the child as described in the child's IEP" (20 U.S.C. Sec. 1412(a)(5)(B)).

If the state does not have policies and procedures to comply with the funding-mechanism requirement, the SEA must provide assurances to the U.S. Department of Education that it will revise its present funding schemes so any such mechanism that it may adopt in the future will not result in placements that violate the LRE rule (20 U.S.C. Sec. 1412(a)(5)(B)(ii)).

Another provision also addresses the issues of money and funding: the "incidental benefit" provision (20 U.S.C. Sec. 1413(a)(4)(A)). This rule allows an LEA to use IDEA funds for the costs of special education and related services and for the costs of supplementary aids and services that benefit a student with a disability even if the use of those funds also benefits nondisabled students. Indeed, these services can benefit nondisabled students, and IDEA's previous restriction on their use (a "disabled student only" benefit) no longer exists. Its elimination now will let LEAs use IDEA money more flexibly and more deliberately to advance the LRE principle.

Governing State Allotments to Advance LRE

Another provision of IDEA related to funding mechanisms and inclusion of students in the general curriculum deals generally with federal aid to the states; it recognizes that some states have overidentified students as having a disability so they could draw down federal special education funds under IDEA. Overidentification can occur at two separate times in a student's life: first, when the student is evaluated initially to determine whether he or she has a disability that affects the student's participation in the general curriculum ("in/entry qualification"); and, second, when it may be appropriate for the student to exit special education altogether ("out/exit qualification").

Accordingly, IDEA authorizes the U.S. Department of Education to distribute IDEA funds to the states on the basis of the state's census and the state's poverty factor. This new basis will supplement the original allocation formula, which now is based on the number of students whom the state qualifies for special education, only after the total federal appropriations for IDEA exceed $4.9 billion.

Thus, the traditional and longstanding head-count basis, which created an incentive to classify students into special education and to retain them there to draw down federal funds, is now supplemented with a classification-neutral formula (census plus poverty) at a predetermined level (when the federal funds exceed $4.9 billion).

Other Statutory Techniques

Still other provisions of IDEA advance the LRE principle:

- Sections 1412(a)(14) and 1413(a)(3) require SEAs to create comprehensive systems of personnel development (CSPD). Without properly trained professionals, education in the LRE would not be successful.
- Section 1401(22) clarifies that therapeutic recreation is a related service and thus emphasizes that students in special education will have opportunities to learn skills that help them participate in community parks-and-recreation programs, which, under ADA, no longer may discriminate against otherwise qualified individuals with disabilities.
- Section 1401(33) defines supplementary aids and services as "aids, services, and other supports" that are provided in general education classes or other education-related settings to enable children with disabilities to be educated with nondisabled children to the maximum extent appropriate.
- Regulation 300.116(e) prevents a school district from removing a child with disabilities from the age-appropriate regular classroom solely because of needed modifications in the general curriculum.

Exception to the LRE Principle

IDEA contains one explicit exception to the mandate that students must be educated in the least restrictive environment. Juveniles who have been incarcerated as adults in adult prisons and who have IEPs are not entitled to LRE placement. IDEA specifically grants to IEP teams for those incarcerated juveniles the authority to disregard the LRE mandate and the rules regarding IEP content, but only if the state demonstrates a "bona fide security or compelling penalogical interest that cannot otherwise be accommodated" (20 U.S.C. Sec. 1414(d)(7)(B)). It is unclear what those two exceptions mean. State and local juvenile justice and special education authorities will give them various meanings, and litigation to define the terms and the students' rights undoubtedly will ensue.

Juveniles who are incarcerated as adults also are not required to participate in general and statewide assessment programs (20 U.S.C. Sec. 1414(d)(7)(A)(i)). Furthermore, incarcerated juveniles are not entitled to transition planning and services if they will be in prison past the age of eligibility for special education services (20 U.S.C. Sec. 1414(d)(7)(A)(ii)).

PART C REQUIREMENTS

The regulations under Part C clearly create a strong preference for community-based services, to the extent appropriate for the child. The purpose of Part C is to enhance infants' and toddlers' development (see chapter 3). Accordingly, states must put into effect a statewide system of "appropriate early intervention services" (20 U.S.C. Sec. 1434).

Under this system, early intervention services must be provided in "natural environments," including the home, in which infants and toddlers without disabilities normally or naturally would participate, to the maximum extent appropriate for infants and toddlers with disabilities (20 U.S.C. Secs. 1432(4)(G) and 1436(d)(5)). The home is considered a natural environment for delivery of early intervention services because the home is the usual environment in which infants and toddlers without disabilities are cared for and educated, even though it does not provide opportunities to interact with children who do not have disabilities. Where group settings are utilized, IDEA leaves no doubt about its preference for integrating infants and toddlers with disabilities in settings that include children without disabilities.

Part C's regulations, however, make it clear that separate environments are permitted when infants and toddlers require extensive medical intervention (34 C.F.R. 303.12(b)). But this exception is narrow and depends on the necessity of medical services for the infant or toddler "during the period in which they require extensive medical intervention," and after which "early intervention services must be provided in natural environments (e.g., the home, integrated child-care centers, or other community settings)."

One significant difference between the LRE principle as set out in Part B and the natural environment mandate of Part C is that while the LRE in Part B suggests a continuum of placements ranging from most inclusive to least inclusive, placements under Part C can be equally "natural" in either of two situations. The home and a fully integrated child-care center are both natural environments, and the mandate does not create a preference for either one over the other. Because selection between these two natural placements cannot be made on the basis of which is more natural, it must be made on the basis of which is more appropriate in securing the two child-related outcomes that Part C and its integration provisions set out—namely, maximizing the child's development and minimizing the likelihood that the child will have a developmental delay. Congress reflected this reality when it amended IDEA in 2004, by providing that

> ... provision of early intervention services for any infant or toddler with a disability occurs in a setting *other than a natural environment that is most appropriate,* as determined by the parent and the individualized family service plan team, only

when early intervention cannot be achieved satisfactorily for the infant or toddler in a natural environment. (20 U.S.C. 1435(16)(B)) (2004 amendment italicized)

So the decision of whether the home or an integrated child-care center is the child's natural environment depends upon which environment will best meet the child's needs—maximizing development and minimizing developmental delay.

SECTION 504 AND ADA REQUIREMENTS

In addition to IDEA, nondiscrimination laws such as Section 504 of the Rehabilitation Act and the Americans with Disabilities Act (ADA) support the concept of inclusion by prohibiting discrimination and unjustified segregation.

Section 504 Requirements

Section 504 applies to students who

- are entitled to Section 504 benefits (they have, are regarded as having, or have a record of a disability that significantly affects one or more of life's major activities, including their ability to learn); and
- are not formally classified into special education and not entitled to IDEA benefits.

Among the so-called 504 students may be those with a contagious disease (see the chapter 3 discussion of AIDS) or another impairment that does not interfere with their ability to learn (e.g., a student with attention deficit/hyperactivity disorder may not need special education but still is entitled to Section 504 benefits because he or she has a disability that may not require special education placement). For these students, Section 504 and ADA are protections against discrimination in education based solely on their disabilities.

The regulations under Section 504 (34 C.F.R. 104–104.61) are substantially similar to those of IDEA. Section 104.34 of the regulations requires that schools provide general education to each qualified student with a disability to the maximum extent appropriate to that student's needs. The school must place students with disabilities in the general education environment operated by the school unless the school can demonstrate that a student's education in the general environment with the use of supplementary aids and services cannot be achieved satisfactorily. Although the student's needs determine what is a proper placement, the Department of Education's comments on Section 104.34 make clear that if a student with a disability is so disruptive in a general classroom that other students' education is significantly impaired or the student's needs cannot be met in that placement, the general setting placement is not appropriate or required.

Students with disabilities also are to be provided with nonacademic services in as inclusive a setting as possible (34 C.F.R. 104.34). This requirement is especially important for students whose academic needs require them to be separated from general education programs during part of each day. In providing or arranging for the provision of extracurricular services and activities, including meals, recess periods, and nonacademic services and activities, a school must ensure that each student with a disability participates with nondisabled students to the maximum extent appropriate for the student in question (34 C.F.R. 104.37(a)(2)). To the maximum extent appropriate, students in residential settings also are to be provided with opportunities to participate with other students.

If an LEA operates a separate facility for students with disabilities, the LEA must ensure that the facility and the services and activities it provides are comparable to its other facilities, services, and activities for nondisabled students (34 C.F.R. 104.34). This is not intended to encourage the creation and maintenance of such facilities. In fact, a separate facility violates Section 504 unless it is necessary for providing an appropriate education to specific students with disabilities.

Among the factors to be considered is the need to place a child as close to home as possible (34 C.F.R. 104.34). When proposing a placement, schools must take the proximity factor into account. The parents' right to challenge their child's placement extends not only to placement in special classes or a separate school but also to placement in a distant school and, in particular, a residential placement. If an equally appropriate educational program exists closer to home, the parent or guardian may raise this LRE issue through a procedural due process hearing.

As the regulations to Section 504 clarify, the education of students with disabilities in the most normal setting feasible means educating them with nondisabled peers "to the maximum extent appropriate" (34 C.F.R. 104.34(a)). Although there is a strong presumption for inclusion, which includes educating them as close to home as possible, that presumption can be overcome. For many students with disabilities, "the most normal setting feasible is that which combines the use of special and regular classes" (appendix to Sec. 504 Regulations).

ADA Requirements

The ADA also is dedicated to the integration principle; it sets the goals of equal opportunity, full participation, independent living, and economic self-sufficiency for individuals, including students, with disabilities (42 U.S.C. Sec. 12101(a)(8)). In short, ADA advances the concept of least restriction and maximum inclusion, requiring accommodations and opportunities to live in an integrated society.

SUMMARY OF THE THREE INTERLOCKING VALUES OF THE LRE PRINCIPLE

The LRE principle is especially value laden because it promotes three sets of public policy values:

1. *The value of an appropriate education for students with disabilities.* LRE promotes this value because it creates a strong impetus toward inclusion of

special education students into general education programs where their education thereby can be enhanced.

2. *The value of conservation of political and fiscal capital.* Equal access for students with disabilities to general education also decreases the likelihood that unequal services (special education) will be thought to be politically untenable and fiscally unfeasible. Duplication of resources, especially in times of economic retrenchment, can be neither politically astute nor economical.

3. *The First Amendment's right of freedom of association.* This value refers to the right of those with disabilities to associate with nondisabled people. The right of association is more than a constitutional imperative. It also is a positive force in broadening individual and cultural dimensions of the citizenry and dispelling stigmatizing and discriminatory attitudes toward people with disabilities. As stigma is less attributable to disability and as *de jure* and *de facto* discrimination recede accordingly, individuals with disabilities acquire greater opportunity to pursue the constitutional value of liberty and choice in association.

A synthesis of these values is illustrated in Table 7.1 by a matrix in which the three basic levels of the policy interact with the two major value assumptions concerning appropriate education and the right of association to produce six dimensions of the LRE policy.

LRE, then, is both a legal principle and an educational strategy that, in combination with each other, circularly produce social effects. The legal principle assures that a student with a disability receives an appropriate education, and thereby the right to associate with nondisabled students and other people. As an educational

TABLE 7.1
Dimensions of the LRE Policy

Value Assumptions	A. That individuals and societies benefit when all are educated to their fullest potential	B. That individuals and society benefit when all its members are free to associate with each other
Produce: Legal Principles *and* Educational Strategies	1. Right to education	4. Right to association
	2. Appropriate education	5. Integration
Resulting in: Social Effects	3. Enhanced individual potential	6. Decreased stigma

strategy, LRE enhances individual potential through appropriate education. Education, in turn, is thought to mitigate the effects of disability by decreasing stigma and thereby increasing associational rights, individual opportunity, and individual potential to contribute to the general welfare of society. These six dimensions provide a framework to organize stated goals of IDEA and the LRE principle. The following list summarizes the goals of IDEA and its LRE component:

- *Right to education*: to provide education to all students with disabilities
- *Appropriate education*: to provide every student an education appropriate to that student's unique strengths and weaknesses
- *Enhanced individual potential*: to provide the opportunity for students with disabilities to develop to their potential
- *Right of association*: to provide education in an environment that promotes association with nondisabled peers
- *Integration*: to provide the opportunity for nondisabled peers to develop sensitivity to individual differences, and to prepare the student with a disability for integration into general education and society in general
- *Decreased stigma*: to enhance the social status of the student with a disability
- *Decreased cost*: to decrease the use of costly segregated schools and placements, as well as to decrease the need for disability services by requiring students with disabilities to achieve to high standards in integrated, real-world settings

Given this understanding of the goals of LRE, we ask: How are these goals to be implemented, and how can the value conflicts embedded in the goals be resolved in practice? To resolve these questions, we have to return to the legal concept of LRE as a rebuttable presumption and translate that principle into an educational strategy.

The relative restrictiveness of an educational environment ideally should be judged only in light of the individual educational need (right to an appropriate education) of each student with a disability. In light of that need, the most "normal" environment—even after it has been modified consistent with IDEA, Section 504, and ADA—still may not always be the least restrictive of the student's right to an appropriate program of education. To determine the least restrictive environment for a given student, the NDE/IEP must make two decisions:

1. The NDE/IEP team must choose the range of available programs or environments to satisfy the student's requirements for an appropriate education. Conceivably, this might include more than one possible environment. Decision-makers, such as the IEP committee, ideally must identify the specific programs or environment, from the range of satisfactory ones, that can contribute most substantially to the student's freedom to interact with students who are not disabled.
2. The NDE/IEP team also must decide (a) how to develop an individualized program that helps the student fit into the program or environment; and (b) how to change the program or environment so the student, with the benefit of an LRE-focused NDE, IEP, and other IDEA entitlements, may accommodate the student.

The principle of dual accommodations requires mutual change—by the student and by the environment. Thus, when making a placement decision, priority is given to providing an appropriate education in an accommodating environment that minimizes infringement on the student's liberty to associate with nondisabled peers.

This principle is illustrated in Figure 7.2. Circle A represents the set of all appropriate educational programs or environments available for a given student with a disability. Circle B represents the set of all environments that allow the same student to

A = All possible educational environments capable of providing an education for an individual disabled child

B = All possible environments capable of maximizing freedom to associate with nondisabled peers

C = Needs of other interested parties

1A = numerous choices available to satisfy both A and B (ideal case)

1B = few choices available to A and B

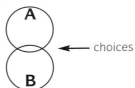

1C = no available alternatives to satisfy needs of both A and B

1D = complex decision process considering needs of A and B as well as other interested parties (C)

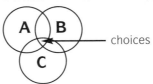

FIGURE 7.2
Choices for Maximizing LRE

interact with nondisabled peers. In an ideal case, circles A and B overlay one another perfectly or nearly perfectly (1A). More likely, they will overlap marginally, providing decision-makers with relatively fewer choices for placement (1B). Or they may not meet at all, even with accommodations, forcing decision-makers to choose environments entirely on the basis of what is available within circle A (1C).

In actuality, the problem is much more complex because the interests and needs of others (e.g., students with and without disabilities) enter the decision process (1D). Moreover, the decision of Congress to have a continuum of services complicates the choices because the continuum allows placement in segregated or special programs and thus reduces the likelihood that appropriate programs always will be developed within more, rather than less, integrated environments.

THE COURTS' INTERPRETATIONS

Having established that LRE is a rebuttable presumption (in IEP decision making, not due process) with a three-part value base and interlocking goals and strategies, we now will explore how the courts have interpreted this complex principle. Although the U.S. Supreme Court has not ruled directly on IDEA's LRE principle, other federal courts have; indeed, the number of cases involving the interpretation and application of the LRE principle is huge and growing. Despite the absence of a definitive ruling by the nation's highest court, there are clear trends and a developing consensus regarding LRE's meaning.

The consensus that had been developing in the courts, culminating with the *Daniel R.R. v. State Bd. of Educ.* (1989) and *Holland* (1994) decisions (discussed fully in the next section), now has been codified into IDEA, as we will point out. Nonetheless, a review of the most significant cases is useful, keeping in mind the statute's historical underpinnings. That is so because, despite IDEA's explicit provisions, controversy will remain: How should courts interpret them and apply them to a given student? The answers will come, in part, from the existing cases; precedents are powerful. The answers also will come from the U.S. Department of Education's regulations.

First Wave: Either–Or Choices

In the time between IDEA's enactment in 1975 and the mid-1980s, the courts faced an unenviable task of interpreting and applying the LRE doctrine to school systems that had not yet developed a capacity, or arguably a willingness, to include students with disabilities into general education programs.

In that (roughly) 10-year period the courts were obliged to make a Hobbesian choice (one that would not be particularly good, no matter what the choice) between (a) ordering a school system to integrate a student with a disability into an unprepared and often resistant general education program, or (b) ordering the student to be placed into a special education program in which the professional staff generally was able and willing to provide an appropriate education—albeit an education separate from the general education program in the school district.

Given this rather difficult choice—one that placed appropriateness above integration and another that placed integration above appropriateness—and also given that parents and professionals did not speak with a unanimous voice regarding integrated placements, the courts more often than not chose the placement that offered the more appropriate education. In making this choice, the courts seemed to say that the student's right to an appropriate education—which is a need-based right because it responds directly to the student's special education needs—is more important than the student's right to an LRE placement and interest in associating with nondisabled peers as a means for acquiring academic and other benefits.

In cases in which the student's need-based rights prevailed over the student's LRE rights, the right to an LRE placement was seen to be a means for securing an appropriate education. LRE itself was not regarded as an independent right but, rather, as an instrumental one, as an aid to the right to an appropriate education. Moreover, in those same cases, the courts more often than not justified the separate non-LRE placement by taking into account the extent, not the nature of, the student's disability. It mattered a great deal whether the student experienced extensive impairments and had substantial education needs; it mattered very little whether the student was classified into any one of the special education categories (Turnbull et al., 1983).

For nearly 10 years, the schools' capacities, parents' attitudes, students' needs, and courts' interpretations of the LRE rule interacted to create a body of case law that favored overall the more separate and less typical placement. During this phase of law development, the courts essentially took what was offered to them: an arguably inappropriate but integrated program, or an arguably appropriate but separate program. Theirs was a relatively passive role in that they simply reacted to the programs the schools offered. They did not require the schools to take any action to make the general education program both appropriate and inclusive.

Moving Out of the First Wave

Not until 1983 did a federal court recognize that it had the power to use the LRE doctrine in a far more proactive, corrective way. In that year, the Sixth Circuit Court of Appeals, in *Roncker v. Walter* (1983), rejected the traditional "take-it-or-leave-it" attitude that had characterized the earlier choice between integration or appropriateness and converted the LRE doctrine into a proactive force for school reform.

In *Roncker,* the court was faced with a relatively clear-cut factual situation. The state of Ohio had operated a dual system of schools for many years. One system served only those students who were classified as having severe-to-profound disabilities; the other served students who were classified as having mild disabilities and those who had none. When a student classified as having trainable mental retardation sought to attend the mild/nondisabled system, the LEA rejected the student's application. The issue, then, was whether the court would simply acquiesce to the school district's take-it-or-leave-it approach, which was based on classification by extent of disability, or whether it would use the LRE doctrine as the rationale for ordering the mild/nondisabled system to change its ways. In keeping with the trend of the cases to date, the trial court adhered to the take-it-or-leave-it approach.

Upon appeal, the Sixth Circuit reversed the trial court and ordered that the student be enrolled in the more integrated system. In reaching this result, the court established a new standard, or test, for determining a student's placement. Sometimes called the "feasibility test" and sometimes called the "portability test," the standard fundamentally requires the school system to take positive, affirmative steps to modify its general education curriculum so the student will be able to receive an appropriate education (one that complies with *Rowley*'s benefit standard) in a more typical, more integrated setting.

Roncker and the Feasibility–Portability Test

The court of appeals observed a strong congressional preference for integration in IDEA's requirement that a student with a disability be educated with nondisabled students to the maximum extent appropriate. The first step in analyzing the inclusion doctrine, the court stated, is to determine whether the student's proposed placement is appropriate under IDEA. The next step is to consider whether the placement is in the least restrictive environment.

Acknowledging that these two different values (appropriate education and least restrictive environment/most typical placement) can be in conflict, the court noted that a placement that may be considered better for academic reasons may, nevertheless, fail to comply with the LRE rule. The perception that a segregated school system facility or institution is academically superior for a student with a disability, said the court, may reflect no more than a basic disagreement with the LRE concept. Such a disagreement is not, of course, a basis for not following IDEA's LRE mandate. Professional and parental disagreements with IDEA's mandates do not override congressional intent.

Furthermore, the court declared, when deciding whether a segregated facility is superior to a more inclusive environment, a court should determine whether the services that make the separate placement superior could be feasibly provided in an inclusive environment. If those services can be provided in a more inclusive setting, the placement in the segregated school is inappropriate under IDEA.

Framing the issue in this manner, the court said, accords the proper respect for the strong preference in favor of the LRE rule while still realizing the possibility that

1. some students with disabilities simply must be educated in segregated facilities either because the student will not benefit from mainstreaming or because any marginal benefits received from a more integrated placement are far outweighed by the benefits gained from services that could not feasibly be provided in the nonsegregated setting, or
2. the student might be a disruptive force in the nonsegregated setting.

The court's use of the term "feasible" is, of course, the basis for the feasibility test: If it is possible (i.e., feasible) for the school to replicate the services that assure benefit (appropriate education) in the more integrated setting, the school system must do so. That is to say, it must "transport" the beneficial services from one setting to another; hence, the "portability" test.

Notice, however, that (a) the court recognized limits as to what was feasible, and (b) it did not require wholesale portability. If the student would receive no or only little benefit from the more integrated system, or if the student's placement there would be disruptive to the education of other students (both those with and without disabilities), the more separate setting was still permissible.

Despite the safety valves (no or little benefit, or disruptiveness), the feasibility and portability test put real force behind the LRE doctrine and established a much different mindset for other courts to follow.

First, the test put pressure on the school system to make accommodations. In that respect, it turned the take-it-or-leave-it choice on its head in two respects:

1. A court should use the LRE doctrine in a proactive, change-oriented way.
2. Schools must make accommodations that they previously had escaped having to make.

Congress's presumption in favor of integration must be honored. It cannot be honored if courts simply take what schools have decided to provide, and indeed it can be honored only with some judicial force behind the presumption, some power to make it come alive for students. *Roncker*, then, converted the LRE doctrine into a force for change.

Second, the test created a different mindset in that it instructed other courts to be more forceful in attempting to reconcile the appropriate education doctrine with the LRE doctrine. They should refuse to simply "take it or leave it" (a posture in which they would not attempt to reconcile IDEA's two commands) and, instead, should seek ways to make IDEA's two commands mutually consistent. Because Congress has created a presumption in favor of integration, the proper role of the courts is to enforce that presumption, even if doing so turns them into activist agents for change.

Roncker and Cost

Recognizing that feasibility and portability will impose a host of financial obligations on a school system, that school budgets have limits, and that other students have interests in IDEA's being enforced on their behalf, the court also held that cost is a factor to consider because excessive spending on one student may deprive other students of services. Cost is no defense, however, if the school district has failed to use its funds to provide a proper continuum of alternative placements for students with disabilities. If a district does not provide a continuum-based alternative to an integrated appropriate program, it may not complain about the cost of modifying the integrated one.

The "cost-is-a-consideration" approach can be criticized on the basis that it permits a school district to raise a defense that the cost is too high to comply with the feasibility or portability test. Stated alternatively, a school district that raises a cost defense in a case involving one student may be able to show that, for this one student, costs of appropriate education in an LRE program are indeed high.

The answer is to think beyond that one student. Although it is true that cost is a defense, it also is true that the cost of complying with the feasibility or portability test should be amortized over a number of students and over a period of time. The student seeking enrollment in a beneficial (appropriate) and integrated (LRE) program should answer the cost defense by saying that expenditures that benefit him or her now will also benefit other students later. The student "amortizes" costs over other benefited students and over time.

The *Roncker* approach is valid for two reasons:

1. It forces courts to make a decision based on the student's rights to both an appropriate education and an inclusive environment for that education. It is a student-centered approach that focuses on individualized determinations, consistent with IDEA's overall approach.
2. It forces the courts to look into what can be done to modify the otherwise inappropriate integrated setting. Thus, the parents can attempt to show how an inclusive setting could be modified or accommodated to the student.

Under this approach, the schools must argue that an inclusive setting (that is, the student's right to an integrated, least restrictive education) cannot possibly satisfy the educational benefit standard of *Rowley* (the student's right to an appropriate education). To inquire into what could "feasibly" make the appropriate-education services "portable" is entirely consistent with LRE as a rebuttable presumption. IDEA presumes that the more integrated setting is the appropriate one. The schools must abide by that presumption if, for a given student, transporting the appropriate education services to the least restrictive setting is feasible.

Although an arguably valid approach, the cost consideration in *Roncker*—and other cases involving cost—may well be decided differently under the 2004 amendments to IDEA. IDEA's new optional provision for creating a high-risk pool provides a means for schools to share the financial burden of integrating students who need particularly expensive services to participate in the general education classroom and general curriculum. Courts may resort to this new option when considering the cost-benefit balance and find that Congress intended the high-risk pool option to help ensure that students with disabilities were not excluded from any aspect of FAPE (including LRE) merely because of cost considerations.

The Second Wave: *Daniel R.R.*

Roncker marked the end of the first wave of take-it-or-leave-it cases, those that regarded the extent of a student's disability as dispositive of where the student would be educated. It also marked the transition from the first wave to the second wave of cases. With *Roncker* as a precedent, courts continued to put pressure on the schools to reconcile the doctrines of appropriate education and LRE. In doing so, they began to view the LRE doctrine more expansively and require schools to make greater accommodations.

The most significant of these second-wave cases arose from the Fifth Circuit Court of Appeals. *Daniel R.R. v. State Bd. of Educ.* (1989) involved a 6-year-old boy with Down syndrome, whom the LEA proposed to place in its segregated special education early childhood class. His parents requested that the LEA place their son in the segregated program for half of the day and an integrated prekindergarten general education class for the remainder of the day. The federal district court sided with the LEA, and the court of appeals affirmed that decision, agreeing that the LEA's refusal to remove the student from the special education academic program was not a violation of IDEA. The court of appeals rested its decision on the finding that the student could not receive an educational benefit in the general education program.

Despite the result in the *Daniel R.R.* case, the court of appeals actually opened up the avenue for that student and others to be included in general education. It did so in two different ways:

1. It observed and approved of the fact that the LEA had tried to accommodate the student in general education and had modified the curriculum "almost beyond recognition," and that the LEA did provide the student with opportunities to eat lunch in the school cafeteria with nondisabled students on three days of the week (provided that his mother was present to supervise him) and to have contact with nondisabled students during school recess.
2. It declined to follow the *Roncker* feasibility standard, finding that that standard "necessitates too intrusive an inquiry into the educational policy choices that Congress deliberately left to state and local school officials." Determining what is feasible was determined to be an administrative decision that "state and local officials are far better qualified to make than we (the court) are." But it also declined to follow the narrow "academic benefits" approach that the lower court used.

In *Daniel R.R.*, the problem with the lower court's standard—basically, whether the student could receive only an academic benefit—was twofold, according to the court of appeals:

1. As a prerequisite to placement in a general education program, it required a court to find that students with disabilities can "learn at approximately the same level as their nonhandicapped classmates" (874 F.2d 1036, 1046).
2. The standard places "too much emphasis on the student's ability to achieve an educational benefit" (874 F.2d 1036, 1046).

The court of appeals noted that some students with disabilities may not be able to master as much of the general education curriculum as their nondisabled peers. This did not mean, however, that students with disabilities were not receiving any benefit from general education. Nor did it mean that they were not receiving all of the benefit that their disabling condition would permit.

> If the child's individual needs make mainstreaming appropriate, we cannot deny the child access to regular education simply because his educational achievement lags behind that of his classmates. (874 F.2d 1036, 1047)

In short, placement in the least restrictive environment of general education is legally required for students with disabilities who can receive some, though not the full, benefit of such a placement. This result casts a somewhat different light on the LRE standard: Some, but not exactly equal, benefit justifies general education placement.

Moreover, the court of appeals found that placement in the general education program "may have benefits in and of itself." The student may learn appropriate language and behavior from nondisabled peers; and the fact that the student may receive benefit from "nonacademic experiences in the regular education environment" must be taken into account when LEAs and parents make placement decisions.

To comply with the presumption in favor of a general education placement, then, the court of appeals laid down a two-part test:

1. Can education in the general program be achieved satisfactorily with the use of supplemental aids and services? This first prong of the test requires a court to make four separate and sequential findings:

    a. Has the LEA taken steps to accommodate the student in general education? Has it provided supplementary aids and services? Has it attempted to modify the general education program? If the answers to these questions are "no," the LEA has violated IDEA. If the answers are "yes," the issue is whether the LEA's efforts are sufficient. Or are they mere token gestures? If so, the LEA must do more, though it need not provide "every conceivable supplementary aid or service."

       The supplemental aids requirement has limits, as the LEA is not required to provide every possible service (see *Greer v. Rome City Sch. Dist.*, 1990). Nor does the LEA have to require general educators to "devote all or most of their time" to the student with a disability. And it need not excuse the student from learning "any of the skills normally taught in regular education." Merely "sitting next to a nonhandicapped student" is not conferring a benefit to the student with a disability.

    b. Will the student receive an educational benefit from general education? To answer this, the court must pay "close attention" to the "nature and severity" of the student's disability and to the "curriculum and goals of the regular education class." If the LEA determines that a student placed in a general education classroom is falling behind similar students with disabilities in segregated classrooms and would make significantly more progress in a self-contained special education environment, an LRE placement may not be appropriate because it actually may be detrimental to the student, depriving him or her of an appropriate education. But the court also must extend its inquiry beyond only the educational benefits of a placement.

c. Accordingly, the next question is whether the student's "overall educational experience" in general education confers other than purely academic benefits. "(E)ven if the child cannot flourish academically," the benefit from "language models that his nonhandicapped peers provide him" may justify the general education placement. (874 F.2d 1036, 1049)

d. Finally, what is the effect of the student's placement in the general education environment and on the education of other students? Behavior that disrupts the education of others may justify placement out of the general program. Also, if the student requires "so much" of the time of a teacher or an aide that the "rest of the class suffers," placement out of general education is justified.

2. If, after answering these questions, the court determines that education in the general education classroom or program cannot be achieved satisfactorily, it must determine whether the LEA has integrated the student into the general education program "to the maximum extent appropriate." The LEA must offer a "continuum of services" and "must take intermediate steps where appropriate," such as placing the student in general education for some academic classes and in special education for others, enrolling the student in nonacademic (as distinguished from academic) general education classes, or providing interaction with nondisabled peers during lunch or recess.

Daniel R.R. is a paradoxical case: It approved the separate special education academic placement of the student, but it also set out a legal standard that contributed to the mix-and-match approach that we discussed earlier. Under that approach, an individualized decision must be made about how to increase both academic and nonacademic integration. The LEA must "mix" the academic and nonacademic opportunities in the general education program and "match" the student's abilities to those opportunities, all the while offering supplementary aids and services to promote integration.

In applying this two-part test, the burden of proving compliance with IDEA is placed on the party that initiates the complaint (*Weast*). In other words, when parents challenge the LEA for not complying with the LRE provision, they must show that the LEA did not sufficiently rebut the presumption in favor of a more inclusive program and thus is not able to justify the proposed separate program.

Not only is *Daniel R.R.* paradoxical, but it also is broadly visionary and highly prescriptive. Unlike *Roncker*, the broad vision of *Daniel R.R.* looks at both academic and nonacademic benefits. It thus acknowledges two values of integration: (a) the student's appropriate (academic) education (benefit), and (b) the student's opportunity to associate with and learn from nondisabled peers.

Unlike *Roncker,* too, *Daniel R.R.* set out highly specific inquiries that a court must make to determine whether a student's placement is consistent with the dual commands of IDEA that the student must receive an appropriate (beneficial) education and one delivered in the least restrictive, most typical setting possible, with the use of supplementary aids and services. Rather than relying on an arguably vague standard of feasibility or portability per the *Roncker* approach, the *Daniel R.R.* case provides courts and educators with highly individualized fact-finding guidelines.

Concluding the Second Wave: *Holland*

In the *Holland* case, the Case on Point at the beginning of this chapter, the court did not accept either the *Roncker* or *Daniel R.R.* tests as dispositive. Instead the court combined the approaches, as well as those of other courts in the second wave, to identify four factors for determining whether a placement is appropriate:

1. What are the educational benefits of a general classroom placement, with supplementary aids and services, as compared to the educational benefits of a special education classroom? A court and the LEA must determine whether the student's disabilities are "so severe that he or she will receive little or no academic benefit" from general class placement. Indeed, even if the special class placement is superior academically to the general class placement, IDEA does not require the "best academic setting" for the student, only an appropriate one. Moreover, to ensure benefit in the general class, the LEA must provide supplementary aids and services.
2. What are the nonacademic benefits to the student from interaction with nondisabled peers? A court and LEA must determine whether a student "may benefit from language and behavior models provided by nonhandicapped children." Likewise, improved self-esteem and increased motivation through general class placement must be taken into account. If nonacademic benefits flow from the general class placement, it, not the special class placement, is appropriate and least restrictive.
3. What are the "possible negative effects" of general class placement? If the student is disruptive to other students or "unreasonably" occupies the teacher's time "to the detriment of other students," the general placement is not appropriate. A student who "merely requires more teacher attention than most students is not likely to be so disruptive as to significantly impair the education of other children." Moreover, the LEA must "keep in mind its obligation" to provide supplementary aids and services, minimizing the "burden on the teacher." The disruptive factor weighs against regular education placement "only if, after taking all reasonable steps to reduce the burden to the teacher, the other children in the class will still be deprived of their share of the teacher's attention."
4. What are the costs involved in accommodating placement? This is a proper consideration, the LEA having to balance the needs of each student with a

disability against the needs of the other students in the school district. If the cost of educating a student with a disability in a general classroom is "so great that it would significantly impact upon the education of other children in the district, then education in the regular classroom is not appropriate."

Holland seems to summarize the factors that the *Roncker* and *Daniel R.R.* courts took into account as

- academic benefit,
- nonacademic benefit,
- disruption, and
- cost.

More than that, it reaffirms the significant criterion of the *Daniel R.R.* case—namely, that the LRE principle presumes that academic and nonacademic benefits alike are available in the general education program, and that both types of benefits must be made available to the student, consistent with the interest of the student to receive an appropriate (beneficial) education, and with the interests of other students to be free of disruption and to have access to a reasonable sum of money for their own educational benefit.

To date, *Holland* stands as the most comprehensive statement of the ways in which the appropriate education and LRE principles can be made mutually consistent. It is not the only case, however, that raises significant integration/LRE issues, as we shall see.

Other Factors Under Cases in Second Wave

Other courts have embraced inclusive education placements for students under IDEA, but under different facts and with different rationale. Although these cases are only of secondary importance, we review some of these other approaches to the legal basis for inclusion to illuminate how courts interpret and apply the LRE provisions of IDEA and to provide examples of some additional arguments used to advocate for a more inclusive setting.

The Associational Trump

In *Hulme v. Dellmuth* (1991), the LEA wanted to change the placement of a 14-year-old student with low-mild, high-moderate mental retardation and cerebral palsy from the school for orthopedically impaired students (where his parents wanted him to be retained) to a general education high school. The student was not orthopedically impaired, and the district acknowledged that the special school was its most restrictive placement. His progress there had enabled him, in the judgment of the district's experts, to function in a school setting with nondisabled students, with age-appropriate peers, and with necessary support services (speech, occupational therapy, and transportation).

In agreeing with the school district and ordering the student's removal from the special school, the court placed a great deal of weight on the "associational rights" approach: "In a mainstream environment, (the student) will be able to interact with nondisabled peers and thus enhance his life support and social interaction skills."

Likewise, *Chris D. v. Montgomery County Board of Education* (1990) used an "associational rights" approach, but with an unexpected, yet defensible result. There, the court held that a residential program was preferable to a homebound program for a student with severe emotional disabilities. The student required extensive positive behavioral support and training in adult and peer relationships. Without these services he was unable to obtain an educational benefit. The court determined that homebound education was the most restrictive placement because it provided only an isolated, sterile environment that hindered the student's educational progress and provided no opportunity for the student to apply newly learned techniques so he could return to a general education environment. Therefore, the court determined that the residential placement offered the least restrictive environment.

As in *Chris D.*, so it is in other cases: The LEA was not the party favoring a more restrictive placement; it was the parents. In *Wall v. Mattituck-Cutchogue Sch. Dist.* (1996), the federal district court approved the LEA's placement of the child in general education for science, English, art, music, library, physical education, and homeroom, and in a self-contained fifth-grade classroom for reading, social studies, spelling, and math. After the student experienced difficulty in English, the IEP team removed the student from only the general education English placement.

Because the student was having difficulty socializing at school and was the subject of teasing and taunting, the parents unilaterally placed their child at a private school for children with learning disabilities and sued for reimbursement. The court denied reimbursement, holding that the student was receiving an educational benefit in the LEA; his test scores indicated that he was making progress and his abilities were within the range of the other students. Although the student had experienced some difficulty with another student, this alone was not sufficient to require a more restrictive placement. Furthermore, accommodating a parent's ideal educational program was deemed to be beyond the scope of IDEA.

Because these cases all rest on the rights to association, and because IDEA emphasizes that the student's participation in the LRE involves extracurricular and other school activities, where the association between disabled and nondisabled students will occur, as well as academics, these cases will continue to be good law.

Neighborhood Schools

As we discussed earlier in this chapter, IDEA creates a preference for students with disabilities to attend the same school they would attend if they did not have a disability—but that preference is limited, as the courts have acknowledged. Many parents who are unhappy with their child's nonlocal placement have argued that their child must be educated in his or her neighborhood school—that the neighborhood school is not just the presumptive LRE but is indeed the mandatory placement, not merely one that can be rejected (rebutted). They have met with little success.

The federal circuit courts that have examined this issue have agreed that these regulations, while creating *a preference* for the neighborhood school, do not require a student with a disability to be educated in the neighborhood school (*Barnett v. Fairfax County School Bd.,* 1991; and *S.H. v. State-Operated Sch. Dist.,* 2003). The neighborhood school component of the LRE mandate is merely a single and, in practice minor, component of the LRE balancing test.

In making decisions in the neighborhood school cases, the courts have balanced several factors:

- The student's needs
- The student's opportunities to benefit academically and by association with nondisabled peers
- The LEA's right to make administrative and fiscal decisions that affect students' placements
- The LEA's need to conserve fiscal resources by operating highly intensive (needs-responsive) programs where there is a critical mass of similarly needy (disabled) students
- The fact that the LRE mandate itself creates a rebuttable presumption, not an iron-clad rule of conduct

The Harmful Effects and Competing Equities Issues

As we already noted, IDEA does not require a student who cannot be educated satisfactorily in general programs or schools, even with supplementary aids and services, to be educated in a general education classroom. This is the *harmful effects standard.* The harmful effect of integrating the student with a disability is a legitimate concern. Likewise, the harmful effect of integration on students without disabilities is a legitimate concern. The underlying issue is to what extent some students should be disadvantaged to give advantage to others and thus accommodate the LRE rule. This is the issue of competing equities. Both issues are factors in the balancing test outlined in *Holland.*

As we pointed out in chapter 4, this balancing approach—benefit versus harm to self or others—is precisely the approach adopted in *Honig* and in the AIDS cases. An SEA's or LEA's responsibilities extend to all students, not just one. If placing a student with a disability in a program with nondisabled children negatively affects the education of the latter, SEA or LEA responsibilities to those students are compromised.

The 2004 amendments related to discipline make clear that harmful effects and competing equities are major concerns (see chapter 4). That is why IDEA addresses issues of weapons and drugs and why it includes a special provision regarding students whose behavior impedes their learning and that of other students. Building on *Honig* but refining it, the 2004 amendments strike a balance between the competing interests of all students (and staff)—a balance that some will quarrel with in its abstract form and many will litigate as it is applied. The last word about harmful effects and competing equities has not yet been written, and the courts likely will continue to look at such issues on a case-by-case basis.

Educability, Expulsion, and Cessation of Services: Not an LRE option

Unlike the harmful-effects cases, which are statutorily grounded in appropriate education/LRE concepts, cases involving the attempted exclusion of allegedly ineducable students or students with contagious diseases and the attempted expulsion of students with disabilities because of disciplinary reasons rely on statutory zero reject principles (see chapter 4). These cases, however, are equally supportive of the LRE provision.

The most restrictive educational placement, after all, is outside any educational program—total exclusion of the purest kind. The most restrictive permissible placement is necessarily one within the continuum (i.e., within a free appropriate education, wherever furnished), not outside it. Total exclusion is, by definition, too restrictive.

BALANCING COMPETING PRINCIPLES AND EQUITIES

Although it is one of the most contentious issues in IDEA, the LRE requirement also has become one of the most clearly defined, strongly supported, and enforceable provisions of IDEA. Nevertheless, issues remain, and the LRE provisions are also some of the most commonly litigated provisions in IDEA. The common underlying question is: How should we balance competing principles and equities?

Of all the IDEA issues, two have produced the greatest consternation among all who are interested in the education of students with disabilities. One, of course, is the matter of expulsion and cessation of services (see chapter 4). The other is the matter of placement that is both beneficial (meets the benefit test of *Rowley* and of 2004 amendments) and inclusive (meets the LRE requirements).

Neither of these issues has been resolved readily or quickly. Each required, and still requires, a considerable amount of litigation. Interestingly, each poses rather similar considerations, though they seemingly are unrelated to each other.

One common issue has to do with placement itself. When a student whose behavior violates school codes, is unlawful, is harmful to self or others, or is subjected to school-initiated discipline, the issue of suspension or expulsion necessarily involves placement. May the school place the student into a less typical, more restricted, or supervised program? May it even expel the student, thereby causing a total cessation of services? The answers (as chapter 4 makes clear) depend on the type of behavior, the proposed disciplinary action, and whether the behavior is a manifestation of the student's disability. One thing is clear: IDEA does not foresee any legitimate circumstances that support or justify long-term cessation of services—not for the students covered by the manifestation rule and not for the students who are not covered by it.

Moreover, in the LRE cases, behavior and placement are related. This is so because the LRE rule allows a school to take into account, when it is making a placement decision, the student's behavior as a factor that could impede the education of either the student himself or herself, or the education of other students.

The student's attributes are related to placement in yet another way. Under the LRE rule, the student's ability to benefit from the services offered, even when the services are augmented by supplementary aids and services, is a determinant of placement. If the student is not able to benefit—academically or otherwise—from an augmented placement, the school may place the student into a program that is more intensive and usually less typical and more restrictive than is available to nondisabled peers or even to some peers with disabilities.

In still one other way the student's attributes are related to placement. For a student who arguably is "ineducable," the placement decision depends on the student's capacities to learn even the most rudimentary skills. The school may not exclude that student wholly from programs that it operates or pays for. Instead, it must continue to provide some beneficial services. Thus, student attributes influence student placements and school decisions about the intensiveness and typicality of services.

The interstitial connections between the zero reject rule, the appropriate education rule, and the LRE are but one aspect of the whole matter of student placement. They demonstrate how interrelated are matters of school obligations and student rights and needs. IDEA makes that interrelatedness explicit by linking the nondiscriminatory evaluation to the IEP and by providing, in both the NDE and appropriate education principles, that evaluation and programming must advance the student's right to be in all three domains of the general curriculum, on a full-time or part-time basis (the mix-and-match and full-/partial-inclusion approaches).

Nowhere were these connections more litigated than in the situation in which a student's needs—that is, the extent (but not the nature) of the student's disabilities—are such that the school's duty to provide an appropriate education apparently conflicts with its duty to do so in the least restrictive, most typical, most integrated program.

In meeting the challenge to comply simultaneously with two apparently different and arguably conflicting duties, courts became increasingly willing to require schools to develop a capacity to meet these two obligations at the same time. For nearly a decade after EHA was enacted in 1975, courts took into account the extent of the student's disability and, if the extent were so great that the student would receive some benefit in a less typical, less integrated setting or program, they opted for that placement over one in which, with accommodations, the student could benefit and would do so in an integrated setting. In this take-it-or-leave-it posture, the extent of the student's disability was decisive and courts usually did not require schools to accommodate the student in a general education program.

SUMMARY

Beginning with the *Roncker* decision, the courts began to be more assertive and less compliant with LEA-proffered either–or choices. That is to say, they began to require the schools to specially justify a less typical, more restrictive placement.

Thus, *Roncker* established the feasibility and portability standard and put pressure on the schools to adapt their general program to students with disabilities. Thereafter, *Daniel R.R.* required schools to take into account the student's right to associate with nondisabled students, and it thus broadened the decision-making process to include more than academic factors.

Returning to our Case on Point, *Holland* represents the last iteration of the LRE rule and requires a four-part calculus:

1. Academic benefit to the student
2. Nonacademic benefit to the student
3. Negative effects of the LRE placement on the student and other students and staff
4. Cost of LRE placement

In *Holland,* the first standard (academic benefit, in which the extent of the student's needs are considered) essentially adopts the type of analysis the courts used in the first decade after IDEA was enacted (the "needs over integration" approach). The second standard (nonacademic benefit) essentially uses the *Daniel R.R.* approach. The third standard (negative effects on student and others) takes into account the appropriate education claims not only of the student in question but of others as well, reflects *Roncker's* concerns, is grounded in the LRE exception that is part of IDEA and Section 504, and adopts the balancing approach that the expulsion and contagious disease cases use (see chapter 4). The fourth and final standard (costs) picks up some of the *Roncker* approach (limitations to feasibility and portability) and constitutes still another form of balancing competing claims.

The *Holland* factors and process remain as valid today as they were when the case was decided. IDEA's provisions related to the least restrictive environment were almost entirely unaffected by 2004 amendments. The President's Commission on Excellence in Special Education (2002) did not identify the least restrictive environment provisions as requiring any amendment. The secretary of the Department of Education and the President's Commission on Excellence in Special Education seemed to go even further than the law's requirements by stating that students with disabilities must be considered regular education students first and by speaking of special and general education as one system of education for all (Report of the President's Commission on Excellence in Special Education, 2002; U.S. Department of Education, 2003 press release).

Simply put, what was once the most contentious issue in IDEA has become widely accepted as the correct and most effective approach to educating children with disabilities. Although the exact balance between inclusion and appropriateness (benefit) is still a much litigated issue, the different perspectives now range only in their extent of support for the least restrictive environment or how to apply it in specific circumstances—not whether such a policy should exist or continue.

Holland created a four-part test, and IDEA as amended in 2004 adopts that test, with one significant change: Unlike the cost test in *Holland*, the IDEA amendments of 2004 make very clear that SEAs and LEAs must not skew their financing patterns in any ways that encourage segregation. When revenues are skewed against inclusion, segregation is bound to prevail. Congress recognized as much in the 1997 amendments and continues to recognize that fact in the 2004 amendments, giving, nevertheless, some flexibility to LEAs to use federal special education funds in general education even if there is an incidental benefit to nondisabled students.

Both *Holland* and IDEA as amended in 2004 acknowledge one of the law's most enduring maxims: Rights run with revenues. But what happens when either revenues, or SEA or LEA action, impairs students' IDEA rights, such as when an LEA ignores the presumption in favor of inclusion? That's the topic of chapter 8.

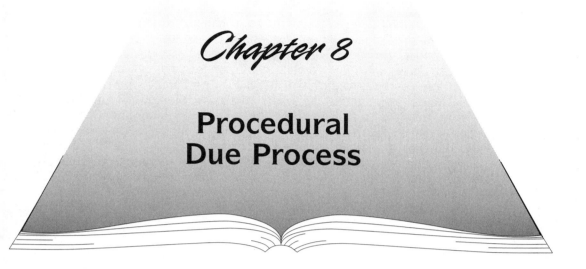

Chapter 8

Procedural
Due Process

Case on Point: *Schaffer v. Weast*
126 S. Ct. 528, 163 L. Ed. 387 (2005)

Power. Think about that word. What does it mean?

The dictionary defines power as the ability to produce an effect, and as the possession of control, authority, or influence over others (Merriam-Webster, 1996). In the lives of students, families, and professionals, power means that either the students and/or families, on the one hand, or the professionals, on the other hand, have the ability to produce a desired effect on the other.

Just who—the students and/or families or the professionals—has that power? Is there a balance of power between these two, or an imbalance? The Supreme Court thinks there is a balance of power. It's worth exploring how and why it came to that conclusion, and the implications of its decision.

When Brian Weast's family disagreed with the IEP that the Montgomery County (Maryland) LEA developed for him, they challenged the IEP under IDEA's procedural due process provisions, enrolled Brian in a private school, and requested that the LEA reimburse them for the private-school tuition they were paying. As a result of their challenge, the LEA changed his IEP, and his family enrolled him in the LEA (from which he eventually graduated) but continued to seek tuition reimbursement. The LEA resisted, and eventually the dispute wound its way up to the Supreme Court.

There, the only question was whether Brian's parents had the burden of proving that his IEP was not appropriate. Because IDEA itself was utterly silent about the burden of proof, the Court had to decide the case based on traditional rules of law and on IDEA's other provisions.

Normally, the person (called a *party, plaintiff,* or *complainant*) who sues another person (*party, defendant,* or *respondent*) has the burden to persuade the court to rule in his or her favor. The Court found no reason to make an exception to this well-settled rule of law. Moreover, it found several reasons to apply that rule to IDEA. Among the most important of those reasons is that the core of IDEA is, in the Court's language, "the cooperative process that it establishes between parents and schools." This process ensures that "no unique informational advantage" accrues to the schools; both the parents and the schools have the same information when developing an IEP.

By writing about advantage—informational or otherwise—the Court itself places its analysis of the burden of proof and IDEA procedural due process within a power framework. But what if, in fact, there is no cooperative process, and what if, in addition, the parents do not have the same experts and the same depth and breadth of information as the schools do? What if there really is no equality between the parents and the schools, and the schools, not the parents, really have the power?

The Court assumed equality. Ironically, as we point out in this chapter, Congress assumed the opposite when it reauthorized IDEA in 2004. It did so by imposing on parents ever-more stringent requirements for informing schools of their reasons for disputing what the educators propose and by requiring parents to take various dispute-resolution actions before facing off against the schools in a due process hearing. Who got it right about power? The Court or Congress? And why is power so important, and why should it be curbed? Those are some of the questions this chapter addresses.

FAIRNESS AS A CONSTITUTIONAL VALUE

As you have learned, the first four principles—zero reject, nondiscriminatory evaluation, appropriate education, and least restrictive environment—set out benefits that the SEAs and LEAs must confer on students: access to public education at no cost, fair evaluations, and an appropriate, individualized, beneficial education in the least restrictive environment. If the SEAs and LEAs do not comply with these principles, what recourse do students and their parents have? Plenty. After all, rights without remedies are essentially worthless. That is why IDEA confers numerous rights on students and their parents to hold those entities accountable.

By the same token, SEAs and LEAs have rights that they can enforce against parents and students. Clearly, IDEA assures mutual enforcement because both the parents and the SEAs and LEAs have an interest in educating students with disabilities effectively. That is why IDEA's fifth principle, procedural due process, exists. It is the mechanism for enforcing these rights and providing remedies for any violations of the rights.

It bears repeating that, without due process, students' rights would have a hollow ring. For those who pioneered the right-to-education doctrine, the procedures for implementing the right were as crucial as the right itself. Procedural due process was, and still is, a means of challenging the multitude of discriminatory practices that schools had followed habitually and that some still practice. Procedural due process also is a constitutional requirement under the provisions of the Fifth and Fourteenth Amendments that no person shall be deprived of life, liberty, or property without due process of law. In terms of the education of children with disabilities, this means that no child with a disability can be deprived of an education without the opportunity to protest what happens to him or her.

It is an axiom of law that fair procedures tend to produce acceptable, correct, and fair results. And fairness is one of the social goals that the law pursues. As Justice Felix Frankfurter once observed, fairness is the essence of due process (*Anti-Fascist Committee v. McGrath,* 1951). In a larger sense, then, the principle of procedural due process encourages SEAs, LEAs, students, and parents to deal fairly with each other, and it prescribes the procedures for fair dealing.

ELEMENTS OF FAIRNESS

There are many "fair dealing" procedures. Although we present them separately here for purposes of clarity, you should bear in mind that each of them drives the parents and SEA and LEA toward being fair in working with each other, even when they disagree with each other.

Rights and Age-Specific Provisions

The procedural due process provisions apply to all educational entities. Each SEA and LEA must give assurances to the U.S. Department of Education that it has adopted appropriate due process procedures (20 U.S.C. Sec. 1412(a)(6), applicable to the SEA; 20 U.S.C. Sec. 1413(a)(l), applicable to the LEA; and 20 U.S.C. Sec. 1415, applicable to both). Except where Part C (birth to age 3) has a special provision regarding due process rights, all of IDEA's due process rights apply to all students—those in Part C programs and those in Part B programs.

The general rule of law is that a person under age 18 is a minor and is presumed incapable of exercising any legal rights on his or her behalf because minors lack the experience necessary to look after themselves. Parents hold minors' rights in custody for their children and exercise those rights on behalf of their children. That is why, for the most part, IDEA refers to the students' parents as the ones who can invoke IDEA rights (see chapter 9, "Parent Participation").

When, however, students attain the age of majority, the general rule is that they become competent to exercise all IDEA rights that they had as a minor, but now they exercise these rights on their own behalf, not through their parents. The exception to this rule is that, if students have been adjudicated to be mentally incompetent under state law, a court appoints the parents or other responsible adults to be the legal guardian(s), and the guardians exercise the rights on the students' behalf (20 U.S.C. Sec. 1415(m)(1)). If a student reaches the age of 18 and has not been deemed incompetent but nevertheless is unable to give informed consent and the parents do not have guardianship rights, IDEA authorizes SEAs and LEAs to establish procedures to appoint the student's parents or other appropriate individuals to represent the student's educational interests (20 U.S.C. Sec. 1415(m)(2)). (We discuss the transfer of rights from parents to students in chapter 9.)

Access to, and Privacy of, Educational and Health- and Discipline-Related Records

"I am my record." That's an interesting statement, wouldn't you agree? In a country where we all have records (birth, Social Security, school, health, employment, and sometimes criminal justice records, drivers' licenses, or other government identification documents, such as passports), it is often the case that other people know each of us solely on the basis of the records that we maintain about ourselves or that others maintain about us. Given that our identity is tied so closely to our records for many purposes, including, of course, for our education, it is obviously true that "I am my record."

But what if the SEA or LEA records about the student are inaccurate, incomplete, outdated, or misleading? The consequence most likely will be that others will not truly know the student. In turn, they may make incorrect judgments about the student—judgments that affect evaluation and eligibility for services (chapter 4, "Zero Reject," and chapter 5, "Nondiscriminatory Evaluation") and the nature and place of services (chapter 6, "Individualized and Appropriate Education," and chapter 7, "Least Restrictive Environment").

Now apply these concerns to the context of IDEA. A student's records most certainly will contain information based on the student's nondiscriminatory evaluation and related to the student's appropriate education (IEP) or placement. It also is likely that the student's records will reveal something about the student's family. That definitely will be the case when the family has an infant or toddler participating in Part C programs and there is a family-originated IFSP.

So what if the records *are* inaccurate, incomplete, outdated, or misleading? Or if they are disclosed randomly to people who have no stake in educating the student or serving the infant or toddler and family?

- At one level, the consequences could seriously impair how educators or other professionals serve the student, infant or toddler, and family.
- At another level, the consequences could be that information the family or student give educators, in the expectation that the information will remain confidential, could be divulged to people who have no reason to know anything, much less any truly private information, about the child or family. If that were the case, there would be a chilling effect on the student and family: They

would be reluctant to disclose educationally useful information, and their reluctance in turn may impair their ability to receive appropriate services from educators or other professionals.

- At still another level, families and students would have a hard time holding LEAs accountable for their actions, because they would not know the reason for the educators' actions, not having full access to the records on which the educators might rely.

To ensure accuracy and privacy (sometimes called confidentiality) and to ensure accountability, Congress (in 1974) enacted the Family Educational Rights and Privacy Act (FERPA, P.L. 93-380, 20 U.S.C. Sec. 1232(g)) and (in 1975) made it apply to IDEA and the records of students, infants and toddlers, and families served under Part B and Part C (20 U.S.C. Secs. 1412(a)(8), 1415(b)(1), and 1417(c)). (Please note that we summarize FERPA here, and you should read it and its regulations carefully to know precisely what they provide.)

FERPA's general rule has several parts. The parents of students and infants and toddlers have the right to

- inspect and review their children's education records;
- have a hearing to challenge the contents of the records to make sure that the records are not inaccurate, misleading, or in violation of the students' privacy rights;
- provide for the correction or deletion of any inaccurate, misleading, or otherwise inappropriate data;
- insert into the records a written explanation respecting the content of the records; and
- consent or not consent, in writing, to the release of the records to any individual, agency, or organization except those that FERPA authorizes to see the records without parental or student consent (20 U.S.C. Sec. 1232g(b)(1)).

FERPA defines "education records" as those that contain information "directly related to a student" and that are "maintained" by an "educational agency or institution" or by a person acting for the agency or institution, such as an SEA or LEA. The term does not include

- records of instructional, supervisory, or administrative personnel that these people keep in their sole possession and do not make accessible to or reveal to others;
- records of an LEA's law-enforcement unit that are separate from the student's other education records, maintained solely for law-enforcement purposes, and disclosed only to law-enforcement officials in the same jurisdiction as the LEA;
- records on a student who is over the age of 18 that are made or maintained by a physician, psychiatrist, psychologist, or other recognized professional or paraprofessional acting in a professional capacity and that are used only for

treating the student and are not made available to people who are not treating the student (34 C.F.R. 99.3) (note that the federal health-records privacy act, Health Insurance Portability and Accountability Act of 1996 [HIPAA, P.L. 104-191], does not apply to these student treatment records [45 C.F.R. 164.501(2)(i)]); and

- directory information, such as the student's name, address, telephone listing, date and place of birth, major field of study, participation in extracurricular and sports activities, dates of attendance, degrees awarded, and most recent previous educational agency or institution the student attended.

What if an LEA disciplines a student? (Chapter 4, "Zero Reject," discusses student discipline.) Is that fact part of the student's records and, if so, should the information about discipline be entirely private or should it be accessible to others? FERPA answers these questions by providing that an LEA may include in the student's records appropriate information concerning "disciplinary action taken against such student for conduct that posed a significant risk to the safety or well-being of that student, other students, or other members of the school community" (20 U.S.C. Sec. 1232g(h)). The FERPA regulations define "disciplinary action" as "the investigation, adjudication, or imposition of sanctions" by an LEA with respect to an "infraction or violation" of the LEA's "internal rules of (student) conduct" (34 C.F.R. 99.3). The regulations do not define "significant risk to ... safety or well-being."

It seems that an LEA may include in a student's records any information about a student's behavior that caused the LEA to take any of the disciplinary action we discussed in chapter 4. FERPA also permits an LEA to disclose that information to teachers and school officials, including teachers and officials in other LEAs, who have a "legitimate educational interest" in the student's behavior.

To ensure privacy, the general rule under FERPA is that parents may consent to the release of their children's education records, but it requires them to do so in writing. The exception to this privacy rule is that the LEA may release a student's education records to

- other educators who have "legitimate educational interests" in the student,
- officials of other schools or schools systems in which the student seeks to enroll,
- federal and state education auditing or accrediting agencies,
- law-enforcement agencies,
- researchers who promise not to reveal the personally identifiable information in their research reports,
- individuals who need the records to protect the health or safety of the student or other individuals in an emergency, and
- individuals or agencies authorized by a court to see the records.

In addition, FERPA requires an LEA to notify a student's parents

- that it maintains personally identifiable information about the student;

- how it intends to collect, maintain, use, and protect that information;
- what its collection, maintenance, use, and protection policies and procedures are; and
- what rights parents have to inspect, correct, add to, explain, or delete information in the student's records, and to copy the records and where they may find the records.

Finally, FERPA provides that the parents' rights transfer to the student when the student becomes 18 years old. At that time, however, some students with disabilities may not be legally competent to act. They will either be adjudicated to be incompetent (the guardianship proceedings in state court) or deemed by their LEA not to be able to exercise their IDEA rights. (We discussed IDEA's devolution and transfer-of-rights provisions under transition in chapter 6, "Individualized and Appropriate Education.") In either of those two events, their legal guardians appointed by a court or individuals whom the LEA designate to act on their behalf own the FERPA rights.

As we noted, FERPA's provisions are highly detailed and involve general rules, exceptions to the general rules, and exceptions to the exceptions. We have described FERPA generally so you will understand its purposes related to accuracy, privacy, and accountability—especially accountability because that is one of the underlying goals of procedural due process.

Consent for Evaluations and Reevaluations

As we discussed in chapter 5, "Nondiscriminatory Evaluation," LEAs must obtain parental consent for an initial evaluation (20 U.S.C. Sec. 1414(a)(1)(D); 34 C.F.R. 300.300)). In addition, LEAs must obtain parental consent for reevaluations of students with disabilities.

Defining Consent and Absence of Consent

In the context of evaluation and in all other contexts, consent means that

- the parents have been informed fully in their native language, or in another suitable manner of communication, of all information relevant to the activity (e.g., evaluation) for which consent was sought (34 C.F.R. 300.9(a));
- the parents understand and agree in writing that the activity may be carried out (34 C.F.R. 300.9(b));
- the consent describes the activity and lists the records (if any) that will be released, and to whom (34 C.F.R. 300.9(b)); and
- the parents understand that they give their consent voluntarily and may revoke it at any time (34 C.F.R. 300.9(b)). (Note that such revocation is not retroactive.)

If the parents refuse to consent for an initial evaluation, the agency may initiate mediation or a due process hearing to obtain authority to do an evaluation. Note that the LEA does not have a duty to initiate mediation or due process. It simply is an option it may pursue. If a hearing officer rules in favor of the agency, the parents' refusal will be overruled and the agency may evaluate the child, notifying the parents of its actions so that they may appeal (34 C.F.R. 300.300(b), 300.506, 300.507, 300.511, 300.512, 300.514). In addition, if an LEA has taken reasonable efforts to reach a parent but a parent has failed to respond, the LEA nevertheless may evaluate the student (20 U.S.C. Sec. 1414(c)(3)).

Consent for Special Education Services

The parents' consent to an evaluation is for the evaluation only. It does not commit a parent to accepting special education or related services (20 U.S.C. Sec. 1414 (a)(1)(D)(i)(I)). That is why the LEA also must seek informed consent from the parent before initiating services (20 U.S.C. Sec. 1414(a)(1)(D)(i)(II)).

A significant change in the 2004 reauthorization provides that if a parent refuses to consent to special education services, the LEA is absolved of any obligations to provide FAPE or develop an IEP (20 U.S.C. Sec. 1414(a)(1)(D)(ii)(III)). Indeed, IDEA prohibits the LEA from using the due process procedures to provide special education or related services (20 U.S.C. Sec. 1414(a)(1)(D)(ii)(II)).

The effect of the 2004 amendment is that by refusing to consent for services, parents essentially forfeit their child's rights under IDEA. They cannot return to the LEA at a later date and claim that their child was denied FAPE. However, this "no claim" rule relates to only the specific refusal of consent for services. Parents can always ask, at a later time, to have their child evaluated again and to consider after that evaluation whether to consent to special education services.

Consent Under Part C

Part C (birth to age 3) has its own rules about consent. Early intervention service providers must obtain written parental consent before evaluating a child (34 C.F.R. 303.404(a)(1)) and before initiating the provision of early intervention services for the first time (20 U.S.C. Sec. 1436(e)). Parents may give or withhold consent to all or any one or more early intervention services (20 U.S.C. Sec. 1436(e)); they may "cherry pick" the services they consent to receive.

If the parents do not give consent to evaluation and assessment, the providers must make reasonable efforts to ensure that the parents (a) are fully aware of the nature of the evaluation and assessment, and (b) understand that their child will not be able to receive the evaluation and assessment (and subsequent services) unless they consent.

Independent Evaluation

Parents also are entitled to an independent (nonagency) educational evaluation of their child (20 U.S.C. Sec. 1415(b)(1); 34 C.F.R. 300.502). The regulation 34 C.F.R.

300.15 defines evaluation as "procedures used in accordance with 34 C.F.R. 300.304–300.311 to determine whether a child has a disability and the nature and extent of the special education and related services that the child needs." The term *evaluation* refers to procedures used selectively with an individual child and does not include basic tests administered to, or procedures used with, all children in a school, grade, or class.

The regulation 34 C.F.R. 300.502(a)(3)(i) defines who may make an independent evaluation—namely, a qualified examiner not employed by the public agency responsible for educating the child. The regulation 34 C.F.R. 300.502(a)(2) also provides that public agencies, upon request, must inform parents about where they may take their child to have an independent educational evaluation. IDEA does not require the list to be exhaustive, giving information about each and every possible independent examiner in the state, county, city, or school district. That is why parents should be vigilant to use that list and other sources of information (such as the state Parent Training and Information Center) to locate independent evaluators.

Under some circumstances, the independent evaluation must be made at public expense, with the public agency either paying for the full cost of the evaluation or ensuring that the evaluation is otherwise provided without cost to the parent. Parents have the right to an independent evaluation at public expense if

- a due process hearing officer requests one for use in a due process hearing, or
- the parents justifiably disagree with the evaluation made by the public agency.

Parents are entitled to only one independent evaluation at public expense each time the LEA conducts an evaluation with which the parents disagree (34 C.F.R. 300.502(b)(5)). But if, in a due process hearing that it initiates, the agency can prove that its evaluation was appropriate, the agency will not be required to pay for the independent evaluation. Parents always have the right to obtain an evaluation at their own expense. When parents obtain an evaluation at their own expense that meets agency criteria (which the agency sets, independently of parent participation), the agency must consider it as a basis for providing the child an appropriate education, as evidence in a due process hearing, or both (34 C.F.R. 300.502(b), (c), (d)).

Notice

Notice takes the forms of prior written notice, notice of procedural safeguards, and rule of actual notice.

Prior Written Notice (Notice of Action)

An SEA or LEA must give prior written notice to a student's parents, guardians, or surrogates whenever it proposes to initiate or change, or refuses to initiate or change, the student's identification, evaluation, or placement, or the provision of a free appropriate public education (20 U.S.C. Sec. 1415(b)(3)). This prior written notice is also called a "notice of action."

Notice-of-Action Requirements

The notice of action must contain

- a description of the action that the SEA or LEA proposes or refuses to take;
- the agency's explanation of why it proposes or refuses to take the action and a description of each evaluation procedure, assessment, record, or report that the agency used as a basis for the proposed or refused action;
- a statement that the parents have certain protections under the procedural safeguards and, if this notice is not an initial referral for evaluation, how the parents may obtain a copy of a description of the procedural safeguards;
- the sources that parents can contact to obtain assistance in understanding the provisions in the notice;
- a description of any other options considered by the IEP team and the reason those options were rejected; and
- a description of other factors that are relevant to the agency's proposal or refusal (20 U.S.C Sec. 1415(c)).

34 C.F.R. 300.503(c) requires that the notice be

- written in language understandable to the general public; and
- provided in the parents' native language or parents' other mode of communication, unless it clearly is not feasible to do so.

If the parents' native language or other mode of communication is not a written language, the SEA or LEA must take steps to ensure that

- the notice is translated orally or by other means to the parents in their native language or other mode of communication,
- the parents understand the content of the notice, and
- there is written evidence that the requirements (of oral translation and parent understanding) have been met. (34 C.F.R. 300.503(c)(2))

Notice of Procedural Safeguards (Rights Notice)

In addition, SEAs and LEAs must provide parents with a procedural safeguards notice (also known as the "rights notice"). The 2004 amendments require LEAs to give the procedural safeguards notice to parents only one time each school year; this provision seeks to reduce the paperwork for LEAs and SEAs. The once-a-year notice has three exceptions:

- When the student is referred for the initial referral or when the parents request an evaluation
- When the parents or agency file the first complaint under subsection 1415(b)(6)
- Upon request by a parent (20 U.S.C. Sec. 1415(d)(1)(A))

Provisions of the Notice of Rights

The notice of rights must contain full explanations of procedural safeguards relating to

- independent educational evaluation (see also Sec. 1415(b)(1));
- prior written notice;
- parental consent;
- access to educational records;
- the opportunity to present and resolve complaints, including the time period in which to make a complaint; the opportunity for the agency to resolve the complaint; and the availability of mediation;
- the child's placement during the pendency of due process proceedings;
- procedures for students who are subject to placement in an interim alternative educational setting;
- requirements for unilateral placement by parents of children in private schools at public expense;
- due process hearings, including requirements for disclosure of evaluation results and recommendations;
- state-level appeals (if applicable in that state);
- civil actions, including the time period in which to file such actions; and
- attorneys' fees (20 U.S.C. Sec. 1415(d)(2)).

An LEA also may place a current copy of the procedural safeguards notice on its Internet Web site (20 U.S.C. Sec. 1415(d)(1)(B)). But simply posting the procedural safeguards notice on the Internet is not sufficient, by itself, to meet the notice requirement. The LEA still must give the notice to the parent. "Constructive notice" through the Internet does not substitute for actual notice by mail, in hand, orally, or by a combination of those methods.

The 2004 amendments require the LEA to provide more specific information as to all of a student's IDEA rights and how parents can enforce those rights. This requirement will help ensure that parents are informed and that SEAs and LEAs do not withhold information regarding parents' or students' IDEA rights.

Rule of Actual Notice

Quite properly, courts ruling on notice requirements have insisted that SEAs or LEAs actually inform the parents of their rights; otherwise, the parents may not know what their rights are or how to assert them. If a parent does not understand a notice, it seems that the parent has the responsibility to ask the LEA or some other source to explain the notice, and then the LEA must make sure that it explains the notice in such a way that the parent actually does understand it. There is every reason to think that the cases decided before the 2004 amendments will continue to guide the courts with respect to actual notice. That is so because nothing in the 2004 amendments suggests otherwise, because the constitutional rule of due process notice requires actual notice, and because IDEA provides that the Web-based notice does not substitute for actual notice.

The simplest way for an LEA to comply with the notice requirement is to follow it word for word. Anything less creates a risk of violation. Word-for-word compliance, however, may mean that the notice uses the language of the law itself, and that language may not be clear or understood by many parents. So it is a safe practice for an LEA to accompany the word-for-word notice with a layman's explanation of the content of the notice.

In addition, an LEA that must give notice to parents who are not literate in English or in any other language, cannot read because they themselves have a disability, or use a language that is not written (as is the case for some American Indians) has the obligation of making sure that the parents actually receive an understandable notice. This is a requirement of due process generally and of the "reasonable accommodations" provisions of the Americans with Disabilities Act as it applies to a parent who has a disability.

MECHANICS OF DUE PROCESS

Few provisions of IDEA are as complicated and difficult to understand as those related to the mechanics of due process—that is, the way that IDEA requires parents and LEAs to behave when they enter into the due process stage. We explain these provisions by stating the general rule, describing two other methods of filing complaints (other than through a due process hearing), and discussing mediation and the new mandatory resolution provisions. We then revisit our discussion about notice and fairness. We conclude by discussing timelines (and offering a flow chart to illustrate them) and the qualifications of the due process hearing officer.

General Rule

An SEA or LEA must give the parents an opportunity to present and resolve complaints relating to any matter concerning the child's identification, evaluation, or placement, or the provision of a free appropriate public education (20 U.S.C. Sec. 1415(b)(6)). If the parents file a complaint with an SEA or LEA, they are entitled to an impartial hearing. Also, the agency must inform the parents about any low-cost or free legal aid in the geographical area (34 C.F.R. 300.507(b)).

Additional Complaint Mechanisms

Parents have the right to present and resolve complaints at any time. Although they may do this in several ways, they must always comply with the SEA's complaint procedures, which are required to be outlined in the procedural safeguards notice (20 U.S.C. Sec. 1415(d)(2)). There are two such mechanisms, over and above the due process hearing mechanism.

1. *Filing a child complaint with the SEA*. Parents may outline in detail the basis of their concerns and any alleged violations. Parents also may submit supporting documentation. The process can vary from state to state, but usually the SEA appoints an investigator who contacts the LEA and requests all relevant documentation. The LEA also has an opportunity to respond to the allegations.
2. *Filing a complaint with the appropriate federal agency*. That agency is the Office of Civil Rights, a branch of the U.S. Department of Education. The Office of Civil Rights has established mechanisms for filing complaints. Under it, parents allege that their child is being discriminated against on the basis of their disability. (We discuss enforcement of IDEA in chapter 10.) Some parents may use both the SEA and OCR methods. If they do, they still may use the due process mechanism, to which we now draw your attention.

Due Process Complaint Notice

When filing a complaint that the parents want to be the basis for a due process hearing, the parents (or LEA if the LEA is proceeding against the parents) must include a due process complaint notice. The notice must remain confidential, be sent to the opposing party and the SEA, and contain the following:

- The student's name and residence address and the name of the school the student is attending
- In the case of a homeless child or youth (within the meaning of section 725(2) of the McKinney-Vento Homeless Assistance Act (42 U.S.C. Sec. 11434a(2)), available contact information for the student and the name of the school the student is attending
- A description of the "nature of the problem of the child relating to (the) proposed initiation or change, including facts relating to (the) problem"
- A proposed resolution of the problem to the extent known and available to the party at the time (20 U.S.C. Sec. 1415(b)(7)(A)

Neither the party making the complaint nor the party responding to the complaint may have a due process hearing until the party files a notice that meets these requirements (20 U.S.C. Sec. 1415(b)(7)(A)). Like the notice of action described previously, this notice requirement prevents the parties to a due process from catching the opposing party unaware.

Response to the Due Process Complaint Notice

The 2004 amendments provide that, upon receipt of the complaint, the noncomplaining party must respond to the issues in that complaint within 10 days (20 U.S.C. Sec. 1415(c)(2)(B)(i)(I)). If the LEA is the noncomplaining party (the parents filed the complaint), the LEA does not have to respond if the LEA had sent a prior written notice (notice of action) previously on the issues raised in the complaint (20 U.S.C. Sec. 1415(c)(2)(B)(ii)). If the LEA had not sent prior written notice, the LEA must, within 10 days, send a response that describes

- the action that the LEA proposed or refused;
- any other options considered by the IEP team and the reason the team rejected those options;
- each evaluation procedure, assessment, record, or report that the LEA used as a basis for its proposed or refused action; and
- any other factors that are relevant to the LEA's proposal or refusal (20 U.S.C. Sec. 1415(c)(2)(B)(i)(I)).

Sufficiency of the Due Process Complaint Notice

Regardless of whether the LEA responds by sending out this notice, the LEA still may assert (within 15 days) that the parents' notice was not sufficient (20 U.S.C. Sec. 1415(c)(2)(B)(i)(II)). If it alleges that the parents' notice is not sufficient, it appears that the LEA still may respond to the notice in substantive terms. Simply saying that it is insufficient does not seem to preclude the LEA from denying or admitting the allegations in whole or part. Thus, it appears that the LEA may claim that parts or all of the notice are insufficient, or that some parts are insufficient but others are not, and with respect to those that do meet the sufficiency test, the LEA may either deny or admit the parents' allegations.

Let's assume that the LEA asserts that the parents' notice is not sufficient. When ruling on the sufficiency of the notice, the due process hearing officer may either dismiss the parents' complaint altogether on the grounds that none of it suffices to show that the LEA violated IDEA, or give the parents and LEA the opportunity to agree that the complaining party may amend the complaint so it meets the sufficiency rule.

If the hearing officer dismisses the parents' complaint on the grounds of insufficiency and if the LEA does not agree to permit the parents to file an amended complaint, the parents may start all over again by filing a new complaint that meets the sufficiency requirement. Because the LEA will have stated why it thinks the first complaint is not sufficient, the parents can use that information as the basis for creating a new, sufficient complaint.

Timelines for Sufficiency Ruling

The sufficiency rule has strict timelines. If the party receiving the notice (assume it is the LEA) believes that the (parents') complaint does not meet the requirements of 20 U.S.C. Sec. 1415(b)(7)(A), that party (the LEA) can notify the hearing officer of that fact, but it must do so within 15 days after it receives the complaint. If the LEA (receiving party) does not contact the hearing officer, the due process complaint is automatically deemed sufficient. If, however, the LEA (receiving party) objects on the grounds of insufficiency, the hearing officer has to make a written decision within 5 days after receiving the notification, ruling whether the notice is sufficient or insufficient (20 U.S.C. Sec. 1415(c)(2)(D)).

If the hearing officer rules that the notice is sufficient, the 30-day timeline for the LEA to resolve the issues in the complaint continues. If the officer rules that the notice is insufficient (as we noted above), the officer may dismiss the case, or the parties can agree to amend, or the hearing officer may order an amendment.

This new sufficiency requirement is a direct response to LEA complaints that parental requests for due process have been too general and do not provide sufficient information so the LEA may attempt to remedy the alleged problem. By creating a sufficiency requirement, Congress required the parents and LEA to present enough information so the complaint actually can be weighed and responded to long before a due process hearing begins. This also starts a discovery process in which the parties will present all of the relevant issues in a paperwork exchange (20 U.S.C. Sec. 1415(c)).

More significantly, this provision highlights the new responsibilities placed on parents to be informed about their child's education. If they do not clearly state the facts that underlie their complaint and describe the remedies they want, parents run the risk of having their case dismissed long before getting to the actual hearing.

Amending the Complaint

If the hearing officer rules that the notice is insufficient (assume, again, that the parents are filing the notice and complaint and must meet the sufficiency test), the parents may amend the complaint only if the LEA consents in writing and is given the opportunity to participate in a resolution session, or if the hearing officer grants permission to amend no later than 5 days before due process is scheduled to begin (20 U.S.C. Sec. 1415(c)(2)(E)). If a complaint is amended, the timeline for due process, as well as the timeline for the resolution session, restarts (20 U.S.C. Sec. 1415(c)(2) (E)(ii)).

This new provision reinforces that a complainant must set out, at the beginning of the dispute, every alleged violation that the party intends to raise in due process and is intended to prevent a long process involving repeated amendments. But, again, it places a heavy burden on the complainant to know exactly all the issues and how to allege them specifically.

Mediation

In an effort to forestall a due process hearing and any subsequent litigation in court and to advance the resolution of disputes by less adversarial means, IDEA (20 U.S.C. Sec. 1415(e)) provides that SEAs and LEAs must offer parents an opportunity to resolve disputes concerning their child's education through mediation (see also 34 C.F.R. 300.506). Each SEA and LEA must establish and implement procedures to ensure that mediation is available and must maintain a list of qualified mediators who have knowledge relevant to IDEA-related issues (34 C.F.R. 300.506(a) and (b)).

Furthermore, the mediator must be impartial, having no personal or professional conflict of interest and may not be an employee of the SEA or the LEA involved in the student's education (30 U.S.C. Sec. 1415(e); 34 C.F.R. 300.506(c)).

If a student's parents decline an agency's offer for mediation, the LEA or SEA may require, before proceeding to a due process hearing, that they meet (at a time and location convenient to the parents) with a disinterested third party who will explain the benefits and encourage the use of mediation (20 U.S.C. Sec. 1415(e)(2)(b); 34 C.F.R. 300.506(b)). The parties must enter into mediation voluntarily, and the mediation provisions may not be used to deny or delay parents' rights to procedural due process or any other rights under Part B (20 U.S.C. Sec. 1415(e)(2)(A)(ii); 34 C.F.R. 300.506(b)(1)(ii)). Thus, even if parents do not participate in the pre-mediation meeting, they may not be denied parents' rights to a due process hearing (34 C.F.R. 300.506(b)(1)(ii)).

If the parents do engage in mediation, the SEA bears the financial responsibility for the mediation, each mediation session must be scheduled in a timely manner (so as to not delay the right to an impartial hearing), and each must be held in a location convenient to both the parents and the LEA. Generally, the mediator can chose the direction of the discussion by having the parties either speak directly to one another or speak only to the mediator. If the parties are speaking to the mediator, they will present their information and offer for settlement, and the mediator will then convey that information to the other party.

If the parents and LEA reach an agreement during mediation, the agreement must be written (and is called a mediation agreement) and signed by the parents and LEA or SEA. An important change under the 2004 amendments is that the agreement is enforceable in any state court of competent jurisdiction or district court of the United States (20 U.S.C. Sec. 1415(e)(2)(F)). Finally, the content of the mediation proceedings must be kept confidential, and any statements the parties make during the mediation process may not be used as evidence in subsequent hearings or trials (20 U.S.C. Sec. 1415(e)(2)(G); 34 C.F.R. 300.506(b)(6)(i)).

Mandatory Resolution Process

For many years following the enactment of EHA in 1975, and certainly during the late 1990s and the early years of the twenty-first century, parents of students with disabilities used IDEA's procedural due process provisions aggressively—arguably, in the judgment of many SEAs and LEAs, too aggressively. Indeed, a major criticism of IDEA has been that it encourages litigation rather than resolution of disputes between educators and parents (Finn, Rotherham, & Hokanson, 2001; President's Commission, 2002).

Those who held this view also argued that the threat of due process and ensuing litigation caused SEAs and LEAs to expend excessive time documenting what they did, to be able to prove that they complied with IDEA, and that this paperwork burden diminished the educators' availability to teach and their willingness to practice their profession as they were taught to practice it. To the contrary, parents and other advocates for students responded, parents had to resort to due process only because SEAs and LEAs were defaulting in their IDEA obligations.

In reauthorizing IDEA in 2004, Congress resolved the dispute by

- retaining all of the procedural due process rights that EHA had established in 1975,

- strengthening the 1997 provisions for mediation, and
- adding new provisions for still another kind of alternative dispute resolution—the "mandatory resolution session."

Congress thereby made clear its intention to beef up alternative dispute resolution, consistent with its finding that "parents and schools should have expanded opportunities to resolve their disagreements in positive and constructive ways" (20 U.S.C. Sec. 1400(c)(8)).

The key change in the 2004 amendments is the addition of a "resolution session." The general rule is that the LEA must

- convene the resolution session within 15 days after it receives the parents' complaint,
- include at the session the members of the IEP team who have "specific knowledge" concerning the facts in the complaint,
- include an LEA representative who has "decision-making authority" on the LEA's behalf,
- allow the parents to discuss their complaint and the facts that form the basis of their complaint, and
- allow the LEA an opportunity to resolve the complaint (20 U.S.C. Sec. 1415(f)(1)(B)).

The parents may not go to a due process hearing unless they and the LEA waive, in writing, the requirement of a resolution session or agree to use mediation in its place. Thus, before the due process hearing begins, the parents must come face to face with the LEA at either the resolution session or mediation.

The LEA may not have its attorney present unless the parents are accompanied by an attorney (20 U.S.C. Sec. 1415(f)(1)(B)(i)(III)). If attorneys do attend, a due process hearing officer or a court may not award attorneys' fees for time spent attending a resolution session to the prevailing party in the dispute. (We discuss attorneys' fees in chapter 10.) But, of course, the parents and the LEA still will be responsible for paying their lawyers for any work done in connection with the resolution session. It is simply the case that, under the 2004 amendments, attorneys' fees may not be awarded for any services related to the resolution session (20 U.S.C. Sec. 1415(i)(D)).

If the parents and the LEA reach agreement at the resolution session, they must execute and sign an agreement that is legally enforceable in any state or federal court (20 U.S.C. Sec. 1415(f)(1)(B)(iii)). A party may void the agreement within 3 business days (20 U.S.C. Sec. 1415(f)(1)(B)(iv)).

The purpose of requiring the parties to participate in either the resolution session or mediation is clear: to give the LEA an opportunity to resolve the issues that the parent has raised in the due process complaint without having to undertake the time and expense of a due process hearing. Only if the LEA has not resolved the problem within 30 days from receipt of the parents' complaint may the due process hearing occur, and at that point the applicable timelines commence (20 U.S.C. Sec. 1415(f)(1)(B)(ii); 34 C.F.R. 300.510(b)(1)).

Thus, the 2004 amendments have not only created the mandatory resolution session, they also have created a mandatory "30-day cooling-off period." That's the period during which the resolution session occurs and the LEA has the opportunity to cure any alleged IDEA violations.

The regulations also impose specific consequences if parents do not participate in the process in a timely manner. Except where the parties have jointly agreed to waive the resolution process or use mediation, if the parents fail to participate in the resolution meeting, all timelines for the resolution process and due process are delayed (34 C.F.R. 300.510(b)(3)). However, the parents cannot delay the resolution period indefinitely. If an LEA is unable to obtain the participation of the parents (after documenting such attempts), the LEA may, at the conclusion of the 30-day resolution period, ask the hearing officer to dismiss the parents' due process complaint (34 C.F.R. 510(b)(4)). The regulations also add a parental remedy if an LEA does not participate. If the LEA does not schedule the resolution meeting in a timely manner or attend the resolution meeting, the parents may petition the hearing officer to begin the due process timelines (34 C.F.R. 300.510(b)(5)).

If the LEA has not resolved the complaint to the parents' satisfaction within those 30 days after it receives the parents' complaint, then and only then may the parents and LEA engage in the due process hearing. Generally, it is only after the 30-day period that the timelines related to due process hearings begin; the timelines are suspended when the parties are in the resolution stage (20 U.S.C. Sec. 1415(f)(1)(B)). However, the regulations have also added several exceptions to the 30-day resolution period timeline. The 45-day timeline for the due process hearing may also start the day after one of the following events:

- Both parties agree in writing to waive the resolution meeting.
- After either the mediation or resolution meeting starts but before the end of the 30-day resolution period, the parties agree in writing that no agreement is possible.
- Both parties agree in writing to continue the mediation at the end of the 30-day resolution period, but later the parents or the LEA withdraw from the mediation process (34 C.F.R. 300.510(c)).

Figure 8.1, the dispute-resolution flowchart, illustrates the new provisions related to notice, response, and mandatory resolution action, which we explain next and for which the figure should prove helpful.

Notice (Revisited) and Fairness (Also Revisited)

Under the 2004 amendments, the parents and LEA must undertake either the mandatory dispute resolution meeting or mediation before going to a due process hearing. As we pointed out, the 30-day period after the complaint is filed then becomes a time when a "quasi-hearing" or "mini-hearing" occurs—one that lacks the formality of a full due process hearing and one in which the LEA may try to cure any alleged IDEA violation and thereby forestall a hearing. That result flows from the notice requirements, which alert the LEA concerning the nature of the complaint, make it possible for the LEA to discover some of the facts on which the complainant-parents rely, and allow the LEA to develop an appropriate response and defense.

Moreover, the LEA has the opportunity to challenge the sufficiency of this notice. By challenging the sufficiency, the LEA obliges the parents to disclose exactly what they claim the LEA did wrong. That, too, gives the LEA the opportunity to cure any alleged wrongs because now it has information about the alleged

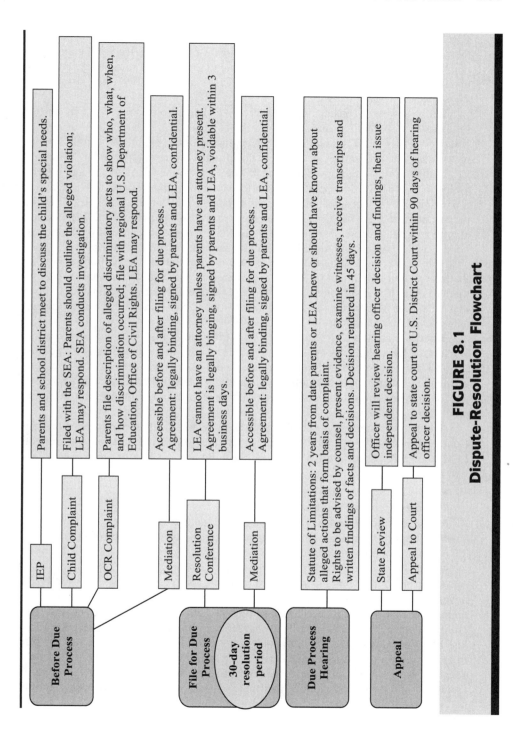

FIGURE 8.1
Dispute-Resolution Flowchart

IDEA violation. The LEA may be able to avoid a due process hearing altogether by taking such action as may satisfy the complainant-parents and lead to the dismissal of the complaint. Obviously, these requirements for notice, sufficiency, and cure underlie Congress's intent that parents and LEAs should resolve their disputes in ways other than due process.

Let's, however, consider this matter of dispute resolution in light of Justice Frankfurter's observation that fairness is the essence of due process and in light of *Schaffer v. Weast,* the Case on Point at the beginning of this chapter. The 2004 amendments make the procedure leading up to due process fair to parents and to SEAs and LEAs alike in this one important respect: They enable the LEA to cure any alleged violation. If the LEA does so, it advances the student's rights under IDEA, and that is fundamentally fair because IDEA intends to benefit the student. It also is fair to the parents and the LEA because any cure may mean that the parents and LEA do not engage in a due process hearing. That is fair to both parties because of the huge economic, psychological, and time-burden costs associated with any hearing.

We have been arguing that fairness results from the new resolution process. Is that really the case? It can be if the LEA does not challenge the parents' notice on the basis that it is insufficient, or if the LEA permits the parents to amend a notice that a hearing officer rules is not sufficient. And it also can be if the LEA indeed cures any IDEA violations.

But those are three "if" conditions. What if none of the "if" conditions occurs? What if the LEA challenges the parents' notice, objects to their amending it, requires them to start over again with a new notice, and makes no changes in how it is educating the student? Arguably, nothing is fair about a law that gives so much power to the LEA during the resolution process. So much for fairness that results from fair procedures.

The fairness matter has yet another side. It has to do with the imbalance that the Court wrote about in *Schaffer v. Weast.* In any face-off between the parents and the LEA, the LEA almost always will have the following advantages that the parents will not have:

- In-house experts whose salary it is already paying
- The advice of skilled lawyers
- The deep pockets of its federal, state, and local tax revenues
- Perhaps the benefits of an insurance policy and the assistance of the insurer's in-house staff and counsel

Contrarily, the parent must hire experts, pay legal counsel (usually in advance in the form of a "retainer fee"), and be prepared for the law's delays, the emotional distress that accompanies any lawsuit (especially one against the child's educators), and the possibility that the complaint itself will make the LEA less likely to educate the student appropriately, for doing so would be tantamount to an admission that it has violated IDEA. It is not unfair to criticize the Court's decision on the basis that the factual premise of the decision—that the statute creates an informational balance and thus a larger balance of power between the parties—is simply wrong.

Timing

Once the 30-day resolution period has ended, the ensuing due process hearing must be held and a final decision reached within 45 days after the expiration of the 30-day period or within the adjusted timeline described previously (34 C.F.R. 300.515). The hearing officer may extend this deadline at the request of either party (34 C.F.R. 300.515(c)). The time and place of a hearing involving oral argument must be reasonably convenient to the parents and student (34 C.F.R. 300.515(d)).

Qualifications and Impartiality of Hearing Officers

Each agency must keep a list of impartial hearing officers and their qualifications (34 C.F.R. 300.511(c)). The hearing officer may not be an employee of the agency involved in educating or otherwise providing services to the child and must not otherwise have any personal or professional interest that might conflict with objectivity in the hearing (20 U.S.C. Sec. 1415(f)(3)(A); 34 C.F.R. 300.511(c)). A person who otherwise qualifies to conduct a hearing is not considered to be an employee of the agency solely because the agency pays him or her to serve as a hearing officer (34 C.F.R. 300.511(c)).

The 2004 amendments added the requirement that the hearing officer must possess knowledge of IDEA statute, regulations, and federal and state case law; possess the knowledge and ability to conduct hearings in accordance with appropriate, standard legal practice; and possess the knowledge and ability to render and write decisions in accordance with appropriate, standard legal practice (20 U.S.C. Sec. 1415(f)(3)(A); 34 C.F.R. 300.511(c)).

CONDUCT OF HEARING AND FINDING (DECISION)

There are several issues related to the conduct of the hearing and the hearing officer's findings of fact and conclusions of law. They involve the stay-put rule; rights at hearing; burden of proof; the no-harm, no-foul rule; the right to free transcript; and the right to appeal.

Stay-Put Rule

The 2004 amendments preserve the basic stay-put rule. That rule generally requires an LEA to keep the student in the student's "then-current educational placement" during the time when any of the due process, mediation, and mandatory dispute-resolution activities are under way (20 U.S.C. Sec. 1415(j)). This rule has two exceptions:

1. The parents and LEA may jointly agree to change the student's placement during the "pendency" of any of those proceedings (that is, while they are ongoing).

2. During dispute proceedings that relate to discipline of any kind (not just discipline for possessing of weapons or illegal drugs or for causing serious bodily injury), the LEA may place the student into an interim alternative educational setting (20 U.S.C. Sec. 1415(k)(4)). (We discuss the disciplinary hearings later in this chapter.)

The purposes of the stay-put rule are

- to preserve the student's presumptively correct placement and program and thereby continue whatever benefits the placement and program offer,
- to prevent the LEA from making any unilateral decisions that might be construed as retaliatory against the parents who filed the complaint, and
- to assure the parents that they may complain without fear that the LEA will retaliate against them.

The regulations have also clarified what constitutes "stay-put" when a complaint is filed during the child's transition from services under Part C to Part B. If the child is no longer eligible for Part C services because the child has aged-out (turned 3), the LEA is not required to provide the Part C services that the child had been receiving (34 C.F.R. 300.518(c)). If, however, the child is found eligible for special education and related services and the parents consent to the initial provision of special education and related services, then the LEA must provide those services that are not in dispute between the parent and the LEA (34 C.F.R. 300.518(c)). The "stay-put" then is in the Part B program.

The general rule, then, is that the stay-put rule applies to disputes concerning the student's evaluation, IEP program, placement, due process rights, or parent/student participation rights (as we describe them in chapters 4 through 9). The exception to this general rule is that the stay-put rule does not apply to complaints and proceedings that involve discipline and the student's behavior. That is so because

- the student's behavior may reflect the fact that the current placement and program are not effective; the presumption that they are effective and appropriate arguably should be overcome solely because the student has engaged in punishable behavior;
- the student's behavior may jeopardize the teaching and learning environment; faculty and other students have an interest in teaching and learning without the interference that a student may cause; and
- the student's behavior may physically or emotionally threaten or injure the faculty or other students; school safety is a valued commodity under both IDEA and NCLB.

Rights at Hearing

At the initial hearing and on appeal, each party has the right to (20 U.S.C. Sec. 1415 (f),(h))

- be accompanied and advised by an attorney and by individuals with special knowledge or training with respect to the problems of children with disabilities;

- present evidence and confront, examine, cross-examine, and compel the attendance of witnesses;
- exclude any evidence offered by any party unless it was disclosed at least 5 business days before the hearing;
- receive a written or (at the option of the parents) an electronic verbatim record of the hearing; and
- receive written or (at the option of the parents) electronic findings of fact and decisions (20 U.S.C. Sec. 1415(h); 34 C.F.R. 300.512(a)).

At least 5 business days prior to a hearing, each party shall disclose to all other parties all evaluations completed by that date and recommendations based on those evaluations that are intended to be used at the hearing (20 U.S.C. Sec. 1415(f)(2)). If either party fails to meet this requirement and attempts to introduce such an evaluation or recommendation without the other party's consent, the hearing officer may bar the introduction of that evidence (20 U.S.C. Sec. 1415(f)(2); 34 C.F.R. 300.512(b)).

Parents involved in hearings must be given the right (34 C.F.R. 300.512(c))

- to have the child present,
- to have the hearing open to the public, and
- to have the records of the hearing provided at no cost to the parents.

The hearing officer's decision must be sent to the state special education advisory panel established under 20 U.S.C. Sec. 1415(h)(4) and 34 C.F.R. 300.167). These findings and decisions also must be made available to the public (34 C.F.R. 300.513(d)).

Burden of Proof

When one party brings a lawsuit against another, the law typically requires the party bringing the suit to prove his or her claim. IDEA does not explicitly assign the burden of proof to any potential party, so in the past, courts have relied on this general proposition, or on state law, to determine which party has the burden of proof. This resulted in an almost even split of opinion among the federal court circuits as to whether parents or the LEA had the burden of proof.

The Supreme Court resolved the matter in *Schaffer v. Weast* (2005) by ruling that the party bringing the suit has the burden of proof. As the opening paragraphs of this chapter make clear, the parents in that case had the burden of proof because they challenged the LEA's proposed IEP, alleging that it did not provide for an appropriate education. Writing for the Court, Justice O'Connor justified the decision on six grounds:

1. Litigation costs, which should be minimized by placing the burden of proof on the party that brings the due process hearing
2. Deference to the LEA's and educators' expertise, consistent with other decisions of the court in which it defers to professional judgment
3. The presumption that a student's IEP is appropriate, as warranted by IDEA's stay-put provision (see chapter 4)

4. The fact that parents already have sufficient procedures on their side, as evidenced by their rights of access to school records and their right to secure and require the school to consider independent evaluations

5. The 2004 requirement that LEAs must provide notices of action in response to any items raised in the filing of a complaint (if not already done)

6. Access to attorneys' fees

The effect of this ruling will be varied. Where state law or regulations already have placed the burden on parents, there will be no change. In states where the burden has shifted, however, parents will have to be even more prepared to present their case in point if they are representing themselves, and they also must face the reality that hiring an attorney is even more necessary now than before. That is so even in those few situations when the LEA has the burden of proof. It has the burden in at least these situations:

- The LEA appeals a decision of the hearing officer or court; on appeal, the LEA must persuade the appeals hearing officer or court of appeals that the initial hearing officer or trial court was wrong in its decision.

- The LEA seeks to override a parent's refusal to give consent for an initial evaluation or reevaluation.

- The parent requests an independent evaluation and wants to charge the cost to the LEA, but the LEA believes that its evaluation is appropriate (34 C.F.R. 300.502).

Because the parents, not an LEA, are more often the complaining party and have, in almost all cases, the burden of proof, it seems clear that the real issue (as the Case on Point argues) is whether the Supreme Court was correct when it concluded that there was no "informational imbalance" and thus no imbalance of power between the parents and the schools. We have discussed that issue and will return to it when we summarize this chapter. We simply ask you to keep that theme about power in your mind as you read more about due process.

Procedural Versus Substantive Violations; No-Harm, No-Foul Rule Now Codified

There also is a significant change in the basis for hearing officer decisions. Under the 2004 amendments, the hearing officer must make a decision on substantive grounds; that is, the hearing officer must determine whether the child has or has not received a free appropriate public education in the least restrictive environment (20 U.S.C. Sec. 1415(f)(3)(E); 34 C.F.R. 300.513(a)). The hearing officer may not hold that the student was denied FAPE solely because an LEA failed to comply exactly with all of IDEA's procedural requirements (the so-called *procedural inadequacies* failure) unless those inadequacies

- impeded the child's right to a FAPE (namely, education provided at public expense, without charge and under public supervision; that meets the SEA's standards; that includes appropriate preschool, elementary, or secondary school education; and that is provided in conformity with the required IEP, 20 U.S.C. Sec. 1401(9));
- significantly impeded the parents' opportunity to participate in the decision-making process regarding the provision of FAPE to their child; or
- caused a deprivation of educational benefit.

As to the first standard, "impeded FAPE," if the way in which an LEA provides services does not conform to the statute's procedural provisions (those that prescribe who must do what, when, and how) and if the result of those procedural violations are so great that the child therefore cannot have access to school (zero reject), a fair evaluation (nondiscriminatory evaluation), an appropriate (beneficial, effective) education, or a placement in the least restrictive environment in the general curriculum, then it seems the LEA is indeed impeding the student's right to FAPE. Just how great those procedural violations must be to actually impede a student's education is a matter that the courts will have to determine. As to the second standard, "significantly impeded" the parents' opportunity to participate, the courts clearly will have to define the meaning of that phrase.

The courts also will have to define the third standard, "caused a deprivation," most likely by relying on the dictionary definition of "deprivation." This word means a disadvantage from losing something or having something taken away and arguably includes, for example, a reduction in the hours a paraprofessional works with a student, a reduction in the number of related services or the number of hours any one or more related services is provided, a reduction in the supplementary services or aids available to a student, or any other loss of a present benefit, even if that loss does not make the student's program inappropriate (chapter 6) or the student's placement to be differently restrictive (chapter 7). These kinds of "losses," however, must be caused by a procedural violation; the courts must follow a strict cause-and-effect test.

The no-harm, no-foul rule reflects Congress's concern that hearing officers were ruling against LEAs and for students solely on the basis of violations of procedural technicalities. These decisions had costly ramifications for school districts, considering that the LEA had to pay for parents' attorneys' fees (S. Rept. 185 108th Cong., 1st Sess., 39 (2003)). The amendment also codifies the decisions of the many courts that laid down a maxim in IDEA cases: no harm, no foul.

Right to Free Transcript

An indigent parent representing himself or herself and the child in an IDEA action against an LEA is entitled to both an electronic tape-recorded record of the due process hearing and a written transcript of the same hearing.

Right to Appeal

Unless a party appeals, the initial hearing officer's decision is final (20 U.S.C. Sec. 1415(i)(1)(A); 34 C.F.R. 300.514(a)). If the hearing is conducted by an LEA, an aggrieved party may appeal to the SEA, which is required to

- conduct an impartial review of the hearing (which includes examining the hearing record, ensuring that hearing procedures were consistent with due process, seeking additional evidence as necessary, and affording the parties the opportunity for oral or written argument as needed);
- reach an independent decision; and
- send a copy of the decision to the parties within 30 days (34 C.F.R. 300.514(b); 34 C.F.R. 300.515(b)).

If the SEA reviewing official determines that oral argument will be held, the time and place of a review involving oral argument must be reasonably convenient to the parents and the child (34 C.F.R. 300.514(b), citing 300.512). Some states have only one level of SEA hearings; others have more than one. The findings and decisions on appeal must be transmitted to the state advisory panel and be made available to the public, as also is required after the initial hearing (34 C.F.R. 300.514(c)).

Persons who are aggrieved by the findings and decision in the initial hearing (who do not have a right to an appeal as described), or who are aggrieved by the findings and decision on appeal, may file a civil action in either a state court or a federal district court. The court, whether state or federal, is to receive the records of the administrative proceedings, hear additional evidence at the request of any party, and, on the basis of preponderance of the evidence, grant appropriate relief (20 U.S.C. Secs. 1415(i)(2)(A) and (B); 34 C.F.R. 300.516).

As the Supreme Court in *Rowley* made clear, when a court hears an appeal, the review includes a *de novo* (new) review of the administrative record and of the legal issues presented. Not only may a court review the record before it, but it also may admit new evidence and must do so if a party requests it.

Then the court must make its decision on the basis of the entire record before it—the administrative record and the new evidence; and it must give due weight to the administrative record and the hearing officer's decision. It must follow that decision unless it is clearly wrong and unless the newly admitted evidence is contradictory and more persuasive.

When, as usual, the review involves mixed questions of fact and law, a court may be tempted to decide on its own exactly what constitutes a free appropriate public education in the least restrictive setting. That, however, would not be entirely proper. The court must give proper deference to the findings of fact of the hearing officer or a lower court; the rule of deference to the previous adjudication applies only with respect to matters of fact.

The court is not required, however, to defer to the hearing officer's or lower court's conclusion of law. It is free to affirm or reverse the conclusion of law, in whole or in part, based on its interpretation of the statute or regulations or other courts' decisions (the principle of precedents and *stare decisis*: let the decisions stand).

Further, a court's role is not to second-guess educators' judgments about the methods they use to educate children appropriately and effectively. When a dispute exists, the court should defer to professionals' expert opinions and, if experts disagree, may side with the experts who are more persuasive and offer more probative testimony (testimony that proves their point) (*Daniel R.R. v. State Bd. of Educ.*, 1989).

Rather, a court's narrow task is to determine whether those officials have complied with IDEA's provisions and regulations as interpreted by other courts. Have the officials followed its process (the *Rowley* standard, also called the process definition), and have they thereby assured that the student will receive some educational benefit (the *Rowley* standard, also called the benefit standard) (*Salley v. St. Tammany Parish Sch. Bd.*, 1995)?

LIMITATIONS ON THE RIGHTS OF DUE PROCESS

You might think that IDEA places no limits on the parents' or LEA's rights to due process. But you would be wrong. The 2004 amendments create limits in two ways:

1. By specifying who may file for a due process hearing
2. By saying when they must file

The courts also have limited due process rights by applying traditional doctrines having to do with involuntary dismissal, waiver and estoppel, and exhaustion of remedies.

Standing to Seek Due Process: Who May File

The 2004 amendments grant the parents, the SEA, LEA, or any other interested party standing to file a complaint with respect to any matter relating to the identification, evaluation, educational placement of the child, or provision of FAPE to the child. The phrase "other interested party" can include a great number of professionals (such as health-care or behavioral-health/mental health professionals, foster-care or adoption social workers, or probation officers attached to courts or juvenile/adult justice agencies) and agencies (health, mental health, social service, or criminal justice), but only if those professionals and agencies are involved in the child's education in some significant way. Otherwise, "interested party" would mean nothing and there would be no limitation on the ability of a stranger to the situation filing a complaint.

Remember, as we pointed out earlier in this chapter, if a parent refuses to allow the student into special education, the parent loses any right to complain under IDEA about the student's education (20 U.S.C. Sec. 1414(a)(1)(D)((ii)(III))(aa)). Of course, as we also pointed out, the parent can always ask for an evaluation and then give consent to special education services. The refusal of consent and the subsequent loss of standing apply to only the specific refusal.

Statute of Limitations

A statute of limitations limits the period of time beyond which a lawsuit may be filed. This rule ensures that disputes are heard when evidence is relatively fresh—when the witnesses have been only recently removed from the time during which the facts arose. The rule also prompts parties to resolve their disputes sooner or later so they may get on with their lives without the inevitable uncertainty and burdens that come with a lawsuit.

The 2004 amendments have added a statue of limitations: Under those amendments, a parent or SEA or LEA must request a due process hearing within 2 years of the date that the parent or agency knew, or should have known, about the alleged violation (20 U.S.C. Sec. 1415(b)(6)). That rule, however, does not apply to the parents if they were prevented from requesting the hearing because of specific misrepresentations by the LEA that it had resolved the problem that formed the basis of the complaint or if the LEA withheld information that it was obliged to give to the parents (20 U.S.C. Sec. 1415(f)(3)(D)).

Involuntary Dismissal

If a parent refuses to participate in any part of an administrative or judicial hearing (for example, the parent refuses to participate in pretrial discovery proceedings), the general rule in civil proceedings is that the court may dismiss the parent's complaint over the parent's objection (involuntary dismissal). There is no reason to believe that IDEA changes this result.

Parental Waiver and Estoppel

Similarly, the general rule in civil proceedings is that a party—in IDEA, a parent, LEA, SEA, or other party authorized to file for due process—may forfeit IDEA rights by waiving them. The doctrine of waiver basically means that a party who has certain rights foregoes them voluntarily; the party surrenders them and therefore is "estopped" (barred) from insisting that schools must follow them. There also is no reason to believe that the 2004 reauthorization changes this result.

Exhaustion of Remedies

A highly vexatious issue is whether parents or an LEA must exhaust their administrative remedies under IDEA before they may file a lawsuit in federal or state courts. To exhaust one's administrative remedies simply means that one first must go through the mandatory resolution session (unless the parents and LEA waive it), the meeting about the benefits of mediation (unless the parents and LEA waive it), mediation (if both the parents and LEA agree to it), and any LEA- and SEA-level due process hearings before being entitled to file a lawsuit in state or federal court. The general rule is that parents must exhaust their administrative remedies. Why is that a good rule?

Purposes of the Rule

The purposes of the exhaustion-of-remedies rule are manifold. The rule

- permits the LEA to exercise discretion and apply the agency's expertise to students' education;
- allows full development of technical issues and factual records before a court hears the case;
- prevents deliberate disregard and circumvention of agency procedures that Congress has clearly established;
- avoids unnecessary judicial decision, and thereby economizes judicial resources, by giving the LEA the first opportunity to correct any errors it may have made;
- ensures accuracy in the findings of fact, because the administrative hearings (the due process hearings) can be scheduled more rapidly than a court trial, given the backlog of cases in state and federal courts, and thus the administrative hearings will occur when the evidence, especially witnesses' memories, are fresh and more reliable; and
- ensures efficiency in the administration of IDEA, because many conflicts can be solved at the administrative level and thus not have to wait on court hearings, rapid resolution being desirable because justice delayed often is justice denied.

For these reasons, 20 U.S.C. Sec. 1415(l) and 34 C.F.R. 300.516(e) requires parties—parents and schools alike—to exhaust their administrative remedies (go through the mandatory resolution session or mediation and then due process hearings) before being eligible to have a hearing in a federal or state court. The statute also requires parties to exhaust their administrative remedies under Sec. 1415(f) (due process hearings) and Sec. 1415(g) (appeal) before proceeding with any complaints under other federal laws, including ADA, Sec. 504, and Sec. 1983 of the Civil Rights Act.

Exceptions to "Exhaustion" Requirement

A rule as simple as the exhaustion rule should not, it would seem, create so many difficulties. Yet that is exactly what the rule has done. Like every general rule, it has its exceptions. The major exception is the *futility exception*.

Because the exhaustion rule can create hardships, the courts, using their equitable powers, have excused parties from exhausting their administrative remedies when doing so would be futile for them—that is, when exhausting the remedies would contribute little or nothing to resolving the disputes between the parties (*Miener v. Missouri*, 1980; *Monahan v. Nebraska*, 1980). The question, then, is what constitutes futility with respect to IDEA's exhaustion rule? We answer that in the following segment.

Exceptions to Exhaustion Rule

Cases in which courts have excused the complaining party (usually the parents) from complying with the exhaustion-of-remedies rule:

- The LEA, as a respondent/defendant, waives the exhaustion rule where a portion of a case already has been adjudicated at the administrative level, as in *North v. D.C. Bd. of Ed.* (1979), or in which the parties were bound by the prior order of the same court (see also *Jose P. v. Ambach,* 1982).
- More than one parent (complainant/plaintiff) files a class action lawsuit (one brought on one's own behalf and on behalf of other parents similarly aggrieved), alleging that an LEA has failed in the past to carry out its IDEA obligations, and another court has so found (*United Cerebral Palsy of NYC v. Bd. of Ed. of City of N.Y.,* 1983).
- Facts are undisputed that an LEA is not complying with IDEA (the student is excluded totally from any IDEA benefits and from school itself) and that the LEA will take no action at all to provide an appropriate education to the student (*Harris v. Campbell,* 1979).
- An SEA has failed, and continues to refuse, to appoint surrogate parents for residents of a state institution for people with mental retardation, thereby making it impossible for the residents (who are IDEA-entitled) to use their administrative remedies (*Garrity v. Gallen,* 1981; *Ruth Ann M. v. Alvin I.S.D.,* 1982).
- A student challenges the SEA's own regulations, alleging that they are inconsistent with IDEA and therefore invalid; at the same time, the student challenges the state education commissioner's performance of his or her duties, alleging that, as a result of the improper regulations and malfeasance in the performance of duty, the student has been expelled from school contrary to IDEA, as in *J.G. v. Bd. of Educ.* (1982, 1983), a lawsuit designed to correct alleged systemwide violation of IDEA's procedures.
- A student seeks a remedy that cannot be provided, in any way, under IDEA—for example, damages from an LEA because of its alleged failure to comply with IDEA (see chapter 9 for the cases on damages under IDEA and other laws) (*J.G. v. Bd. of Educ.,* 1987; *Kerr Center Parents Association v. Charles,* 1983; *Loughran v. Flanders,* 1979; *Quackenbush v. Johnson City School District,* 1983).
- A student seeks a remedy that cannot be provided under IDEA— namely, a systemwide remedy (cutoff of federal funds to an SEA or LEA) that is available under Section 504 (*New Mexico Association for*

Retarded Citizens v. New Mexico, 1982; *United Cerebral Palsy of NYC v. Bd. of Ed. of City of N.Y.*, 1982).

- A student will experience severe harm, not of his or her own making, as a result of having to exhaust his or her remedies (*Crocker v. Tennessee Secondary School Athletic Ass'n.*, 1989; *Phipps v. New Hanover County Bd. of Educ.*, 1982; *Vander Malle v. Ambach*, 1982; *J. G. v. Bd. of Educ.*, 1987). But if a student is dangerous to others and the LEA uses the *Honig* safety valve to suspend the student temporarily (for up to 10 days) or to seek a court order enjoining a dangerous student from attending school temporarily (see chapter 3, explaining that under *Honig* the Supreme Court allowed an LEA to take all necessary steps to safeguard other students in the extreme likelihood of danger to them from the expelled student), the LEA itself need not exhaust IDEA administrative remedies (64 Fed. Reg. 12,621—discussion on 34 C.F.R. 300.521) (*Honig v. Doe*, 1988; *School Board of Hillsborough County v. Student 26493257S*, 1995).

- An SEA or an LEA absolutely denies the student access to an administrative remedy, refusing to appoint a hearing officer or to attend a due process hearing (*Christopher W. v. Portsmouth School Committee*, 1989; *Ezratty v. Commonwealth of Puerto Rico*, 1981; *Kerr Center Parents Association v. Charles*, 1983; *Mrs. W. v. Tirozzi*, 1987; *Quackenbush v. Johnson City School Dist.*, 1983).

- An LEA fails to carry out the order of a due process hearing officer (*Porter v. Board of Trustees of Manhattan Beach Unified Sch. Dist.*, 2003).

What does not constitute futility?

- The fact that the administrative process is protracted does not constitute futility.
- The fact that a case involves many students and requires a finding of fact and conclusion of law regarding each of them (as to their IDEA rights) does not constitute futility.

Later-Occurring Grievances

What if a student, who already has concluded a due process hearing on one or more grievances, finds that he or she has yet another, later-occurring grievance against the same LEA? Must the student exhaust the administrative remedies as to the later-discovered grievance, or may the student consolidate that grievance with the other grievances in the appeal to a court? To require the student to exhaust his or her administrative remedies on the later-discovered grievance would be consistent with IDEA and the purposes and principles of exhaustion, but it also would prevent the student from having a hearing on all of the claims, those being appealed and those just discovered—hardly an efficient process for the student or the LEA.

The answer usually has been that the student must exhaust his or her IDEA remedies as to the later-discovered claims (*Jeremy H. v. Mt. Lebanon Sch. Dist.*, 1996). It seems that the notice requirements of the 2004 amendments—those that require the complaining party to set out all of the facts and proposed remedy—do not change this rule because they do not address later-occurring (alleged) violations per se and are very clear about requiring the complaining party to set out all of the facts and proposed remedy for the particular (alleged) violation. There is no reason to think that any later-occurring (alleged) violation is exempt from that requirement.

Administrative, Fiscal, or Organizational Issues Affecting More Than One Child

Although IDEA grants a due process hearing as a matter of right to any party in matters involving child identification, classification, or services, the courts have limited students' right to obtain a hearing if the party (typically, a parent) seeking the hearing is trying to prevent an SEA or LEA from carrying out administrative, organizational, or fiscal decisions that affect more than one child (*Behavior Research Institute v. Secretary of Administration*, 1991; *Concerned Parents and Citizens for Continuing Education at Malcolm X (PS 79) v. New York City Bd. of Educ.*, 1980; *Dima v. Macchiarola*, 1981; *Tilton v. Jefferson County Bd. of Educ.*, 1983; *Windward School v. State*, 1978).

Notwithstanding these decisions, any parent who alleges that any change of placement, even one resulting from administrative, organizational, or fiscal decisions about the education of a group of students, may go to due process to challenge the change as it affects the one child; access to due process is still open if the systemwide change alters the particular special education program or services for an individual child (*Brown v. Dist. of Columbia Board of Educ.*, 1978; *Concerned Parents and Citizens for Continuing Education at Malcolm X (PS 79) v. New York City Bd. of Educ.*, 1980).

The reasons for the courts' reluctance to allow parents to use the due process hearing remedy in cases involving administrative, organizational, or fiscal decisions are fairly well grounded:

- Although Congress intended a hearing to be available when placement changes (the child is moved from one type of program, such as a residential one, to another, such as an integrated one; or from one type of setting, such as a resource room, to another, such as a fully integrated program), the due process route is not needed unless the change in placement or program substantially affects the student's rights to an appropriate education.
- Allowing a due process hearing in all changes of placement or program, even those that are not likely to affect the student's rights to an educational benefit, would open up the floodgates for many insubstantial claims. The administra-

tive and judicial hearing process could become clogged with essentially frivolous cases.

- Allowing a due process hearing in all changes of placement and program would involve the courts in oversight of school district decisions that are based on administrative grounds. To function effectively and efficiently, school authorities have to redraw school boundaries, open or close schools, move students from one building to another, and so on. If every such administrative decision can be challenged, the courts will become super-ordinary school boards and the administrative efficacy of the schools will be impaired.

- Allowing a due process hearing in all such changes may put the courts in the position of having the opportunity to substitute their educational or administrative policy decisions for those of the elected or appointed school boards and their professional staffs. As has been argued throughout this book, courts are reluctant to take on that kind of authority, preferring to defer to the experts in those matters.

- IDEA's reference to placement—challengeable in a due process hearing—is limited to basic decisions regarding evaluation and appropriate education. A broad interpretation might impair an LEA's ability to implement even minor changes.

Disciplinary Hearings

One of the most serious issues leading up to the 1997 amendments and again in the 2004 amendments to IDEA was the matter of student discipline and school safety. (We pointed this out in chapter 3, "IDEA, Antidiscrimination Laws, and General Education Laws," and discussed in depth in chapter 4, "Zero Reject"). Why are discipline and safety so significant, and why does IDEA pay particular attention to them?

Discipline is valued for two reasons:

1. Discipline can teach a student how and why to behave in certain ways.
2. Discipline can enhance educators' ability to teach and students' ability to learn.

School safety is valued for two related reasons:

1. Safety is essential if there is to be an effective environment for teaching and learning.
2. Safety is essential to safeguard against physical or emotional harm.

Given the values attached to discipline and school safety, it was only reasonable for Congress to enact provisions preserving these values while also affording parents and an LEA the opportunity to resolve their differences around discipline through specialized due process procedures. Let's now analyze those procedures, bearing in mind that we discussed the substantive standards related to discipline in chapter 4, "Zero Reject."

General Rule: The 10-Day Change of Placement and Manifestation Determination

If an LEA seeks to order a change in placement that would exceed 10 school days, the student's IEP team must conduct a manifestation determination to confirm if the student's behavior was a manifestation of the student's disability (20 U.S.C. Sec. 1415(k)(1)). Within 10 school days after the LEA decides to change a student's placement because the student violated a student code of conduct, the members of the manifestation-determination team must conclude that the behavior was or was not a manifestation of the student's disability (34 C.F.R. 300.530(e)). If the LEA, the parents, and members of the child's IEP team determine that the child's behavior was a direct result of the LEA's failure to implement the child's IEP, the LEA must take immediate steps to remedy those deficiencies of failure to implement (34 C.F.R. 300.530(c)(3)).

If a parent disagrees with any decision regarding placement or the manifestation determination, the parent may appeal the decision by requesting a hearing before a due process hearing officer (20 U.S.C. Sec. 1415(k)(3)). In addition, an LEA may request a hearing if the LEA believes that maintaining the student's current placement is "substantially likely to result in injury to the child or to others."

Expedited Hearing

If there is a hearing request, the LEA or the SEA must arrange for an expedited hearing. The statute provides that the hearing has to occur within 20 school days of the date it is requested and that the hearing officer must render a decision within 10 school days after the hearing (20 U.S.C. Sec. 1415(k)(4)(B)).

The regulations (34 C.F.R. 300.532(c)) clarify the timeline under the expedited hearing and may lead you to conclude that "expedited" is a rather inaccurate word if one understands it to mean fast or swift. But if one understands "expedited" to be relative to the ordinary due process hearing timelines, the expedited hearing rule does require faster and swifter action. It is best to explain the expedited hearing timeline by using an actual calendar of events and to illustrate the narrative explanation in Figure 8.2.

Assume that the parent requests an expedited hearing on Wednesday, April 5, 2006 (the "request day"). The LEA must convene a resolution session and hold that session ("resolution session day") by Wednesday, April 12 (within 7 calendar days after the parent files the request). The regulations allow 8 days for the resolution period.

If, however, the parents and LEA do not reach a resolution within those 8 calendar days or within 15 calendar days after the parent requests the expedited hearing, a hearing may occur. That earliest date is Thursday, April 20 (the "hearing day"). That is the very first day when a hearing can begin (because of the mandatory resolution period), but it is not the last. The hearing must be held before Monday, April 3.

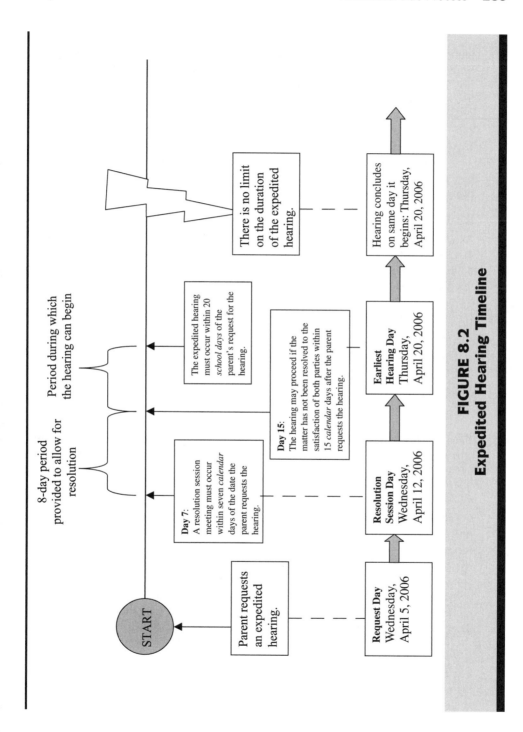

8-day period provided to allow for resolution

Period during which the hearing can begin

Day 7: A resolution session meeting must occur within seven *calendar* days of the date the parent requests the hearing.

Day 15: The hearing may proceed if the matter has not been resolved to the satisfaction of both parties within 15 *calendar* days after the parent requests the hearing.

The expedited hearing must occur within 20 *school days* of the parent's request for the hearing.

There is no limit on the duration of the expedited hearing.

START

Parent requests an expedited hearing.

Request Day Wednesday, April 5, 2006

Resolution Session Day Wednesday, April 12, 2006

Earliest Hearing Day Thursday, April 20, 2006

Hearing concludes on same day it begins: Thursday, April 20, 2006

FIGURE 8.2
Expedited Hearing Timeline

The expedited hearing must occur no later than 20 school days after the parent requests it. Note that the regulation now uses school days instead of calendar days. Thus, the hearing must begin by no later than Tuesday, April 25.

There is no limitation on how long the hearing may last. It can be as short as one day, or as long as a week or more.

Assume that the hearing takes only one day and is held on the earliest hearing day, Thursday, April 20. In that event, the hearing officer must render a decision within 10 school days, or by no later than Tuesday, May 4 (the "decision day").

Assuming that these dates hold, the expedited hearing period begins on Wednesday, April 5 (the request day), and ends on Tuesday, May 4 (the decision day). That is a period of just a day under 4 weeks.

No Stay-Put During Disciplinary Proceedings

As we pointed out earlier in this chapter and in chapter 4 ("Zero Reject"), the basic stay-put requirement (20 U.S.C. Sec. 1415(j)) states that students will remain in their then-current educational placementt. However, 20 U.S.C. Sec. 1415(k)(4) provides the exception to this rule for disciplinary placements:

> When an appeal under paragraph (3) has been requested by either the parent or the local educational agency—the child shall remain in the interim alternative educational setting pending the decision of the hearing officer or until the expiration of the time period provided for in paragraph (1)(C), whichever occurs first, unless the parent and the State or local educational agency agree otherwise.

Thus, for the duration of any appeal of a more-than-10-day suspension, the student will remain in the interim placement, not the student's then-current placement, if the LEA so chooses.

Burden of Proof

On an appeal from the team's determination, it appears that the appealing party must prove that the team's decision (to place the student into an interim alternative placement, to conclude that the student's behavior was not a manifestation of the disability, or to apply disciplinary sanctions) is not supported by the evidence that it considered. The burden of proof is on the party bringing the appeal and consists of persuading the hearing officer or, later, a judge that the team's manifestation determination is clearly factually erroneous. This is consistent with the Supreme Court's decision in *Schaffer v. Weast*, the Case on Point.

Conduct of Hearing and Findings by Hearing Officer

The hearing officer must "hear and make a determination regarding an appeal" from the manifestation determination. The hearing officer also may order a change in the student's placement by either

- returning the student to the student's current placement, or
- ordering a change of placement to an appropriate alternative educational setting for not more than 45 school days if the hearing officer determines (by a preponderance of the evidence—more than 50% of it) that maintaining the current placement of such child is "substantially likely to result in injury to the child or to others" (20 U.S.C. Secs. 1415(k)(3)(B)(i)–(ii)).

Preemptive Strike

A student can claim to be eligible for IDEA protection even though the student was not yet classified into IDEA. This claim is known as a "preemptive strike" against an LEA: The student "strikes first" by invoking IDEA and its special protections.

IDEA (20 U.S.C. Sec. 1415(k)(5)(A)) provides that the student who has violated a code of student conduct or otherwise engaged in punishable behavior may invoke IDEA protections "if the (LEA) had knowledge … that the child was a child with a disability before the behavior that precipitated the disciplinary action occurred." The LEA is deemed to have that knowledge if

- the student's parent has expressed concern in writing (unless the parent is illiterate or has a disability that prevents compliance with these requirements) to "supervisory or administrative personnel of the appropriate educational agency, or a teacher of the child, that the child is in need of special education and related services";
- the parent has requested an evaluation of the child pursuant to 20 U.S.C. Sec. 1414(a)(1)(B); or
- the student's teacher or other LEA personnel has "expressed specific concerns about a pattern of behavior demonstrated by the child, directly to the director of special education of such agency or to other supervisory personnel of the agency" (20 U.S.C. Sec. 1415(k)(5)(B)).

An LEA is not deemed to have knowledge that the student is an IDEA student if

- the student's parent has not allowed the LEA to evaluate the student pursuant to 20 U.S.C. Sec. 1414 or has refused services under Part B after the LEA evaluated the student and found him/her eligible for IDEA, or
- the LEA has evaluated the student and found that he/she is not "a child with a disability" (20 U.S.C. Sec. 1415(k)(5)(C)).

In other words, parents cannot protest a change of placement because of their child's behavior if they refused to admit their child to special education before the behaviors occurred.

Figure 8.3 organizes the dispute-resolution timelines in a flowchart to help with understanding.

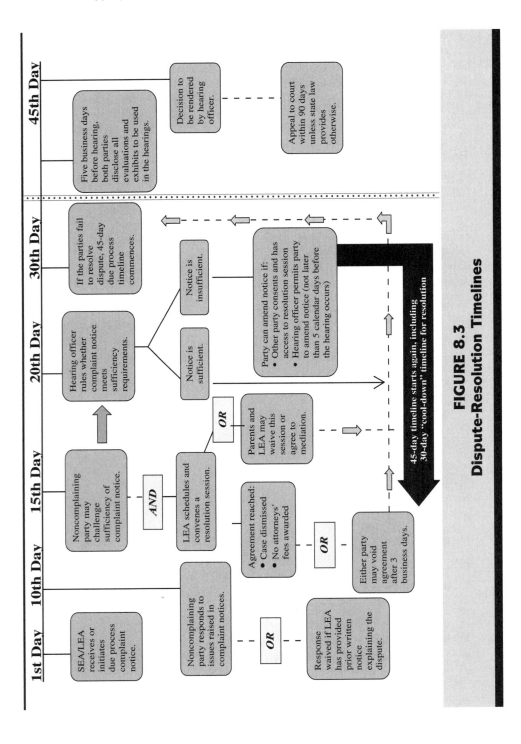

FIGURE 8.3
Dispute-Resolution Timelines

SUMMARY

Let's return to the Case on Point, *Schaffer v. Weast,* and the point of the case. Narrowly understood, the Court held that parents have the burden of proof when challenging the LEA's IEP. Broadly understood, the Court assumed that parents and LEAs were in a relationship in which there was a balance of power. Did Congress, in the 2004 reauthorization, agree?

It is doubtful, for Congress imposed on parents various new due process duties and required the mandatory resolution session. Given that Congress was responding to the recommendations of the President's Commission on Excellence in Special Education (2002) to reduce paperwork, adversarial relationships, and administrative burdens that IDEA allegedly had created, and given further that Congress itself found that "parents and schools should have expanded opportunities to resolve their disagreements in positive and constructive ways" (20 U.S.C. Sec. 1400(c)(8)), it seems difficult to conclude that the Court got it right in finding that the "core" of IDEA is its "cooperative process" and that there is not such a great "informational imbalance" to justify placing the burden of proof on the party filing a compliant (typically, the parents).

Historically, there was no cooperative process. That fact alone was one of the reasons Congress enacted EHA (now, IDEA) in 1975, as we pointed out in chapters 1–3. Over the years since then, the cooperative process has improved, but the adversarialness did, too. And what was true in 1975 remained true in 2004: Schools enjoyed the home-court advantage—the power—when dealing with parents. They had a larger talent bank (experts) and deeper pockets (public funds, lawyers, and insurance policies) than parents.

For those reasons alone, IDEA gave parents and students (when of age) access to due process safeguards. But not for just those reasons: Due process is, as we pointed out early in this chapter, a requirement of the Constitution and the means for assuring fairness between the government and the governed. The question that you must answer is whether it is fair for the parents to have to prove that a school's proposed IEP is not appropriate. Before answering that question, consider the last of IDEA's six principles, the principle of parent participation—or, in the Court's words, "the cooperative process" that is the "core" of the statute.

Chapter 9

Parent Participation

Case on Point: *Burlington School Committee v. Massachusetts Department of Education*
471 U.S. 359 (1985)

Desperate needs produce desperate action. And desperate action often requires unusual legal responses.

Take, for example, the education of Michael Panico, a student in the Burlington, Massachusetts, public schools. For eight years, the Panicos and the LEA had been negotiating with each other about Michael's education. There was no question about the fact that he had a disability (specific learning disability with secondary emotional disturbance) and was entitled to IDEA benefits. The issue was whether the LEA was providing FAPE. The Panicos thought not; the LEA thought so. The LEA and his parents reached an impasse; neither was willing to yield to the other.

Michael's father broke the impasse by refusing to enroll him in an LEA program and, instead, enrolling him in a state-approved private school. Then, Michael's father sought to recover the tuition and related costs of that school from the LEA.

At a due process hearing, Michael's father carried the day, and the SEA ordered the LEA to pay the tuition and related costs. The LEA refused, and in due time the dispute went from the due process hearing, to a federal district court, then on appeal to the federal court of appeals, and eventually to the

U.S. Supreme Court. The LEA was pitted against the SEA because the LEA refused to pay, and the SEA ordered that it must pay the private-school tuition and related expenses.

The Court faced two issues. First, does IDEA, which authorizes a court to grant "such relief as the court determines is appropriate," permit a court to order an LEA or SEA to reimburse parents for the tuition and related expenses of a private-school education? Second, may the court award that relief when the parent places the child in that school without the LEA's consent?

The Court answered both questions with a resounding "yes." Why? Because IDEA itself provides for placement in a private school at public expense as a means for providing FAPE. And because, on a more fundamental level, the IDEA procedural due process safeguards constitute a "ponderous" process. Often, a final judgment from a court about the merits of a student's IEP and placement will take a year or more after the school term covered by that IEP has passed.

In the meantime, parents who disagree with the proposed IEP are faced with a choice: go along with the child's IEP to the detriment of their child if it turns out to be inappropriate or pay for what they consider to be the appropriate placement. If they choose the latter course, which conscientious parents who have adequate means and who are reasonably confident of their assessment normally would, it would be an empty victory to have a court tell them several years later that they were right but that these expenditures could not in a proper case be reimbursed by the school officials. If that were the case, the child's right to a free appropriate education, the parents' rights to participate fully in developing a proper IEP, and all of the procedural safeguards would be less than complete.

Congress, the Court said, "undoubtedly did not intend this result." So parents may recover the tuition and related costs if they place their child in a private school because the public school did not provide FAPE. But the private school itself must provide FAPE. There is no reason to substitute a public school that does not provide FAPE for a private school that also does not provide FAPE.

Desperate needs for FAPE produce desperate action—expensive private-school education. Likewise, an IDEA violation produces a legal remedy. That's one lesson from the *Burlington* case.

Another lesson is that LEAs cannot simply stonewall parents, refusing to deal with them. *Burlington* teaches us that parents and LEAs have duties to deal with each other in good faith—if not as partners in the child's education, then at least in ways that conclusively resolve their differences.

Finally, *Burlington* instructs us that, despite all of the IDEA rights and remedies that parents have, LEAs still have the power advantage. We made that case in chapter 8, especially when we discussed *Schaffer v. Weast,* the burden-of-proof case. *Burlington* makes it again: The parents must face off against the LEA and may recover private-school tuition *only*—that's the governing word—if the LEA agrees to pay for it or is ordered to pay for it. In that face-off, the LEA has more expertise and deeper pockets than parents, despite the IDEA parent participation provisions that we discuss next.

THE PARENT PARTICIPATION PRINCIPLE: RELATIONSHIPS AND FUNCTIONS

Having reviewed IDEA's first five principles, let's now examine how IDEA makes it possible for parents and professionals to be partners in educating a student with a disability. The last of IDEA's principles, parent participation, promotes partnership but it cannot compel it; that's up to the parents and professionals. Further, the parent participation principle has other functions, as you will soon learn.

Protect Parent and Student Rights

One of IDEA's original and continuing purposes is to protect the rights of children with disabilities and their parents or guardians (20 U.S.C. Sec. 1401(d)(1)(B)). Like the procedural due process principle, the parent participation principle is a check-and-balance technique, enabling parents to monitor SEAs and LEAs with respect to how they implement the first four IDEA principles. It is, however, more than that. It is also, and most significantly, a means for assuring that the key stakeholders in a student's education may collaborate as partners worthy of each other's trust. But, with the opportunity to participate comes accountability for these decisions, just as is the case with respect to the principle of procedural due process.

Require Parents to Be Accountable

As we emphasized in earlier chapters, there is increased accountability for parents under IDEA's 2004 amendments. The amendments state that the education of children with disabilities will be made more effective by "strengthening the role and responsibility of parents and ensuring that families of such children have meaningful opportunities to participate in the education of their children at school and at home" (20 U.S.C. Sec. 1400(c)(5)(B)). This language conveys a message that has long been part of IDEA, namely, that parents have roles in their children's education and accordingly should have rights to participate in decisions affecting their education. But it also conveys a new message, which is that parents have responsibilities, not just to their children but also to the professionals charged with educating their children. In chapters 4–8, we discussed some of those responsibilities, and we will summarize them again. The key point is that there are no rights without corresponding responsibilities.

The consequence of the responsibilities emphasis is that parents themselves must acquire information and training on IDEA and its provisions or risk losing the many benefits and rights that IDEA confers.

Advance Democratic Values

Making parents partners in the education of their children is also another way to prevent unilateral decision making and promote democratic values. Shared decision making in the schools and in other public agencies is called participatory democracy. It refers to the legal right or political opportunity of those affected by a public agency's decisions to participate in making those decisions.

Although it is a longstanding tenet of our democracy, it has not always been in good standing. Too often it has been given little more than lip service. As this chapter shows, however, IDEA makes inroads against unilateral decision making in the schools.

Recognize the Family as the Core Unit of Society

Although the legal foundations for parents' participating in their children's education are not well articulated in IDEA or in other laws, they nevertheless exist and can be identified and explained. At the core of these principles is the common-law doctrine that parents have a duty to support their children and a corollary right to their children's services and earnings for as long as the children have the legal status of minors. Under common law, and even by today's statutes, these rights and interests mean that parents may control their children in various ways.

For example, parents have the right to consent (on the minor's behalf) to their child's medical treatment. Further, compulsory school-attendance laws usually make the parents criminally liable if they do not require their child to attend the public schools. Also, state statutes make parents criminally liable for failing to support their minor children. The reason for these and similar laws is that a minor is presumed incapable, because of age, of acting on his or her own behalf except in limited ways, as granted by statute or, as recognized recently under the constitutional "privacy interest," by the courts (for example, the rights to abortion, contraception, and treatment for substance abuse). Parents, then, have rights that they can exercise on behalf of their child, and in many instances the parents exercise the child's right to have an education.

Finally, it is a cardinal principle of constitutional law that parents have the fundamental right and duty to raise their children relatively free of governmental influence. The Supreme Court announced that principle nearly a century ago and has adhered to it ever since (Stowe, Turnbull, & Sublet, 2006).

CONTEXT FOR PARENT PARTICIPATION

Historical Roles

Clearly, IDEA recognizes a new role for families and parents—that of education decision-makers. This is not, however, a perfectly realized role, in part because some parents still play (and some professionals still expect them to play) other, more traditional roles. As Turnbull, Turnbull, Erwin, and Soodak (2006) point out, there have been seven basic roles:

1. Parents or families as the source or causes of their children's disabilities
2. Parents and families as members of family-centered, family-directed organizations that exist to satisfy families' needs
3. Parents and families as developers of services for their children, including education, recreation, residential, and vocational services
4. Parents and families as the relatively passive recipients of professionals' decisions, as the second (and less active) party in the principle of deference to expert opinion
5. Parents and families as the follow-through educators of their children, as auxiliary teachers who are expected to carry out school-planned education and other interventions
6. Parents and families as political advocates, as the primary constituency behind laws such as IDEA and others that create rights or entitlements or protection from discrimination
7. Parents and families as education decision-makers, as partners with educators in developing "I-plans" and helping to carry them out—this being the current role envisioned by IDEA

An emerging eighth role extends the decision-maker partner role: parents, family members, and professionals as trust-driven collaborators (Turnbull, Turnbull, Erwin, & Soodak, 2006). This role transforms the decision-making partnership into a relationship in which trust is the core ingredient. It's not simply a matter of being partners in making decisions abut the child. Instead, it's a matter of earning each other's trust and thereby entering into a relationship that is richer and deeper than a partnership.

Further, this role involves more than just the parents; it also includes the students themselves and other family members and friends. In that respect, this role recognizes that families are systems; whatever happens to one member affects all others. It also acknowledges that families receive a great deal of informal support—that is, non-paid support—from relatives and friends. We will describe this role later in this chapter, under "Partnerships and Trust."

Relationship to NCLB

As we pointed out in chapter 2, IDEA aligns with NCLB and its parent-choice principle. Under NCLB, LEAs must provide parents with annual report cards on the performances of schools in the district. Based on this information, parents have the right to choose to transfer their child from a school that fails to meet the standard of "adequate yearly progress" to one that does, making it possible for their child to attend a more effective school. With this right comes the additional responsibility to make a decision, find the better school, arrange for the transfer out of one school to the other, and attend to all of the other issues regarding their child's IDEA rights in the new school.

NCLB also requires schools to involve parents in the development of various school programs, such as violence- and addiction-prevention classes, to grant parents access to reports on school safety and drug use among students, and to provide parents information about teachers, such as their state certification and educational backgrounds.

Together, IDEA and NCLB give parents both roles and responsibilities to participate in their children's education. As we emphasized in chapter 8 ("Procedural Due Process"), it's no longer the case that IDEA is primarily about rights; it's now well balanced between granting rights and imposing responsibilities on parents to be critically involved in their children's education, not just as valuable decision-makers but also as trusted and trustworthy partners.

PARTNERSHIPS AND TRUST

Partnerships and trust are important for two reasons:

1. They contribute to positive student outcomes (Turnbull, Turnbull, Erwin, & Soodak, 2006).
2. They convert IDEA from a law that is primarily about student and parent rights to one that is also about parent responsibilities.

Before we summarize IDEA's parent rights and responsibilities provisions, let's examine the essential elements of parent and professional partnerships.

Partnerships consist of seven principles: communication, professional competence, respect, commitment, equality, advocacy, and trust (Turnbull, Turnbull, Erwin, & Soodak, 2006). It may help you to think of an arch. On one side of the arch are three of these principles: communication, professional competence, and respect. On the other side are the other three: advocacy, equality, and commitment. Holding these six together, as they lean in toward each other is the keystone of the arch, trust. A keystone is that piece of the arch without which the other pieces do not connect and singly are weaker than they can be when joined with each other. The metaphor of the arch conveys the point that, without trust, the other partnership principles will be effective but not as effective as with trust.

Let's consider each of the partnership principles in light of IDEA's 2004 amendments.

Seven Principles of Partnerships

1. Effective communication requires parents and professionals to be friendly, listen to one another, be clear in describing their wants and needs, and be honest and open to providing information. IDEA's parent participation provisions require parents to be clear in describing

what they want and believe their child is entitled to have (as we showed in the chapters on nondiscriminatory evaluation, appropriate education, and procedural due process).

2. Professional competence reflects NCLB and IDEA requirements that LEAs employ highly qualified personnel.

3. Respect requires parents and professionals to regard each other with esteem and communicate that esteem through words and actions, with professionals being sensitive to families' cultural diversity and personal beliefs and choices, affirming students' and families' strengths, and treating parents and students with dignity. IDEA provides that LEA decision-making teams must respond to families' diversity and consider families' and students' strengths (as we discussed in chapter 5, "Nondiscriminatory Evaluation," and chapter 6, "Individualized and Appropriate Education").

4. Commitment means that professionals should regard their relationships with their students and the students' families not just as work but as a transcendent calling. IDEA can facilitate that commitment, but it cannot command educators to be committed.

5. Equality is the condition that arises when families and professionals feel that they are equal contributors and partners in a student's educational program. Again, IDEA can facilitate equality, but it seems unlikely to do so because the power advantage remains with the LEAs.

6. Advocacy attempts to identify a problem, the barriers to solving the problem, and the action to be taken to overcome the barriers and solve the problem. IDEA gives parents and professionals opportunity to advance their perspectives face to face as members of evaluation and IEP-development teams (chapters 5 and 6) and through the mediation and mandatory dispute-resolution provisions (chapter 8). But as we pointed out in chapter 8, advocacy can turn into an adversarial relationship and lead to due process hearings and even trials in federal or state courts.

7. Trust is the keystone that holds all of the other principles together. Parents trust professionals to educate their children effectively, and professionals trust parents to acknowledge and appreciate their efforts to educate their children. As is the case with other partnership principles, IDEA cannot command parents and professionals to trust each other. It simply provides the procedures within which they must deal with each other and thereby the means by which their dealings can be based on trust. The lack of trust or a breach of trust inevitably leads to disputes and in turn to the mediation, mandatory resolution session, and even due process and court proceedings. So, while providing the means for trusting and trustworthy partnerships, IDEA also provides the means for resolving disputes when trust dissolves.

IDEA AND PARENT PARTICIPATION IN DECISION MAKING

We have described the relationship of the parent participation principle to IDEA's other five principles, the context of the principle, the roles that parents have played historically and are now expected to play, and the seven principles of parent and professional partnerships. Let's now review the parent participation provisions and their significance.

One more thing: As you read about the parent participation provisions, bear in mind that the due process principle is about power and that the parent participation principle can be a means for replacing power relationships with partnerships based on trust.

Defining "Parents"

The 2004 amendments expand the definition of "parents" by providing that, unless state law provides otherwise, the term includes a natural, adoptive, or foster parent, a legal guardian, an individual acting in the place of a natural or adoptive parent (including a grandparent, stepparent, or other relative) with whom the child lives, an individual who is legally responsible for the child's welfare, or an individual assigned to be a surrogate parent (20 U.S.C. Sec. 1401(23)). This new definition takes into account the changing demographics of families; there are now both the traditional two-parent nuclear family and many other variations as well. The regulations further revise the term "parent" by substituting "biological" for "natural" and clarifying that a guardian must either be specifically authorized to make educational decisions or generally authorized to act as a child's parent to be considered a parent under IDEA (34 C.F.R. Sec. 300.30).

Parents as Team Members

As we noted in chapter 5 ("Nondiscriminatory Evaluation") and chapter 6 ("Individualized and Appropriate Education"), parents are members of and participate in two teams that are charged with making critical decisions regarding a student's educational program: the evaluation team (20 U.S.C. Sec. 1414(c)) and the IEP team (20 U.S.C. Sec. 1414(d)). To ensure that parents participate in these teams' deliberations, IDEA requires LEAs to take specific steps, including

- advance notice of meetings;
- mutually convenient scheduling;
- interpreters when necessary (the parents may have language, sight, or hearing limitations);
- meeting without parent participation only when attempts to include parents have failed; and
- allowing parents to participate by videoconference and conference calls (20 U.S.C. Sec. 1414(f)).

As we discussed in chapter 4 ("Zero Reject"), parents, along with the LEA and other relevant members of the IEP team, have the right to participate on the manifestation-determination team. That team determines whether a child's behavior was caused by or had a direct and substantial relationship to the child's disability or if the conduct in question resulted from the LEA's failure to implement the IEP (20 U.S.C. Sec. 1415(k)(1)(E)). Parents and the LEA jointly determine who on the IEP team is considered relevant for the purposes of determining manifestation.

IDEA still does not provide whether any single member of the NDE, IEP, or manifestation-determination team may veto other team members' decisions. Indeed, it seems that IDEA establishes only the membership on teams and the process by which the team members must act. It does not grant or deny a veto right to any particular team member and expects the team to be guided by consensus. Of course, if the parent or the LEA disagrees with the other, recourse to the dispute-resolution provisions, mediation, and due process exists (see chapter 8, "Procedural Due Process"). The right to dispute-resolution provisions, mediation, and due process basically prevent either the parents or, more likely, the LEA team members from making unilateral decisions. It balances the power among the team members and holds each accountable to the others.

Parental Rights and Responsibilities Regarding Evaluations, Services, and Placement

As we pointed out in chapter 5 ("Nondiscriminatory Evaluation"), parents may request an initial evaluation to determine if the child has a disability (20 U.S.C. Sec. 1414(a)(1)). They also may request a reevaluation (during the three-year period between the initial evaluation and the mandatory reevaluation) because they may have or need new information about the student to make the student's special education more effective (20 U.S.C. Sec. 1414(a)(2)). Note that the parents have the burden to request a reevaluation and that they must justify their request on two grounds: new information and its relevance to the child's appropriate education in the least restrictive environment.

Similarly, LEAs must obtain the informed consent of the child's parents to each evaluation. Remember that the consent is for that particular evaluation, not for special education placement and services (20 U.S.C. Sec. 1414(a)(1)(D)). There are, however, consequences if a parent does not give consent, and these consequences also demonstrate that IDEA grants rights while also imposing responsibilities.

If the parents do not respond or refuse to consent to an initial evaluation, their child will not be evaluated for special education eligibility. In response, the LEA has two choices:

1. It may use mediation or due process procedures (which we explained in chapter 8) to secure approval for an initial evaluation. If the LEA does not resort to these procedures, it has no responsibility to provide IDEA benefits to the student and it may treat the student as it does any other student who does not qualify for IDEA, including disciplining the student in the same way it disciplines students without disabilities, subject only to the protections of Sec. 504 and ADA. The regulations emphasize that an LEA does not violate its obligations under either

child find or the evaluation procedures by declining to pursue an initial evaluation (34 C.F.R. 300.300(a)(3)(ii)). So the parents need to consider carefully the consequences of refusing to consent to have their child evaluated, especially if the child is experiencing any difficulty academically or behaviorally.

2. It may proceed with the evaluation if it can "demonstrate that it had taken reasonable measures to obtain such consent and the child's parent has failed to respond" (20 U.S.C. Sec. 1414(c)(3)). Here, again, the parents' action (really, inaction by not responding to the LEA's request for an evaluation) has consequences. The LEA may choose not to proceed with the evaluation. That decision essentially will exclude the child from special education. Or the LEA may conduct the evaluation; it does not have to be bound by parents' inaction.

Similarly, if the parents do not respond or refuse to consent to a reevaluation, an LEA may but is not required to pursue the consent override procedures described above—due process or mediation (34 C.F.R. 300.300(c)(1)). Again, the LEA does not violate any obligations under IDEA by declining to pursue these options (34 C.F.R. 300.300(c)(iii)).

If the parents of a child who is home-schooled or placed in a private school at their own expense refuse to respond or provide consent for either an initial evaluation or a reevaluation, the LEA is prohibited from using either mediation or due process to override the lack of consent. Instead, the LEA is not required to consider that child as eligible for services (34 C.F.R. 300.300(d)(4)(i)-(ii)).

The parents' failure to consent is discussed later in this chapter as one of the limitations that a court may impose to limit the parents' tuition reimbursement claim.

Even if the parents consent to an initial evaluation, their consent is not considered a consent for the child to receive special education services (20 U.S.C. Sec. 1414(a)(1)(D)). An LEA is required to make reasonable efforts to obtain informed consent from the parents for placement (34 C.F.R. 300.300(b)). However, the LEA may not use mediation or due process to override the parents' refusal to consent (20 U.S.C. Sec. 1414(a)(1)(D)(ii)(II)). If the parents refuse to consent to special education services, they essentially free the LEA from any obligations to provide their child with special education and related services (20 U.S.C. Sec. 1414(a)(1)(D)(ii)). That is a heavy responsibility, one that the parents must be careful about assuming.

The regulations also require that in order to meet the reasonable effort requirements to get parents' consent for initial evaluations, reevaluations, and services, the LEA must document its efforts through records such as phone logs, copies of correspondence, and detailed records of visits with the parents (34 C.F.R. 300.300(d)(5)).

Private-School Placements and Tuition Reimbursement

As you learned in chapter 4 ("Zero Reject"), parents may remove their children from the public school system and enroll them in a private school at their own expense. LEAs also may pay for a student's private-school placement if the IEP team determines that the private-school placement is appropriate. Disputes arise, however, when parents enroll their child in a private school without LEA approval and then ask the LEA to reimburse the tuition. That's what the *Burlington* case involved and what several post-*Burlington* IDEA amendments address.

Parents are well aware of the damage that an inappropriate education can have on their child's future and sometimes act to prevent that damage by enrolling their child in a private school. In doing so, the parents are exchanging the potential harm to their child's education for a potential financial harm to their family—the cost of private-school tuition and services. In order to recoup this loss, parents must be able to recover the tuition that they paid. There is no right to a free appropriate education without the remedy of tuition reimbursement. Just how extensive is their right to recover tuition? Clearly, it is not unlimited.

In *Burlington*, the Supreme Court held that IDEA requires LEAs to reimburse parents for their expenditures for private placement if the LEA does not provide the student an educational benefit but the private-school placement does. Parents' ability to recover private-school tuition from an LEA thus depends on two factors: (a) the LEA does not provide an appropriate education, but (b) the private school does. Without this remedy, parents would be paralyzed in seeking an appropriate education for their child.

IDEA Provisions: Federal Court Decisions Codified

Following *Burlington*, courts dealt with many different aspects of the right-to-tuition reimbursement. As they increasingly awarded reimbursement and simultaneously established limits on that right, it became more and more obvious that Congress would have to clarify the right, with respect to both its substantive and its procedural aspects. IDEA now, for the most part, codifies the tuition reimbursement rules and requirements.

The general rule is that the LEA is not obliged to pay for the cost of the education, including related services, of a child whose parents enroll him or her in a private school. One reason for the rule is that the IDEA funds public education, not private education. The other is that parents have the right to raise their children as they see fit (subject to abuse, neglect, and maltreatment protections). If they elect private education, they should pay for it.

This rule has some exceptions that derive from the *Burlington* case. If the parents enroll their child in a private school or facility without the consent of the LEA or a referral to that school by the LEA, the parents may recover the cost of the tuition and related services only if

- the student previously had received special education and related services from the LEA,
- a due process hearing officer or court finds that the LEA did not make a free appropriate public education available to the student in a timely manner before the parents enrolled their child in the private school or facility, and
- the private school or facility provides an appropriate education to the child (20 U.S.C. Sec. 1412 (a)(10)(C)(ii)).

This provision codifies the prior case law, which held that the parents may receive tuition reimbursement only if the LEA did not provide an appropriate education and the private school did. But it adds the limitation that the student must have been enrolled in the LEA and receiving special education and related services; this limitation prevents parents from avoiding the LEA's programs altogether and then seeking to charge private education to the LEA.

Limitations on Tuition Reimbursement

As they followed the *Burlington* decision, courts had to decide not only whether to award tuition reimbursement but also how much reimbursement they must award. IDEA now guides the courts by detailing the procedures that parents must follow as they seek reimbursement and then by limiting the amount of reimbursement if parents do not follow these procedures. IDEA allows a hearing officer or court to reduce or even to deny reimbursement in three instances: failure to notify the LEA, failure to make the child available for an evaluation, and unreasonable actions.

Failure to Notify

The first instance relates to parents and their duty to comply with "notice and cure" conditions. The parents, at the most recent IEP meeting they attended before removing their child from the LEA, must (a) inform the IEP team that they are rejecting the LEA's proposed placement and its proposed FAPE, and (b) state their concerns and their intent to enroll their child in a private school at public expense (20 U.S.C. Sec. 1412(a)(10)(C)(iii)(I)(aa)). This provision codifies early case law requiring parents to give notice, but it extends that case law by requiring them to state also why they reject the LEA's placement and program. More than that, it gives the LEA an opportunity to offer a placement and program that the parents may accept as appropriate. Thus, it secures notice for the LEA, it eliminates the element of surprise, and it encourages the LEA to respond to the parents' concerns.

If the parents have not attended a recent IEP meeting requirement, they must, at least 10 business days (including holidays that occur on a business day) before removing their child from the LEA, give the LEA written notice that they intend to enroll their child in a private school and seek reimbursement, and what their concerns are about the LEA program and placement (20 U.S.C. Sec. 1412 (a)(10)(C)(iii)(I)(bb)). This requirement has the same purpose and effect of the IEP meeting requirement, but it applies to parents who did not attend their child's most recent IEP meeting.

Because the notice requirements imposed on parents may prove difficult for some parents or problematic for their child, IDEA creates three exceptions (20 U.S.C. Sec. 1412(a)(10)(C)(iv)):

- The LEA prevented the parent from providing the notice.
- The parents themselves have not received the notice, pursuant to 20 U.S.C. Sec. 1415, that the LEA must give them concerning their rights and responsibilities (including that they are responsible for providing the aforementioned notice to the LEA) (see chapter 7 for a description of the LEA-required notices to parents).
- Compliance with the notice requirement likely would result in physical harm to the child (20 U.S.C. Secs. 1412(a)(10)(C)(iv)(I)(aa)–(cc)).

The first two exceptions recognize that LEAs sometimes do not comply with IDEA deliberately and thus can thwart parents' and students' rights; the third recognizes that special emergency circumstances related to the child's physical well-being may exist and justify the notice omission. In addition to the three required exceptions, the court or hearing officers, at their discretion, may apply two additional exceptions to the notice requirement, if

- the parent is illiterate and cannot write in English,

- compliance with the notice would likely result in serious emotional harm to the child (20 U.S.C. Secs. 1412(a)(10)(C)(iv)(II)(aa) and (bb)).

Failure to Make the Child Available for an Evaluation

The second major limitation on reimbursement relates to nondiscriminatory evaluation. In its effort to ensure that the LEA may respond to parents' concerns and perhaps avoid the duty to reimburse for private education, IDEA entitles the LEA to notify the parents, in writing and at some time before the parents actually remove their child from the LEA, that the LEA wants to evaluate the child and why. If the parents refuse to make their child available for the LEA's evaluation, a hearing officer or court may reduce or deny reimbursement on that account (20 U.S.C. Sec. 1412(a)(10)(C)(iii)(II)).

This limitation is designed to prevent private-school tuition from being awarded when the LEA is trying to reevaluate the student and revise the student's IEP. Consider, for example, the situation in which the parents say the public school's IEP is inappropriate, and the school agrees but requests a reevaluation to determine what changes to make to the IEP. If the parents were able to simply end the collaboration process at that point, they could put their child in a private school and claim reimbursement based on the fact that the LEA agreed that the IEP was inappropriate—without regard to the LEA's attempts to work with the parents to identify the student's needs and create an appropriate IEP. In other words, the evaluation limitation is designed to allow LEAs an opportunity to cure the complaints about the IEP through the evaluation and planning process.

Unreasonableness

Another major limitation on reimbursement allows a court to reduce or deny reimbursement if it finds that the parents acted unreasonably (20 U.S.C. Sec. 1412 (a)(10(C)(iii)(III)). This is a curious provision in two respects:

1. It addresses only the power of a court to reduce or deny reimbursement; it does not grant that authority to a hearing officer, although a hearing officer may reduce or deny reimbursement under the other LEA safeguards.
2. It does not define "unreasonable," although it is safe to assume, based on prior case law, that parents will be found to act unreasonably if they are not straightforward and candid in their dealings with the LEA or if they enroll their child in an unnecessarily expensive, albeit appropriate, private program.

Having described IDEA, it still is appropriate to describe the case law on tuition reimbursement, because some of it is codified into IDEA and thus provides precedent for interpreting it.

Will a Court Award Tuition Reimbursement for Procedural Violations?

The process definition is a road map for schools to follow to ensure that each student receives a free appropriate education. It has been a longstanding rule in the courts that if an LEA fails to comply with the process definition and especially IDEA's procedural rules and if, as a consequence, the student experiences actual harm, the student's IEP is inappropriate and the parents are entitled to tuition reimbursement for any appropriate private placement. The 2004 amendments limited the process definition of appropriateness by requiring hearing officers to base any findings of a denial of FAPE on substantive grounds except in three situations—when the procedural violation

1. impeded the child's right to FAPE,
2. significantly impeded the parents' opportunity to participate, or
3. caused a deprivation of educational benefit.

Yet, these limitations are not likely to change this rule of actual harm. If anything, they codify it by making the LEA liable for procedural violations that actually result in a negative outcome for students with disabilities or their parents. The following cases, in which the courts ruled that a procedural violation caused actual harm, illustrate the similarity between the court-made rule and the new 2004 provisions regarding procedural violations. For each case, we provide the basis for the court's decision and then state how a similar result is likely pursuant to the three procedural bases for a violation of FAPE in IDEA 2004.

- An IEP that fails to identify a student's disability accurately and/or fails to respond to the student's specific disability (as determined by the nondiscriminatory evaluation) by providing appropriate services violates the process definition principle and thus fails to provide an education reasonably calculated to enable a child to obtain an educational benefit (*Bonadonna v. Cooperman*, 1985; *Metropolitan Nashville & Davidson County Sch. System v. Guest*, 1995; *Russell v. Jefferson School Dist.*, 1985). Under IDEA 2004, the failure to properly identify the student's disability arguably causes a deprivation of educational benefit by making it impossible for an IEP to appropriately and effectively address the student's needs.
- When a student moves from a state in which she received special education services, the new state of residence must inform the parents or guardian if it proposes to change the student's identification, evaluation, or placement in the present out-of-state residential placement (*Salley v. St. Tammany Parish Sch. Bd.*, 1995). Under IDEA 2004, the failure to inform the parents about changes to the student's identification, evaluation, and placement arguably has a significant impact on the parents' ability to participate in the development of their child's IEP (since they are excluded from substantive decisions).
- An LEA may not try to remove a student from a residential program and place the student in its program without assessing first whether it is capable of implementing the student's IEP (*Day v. Radnor Township School Dist.*, 1994).
- In *Christen G. v. Lower Merion School Dist.* (1996), the court found that a procedural violation was sufficient to deny a student a free appropriate education when the LEA failed to make any formal offer of placement until 10 months after the LEA offered an inappropriate placement and 7 months after a hearing officer deemed the placement inappropriate. Under IDEA 2004, such delays deny the student's right to FAPE.

In all of these cases, the procedural violation actually impaired the student's right to an appropriate education and left the parents with no choice but to enroll their child in a private school and seek tuition reimbursement. These same situations are arguably still violations under IDEA 2004 despite the increased limitations on procedural recovery. That is so largely because Congress was not so much creating new limitations as codifying one that the court had already employed in numerous cases: the harmless-error rule.

The Harmless-Error Rule Codified

Stated briefly, the harmless-error rule says that if the LEA commits a procedural violation but the violation does not result in denial of an appropriate education and the LEA confers a benefit, the LEA has not deprived the student of IDEA rights and the student's parents are not entitled to a reimbursement award. In *Urban v. Jefferson County School Dist R-1* (1996), for example, the LEA provided an IEP that (a) lacked an explicit statement of transition services, (b) did not designate a specific outcome or goal for the student to meet upon turning 21 years of age, and (c) did not include a specific set of activities for the student to accomplish that goal.

The court ruled, however, that these deficiencies did not deprive the student of a free appropriate education, especially because the IEP provided for need-responsive services such as community awareness, daily living skills, and functional math for purchases. Further, the IEP emphasized the need for the student to transfer the skills learned in the educational setting to everyday life. Although the court ordered the LEA to rewrite the student's IEP, it concluded that, even in its deficient condition, the IEP was reasonably calculated to enable the student to receive an educational benefit.

Nor is the procedural defect fatal if (a) the process is only slightly flawed (in that the IEP does not contain all of the relevant information IDEA requires); and (b) the parents, as well as the school, are aware of the missing information (*Burke County Bd. of Educ. v. Denton*, 1990; *Doe v. Defendant I*, 1990). Furthermore, if a student's parents interrupt or block the process or procedures from being carried out, they are not entitled later to claim that the process definition has not been satisfied (*Burke County Bd. of Educ. v. Denton*, 1990; *Doe v. Defendant I*, 1990).

The harmless-error rule, then, does not stand for the proposition that any procedural error is excusable. It does mean that errors that result in little, if any, harm cannot support a claim for reimbursement. Congress was undoubtedly aware of the courts' use of the harmless-error rule when it reauthorized IDEA in 2004, as well as of the President's Commission Report's (2002) suggestion that IDEA compliance focus on outcomes rather than process. Arguably, then, Congress intended the procedural recovery limitations in IDEA 2004 as a codification of the courts' use of the harmless-error rule—to ensure widespread and consistent application of the rule and to restrict recovery based solely on procedural violations, or, in other words, to limit recovery when no actual harm occurred.

When Will Courts Award Reimbursement for Substantive Violations?

To satisfy the second prong of the *Rowley* standard—the benefit test—the LEA must provide an IEP that is reasonably calculated to enable the student to obtain an educational benefit. Thus, the student's IEP must be devised to meet the unique needs of that student. Individualization is the key. The following cases illustrate LEA failures to comply with the second prong of the test, and thus failures to provide an appropriate education. IDEA's provisions are not likely to change this rule. Indeed, they seem to codify it by insisting that an LEA must reimburse tuition and related expenses if the LEA has not provided the student with FAPE. After all, the substantive standard of appropriate, established by the *Rowley* decision, is that the LEA's program and placement must actually benefit the student.

The Supreme Court in *Florence County Sch. Dist. Four v. Carter* (1993) approved private-placement reimbursement for a student classified as having a learning disability who did not make educational progress in the public placement. The public school's IEP resulted in her achieving only 4 months of progress in a 9-month year, the student having received only three periods of resource classroom work per week. Its program also resulted in her regression and failed to ensure her passing from grade to grade (in compliance with the *Rowley* standard as appropriately applied to this student, who has a learning disability and thus is capable of grade-to-grade advancement during the high school years).

The Court held that the parents may recover private tuition, even though the private school did not meet state accreditation standards, if (a) the public school placement is not appropriate, (b) the private-school placement is appropriate in that it is reasonably calculated to provide an educational benefit to the student, and (c) the costs assessed by the private school are reasonable.

In this case, the Supreme Court reasoned that IDEA's state accreditation requirement cannot be applied to unilateral placements by parents because it would condition tuition reimbursement on state approval of the private school, thereby enabling the state to avoid its duty to provide a free appropriate education. By withholding its approval, the state would foreclose the student's placement and thereby relegate the student to only the inappropriate program in the public school. Moreover, the parental right of placement, established in the *Burlington* case, would be nullified if the parent could not make a private-school placement. Finally, IDEA's requirement that a student's education be provided under public supervision and that the student's IEP be developed and annually reviewed by a local agency does not apply because it cannot feasibly be met in the case of a unilateral parental placement; for that reason, these requirements do not apply to such a placement.

When the LEA in *Union School Dist. v. Smith* (1994) offered to place a student with autism in a "communicatively handicapped class," supplemented by one-on-one behavior modification counseling, the parents placed their child in a private, nonaccredited placement and requested reimbursement. The court determined that the public program was inappropriate, as it did not address the student's need for a more restrictive and less stimulating environment. Experts testified that he required full-time, one-on-one instruction to benefit from group instruction. Furthermore, all of the witnesses testified that the student needed to acquire attending skills, which he had not yet attained, before he would be able to learn from language instruction and therefore would not benefit from the LEA's placement.

In *Murphysboro Community Unit School Dist. v. Illinois State Bd. of Educ.* (1994), the LEA wanted to place a student with mental retardation and speech and language impairments and possible autism in its "Choices" program, an education program designed to promote interaction between students with disabilities and students without disabilities, and to supplement that program with speech training and summer school. The LEA wanted to enroll the student in this program so she would develop good modeling habits. The parents thought their child's language skills were regressing and did not believe that behavior modeling should be a primary objective, considering her other needs.

The court determined that the LEA denied the student a free appropriate education because it failed to present an IEP with an appropriate placement and failed to offer any viable alternative. The court based its decision on the testimony of expert witnesses who found the student's IEP and "Choices" program inadequate to meet the student's unique needs.

To summarize, an LEA may fail to offer an educational benefit if the student is regressing or not progressing, or if the student's IEP or IFSP inadequately addresses the student's individual needs. In those cases, appropriate private placement and tuition reimbursement are fully warranted, consistent with *Burlington*.

Other Aspects of *Burlington* and the Tuition Reimbursement Award

Several other aspects of the *Burlington* tuition reimbursement rule concern the award itself and are worth noting:

- If an LEA agrees to a private-school placement and the placement has been made, it may not unilaterally refuse to pay tuition on the grounds that it now has an appropriate program (*Colin K. v. Schmidt*, 1983; *Leo P. v. Board*, 1982; *Parks v. Pavkovic*, 1982). As would be the case if the student were not in a private school but, instead, in a public one, the LEA may conduct the required NDE, reconvene the IEP team, and propose a new program or placement. It also may go to a due process hearing to try to get an order that its proposed program is appropriate and thus try to get relief from the private-school tuition burden. But it may escape the tuition burden only if the LEA's program or placement is ordered to be appropriate, and until that order is entered and becomes final, it must continue to pay the tuition (*Bonadonna v. Cooperman*, 1985). IDEA's 1997 amendments codified the essential holding of these cases. IDEA now explicitly entitles a hearing officer or court to reduce or deny tuition reimbursement if a parent refuses to comply with an LEA's request to evaluate the student.
- Tuition is not the only reimbursable expense. If parents must spend funds to obtain related services so that the student receives an educational benefit, the parents may recover those expenses (*Ojai Unified School Dist. v. Jackson*, 1993). IDEA explicitly provides that parents may recover not only tuition but also related service expenses.
- If the LEA illegally suspends or expels a student and parents incur additional education expenses during the period of suspension or expulsion, they may recover those expenses (*Scituate School Committee v. Robert B.*, 1985).

When Will a Court Deny Tuition Reimbursement?

Simply, a court will deny reimbursement when the LEA's IEP and placement are appropriate. IDEA does not require public funding of a superior private program, only that an LEA offer an appropriate program (*Doe v. Bd. of Ed. of Tullahoma City Schools*, 1993). Also, even if a private-school program may be ideal for a student, tuition reimbursement is still unavailable when the LEA can provide a free appropriate education under *Rowley* (*Lenn v. Portland School Committee*, 1993).

The difficult aspect of the *Rowley* standard is knowing how much educational benefit is adequate. In *Petersen v. Hastings Public Schools* (1994), tuition reimbursement was denied because the level of educational benefit that the LEA provided was sufficient to support the LEA's defense that it offered an appropriate education to the student. There, the parents of three children with hearing impairments sued because the LEA chose to use a modified signing system that did not provide sign interpreters during nonacademic portions of the school day. The court, however, found that the LEA had conferred an educational benefit on each student, as each had progressed and continued to show academic and lingual improvement, both on standardized tests and in areas of word comprehension, language and communicative skills, reading, and math.

As stated earlier, a student receives a free appropriate education if the IEP substantively addresses that student's needs. If a court believes that the LEA has provided services beyond IDEA's minimum standard, it will conclude that the LEA has complied with IDEA and accordingly will deny reimbursement.

The Role of LRE

The principles of appropriate education and least restrictive environment complement one another and are inextricably connected (see chapter 6). It is proper for a court to balance academic progress with a student's right to associate with nondisabled peers under the LRE doctrine and to refuse to award private-placement reimbursement when the LEA program is less restrictive (provides more association with nondisabled students than the private placement) and still provides academic benefit (*Amann v. Stow School System*, 1992). Similarly, in *Teague Indep. School Dist. v. Todd L.* (1993), the court denied tuition reimbursement and concluded that a student with severe emotional and behavioral disabilities should be placed in the LEA's program, not a psychiatric facility, because the LEA placement would yield an academic benefit for the student and because the student also would have the opportunity to associate with nondisabled peers and participate in the community more fully.

When, however, a student's disruptive and violent behavior persists in day school and in homebound placements even after the LEA has made efforts to support the student in those placements, the LEA may place the student in a residential program. Indeed, the LRE principle not only does not forbid that placement but actually requires it (*Johnson v. Westmoreland County School Bd.*, 1993) (see chapter 7).

Other Than Educational Reasons

Often parents with children with severe emotional disorders seek a private placement when their child is presenting extremely challenging behaviors at home. Although sympathetic with the frustration these parents experience, the courts deny reimbursement if they believe a child is placed in a private facility for other than educational reasons. These cases, which are not disturbed or changed by the 2004 amendments, can be subdivided into two categories. The "four-corners" cases constitute the first category. In these cases, the courts are not willing to examine the student's behavior outside the school setting; they look only to the "four corners" of the school environment. The following case is illustrative of this approach.

In *Hall v. Shawnee Mission School Dist.* (1994), the LEA placed a student with pervasive developmental disorder and attention deficit disorder in a "behavior disorder" classroom part time and in a general fourth-grade classroom for the remainder of the day. The parents unilaterally placed him in a private facility and sought reimbursement. The student's teachers testified that he was being included gradually in the general program for more of the day, that he was a model student in the special education classroom, and that he was performing at grade level in all subjects except reading, where he was performing above grade level.

The student's parents testified that his behavior had deteriorated at home to a point at which they could tolerate it no longer. His private physician testified that the student was unmanageable at home and should be placed in a residential facility. Based on the teachers' testimony, the court determined that the LEA indeed did provide an educational benefit and that the residential placement was for other than educational reasons.

The second line of cases involves those in which the court denies reimbursement for a private facility because it believes that parents seek private placement only as a last resort and to obtain respite care from the duty of caring for their child. *Sanger v. Montgomery County Bd. of Ed.* (1996) involved a 17-year-old student with severe emotional disorders who suffered additional emotional trauma from having injured a baby in an automobile accident; shortly thereafter, he attempted suicide. The student's physician recommended private placement after determining that the student refused to take his medication or commit to therapy on his own. His parents unilaterally withdrew him from his public placement and enrolled him in a private psychiatric facility, apparently as the last resort for treatment. The court denied reimbursement, stating that residential placement necessitated by emotional problems was separate from the learning process and not fundable under IDEA. The court stressed that his parents, not the LEA, were responsible to pay for his medical needs.

Agreements Between Parents and an LEA

The 2004 amendments strengthen the collaboration between parents and the LEA by allowing the parents and LEA to agree that

- a reevaluation may occur more often than once a year or that they waive the requirement of an evaluation at the 3-year mark (20 U.S.C. Sec. 1414(a)(2)(B));

- an IEP team member may be excused from an IEP meeting if the member's area of the curriculum or related service is not going to be modified or discussed at the meeting (20 U.S.C. Sec. 1414(d)(1)(C)(i)); the parents' consent must be in writing (20 U.S.C. Sec. 1414(d)(1)(C)(iii));
- changes to an existing IEP may be made without convening an IEP team meeting (20 U.S.C. Sec. 1414(d)(3)(D));
- alternative means of parent participation are acceptable, such as video conferences and conference calls (20 U.S.C. Sec. 1414(f)).

Note that each of these provisions has the potential for reducing the amount of paperwork and the administrative burden that LEAs face, for putting the parent–professional relationship on a more informal, less arms-length basis, and for assuring prompt and appropriate action on the child's behalf.

Reviewing Parent Participation Rights

There are so many parent participation rights that it may help you to picture them as depicted in Figure 9.1. Figure 9.1 begins with the circle defining "parents." It then places them in various teams. Next, it shows how they are involved in evaluations, may choose private-school placements, have access to records and may control the distribution of the records, and may attempt to resolve their disputes and even go to a due process hearing.

The regulations have expanded the importance of parent participation by strengthening the assumption that an IEP meeting should not be conducted without the parents present unless the LEA can demonstrate the parents cannot be convinced to attend. The LEA must document its attempts to secure the parents' attendance by maintaining records of phone calls, copies of correspondence, and even visits to the parents' home or places of employment (34 C.F.R. 300.322(d)). An LEA must take whatever actions are necessary to ensure that a parent understands the process and content of an IEP meeting by providing interpreters for a parent who is deaf or whose native language is other than English (34 C.F.R. 300.322(e)).

Parent Responsibilities if Collaboration Fails: File for Due Process

As we discussed in chapter 8 ("Procedural Due Process"), IDEA imposes responsibilities on parents. If parents fail to exercise these responsibilities, they may jeopardize their children's IDEA rights. For example, they must comply with the action notice when they file a due process complaint by including in the complaint

- the student's name, residential address, and the school the student is attending; or in the case of a homeless child or youth (within the meaning of section 725(2) of the *McKinney-Vento Homeless Assistance Act* (42 U.S.C. 11434a(2)), available contact information for the student and the name of the school the student is attending;

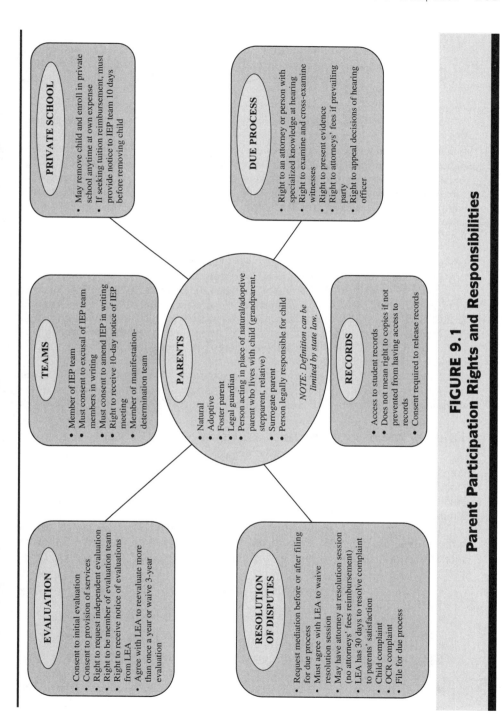

FIGURE 9.1
Parent Participation Rights and Responsibilities

- a description of the nature of the student's problem relating to the proposed initiation or change in the student's identification, evaluation, placement, or free appropriate public education, including the facts relating to the problem; and
- a proposed resolution to the problem to the extent known and available to the parents at the time (20 U.S.C. Sec. 1415(b)(7)(A)).

The most significant of these provisions compel the parents to set out facts describing the student's problem and how to resolve it. (Note that the law requires the parents to identify the student's problem, causing them to place the problem within their child rather than within the LEA, which is really what they are complaining about.) That is so because the provisions require the parents to monitor what the LEA is doing to educate their child, how the LEA is failing to do its job, and what the LEA must do to fully comply with IDEA. These provisions raise the bar for parental oversight and, at the same time, may make it possible for parents and professionals to work more closely together, as partners with comparable responsibility for the child's education.

The LEA must notify the hearing officer and the parents within 15 days if it believes the parents have not complied with these notice requirements. The hearing officer then determines whether the notice is sufficient (20 U.S.C. Sec. 1415(c)(2)). If the notice is not sufficient, parents may amend the notice only if the LEA consents in writing and is given the opportunity to resolve the complaint in a meeting (20 U.S.C. Sec. 1415(c)(2)). Also, if an attorney fails to include the above information in a complaint filed on behalf of a student's parents and the parents eventually prevail in court, the court may reduce the amount of attorneys' fees awarded to the parents (20 U.S.C. Sec. 1415(i)(3)(F)).

However, parents do have sources for securing this information. SEAs must develop a model form to assist parents in filing complaints that contain this information as well as the new due process complaint notices (20 U.S.C. Sec. 1415(b)(8)).

Family Systems Approach and Benefits to Family

As we pointed out in chapter 6, IDEA defines an appropriate education as special education and the related services and other support services that are necessary for the student to benefit from special education. Related services commonly are targeted to students only, but they can benefit the student's family as well. That is because of a simple fact: Whatever benefits the student also benefits the student's family.

In addition to this "family systems" approach, families or parents are entitled to a much more direct benefit from related services. This is so because the following related services, as defined in IDEA regulations, are available to the student's parents or family members:

- Training and technical assistance related to "assistive technology services" (34 C.F.R. 300.6(e))
- Counseling and guidance for parents related to the student's hearing loss, as part of the related service of "audiology" (34 C.F.R. 300.34(c)(1)(v))
- Parent counseling and training (34 C.F.R. 300.34(a))
- Psychological counseling for parents, as part of the related service of "psychological services" (34 C.F.R. 300.34(c)(10)(v))
- Group and individual counseling with the student's family, as part of the related service of "social work services in school" (34 C.F.R. 300.34(c)(14)(ii))

- Counseling and guidance of parents, as part of the related service of "speech pathology" (34 C.F.R. 300.34(c)(15)(v))

These services do not depend on the student's age; the parents or family of any student in special education (birth through 21) may receive these services, but only if the services are regarded as necessary to help the student benefit from special education and are included in the student's IEP.

Age-limited services, however, also can directly benefit the student's family or parents. Foremost among these, of course, are those set out in IDEA in Part C (birth to age 3—infants and toddlers), as long as they are incorporated into the individualized family service plan (IFSP) (see chapter 6 for a full discussion of Part C).

Here again, IDEA grants rights to parents (the right to benefit from some related services). But it also imposes a responsibility on parents to persuade their child's IEP team to include these services in the IEP (as necessary for the student's education) and then to take advantage of them when the LEA does offer them.

Participation on Policy-Making Advisory Committees

SEAs must create an advisory panel whose members are appointed by the governor or any other authorized official. The panel should be representative of the state's population and be composed of individuals involved in or concerned with the education of children with disabilities, including those listed next.

Membership of SEA Advisory Panel (20 U.S.C. 1412(a)(21))

- Parents of children with disabilities
- Individuals with disabilities
- Teachers of children with disabilities
- Representatives of institutions of higher education that prepare special education and related services personnel
- State and local education officials, including officials who carry out activities under the *McKinney-Vento Homeless Assistance Act*
- Administrators of programs for children with disabilities
- Representatives of other state agencies involved in the financing or delivery of related services
- Representatives of private schools or public charter schools
- At least one representative of a vocational, community, or business organization concerned with the provision of transition services
- A representative from the state child welfare agency responsible for foster care

---

The state advisory panel must

- draw a majority of its membership from individuals with disabilities or parents of children with disabilities (ages birth through 26) (20 U.S.C. Sec. 1412 (a)(21)(C)),

- advise the SEAs on the corrective-action plans to cure any defaults that federal monitoring panels discover,
- assist in developing policies for coordinating services and for meeting the unmet needs of students with disabilities,
- have the opportunity to make public comments about any SEA rules or regulations, and
- assist the SEA in developing and reporting data the U.S. Secretary of Education might require (20 U.S.C. Sec. 1412(a)(21)(D)).

A parent who has the time, energy, and desire to serve on the state advisory committee will soon find that service has its benefits to their child and others as well: access to key decision-makers in the SEA and among LEAs; the prestige and purported power associated with holding a position on the committee; and a plethora of information about IDEA, its regulations, the state plan, and how the SEA and LEAs implement (or do not implement) IDEA.

Access to System Records

Certain information about school programs for children with disabilities and about the children themselves is public information, available to all, including

- the SEA's and LEAs' applications for IDEA assistance;
- information necessary for an SEA to perform its evaluation duties;
- information relating to the educational achievement of children with disabilities in IDEA-financed programs (20 U.S.C. Sec. 1416(a)(16)(D)); and
- notice of proposed amendments to the state plan, including when and where public hearings will be held to solicit public comment about the amendments (20 U.S.C. Sec. 1412(a)(19)).

Special Significance of Part C

As you know from reading chapter 3, Part B establishes rights for students ages 3 through 21 and for their parents, and Part C establishes different rights for infants and toddlers and their families. We described those rights and their differences in chapters 4 through 8. But it will be helpful to reconsider Part C as the means by which IDEA grants much more extensive rights and responsibilities to parents than Part B does. For example, Part C provides that

- parents may veto an offer of early intervention services;
- parents may consent to some services but reject others;
- parents have some responsibilities to pay for early intervention services;
- parents may provide the "natural environment"—the home—in which their infant or toddler receives early intervention services;
- parents also may enroll their child in center-based early intervention services;

- parents and other family members are beneficiaries, along with their infants and toddlers, of early intervention services; and
- parents and families are, in sum, partners with professionals in planning services, they also are service providers (through the natural environment of in-home services), and they are service recipients.

In all of these ways, Part C explicitly recognizes that families are "systems." Whatever happens to one member has an effect on other family members. By contrast, Part B focuses far more on the rights of the students and designates them as the primary beneficiaries of special education. Likewise, Part B regards their parents (as defined), not their other family members, as secondary beneficiaries, not primary beneficiaries or at least co-primary beneficiaries (as Part C does). Accordingly, it minimizes the family systems theory and arguably may thereby dilute the effect of special education.

Unless general and special educators pay direct attention to parents and other family members, what they do in schools for the students may not carry forward to the students' homes or communities. That would be an unfortunate result, but it is one that may well follow from the different emphases that Part C and Part B give to family and parent participation.

In addition, Part C adds still other opportunities for parents and family members to participate in the early intervention for their infant and toddler members. Under Part C, all of the access and confidentiality rights under Part B are available to parents of infants and toddlers (20 U.S.C. Secs. 1439(a)(2) and (a)(4)). In addition, the SEA and LEA must

- grant parents and other members of the public access to information about state and local early intervention programs and the programs that the state or local agency runs;
- publish its proposed plan for delivering early intervention services, give notice of when hearings will be held, allow for public opportunity to comment on the plan, hold public hearings, and review and comment on the public comments (20 U.S.C. Sec. 1437(a)(8));
- establish a public-awareness program, comprehensive child-find system, and a central directory of information (20 U.S.C. Secs. 1435(a)(5)–(7)); and
- create a State Interagency Coordinating Council, 20 percent of whose members must be parents of infants or toddlers with disabilities (20 U.S.C. Sec. 1441(b)(1)(A)).

Student Participation

Eventually, the rights and responsibilities of parents under IDEA transfer to the student. No later than one year before the student reaches the age of majority under state law, the student's IEP must contain a statement that the student has been informed of the IDEA rights that will transfer. These are the "devolution" provisions;

they provide that the rights of the student's parents will devolve to the student when the student achieves the age of majority (usually 18) and acknowledge that adults (those who have turned 18) are competent by reason of age and capacity to make decisions and participate in shared educational decision making (20 U.S.C. Sec. 1415(m)). The devolution provisions are significant for several reasons:

- They tell the LEAs and parents that they should teach students self-determination skills and use research-based and easily accessible self-determination curricula.
- They tell the parents that there will be a time when, legally, they must let go of their parental rights, and to prepare for that time.
- They tell the LEAs and parents that they must consider what action to take to protect the rights of a student who clearly does not have the competence to look after himself as an adult (in legal terms, the capacity to make and communicate decisions about his health, safety, and resources).

In short, the devolution provisions push the LEA and parents to decide the issue of responsibility for an adult child and not to put off the decision until the child becomes an adult.

SUMMARY

Let's return now to the Case on Point. *Burlington* held that parents may recover the tuition they pay to private schools when an LEA defaults in its duty to offer an appropriate education to their child. In that case, the Court observed that "conscientious parents" normally would seek a private education to replace an inappropriate public one, but that their resort to procedural due process safeguards would be "less than complete" if they could not recover the tuition.

When we discussed *Burlington* at the beginning of this chapter, we argued that desperate needs lead to desperate action. As the Court observed, the conscientious parents want, indeed, they need, to have their child educated appropriately, so they place the child in a private school. But they do so at their own risk. That is so because a due process hearing officer or judge may rule that the LEA offered an appropriate education and therefore disallow tuition reimbursement. IDEA still allows them to recover the tuition, but they have many more duties now than before the 2004 amendments to notify the LEA and allow it to cure any default, and they must be sure that the private school does offer an appropriate education and that the LEA does not.

For these reasons, *Burlington* teaches us something about the way the Court regards parental duties: to be conscientious. In this respect, IDEA's 2004 amendments track the Court's view of parents: They have a duty to be conscientious—to be responsible, not just in exercising rights on their and their child's behalf but also in dealing with the LEA and (to a lesser degree) the SEA.

We also said that *Burlington* makes it clear that the LEA has a duty to deal with a student's parents in good faith. That duty remains, but the 2004 amendments also require the parents to deal in equally good faith with the LEA.

Finally, we asserted that *Burlington* shows that LEAs have the power advantage when dealing with parents, and in chapter 8 we argued that the burden-of-proof case, *Schaffer v. Weast,* reinforces that power advantage. The 2004 amendments preserve parent participation rights but ironically tip the power advantage even more to the LEAs by imposing additional duties on the parents and creating serious consequences for them if they fail to carry out those duties.

Having described IDEA's six principles, we are at the point where we must tell how parents can use other means for enforcing IDEA (chapter 10, "Compliance, Rights, and Remedies") and then why IDEA is an ideal example to illustrate the core concepts of disability policy (chapter 11, "The Core Concepts of Disability Policy").

Part Three

Policy, Enforcement, and Core Concepts

Chapter 10

Compliance, Rights, and Remedies

There is no single case that best exemplifies the issues concerning enforcement of IDEA. There are simply too many different issues that no one case captures them especially well. Nor are any of the decided cases particularly relevant, now that Congress has substantially changed IDEA's enforcement provisions (as we will explain).

RIGHTS, DUTIES, AND REMEDIES

Litigation has been a major—and indeed was the original—source for establishing the educational rights of children with disabilities. Were it not for the early landmark decisions (especially *PARC* and *Mills*), it is doubtful whether Congress would have enacted IDEA.

Court orders, however, are not self-executing. Although they demand compliance by the parties involved, they cannot assure or guarantee compliance, and they are truly effective only if the school authorities are willing or able to carry them out. When, as sometimes happens, these authorities are neither willing nor able to do so, students and their parents have been compelled to return to court and seek additional relief. That was the case before Congress enacted IDEA (as Education for All Handicapped Children Act, 1975) and still remains true today.

Moreover, court orders usually are not as specific as statutes and related regulations. They tend to be more general, and of course they are not accompanied by appropriations (funds).

For these reasons, advocates for students with disabilities (parents, civil rights attorneys, and, in the 1970s, state and local legislators and education policy-makers) sought Congress's aid and received it through the 1975 law and its subsequent amendments. Congress acted under two types of authority:

1. It acted to enforce the equal protection clause of the Fourteenth Amendment (see chapter 4).
2. It acted to create a federal grant-in-aid program (see chapter 3).

Rights and Duties

By creating rights for students with disabilities, Congress also imposed corresponding duties on SEAs and LEAs. It is axiomatic that, for every right, there is a corresponding duty; and for every wrong, there should be (and usually is) a remedy.

As we pointed out in chapters 4–9, students' and parents' rights derive from IDEA's six principles. So do the duties of agencies and professionals. Those rights and duties are the bases on which remedies rest—remedies that are available through procedural due process (chapter 8) and through administrative-regulatory means. Before explaining those remedies, let's review IDEA's principles as applied to these rights and duties.

- The right to attend school—the principle of zero reject (chapter 4)—means that agencies and professionals may not indefinitely expel or suspend students for certain behaviors or without following certain procedures; they may not exclude students on the basis that they are incapable of learning; and they may not limit their access to school on the basis of their having contagious diseases.
- The right to a fair appraisal of their strengths and needs—the principle of nondiscriminatory evaluation (chapter 5)—means that agencies and professionals must obtain an accurate, unbiased portrait of each student.
- The right to a beneficial experience in school—the principle of individualized and appropriate education (chapter 6)—means that schools must individualize each student's education, provide needed related services and supplementary aids and services, engage in a fair process for determining what is appropriate for each student, and, given how much more results oriented IDEA is now than in the past, ensure that the student's education indeed confers a benefit.
- The right to be included in the general education settings, the general curriculum, extracurricular activities, and other school activities—the principle of the least restrictive environment (chapter 7)—means that schools must include students with disabilities in the general education program and may not remove them from it unless they cannot benefit from being in that program, even after the provision of supplementary aids and services and necessary related services.
- The right to be treated fairly—the principle of procedural due process (chapter 8)—means the schools must provide certain kinds of information (notice and access to records) to students, special protection when the natural parents are unavailable (surrogate parents), and access to a fair-hearing process and judicial appeals.

- The right to be included in the decision-making process—the principle of parent and student participation (chapter 9)—means the schools must structure the statewide and local decision-making process in such a way that parents and students have opportunities to meaningfully affect the education they are receiving.

Remedies, Generally

Remedies serve two purposes:

1. Remedies forestall any future damage by requiring the SEA or LEA to cease violating IDEA and begin carrying out its duties to fulfill the student's rights. Injunctive relief—a court order commanding the SEA or LEA to take certain action or to not continue certain action—provides the legal mechanism for requiring the LEA to provide the "start-over" remedy.
2. Remedies are intended to compensate for any damage by making the individual "whole," that is, putting the student (or other victim of a rights violation) in the same situation he or she would have been in were it not for the violation. IDEA provides three forms of "making-whole" remedies:

   a. Extended school year (ESY)
   b. Tuition reimbursement
   c. Compensatory education

A remedy for violating any of these or other rights includes a court order requiring the LEA to repair its procedural and substantive failures to fulfill its duties. Essentially, the remedy is a start-over remedy: The LEA must restart the process of evaluation, IEP development and implementation, and inclusion, even if the restart entails a great cost to the school (such as in a private or public out-of-state program).

In addition to the process-based start-over remedy and the three substantive, make-whole remedies expressly provided for in IDEA, students and their parents may invoke other clearly and explicitly stated remedies. IDEA is unequivocal in granting access to other remedies. IDEA provides that none of its provisions, including the remedies it explicitly grants, may be construed to restrict or limit the rights, procedures, and remedies available under the federal Constitution, the Americans with Disabilities Act, the Rehabilitation Act of 1973, particularly the Section 794 antidiscrimination provisions (also known as Section 504 in the original public law), and the Section 795 attorneys'-fees recovery provisions (also known as Section 505), or other federal laws protecting the rights of children with disabilities (20 U.S.C. Sec. 1415(l)).

This is an extraordinarily important provision because it means that a student may sue an SEA or an LEA under IDEA, the ADA, the Rehabilitation Act, Section 1983 of the Civil Rights Act, and any other federal law. Students who have sued under IDEA and these other laws have found that, in many cases, it has helped them tremendously to be able to resort to these other laws to enforce their rights to equal educational opportunities and to FAPE.

In addition, students and parents have a variety of essentially administrative remedies involving monitoring of executive agencies and enforcing IDEA's provisions. The U.S. Department of Education may withhold federal funds from a state that does not comply with IDEA; the SEA may withhold funds from a noncomplying LEA; and the SEA may have to provide services directly to students when a local agency does not or cannot (20 U.S.C. Sec. 1416). Further, as we described in chapter 8, a parent may file a complaint with either the SEA or the Office of Civil Rights of the U.S. Department of Education.

In this chapter we describe and discuss all of these remedies and enforcement mechanisms, indicating where they are clear and where they are tenuous. We start by discussing monitoring and compliance remedies under IDEA, and then the primary judicial remedies for claims under IDEA, including tuition reimbursement, compensatory education, extended-school-year services, and injunctive relief. We continue by discussing suits for monetary damages under IDEA and judicial remedies available under other disability laws. Finally, we discuss attorneys' fees and access to remedies and relief.

Note that when IDEA refers to the "state," it basically refers to the SEA. That is because the state itself acts through its SEA. So we sometimes use "SEA" when IDEA uses "state."

MONITORING AND COMPLIANCE

IDEA includes monitoring and compliance mechanisms, but, historically, actual administrative oversight and enforcement have been notably absent from the struggle to ensure that the promise of FAPE is upheld. In a sharp criticism of the Office of Special Education Programs (OSEP), the report of the President's Commission on Excellence in Special Education (2002) concluded that OSEP "has not been effective both in implementing technical assistance and in monitoring compliance program performance in states" (p. 15).

The Commission noted that despite the fact that "no state has ever been found to be in full compliance with federal special education law" and that, even "though such authority was incorporated into the 1997 IDEA amendments, ... the Department of Education has not sent a single case to the Department of Justice for 'substantial noncompliance'" (p. 15).

The Commission (2002) offered several reasons for these enforcement problems:

- OSEP's organizational structure does not sufficiently separate those who provide assistance to state and local agencies from those who enforce compliance at the federal level.
- An emphasis on good relations between OSEP staff and state directors of special education, intended to facilitate technical assistance, hampers OSEP's ability to enforce IDEA's provisions meaningfully.

- OSEP lacks the necessary authority and resources to pursue and investigate individual complaints of violations.
- Systems of accountability among the various agencies that have jurisdiction over some part of IDEA claims (OSEP, Office of Civil Rights, etc.) are not well integrated. The agencies often fail to communicate and do not have a system for systematically collecting and disseminating data about student performance by and across all pertinent federal agencies. This leads to duplication of effort and wastes time and resources of both federal and state agency staff (p. 62).

In reauthorizing IDEA in 2004, Congress took at least some of these issues to heart and significantly amended the monitoring and enforcement provisions to improve the ability of federal agencies to hold states accountable for compliance with and outcomes under IDEA. The amendments include changes to monitoring requirements, application of enforcement mechanisms, and the required reports to Congress and the public.

Monitoring

IDEA places the responsibility for monitoring and oversight of state IDEA implementation on the federal Department of Education, of which OSEP is a part. The statute directs the Secretary of Education to focus the department's monitoring efforts on

> improving educational results and functional outcomes for all children with disabilities; and ensuring that States meet the program requirements under this part (Part B), with a particular emphasis on those requirements that are most closely related to improving educational results for children with disabilities. (20 U.S.C. Sec. 1416(a)(2))

IDEA clarifies what focusing on educational results and functional outcomes means by creating three broad priority areas for monitoring. Those areas are as follows:

1. Provision of a free appropriate public education in the least restrictive environment (FAPE) (20 U.S.C. Sec. 1416(a)(3)(A)). Note that this area covers the first four of IDEA's six principles (zero reject, nondiscriminatory evaluation, appropriate education, and least restrictive environment) and arguably its last one, parent and student participation.
2. State exercise of general supervisory authority, including child find, effective monitoring, the use of resolution sessions, mediation, voluntary binding arbitration, and a system of transition services (20 U.S.C. Sec. 1416(a)(3)(B)). Note that this area covers IDEA's principle of procedural due process.

3. Disproportionate representation of racial and ethnic groups in special education and related services, to the extent the representation is the result of inappropriate identification (20 U.S.C. Sec. 1416(a)(3)(C)). Note that this area covers IDEA's principle of nondiscriminatory evaluation.

Furthermore, and to ensure that monitoring in these priority areas adequately evaluates the states' performances, IDEA requires monitors to use quantifiable indicators and qualitative indicators as needed to collect valid and reliable data from states on measurable and rigorous targets related to each priority area (20 U.S.C. Sec. 1416(a)(3)). This approach is comparable to the approach that NCLB authorizes under its accountability principle.

The focus on these priority areas does not preclude the Department of Education from also monitoring other areas. IDEA, in fact, requires that each state provide certain other data to the Secretary of Education and the public, including program information.

Program Information

The following program information is required (20 U.S.C. Sec. 1418):

- The number and percentage of children with disabilities, by race, ethnicity, limited English proficiency status, gender, and disability category, who are in each of the following separate categories:
  - □ Receiving a free appropriate public education
  - □ Participating in general education
  - □ In separate classes, separate schools or facilities, or public or private residential facilities
  - □ For each year of age from age 14 through 21, stopped receiving special education and related services because of program completion (including graduation with a regular secondary school diploma), or other reasons, and the reasons why those children stopped receiving special education and related services
  - □ Removed to an interim alternative educational setting under Section 1415(k)(1)
  - □ The acts or items precipitating those removals
  - □ The number of children with disabilities who are subject to long-term suspensions or expulsions

- The number and percentage of children with disabilities, by race, gender, and ethnicity, who are receiving early intervention services
- The number and percentage of children with disabilities, by race, gender, and ethnicity, who, from birth through age 2, stopped receiving early intervention services because of program completion or for other reasons
- The incidence and duration of disciplinary actions by race, ethnicity, limited English proficiency status, gender, and disability category of children with disabilities, including suspensions of 1 day or more

- The number and percentage of children with disabilities who are removed to alternative educational settings or expelled, compared to children without disabilities who are removed to alternative educational settings or expelled
- The number of due process complaints filed under Section 1415 and the number of hearings conducted
- The number of hearings requested under Section 1415(k) and the number of changes in placements ordered as a result of those hearings
- The number of mediations held and the number of settlement agreements reached through such mediations
- The number and percentage of infants and toddlers, by race and ethnicity, who are at risk of having substantial developmental delays (as defined in Section 1432), and who are receiving early intervention services under Part C
- Any other information that may be required by the Secretary

Each SEA must provide this information to the Department of Education, but the Secretary has discretion in determining whether to use this information for monitoring or oversight purposes. In any case, that information must be reported to the public, and—to protect the privacy of students with disabilities and their families—the reporting must be done "in a manner that does not result in the disclosure of data identifiable to individual children" (20 U.S.C. Sec. 1418(b)).

Furthermore, the Department of Education must ensure that the SEAs monitor their LEAs (20 U.S.C. Sec. 1416(a)(3)). By creating this system of tiered monitoring—the federal agency monitors the state; the state monitors the local agencies—Congress has tried to address the concern about limitations on resources and personnel in the federal monitoring agency. After all, it certainly is easier, and more efficient, for the U.S. Department of Education to monitor 50 state agencies than it is for it to monitor the thousands of local education agencies that exist across the United States.

Of course, if the federal agency is to monitor the state agencies and focus on the priority areas, it must have a data source that includes the information necessary for monitoring. That is why IDEA requires the SEA to provide the Secretary of Education with a significant amount of program information, but IDEA allows the Secretary to determine the extent to which the DOE will use those data for monitoring activities.

IDEA provides for two more additional mechanisms for monitoring and requires the Secretary to use these mechanisms for monitoring:

- Oversight and review of required state performance plans
- Oversight of the exercise of general supervision by the states

Performance Plans

A performance plan is simply a written document that "evaluates that state's efforts to implement the requirements and purposes of (IDEA Part B) and describes how the state will improve such implementation" (20 U.S.C. Secs. 1416(a)–(b)). IDEA requires SEAs to create and submit a performance plan to the Department of

Education. If the Department of Education approves the SEA performance plan, the SEA must implement it, review it at least every 6 months, and inform the Department of Education about any changes in the plan that the SEA intends to make (20 U.S.C. Sec. 1416(d)).

A performance plan is simply a plan for how the SEA will evaluate its implementation of IDEA and how it will improve its implementation. The only content requirement for SEA performance plans is that they must provide the measurable and rigorous targets for the monitoring indicators used by the Department of Education in all priority areas (20 U.S.C. Sec. 1416(b)). IDEA thus grants SEAs a certain amount of leeway in developing the content of their performance plan.

That is not to say that SEAs do not have some requirements and responsibilities in creating their performance plans. The SEA plan must be subject to scientifically sound methods of evaluating improvements in the provision of FAPE, the SEA's exercise of its supervisory duties, and the nondiscriminatory classification of children into special education (e.g., any reduction in the misclassifications of minority students into special education) (20 U.S.C. Sec. 1412(a)). In reporting IDEA out of committee and for vote by the Senate and House of Representatives, Congress said: "It is our expectation that state performance plans, indicators, and targets will be developed with broad stakeholder input and public dissemination" (U.S. Congress, 2004). Not only does this quote reflect an expectation that the SEA will use democratic processes in developing its plan and targets, but it also places that expectation upon the Department of Education as it develops its own indicators.

After an SEA creates its performance plan, it must submit it to the Secretary of Education for approval. The Secretary may disapprove the plan, expressly approve the plan, or allow the plan to be deemed to be approved. If the Secretary has not disapproved a performance plan within 120 days of the Secretary's receiving it, IDEA provides that the plan shall be deemed to be approved. If the Secretary does disapprove the plan, the Department of Education must provide notice of the disapproval to the SEA and include in that notification

- the specific provisions in the plan that do not meet the requirements, and
- additional information related to those provisions needed for the plan to be approved.

The notice also must offer the SEA the opportunity to challenge the Secretary's decision in a due process hearing. But before the SEA invokes due process, it is entitled to one more opportunity to correct its plan's insufficiencies by providing the requested information. Also, an SEA's right to repair before due process is not without limits. If the SEA wishes to amend its performance plan to comply with these requirements, it must do so within 30 days of receiving the notice of disapproval.

After the SEA's performance plan has been approved, it must collect data and report those data annually to the public and to the Secretary "on the performance of each local educational agency located in the state on the targets in the state's performance plan" (20 U.S.C. Sec. 1416(b)(2)(C)). Based on the performance report as well as information obtained through monitoring visits and public information, the Secretary must determine if, with respect to Part B, the SEA

- meets its requirements and purposes,
- needs assistance in implementing its requirements,
- needs intervention in implementing its requirements, or
- needs substantial intervention in implementing its requirements (20 U.S.C. Sec. 1416(d)(2)).

Enforcement

Obviously, if the Secretary finds that the SEA meets the requirements for implementing IDEA, no specific action is required. But what if the SEA's report and other monitoring data show that the SEA is not implementing IDEA effectively? What actions does IDEA require to compel compliance and to assist the SEA in improving its implementation? The answer depends on the extent to which the SEA is failing to meet IDEA's implementation goals and the length of time the failure has lasted.

States in Need of Assistance

If the Secretary finds that a state needs assistance in implementing Part B for 2 or more consecutive years, the Secretary must do one or more of the following:

- Advise the state concerning available sources of technical assistance that may help it address the areas in which it needs assistance. These sources may include assistance from the Office of Special Education Programs, other offices of the Department of Education, other federal agencies, technical assistance providers approved by the Secretary, and other federally funded nonprofit agencies. The Secretary may require the SEA to work with any of these entities.
- Direct the use of state-level funds (the so-called Section 1411(e) funds that the SEA retains and does not pass through to LEAs) on the areas in which the state needs assistance.
- Identify the state as a high-risk grantee and impose special conditions on how the state may use federal funds under Part B (20 U.S.C. Secs. 1416(e)(1)(A)–(C)).

IDEA does not specifically prescribe the type or form of technical assistance the Secretary must authorize, but it does list four technical assistance activities:

1. The provision of advice by experts to address the areas in which the state needs assistance, including explicit plans for addressing the area of concern within a specified period of time
2. Assistance in identifying and implementing professional development, instructional strategies, and methods of instruction based on scientific research
3. Designating and using distinguished superintendents, principals, special education administrators, special education teachers, and other teachers to provide advice, technical assistance, and support

4. Devising additional approaches to providing technical assistance, such as collaborating with institutions of higher education, educational service agencies, national centers of technical assistance supported under Part D, and private providers of scientifically based technical assistance (20 U.S.C. Secs. 1416(e)(1)(A)(i)–(iv))

States in Need of Intervention

If the Secretary determines that a state needs intervention for 3 or more years, the Secretary may take any of the actions just described and, in addition, must take one or more of the following actions:

- Require the state to prepare a corrective action plan or improvement plan if the Secretary determines that the state should be able to correct the problem within 1 year
- Require the state to enter into a compliance agreement under Section 457 of the General Education Provisions Act if the Secretary has reason to believe that the state cannot correct the problem within 1 year
- For each year of the determination that the state needs intervention, withhold not less than 20% and not more than 50% of the state's funds until the state has sufficiently addressed the areas in which the state needs intervention
- Seek to recover IDEA funds from the state, relying on Section 452 of the General Education Provisions Act
- Withhold, in whole or in part, any further payments to the state
- Refer the matter for appropriate enforcement action, which may include referral to the Department of Justice (DOJ) (20 U.S.C. Secs. 1416(e)(2)(B)(i)–(vi))

The scope of the Secretary's enforcement power when a state is in need of "intervention" is far more extensive than it is when a state is simply in need of "assistance." Not only may the Secretary refer the matter to the DOJ for appropriate enforcement action through a lawsuit to compel the state to comply, but the Secretary also may tighten the federal purse strings with regard to federal IDEA funds earmarked for the state.

The Secretary has wide discretion in how to apply the withholding power. The Secretary may limit such withholdings to the programs or projects involved or may restrict payments to specific state and local agencies that have failed to successfully implement the law (20 U.S.C. Sec. 1416(e)(3)). The Secretary may withhold the funds until the problems identified as the reason for the withholding are rectified and the state is in compliance with IDEA (20 U.S.C. Sec. 1416(e)(6)(B)).

States in Need of Substantial Intervention

Finally, if for any period the Secretary finds that a state "needs substantial intervention" or there is substantial noncompliance with a required condition for the SEA's or LEA's eligibility, the Secretary must take one or more of the following actions:

- Recover IDEA funds under Section 452 of the General Education Provisions Act

- Withhold, in whole or in part, any further payments to the state under Part B
- Refer the case to the Office of the Inspector General at the Department of Education
- Refer the matter for appropriate enforcement action, which may include referral to the DOJ

Note the important adjective "substantial" and how that single word distinguishes this level of federal oversight from the other two levels. The "need of substantial intervention" is perhaps the most important part of the enforcement provisions of IDEA because it does not allow for any time period to elapse before it requires the Secretary to take action. If a state is in "need of assistance" or in "need of intervention," it must continue to be so for a number of years before the Secretary is authorized (and required) to act. But if a state is found to be in "need of substantial intervention," the Secretary must act immediately and undertake one or more of the above actions—all of which are fairly significant enforcement activities involving a full investigation of the violations, court action, or a restriction of funds.

Opportunity for Hearing and Judicial Review

To balance out the discretion afforded the Secretary of Education in withholding payments to states, IDEA provides a system for SEAs to challenge the Secretary's actions. Before withholding funds, the Secretary must notify the SEA that he or she intends to withhold funds, and then must allow the SEA an opportunity for a hearing (20 U.S.C. Sec. 1416(e)(4)). The Secretary still may suspend payments or revoke the SEA's authority to obligate funds (distribute them to LEAs) while awaiting the outcome of the hearing if the SEA has been given a reasonable opportunity to show cause why future payments should not be suspended (20 U.S.C. Sec. 1416(e)(4)(B)). In addition to challenging the Secretary's actions through an administrative hearing, the SEA may dispute the Secretary's actions to any U.S. Court of Appeals (a circuit court) and may appeal that court's decision to the Supreme Court.

It is important to note that the SEAs are not passive recipients of federal oversight. SEAs also have enforcement powers to ensure that their LEAs comply with IDEA and implement the law to meet the goals of the state performance plan. When an LEA has failed in meeting these requirements, the SEA may restrict the outlay of funds to the LEA to force compliance (20 U.S.C. Sec. 1413(d)(1)).

The extensive amendments to the monitoring and enforcement provisions of IDEA in 2004 and the detailed accountability system they created (grounded in NCLB and IDEA alike) justify higher expectations for future monitoring and enforcement of IDEA. Yet, these amendments do not directly address many of the problems highlighted in the report of the President's Commission (2002). For example, the extensive discretion of the Secretary for monitoring and enforcing IDEA suggests that the relationship between state directors of special education and the DOE still may limit the actual use of enforcement mechanisms. But even if this limiting factor is overcome, the primary enforcement mechanism for IDEA always has been, and is likely to remain, parents' use of procedural due process and the remedies that due process hearing officers and courts may authorize.

JUDICIAL REMEDIES: NONMONETARY DAMAGES AND RELIEF UNDER IDEA

When a student receives educational services that are not tailored to his or her needs or do not provide an educational benefit, the student falls behind. Those weeks, months, or even years in an ineffective program represent lost educational opportunities (and lost outcomes based on an appropriate education) as well as an LEA's or SEA's failure to meet IDEA's requirements. Within IDEA, the legal maxim, "no rights without remedies," translates into three basic remedies:

1. Tuition reimbursement
2. Compensatory education
3. Extended school year

Because we discussed tuition reimbursement and the Supreme Court's *Burlington* case in chapter 9 ("Parent Participation"), we discuss only compensatory education and extended school year in this chapter.

Compensatory Education

Although *Burlington* held that parents and students are entitled to tuition reimbursement, it also stands for the analogous proposition that students are entitled to receive compensatory education if they are denied a free appropriate education. Compensatory education is an equitable remedy that entitles students to obtain services from the LEA beyond their 21st birthday. IDEA's 2004 amendments do not preclude the compensatory education remedy, and the cases on compensatory education remain as good law.

Compensatory education is awardable when the LEA denies a "basic floor of opportunity" under *Rowley*. Parents are not required to allege bad faith by the LEA, because, under *Burlington*, tuition reimbursement cases do not require that kind of showing and because compensatory education is equivalent to tuition reimbursement (*Harris v. D.C. Bd. of Ed.*, 1992; *McManus v. Wilmette School Dist. 39 Bd. of Ed.*, 1992).

The issues surrounding compensatory education are manifold. Because compensatory education is an equitable remedy, courts are free to exercise their discretion when awarding it. Thus, three aspects of the claim must be evaluated:

1. The legal standards that courts use to award compensatory education and to determine its duration
2. Facts that constitute a sufficient deprivation to warrant this award
3. Defenses to a student's claim

The Legal Standard

The Supreme Court has not articulated a legal standard for awarding compensatory education, and the regulations also are silent. Lower courts, however, evaluate a compensatory education claim on a case-by-case basis, examining the facts closely to determine whether the LEA's violation is so flagrant as to warrant such an award. Consider, for example, *M.C. v. Central Regional School Dist.* (1995).

That case involved a 16-year-old student with severe mental retardation. Since 1987, the student's IEP had stressed personal and self-help goals, including toileting, eating, general communication, and community training skills. The student's progress plateaued in 1989 and thereafter regressed in all areas. In addition, the student's IEP failed to address the important goal of reducing his self-stimulatory behavior.

Finding that compensatory education is proper if (a) an LEA knows or should have known that a student's IEP is inappropriate or the student is not receiving more than a *de minimis* (slight) educational benefit, and (b) the LEA fails to correct the situation, the court awarded compensatory education based on a physician's testimony that the student's minimal progress resulted from a program that failed to address his needs and that the student would have progressed had the LEA placed him in a residential facility rather than a local day program.

Facts Constituting Deprivation

Another standard—seemingly more stringent than inadequate IEP and *de minimis* benefit—is represented by *Mrs. C. v. Wheaton* (1990), which held that the appropriate standard for awarding compensatory education is a finding of such a "gross" deprivation of the student's procedural rights that it results in denial of a free appropriate education. The court held that the LEA grossly deprived a student of his rights by attempting to coerce him into terminating his right to further education and by engaging in undue delay in holding required hearings.

Although many courts have awarded compensatory education, the courts in the cases noted above have developed a legal standard for lower courts to follow: the inadequate IEP and *de minimis* benefit standard and the gross deprivation standard. To fully understand when a court may award compensatory education, then, we have to examine what constitutes compensable deprivation of a free appropriate education.

In *Lester H. v. Gilhool* (1990), the court awarded compensatory education when the LEA (a) failed to admit for 30 months that the student's in-district placement was inappropriate, and (b) refused to locate another placement for him despite the availability of at least six acceptable schools within the state. Similarly, the court in *Miener v. Missouri* (1986) awarded compensatory education against an LEA for denying educational services to a student with a severe emotional disorder who, as a result of that denial, spent 3 years in a mental health ward of a state hospital.

Likewise, in *Murphy v. Timberlane Regional Sch. Dist.* (1994), the court awarded compensatory education to a 25-year-old adult with multiple disabilities after determining that the LEA previously had denied the student a free appropriate education for a 2-year period when it failed to provide an adequate IEP or initiate proceedings to resolve the inadequacy.

Thus, the length of time during which an LEA refuses to confer an educational benefit and the consequences of that denial are the controlling factors. Both must be gross or flagrant.

Defenses

It also will be helpful to consider the cases in which courts have refused to award compensatory education. *Carlisle Area School Dist. v. Scott P.* (1995) denied compensatory education to a student because he had progressed, albeit slowly, under the LEA's IEP. The court rejected the parents' assertion that their child had not progressed at a sufficient rate. In addition, *Parents of Student W. v. Puyallup* (1994) refused to order compensatory education for a student even though the LEA violated IDEA by allowing the student to unilaterally disenroll himself from special education without consulting his parents.

Upon realizing that the student qualified for special education, the LEA attempted to remedy the situation by offering tutoring services and an appropriate IEP, which the parents refused. The court based its decision on both the parents' refusal of services and the fact that the student completed high school, graduating with his class without additional services.

These cases stand for the proposition that student progress nullifies a claim for compensatory education. The progress is proof of benefit.

Finally, where an LEA takes reasonable steps to integrate a student, evaluate and pay for an independent evaluation, and provide some related services in the general education program (but not all the services the family wants), the district is not liable for providing compensatory education just because other related services were withheld (*Jeanette H. v. Pennsbury School District*, 1992; *Murphy v. Timberlane Regional Sch. Dist.*, 1994). Substantial compliance, together with benefit, is a defense to a compensatory education claim.

Summary: Quantitative and Qualitative Standards

Courts may determine the duration of a compensatory education award based on both a qualitative and a quantitative analysis. The court used a quantitative formula to determine duration in *M.C. v. Central Regional Sch. Dist.* (1995), holding that a student is entitled to compensatory education for a period of time equal to the period of deprivation minus the time required to rectify the situation. Other courts have awarded compensatory education based on both the length of the deprivation and the magnitude of that deprivation, which is a more qualitative measurement. Whatever the analysis, courts clearly have a great deal of discretion in determining the duration of compensatory education.

Although *M.C. v. Central Regional Sch. Dist.* held that bad faith by the LEA is not a prerequisite for an award of compensatory education, the LEA in each of the cases where the court awarded compensatory education acted flagrantly and therefore culpably. Each LEA displayed deliberate and egregious action, through either undue delay or failure to act. This type of reckless disregard of a student's rights to FAPE caused significant negative consequences for the student.

Extended-School-Year Services (ESY)

Rowley's tenets that professionally developed, individualized education programs are deemed to be appropriate flies squarely in the face of legislative judgments, usually based on fiscal policy, that a school year should be limited to a fixed number of days a year. Although fiscally and politically defensible, the length-of-school-year decision does not satisfy *Rowley*'s demand for individualization of education, based on professional judgment. Not surprisingly, inflexible school-year limits have been tested, with parents arguing and courts agreeing that an extended school year (summer school) is a remedy for the denial of an appropriate education.

The earliest case is *Armstrong v. Kline* (1979), which held that the state's refusal to pay for more than 180 days of schooling each year for students with severe or profound mental retardation and those with serious emotional disturbances violates their rights to an appropriate education under IDEA—an appropriate education being one that allows the children to become self-sufficient within the limits of their disabilities, not just one that allows them to share equally in programs provided to nondisabled students or to reach one of several other goals.

In *Geis v. Bd. of Ed. of Parsnippany-Troy Hills* (1985), the court noted that some children regress significantly during breaks in their education and recoup their losses more slowly, and accordingly are denied an appropriate education unless they are given year-round education. Likewise, *Johnson v. Indep. Sch. Dist. #4* (1990) held that "under the Act itself, states must provide a continuous educational experience throughout the summer under the child's IEP if that is the appropriate educational experience for the handicapped child's situation."

The 2004 regulations codify these results. Sec. 300.106 states that each public agency must ensure that extended-school-year services are available as necessary to provide FAPE—that is, only if it is determined by the IEP team to be necessary to meet the specific needs of a child with a disability. The regulations also explicitly prohibit LEAs from limiting the availability of ESY services to particular categories of disability or from unilaterally limiting the type, amount, or duration of ESY services. Finally, the regulations provide a long-missing definition for ESY services. Extended-school-year services are special education and related services that

- are provided to a child with a disability,
- beyond the normal school year of the public agency,
- in accordance with the child's IEP,
- at no cost to the parents, and
- meet the standards of the SEA.

In summary, ESY, like compensatory education, is an equitable remedy, available at a court's discretion, for violating the right to an appropriate education. As a rule, the extent of the student's disability, as measured by regression and recoupment factors, is the basis for the award of ESY benefits, sometimes exacerbated by LEA dissembling about student rights.

JUDICIAL REMEDIES: DAMAGES UNDER IDEA, SECTION 504, AND ADA

Perhaps the most tenuous remedy under IDEA is the one we have not yet mentioned—a lawsuit to recover monetary damages. Here, the case law is extraordinarily conflicted and the legal doctrines extraordinarily subtle and ever-changing in their application to people with disabilities. For these reasons and because the 2004 reauthorization of IDEA will focus the attention of SEAs, LEAs, and parents and their children's other advocates on the new monitoring and enforcement provisions that we have just reviewed, we state the issue and summarize the case law but do not go into depth in our discussions of the issues.

Courts' Refusal to Allow Monetary Damage Claims

Shortly after Congress enacted IDEA, students and parents began to seek monetary damages for its violations—almost invariably without success. These plaintiffs learned that state law generally does not allow them to recover damages because no "educational malpractice" has been committed, and thus they have no recovery for what an education agency may do or not do to a student. (For an early case that reviews all previous education malpractice cases and discusses the reasons they have failed, see *Hunter v. Board of Education of Montgomery Co.*, 1982.) These families also learned a second lesson: IDEA also does not allow them to recover damages regardless of negligence arguably involved in the LEA's actions. The courts reached these conclusions for several reasons:

- IDEA does not explicitly provide for money damages.
- Damages will encourage the LEA to practice "defensive" education and impair an LEA's willingness to use innovative (but evidence-based) interventions.
- Damages will negatively affect an LEA's budget.
- Damages may subject an LEA to endless litigation (with associated financial expenses and other costs that we reviewed in chapter 8, "Procedural Due Process"); this is the "floodgates" argument (the right to recover damages will open up the floodgates to all sorts of lawsuits).

Despite this overwhelming body of case law, students and families have been somewhat successful in holding education agencies liable for damages in certain situations. They have been successful, to some extent, because there are some valid policy reasons to award damages:

- Compensatory damages are available traditionally whenever any person or agency (such as a state or local education agency) violates a duty (such as the IDEA duty to provide FAPE to a student). The "private enforcement model" (a private person brings a lawsuit for damages to enforce a right owed him or her by another person) is a longstanding and effective way to recover for harm suffered. Because IDEA creates identifiable rights, there is every reason why, like other rights-creating and duty-imposing laws, violations should be compensated by money damages.

- If compensatory damages are awarded under IDEA, education agencies will be far more inclined to comply with IDEA. Damages are powerful incentives for schools to comply. A proclivity toward compliance is created when schools have to worry about paying damages.

- Even though Congress intended IDEA to be a vehicle for distributing federal aid to the states, it also intended IDEA to be the means for implementing the federal Constitution's guarantee of equal protection—i.e., equal educational opportunity. In other laws enacted to carry out the Constitution, Congress has provided that persons who are denied their rights under those laws may recover damages. Similarly, students and families should be able to recover under IDEA.

- Congress has not explicitly forbidden students and their families to secure damages for violations of IDEA. From the moment it was enacted, IDEA has allowed courts to "grant such relief as [they deem] appropriate" (20 U.S.C. Sec. 1415(i)(2)(C)(iii)), and the Supreme Court has interpreted "appropriate" to mean "appropriate in light of the purposes of the Act" (*Burlington*).

In light of these policy reasons, some courts have awarded damages or recovery that seems very much like damages, and others at least hold open the prospect that they would award damages—but generally they do so through the application of other related disability law rather than reading IDEA as explicitly creating a right of action for monetary damages. This method of extending damages to special education claims involves coupling the claims of violation under IDEA with claims that an LEA violated a student's rights under Section 504 or under ADA.

IDEA Damages Through Coupled Claims

Section 1415(l) of IDEA provides that nothing in IDEA shall be construed to restrict or limit the rights, procedures, and remedies available under the Constitution, Section 504 of the Rehabilitation Act, or other federal statutes protecting the rights of children and youth with disabilities. This section allows students to couple their claims of an IDEA violation with claims of Section 504 or ADA violations (or both).

Majority View: Identical Facts for Coupled Claims—No Damages

In deciding whether a student in a coupled lawsuit may recover damages, most courts have considered whether a student's claim under Section 504, ADA, and Section 1983 is factually the same as the student's IDEA claim. If there is no factual distinction between the IDEA claim and the other claims, the majority of the courts have held that the student may not recover damages.

The leading case is *Barnett v. Fairfax County Sch. Bd.* (1989), in which the court held that the student may not base a damage claim under Section 1983 "solely upon the same violation" of IDEA and Section 504. To allow the student to "merely" re-allege a violation of IDEA and convert it into a violation of Section 1983 would allow the student to "circumvent the comprehensive scheme" of IDEA remedies.

Reasons for Disallowing Coupling

What explains this result? Several factors are at work, some of which are familiar reasons for denying recovery in the "malpractice" cases.

- When courts determine that a student's factual allegations concerning an IDEA violation are exactly the same as the student's factual allegations of a violation of Section 504, ADA, or Section 1983, they favor IDEA and its traditionally restricted remedies over Section 504, ADA, and Section 1983. Although they do not make it explicit, courts seem to conclude that education disputes should be settled under IDEA, the education statute.
- Courts interpret the purpose of IDEA as to assist the states in implementing the substantive and procedural rights of students with disabilities (*Ft. Zumwalt Sch. Dist. v. Missouri State Bd. of Ed.*, 1994). Accordingly, they hold that an appropriate remedy is education or the tuition spent to secure an education (the *Burlington* approach); an appropriate remedy is not damages.
- The reasons for denying damages for educational malpractice simply seem to be too ingrained and persuasive (*Barnett v. Fairfax County Sch. Bd.*, 1989).
- Because IDEA creates a comprehensive and exclusive remedy and does not specifically include damages among those remedies (*Smith v. Robinson, 1984)*, the right to damages does not exist.
- Courts that allow students to recover damages from a school district expose the district's limited budget to unpredictable financial liability, to the detriment of all students and their teachers (*Anderson v. Thompson*, 1981; *Barnett v. Fairfax County Sch. Bd.*, 1989).
- Some courts have held that Section 504 does not create tort liability for education malpractice unless the student can prove that the school district acted in bad faith (*Barnett v. Fairfax County Sch. Bd.*, 1989, citing *Monahan v. Nebraska,* 1982, and *Timms v. Metro School District,* 1983).

Minority View: Coupling Allowed

Not surprisingly, a minority of courts disagree with the majority view that coupled claims must present different violations under each statute. These courts (*Jonathon*

G. v. Caddo Parish Sch. Bd., 1994; *Mrs. W. v. Tirozzi*, 1987; *Rodgers v. Magnet Cove Pub. Schs.*, 1994; *Susan N. v. Wilson Sch. Dist.*, 1995; *W.B. v. Matula*, 1995; *Whitehead v. Sch. Bd.*, 1996) have held that the student may sue under IDEA as well as under Section 504, ADA, or Section 1983 simultaneously and for the same factual violation.

Three rationales underlie these "recovery of damages" cases:

1. *IDEA's clear language in Section 1415(l).* Section 1415(l) says that nothing in IDEA shall be construed to restrict or limit a student's rights under the federal Constitution, Section 504, or other federal statutes protecting the rights of children and youth with disabilities. To the courts in the minority, "nothing" means just that: nothing—not fears about educational malpractice, not the other reasons given by the majority of the courts—may prevent a student from suing under IDEA, Section 504, ADA, and Section 1983.
2. *IDEA's legislative history (Section 1415(l)*; S. Rep. No. 112, 99th Cong., 2d Sess., p. 2, 1986; H. Conf. Rep. No. 687, 99th Cong., 2d Sess., p. 7, 1986). This history clearly reveals Congress's strong and unequivocal intent to allow coupling and damages.
3. *The Supreme Court's decision in a sex-discrimination case, Franklin v. Gwinnett County Pub. Sch.* (1992). *Franklin* involved a member of a high school faculty who sexually harassed a student. The student sued the district under Title IX of the Civil Rights Act of 1964, which prohibits discrimination based on sex and allows an aggrieved person to recover damages. The Supreme Court restated the general rule that "absent clear direction to the contrary by Congress, the federal courts have the power to award any appropriate relief in a cognizable cause of action brought pursuant to a federal statute." Stated alternatively, the Court held that Congress must explicitly prohibit a person from recovering damages; otherwise, damages may well be "appropriate relief"—the same term the Court used in *Burlington*, where it interpreted IDEA as authorizing courts to award tuition reimbursement.

Inasmuch as Section 504 allows damages, and inasmuch as Section 1415(l) provides that a student may not be restricted or limited in pursuing his or her rights, procedures, and remedies under the Constitution, Section 504, or any other federal statutes protecting his or her rights, some courts have relied on *Franklin v. Gwinnett County Pub. Sch.* and allowed a student to combine an IDEA claim with a Section 504 claim and recover damages.

To summarize: The courts that allow damages under coupled cases are in the minority, and it is fair to conclude at this time that, unless and until the Supreme Court resolves the conflict, the student's ability to recover damages under IDEA, via Section 504, ADA, or Section 1983, will depend on whether the student has an "over-and-above" claim and whether he or she is in a jurisdiction disfavoring or favoring the damage claim.

Violations Over and Above IDEA

But what if the factual allegations of the coupled claim are not the same and the student can prove that he or she experienced one violation under IDEA but a factually different violation under Section 504, ADA, or Section 1983? *Barnett* recognized this possibility and the propriety of allowing such coupled claims to proceed.

In the situation where the violation of Section 504, ADA, or Section 1983 is "over and above" the IDEA violation, the student may sue under IDEA and the other federal statutes and recover damages (but first must exhaust IDEA administrative remedies of due process hearing and appeal) (20 U.S.C. Sec. 1415(l)).

For example, in *Begay v. Hodel* (1990), a student was denied both her IDEA rights (the school district failed to notify her about her due process rights and later refused to convene a due process hearing at her request) and her Section 504 rights (to a barrier-free school). In addition, she experienced physical damage as a result of having to commute to an accessible school that was not in her school district. Thus, the student experienced two Sec. 504 violations—a single Section 504 violation and physical injury as a result of the Section 504 violation. Under these circumstances, she was entitled to bring a lawsuit based on IDEA, Section 504, and Section 1983.

In summary, although the majority of courts will not allow a student to sue under both IDEA and Section 504, ADA, or Section 1983 if the factual allegations are the same, the majority view also is that if the violations are different from and "over and above" the IDEA claim, the student may recover damages. Later in this chapter we discuss the specific remedies available through these other laws, whether over and above an IDEA dispute or brought independently,

For now, it is reasonable to say that the issue of damages is one of the most complex in special education. It also is the one most likely to remain unsettled for some time to come. To reach any firm conclusions about liability and damages, then, is premature. The most one can conclude is that, on balance, the courts disfavor awarding damages and are much more likely to favor remedies such as tuition reimbursement or extended-year services when a violation has occurred.

REMEDIES PROVIDED BY OTHER DISABILITY LAW

Although IDEA unarguably is the primary law governing special education, it is not the only one that provides remedies for discriminatory actions against students with disabilities. We will examine these other sources for relief and the limitations on their use.

Section 504 and ADA Claims

Section 504 prohibits a recipient of federal funds from discriminating against an otherwise qualified person with a disability solely on the basis of the person's disability. Under Section 504, students who have disabilities are entitled to attend school, receive a nondiscriminatory evaluation, receive an education that makes reasonable accommodations to their disabilities, be placed into the least restrictive education environments and programs, and sue education agencies that violate these rights (34 C.F.R. Secs. 104.31–104.39).

Courts have had no difficulty in using Section 504 to benefit students with disabilities who are not classified into special education under IDEA (*Alexander S. v. Boyd*, 1995; *Glenn III v. Charlotte Mecklenburg School Bd. of Educ.*, 1995; *Thomas v. Davidson Academy*, 1994). Nor have most courts been reluctant to hold that Section 504 allows an aggrieved person, including a student and family, to (a) secure an injunction (court order) commanding the schools to comply with Section 504's reasonable accommodations and other commands, and (b) recover monetary damages for the school's failure to do so (*J.B. v. Indep. Sch. Dist.*, 1995; *Jonathon G. v. Caddo Parrish School Bd.*, 1994).

Similarly, ADA prohibits state and local governments, including school districts, from discriminating against an otherwise qualified individual with a disability and requires them to make reasonable accommodations in their programs, including education and schools, to benefit students with disabilities. ADA also allows courts to award damages to persons whose rights under ADA have been violated (*Goodman v. Georgia*, consolidated with and reported under the title of *U.S. v. Georgia, 2006*).

Sovereign Immunity: State and Municipal Liability

The student normally may not sue a state itself. This is so because the state is a sovereign government and normally is immune from suit. The Eleventh Amendment to the federal Constitution establishes the doctrine of sovereign immunity (*Dellmuth v. Muth*, 1989; *Will v. Michigan Dep't. of State Police*, 1989). The defense of sovereign immunity grants "absolute immunity": The state simply may not be sued. That is the general rule, but, of course, the doctrine of sovereign immunity and the defense of absolute immunity has exceptions.

Congress can remove state immunity from a lawsuit in two ways:

1. Congress may provide, in a federal grant-in-aid program, that a state waives its immunity and agrees to be sued as a condition of receiving the federal aid (*Quern v. Jordan,* 1979). Typically, a state waives its immunity so it can receive federal funds and participate in a federal–state program. If, however, a state is to waive its immunity to secure federal funds, Congress must state expressly and unequivocally its intention that a state will waive its immunity as a condition of its receiving federal aid; the state must know exactly and precisely the terms on which Congress grants the federal aid (*Edelman v. Jordan,* 1974; *Pennhurst State School and Hospital v. Halderman*, 1984). IDEA is a grant-in-aid program that explicitly provides that a state waives its immunity by receiving IDEA funds (20 U.S.C. Sec. 1404).

2. Congress simply may abrogate (invalidate or overrule) the state's sovereign immunity in order to enforce the Fourteenth Amendment (guaranteeing due

process and equal protection of the laws to persons in a state) (*Fitzpatrick v. Bitzer*, 1976; *Goodman v. Georgia*, consolidated with and reported under the title of *U.S. v. Georgia*, 2006). As in the situation of a grant of federal funds conditioned on the state's waiver of immunity, Congress must make perfectly clear that it is abrogating the state's immunity and that it has authority to do so under the Fourteenth Amendment. Because the Supreme Court had ruled in *Dellmuth v. Muth* (1989) that IDEA did not abrogate a state's immunity, Congress, responding to that decision, amended IDEA in 1990 to provide that a state shall not be immune, under the Eleventh Amendment, from suit in federal court for a violation of IDEA. The 2004 reauthorization continues to abrogate the states' sovereign immunity (20 U.S.C. Sec. 1404).

Municipal Corporations/Local Governments: No Immunity From Liability

Students may sue a municipality or other subdivision of a state (*Monell v. New York Dep't. of Social Services,* 1978). Unlike a state, a municipality (such as an LEA) may not claim absolute immunity from lawsuits because it is not, itself, a sovereign government. The municipality will be liable to the student if the student can prove that its action or actions of its employees (a) are based on official policies made by the municipality's policy-making officials, (b) reflect deliberate indifference to the rights of the student, or (c) are part of the municipality's custom or practice.

The Supreme Court, however, has limited a municipality's liability (and that of an LEA) to a situation where the plaintiff (student) can prove that "deliberate action attributable to the municipality itself is the 'moving force' behind the plaintiff's deprivation of federal rights" (*Monell; Bd. of County Comm'rs v. Brown,* 1997, clarifying that "moving force" requires wrongdoing that is a "direct causal link between the municipal action and the deprivation of federal rights" and was authorized by the municipality's legislative body or other authorized decision-maker).

State and Municipal Employees: Limited Immunity From Liability

Because a state itself normally is immune from suit, so are its officials and employees when they are acting in their official capacities. The concept of sovereign immunity (expressed in the Eleventh Amendment) would be violated if the state's officials were liable for acts taken to carry out the state's business. This is so with respect to their acts that require them to exercise discretion and judgment (*Supreme Court v. Consumers Union of United States*, 1980; *Tenney v. Brandhove*, 1951). Likewise, municipal officials are immune when they, too, exercise their discretion and judgment about how to conduct the municipality's official business (*Lake Country Estates, Inc. v. Tahoe Regional Planning Agency*, 1979).

The rationale for granting immunity to state and municipal officials when they act in their official capacities is straightforward: They should not be deterred from exercising their best judgment by fear of a lawsuit. The public's business demands them to exercise their best judgment, and public needs must prevail over a private citizen's needs.

Although state and municipal officials are immune when they exercise their discretion and judgment, they are not immune when they are obliged to carry out duties over which they exercise no discretion and about which they may not exercise discretion. These are the so-called mandatory functions of government, as distinguished from the discretionary functions. In the case of mandatory functions, the officials have no choice but to act according to the law's command. If they do not carry out the law's command and thereby cause someone to be harmed, they may be sued for damages or they may be enjoined (required by a court's order or injunction) to perform the duty that the law commands (*Edelman v. Jordan*, 1974; *Harlow v. Fitzgerald*, 1982; *Will v. Michigan Dep't. of State Police*, 1989).

When an official is sued in his or her individual or official capacity, he or she may defend by a claim of "qualified immunity." Under this defense, the official may not be held liable if he can prove that he did not violate clearly established federal law and the student's rights under that law (*Harlow v. Fitzgerald*, 1982; *Wood v. Strickland*, 1975). The defense is that he acted "in good faith" and should not be held liable; he has "qualified" to be immune. The good-faith defense is available to school officials who allegedly have violated a student's IDEA rights (*Christopher P. v. Marcus*, 1990; *W.B. v. Matula*, 1995).

To be successful with a qualified-immunity, good-faith defense, the defendant must prove that the law he or she allegedly violated was not clear at the time he or she acted. As the Supreme Court stated in *Harlow v. Fitzgerald*, a government official is immune if his conduct does not violate "clearly established statutory or constitutional rights of which a reasonable person would have known." "Clearly established" means that the "contours of the right must be sufficiently clear that a reasonable official would understand that what he is doing violates that right" (*Anderson v. Creighton*, 1987). If the law and the student's rights are not clearly established, the official will not be held liable because he cannot reasonably be expected to anticipate some future legal development or doctrine (*Harlow v. Fitzgerald*).

If the official raises a qualified-immunity defense, the student must prove that the official acted "in bad faith." The essence of bad faith is that an official acts with deliberate indifference to the consequences of his or her action. For example, a prison official who fails to provide necessary medical attention to prisoners acts in bad faith (*Estelle v. Gamble*, 1976).

If the student sues a municipality (school district) and its officials, the municipality itself may not raise a defense of qualified immunity. It either did or did not have a policy or custom of violating a student's federal rights; that is all the student has to prove. Moreover, the municipality may not shield itself behind the qualified-immunity/good-faith defense that its employees may use (*Owens v. Independence*, 1980). Finally, a private citizen or private corporation is not entitled to the good-faith/qualified-immunity defense (*Wyatt v. Cole*, 1992).

Section 1983 of the Civil Rights Act

A student's coupling of IDEA with claims under Section 504 and ADA is made all the easier because of Section 1983 of the Civil Rights Act (and because IDEA itself provides that nothing in IDEA prevents a person from asserting any rights the person may have under "federal laws protecting the rights of children with disabilities" [20 U.S.C. Sec. 1415(l)]). Section 1983 provides that an individual whose rights under the federal Constitution or a federal statute have been violated by any other person who has acted under color of state law may recover damages that compensate for the harm suffered and also get an injunction ordering the defendant to cease the harmful activity. This statute is the primary means by which private citizens enforce their federal rights against state and local governments and their employees. To be successful in a Section 1983 lawsuit, a student must prove the "elements" of Section 1983.

Action Under Color of State Law

The student must prove that the person who deprived him of one or more of his federal rights acted "under color of law." That means the person took action pursuant to powers granted to him or her by virtue of the state's laws; his or her action must be possible only because of the authority of the state's laws (*Monroe v. Pape*, 1961, applicable to police officers; and *Wood v. Strickland*, 1975, applicable to school officials). The action taken, however, must be within the scope of the authority granted. An LEA, for instance, cannot be held liable when a teacher, acting outside the scope of her employment, improperly punishes a student with disabilities (*Tall v. Bd. of Sch. Commissioners of Baltimore City*, 1998).

Deprivation of Rights

The student also must prove that he or she is entitled to certain rights, privileges, or immunities under the federal Constitution or under any federal statute and that he or she has been deprived of one or more of those rights, privileges, or immunities by the color-of-law actor (*Maine v. Thiboutot*, 1980; *Wood v. Strickland*, 1975). Proof of a violation under IDEA, Sec. 504, or ADA is, therefore, required.

Section 1983 as a Vehicle for Enforcing IDEA

What if a student prevails in a due process hearing (at the local or state level), the school district does not appeal, and yet the school district refuses to implement the hearing officer's decision? How can the student enforce the favorable judgment? The answer is that the student may sue the school district under Section 1983 (*Hoekstra v. Indep. Sch. Dist. No. 283*, 1996; *Jeremy H. v. Mount Lebanon Sch. Dist.*, 1996).

Under IDEA, the students clearly are the persons whom IDEA intends to benefit: They either have or should be classified as having a disability. Likewise, IDEA explicitly imposes mandatory and direct obligations on a state that accepts IDEA funding; the state has a clear and binding obligation to comply. Finally (as we pointed out early in this chapter), the fundamental federal enforcement scheme is for the U.S. Department of Education to withhold federal funds from the state. That, however, is not a remedy available to an individual student who has prevailed at a due process hearing and encounters a district that refuses to comply with the hearing officer's order. In such a situation, no comprehensive IDEA remedy is available to the student (*Blazejewski v. Bd. of Educ.*, 1985; *Grace B. v. Lexington Sch. Comm.*, 1991; *Reid v. Bd. of Educ.*, 1991; *Robinson v. Pinderhughes*, 1987).

The only way a student can enforce the hearing officer's decision is to sue under Section 1983. As noted above, the student may secure an injunction requiring the state or local school district to comply with the hearing officer's decision (or to be in contempt of court if it does not comply), and, in some jurisdictions and under some circumstances, the student also may be able to secure monetary damages if he or she suffers an injury as a direct result of the district's failure to comply with the hearing officer's decision or a court order that enforces it. Accordingly, Section 1983 is a vehicle for enforcing a student's or family's rights under FERPA (*Belanger v. Nashua Sch. Dist.*, 1994; *Maynard v. Greater Hoyt Sch. Dist. No. 61-4*, 1995; *Sean R. v. Bd. of Educ.*, 1992).

Likewise, it seems that the provisions of the 2004 reauthorization of IDEA that give the LEA or the student's parents the right to enforce a binding arbitration agreement or the agreement reached in the mandatory resolution session (20 U.S.C. Sec. 1415(e)(2)(F)) will be enforceable under Section 1983 (34 C.F.R. 300.516(e)).

Section 1983 Remedies

If students receive a verdict in their favor, they also may receive either or both of two remedies:

1. An injunction (court order), enjoining a defendant from repeating the wrongful act
2. Money, called damages

Two kinds of damages are available under Section 1983:

1. *Compensatory damages* restore the student to the position he or she was in before his or her rights were violated. These damages compensate the student for the value of any injury incurred.
2. *Punitive damages* provide the student with retribution against the wrongdoer. They also deter others from committing similar wrongs. Punitive damages, however, will be awarded only if the wrongdoer acted with an evil motive or in reckless or callous disregard for the rights of the student (*Smith v. Wade*, 1983). Accordingly, punitive damages are assessable against a public official and a private citizen or corporation.

Because a state (if it is subject to suit) and a municipality, however, cannot be said to have acted with such motive or disregard (after all, it cannot form the requisite animus and evil intent or act in such a negligent way, not being capable of having the state of mind that is so callous), the state and municipality are free from punitive damages. Moreover, they are free from those damages because the injured party has been compensated and because assessing the "windfall" of punitive damages against them is unfair to the taxpayers (*Newport v. Fact Concerts, Inc.*, 1981).

In summary, students and their families have three other bases for suing and seeking damages—Section 504, ADA, and Section 1983—and they couple these statutes with IDEA to try to get damages. As a result, courts must decide whether those coupled claims allow students and families to recover for what are essentially IDEA violations. If the students and families may recover damages, the cases prohibiting damages under IDEA are meaningless; if they may not, students and families must find other ways, over and above IDEA, to recover damages.

Restrictions on Recovery Under Section 504, ADA, and Section 1983

The student's right to recover damages under these statutes is limited. In one of the earliest cases awarding damages, *Monahan v. State of Nebraska* (1982), the Eighth Circuit Court of Appeals interpreted Section 504 to require either "bad faith or gross misjudgment" in the education of children with disabilities. The court stated that as long as educators have exercised

> professional judgment, in such a way as to not depart grossly from accepted standards among educational professionals, we cannot believe that Congress intended to create liability under Section 504.

Bad Faith or Gross Misjudgments

The standards of bad faith or gross misjudgment adheres to the Supreme Court's standard in *Youngberg v. Romeo* (1982), which held that professional judgment is presumed to be valid unless a professional in fact did not exercise any judgment at all. That standard was followed in *Monahan* and also was applied in *John G. v. Bd. of Educ.* (1995). In *John G.*, the student proved that the district failed to comply with IDEA's nondiscriminatory evaluation provisions because it was intent on holding down the cost of special education by using the evaluation process to screen out students who otherwise would be screened into special education. Under those facts, bad faith existed and damages were allowed.

This bad-faith standard was directly at issue in *Heidemann v. Rother* (1996), a case that involved a teacher who subjected a student to a procedure known as "body wrapping." Under that procedure, the person is wrapped into a blanket, the effect being to physically restrain his or her arms, hands, and legs. The teacher applied this procedure to a 9-year-old, nonverbal student with severe mental retardation, visual impairment, epilepsy, and learning disability.

The teacher defended her behavior by saying that she used the procedure upon the recommendation of a licensed physical therapist and to provide "security and comfort" and "warmth and stability" and to induce a "calming effect" in the student.

The court had no difficulty holding that there was no violation of the student's rights to be free from physical restraint (the constitutional right to "liberty" that was involved in the *Romeo* case) and thus the student could not recover damages under Section 1983.

In this case, the professional—a licensed physical therapist—prescribed the body wrapping. The student's teacher, who did the wrapping, was following the therapist's orders. Neither the physical therapist nor the teacher and employer school district had any reason to believe that the prescribed wrapping was a substantial departure from professional norms, and indeed the wrapping was not such a departure. Thus, the facts presented no indication of bad faith or gross misconduct on the school district's part; the school district attempted to comply with the student's educational program and no intentional violation of the student's rights could be inferred.

The gross-misjudgment standard came into play, albeit under somewhat different terminology, in *Todd v. Elkins Sch. Dist. No. 10* (1998). There, a school district allowed a student to push another, who was confined to a wheelchair, over a rough and uneven playing field. After the student fell from his unbuckled chair and broke his leg, his parents sued the school district, claiming that the school acted with "thoughtless indifference and an intentional disregard" for their son's safety. Although the Eighth Circuit agreed that thoughtless indifference and an intentional disregard for safety could indicate gross misjudgment, it ruled that the school district's decisions were not such a substantial departure from accepted professional judgment to create liability.

Intentional Harm

Jonathan G. v. Caddo Parish School Board (1994) illustrates the intention-to-harm rule. There, the court, while conceding that the Fifth Circuit Court of Appeals (which has jurisdiction in Louisiana) had not adopted the *Monahan* bad-faith/gross-misjudgment standard, acknowledged that the *Monahan* language was "useful in assessing whether the school district engaged in an intentional refusal of services sufficient to allow an award of damages."

In *Jonathan G.* the LEA expelled a student in violation of IDEA, there being a clear causal connection between the student's behavior and disability, and then violated the "process" definition of an appropriate education. Nonetheless, the court refused to award damages, finding that the LEA had not acted intentionally, that the student was not the victim of intentional discrimination, and that the LEA did not have an official policy of discriminating against the student and others like him. The court did not find that the LEA discriminated intentionally, and thus it disallowed damages under Section 504.

Moreover, the court interpreted Section 1983 to require proof that the LEA discriminated against the student as a result of its official policy (citing *Monell v. New York Dep't. of Social Services*, 1978), which the facts failed to show. There seems to be no doubt that intent must be proved before a court will allow a student to recover under Section 504 (*Thompson v. Bd. of Special Sch. Dist. No. 1*, 1996; *Whitehead v. Sch. Bd.*, 1996).

In summary, a minority of courts have allowed a student to combine an IDEA claim with a Section 504 or Section 1983 claim and to recover, but they have imposed three limitations:

1. The student must prove bad faith or gross misjudgment to recover under Section 504 or ADA.
2. The student must prove intentional discrimination to recover under Section 504 or ADA.
3. The student must prove that the LEA adopted an official policy of discrimination to recover under Section 1983.

Parents' Lack of Good Faith

The coupled cases seem to have yet another limitation. Just as an LEA's acting in good faith (though technically violating IDEA) and not acting intentionally are defenses to a student's damage claim, so some courts have allowed an LEA to assert the parents' lack of good faith as a defense. For example, in *Marvin H. v. Austin Indep. Sch. Dist.* (1983), the parents failed to utilize state administrative procedures, as outlined in the statute, and the court declined to award damages against the LEA. The same court in another case took note of the parents' refusal to allow their child to be placed appropriately and refused to award damages (*Jackson v. Franklin County Sch. Bd.*, 1985). Likewise, in *Hudson v. Wilson* (1987) the parents refused to allow their child to be tested to determine whether special education was necessary, and a court reduced the extent of their tuition reimbursement. Under the attorneys' fees provisions of the reauthorized IDEA, it is now possible for a court to award attorneys' fees to the LEA against which a parent has proceeded in bad faith (20 U.S.C. Sec. 1415(i)).

ATTORNEYS' FEES

As we explained in chapter 9, a parent has various procedural due process rights, including the right to an attorney at any due process hearing or trial or appeal before any state or federal court. Although parents usually have the right to represent themselves, IDEA's complexities and the process of going to a hearing and trial often mean that the parents should hire an attorney to represent their and the student's interest.

Recognizing that many parents do not have the financial resources to mount a time-consuming and expensive lawsuit against the state or local education agency and that few resources are available for parents who cannot pay an attorney, Congress amended IDEA in 1986 and overturned the Supreme Court's decision in *Smith v. Robinson* (1984), which had disallowed attorneys' fees under IDEA. In the 1986 amendments, also known as the Handicapped Children's Protection Act (HCPA), and in the 2004 amendments to IDEA, Congress has made it clear that courts may award attorneys' fees for violations of IDEA—but only under certain circumstances.

The Prevailing Party Rule

IDEA provides that a court may award reasonable attorneys' fees to the parents of a student if the parent is the prevailing party in any action or proceeding brought under IDEA (20 U.S.C. Sec. 1415(i)(3)(B)). Fees are to be based on the current rates in the party's community for the kind and quality of services rendered. No bonus or multiplier (e.g., three times the actual fee) is allowable (20 U.S.C. Sec. 1415(i)(3)(C); 34 C.F.R. 300.517).

Amount of Fee

The most important factors in determining the amount of the fee are the attorney's compliance with the duty to give notice to the LEA (20 U.S.C. Sec. 1415(i)), the attorney's time (multiplied by the attorney's billing rate), the customary fee for similar services, the amount of money (or its equivalent) involved in the case, the results the attorney obtained, and the attorney's ability and experience.

Exceptions on Right to Recover Fees

The IDEA provides two exceptions to the parents' rights to recover attorneys' fees:

1. No fees may be awarded after an LEA makes a written offer of settlement if

   a. the offer is timely (according to Rule 68 of the Federal Rules of Civil Procedure or within 10 days before an administrative procedure—due process hearing—begins) (34 C.F.R. 300.517(c)(2)(i)(A));
   b. the offer is not accepted within 10 days after it is made; and
   c. the court or administrative hearing officer finds that the relief finally obtained is not more favorable to the parents than the offer of settlement (20 U.S.C. Sec. 1415(i)(3)(D)(i)) (fees may be awarded, however, if the parents prevail and if they are substantially justified in rejecting the settlement offer) (20 U.S.C. Sec. 1415(i)(3)(E)).

2. Attorneys' fees cannot be recovered for legal services provided at IEP meetings unless those meetings are convened as a result of administrative proceedings, judicial action, or at the discretion of the state for mediation (20 U.S.C. Sec. 1415(i)(3)(D)(ii)). The required pre-hearing resolution session is not considered to be a meeting convened as a result of administrative or judicial proceeding or action (20 U.S.C. Sec. 1415(i)(3)(D)(iii)).

Limitations and Reductions in Amount of Fees

The court also may reduce attorneys' fees in four circumstances—namely when

1. the parents, or parents' attorney, unreasonably protracts final resolution of the controversy;
2. the amount of the fees unreasonably exceeds the prevailing rate in the community for attorneys of reasonably comparable skill, reputation, and experience;

3. the time spent and legal services rendered were excessive in light of the nature of the action or proceeding; or

4. the attorney representing the parents did not provide the LEA with the appropriate information (such as the child's name, address, school, a description of the child's problem, and a proposed resolution to the problem) in the notice of the complaint (20 U.S.C. Secs. 1415(i)(3)(F)(i)–(iv)).

None of these limitations applies if the court finds that the LEA itself unreasonably protracted final resolution of the controversy or if the LEA violated the procedural safeguards, particularly those relating to due process hearings (20 U.S.C. Sec. 1415(i)(3)(G)).

Status of Prevailing Party

The "prevailing party" rule states that parents must succeed on a significant issue in the litigation and that this success must achieve some benefit for the student or them (*Kattan v. District of Columbia*, 1993; *Texas State Teachers' Ass'n. v. Garland Indep. Sch. District*, 1989) or must cause major legislative changes (*Grinsted v. Houston County Sch. Dist.*, 1993; *Holmes v. Sobol*, 1991). The key is whether the parents' action in bringing the litigation caused the school or the state to take some action to satisfy the parents' demand and whether the parents' action altered the status quo (*Borgna v. Binghampton City School District*, 1991; *Harris v. McCarthy*, 1986; *Joiner v. District of Columbia*, 1990).

Even if the parents obtained a slight change in the defendant's behavior or the student's evaluation, program, placement, or provision of FAPE, a court *may* award fees (*Howey v. Tippecanoe School Corp.*, 1990). Some federal courts of appeals, however, have backed away from the "slight change" approach (*Monticello School Dist. No. 25 v. George L.*, 1996; parents win on limited private-school reimbursement but lose on the more significant LRE issue).

Note that parents may recover attorneys' fees even if they do not prevail in an administrative hearing if they later prevail in court (*Moore v. District of Columbia*, 1990). And they may recover fees even when a court enters a consent order (a judgment that the parties and the court agree should be entered) (*Barbara R. v. Tirozzi*, 1987) so long as the consent order or settlement explicitly provides that the prevailing party may recover attorneys' fees from the opposing party.

Attorneys' Fees for the LEA

Before Congress reauthorized IDEA in 2004, there was some question whether a prevailing LEA or SEA could recover attorneys' fees and, if so, under what circumstances. The 2004 amendments put this issue to rest and allow LEAs to recover attorneys' fees in three circumstances. The first two circumstances allow the LEA to recover fees from the parents' attorney, and the third from the parents' attorney or the parents themselves. 20 U.S.C. Sec. 1415(i)(3)(B) provides that a court may award reasonable attorneys' fees to an LEA or SEA

- against the attorney of parents who file a complaint or subsequent cause of action that is frivolous, unreasonable, or without foundation;
- against the attorney of parents who continue to litigate after the litigation clearly becomes frivolous, unreasonable, or without foundation; or
- against the attorney of parents, or against the parents, if the parents' complaint or subsequent cause of action was presented for any improper purpose, such as to harass, cause unnecessary delay, or increase needlessly the cost of litigation.

Unlike the attorneys'-fees provision for parents, the option for LEA or SEA recovery of fees is not intended to increase access to the courts for legitimate claims. The LEA and SEA arguably already have the resources to support sufficient access to administrative and judicial remedies. Rather, these provisions are designed to discourage the filing of unjustified complaints by parents and to punish intentional misconduct (filing of frivolous claims or filing for improper purposes).

By making the attorney liable or jointly liable with the parents for LEA or SEA attorneys' fees in these situations, IDEA recognizes that parents depend largely upon their attorney to determine whether a claim is properly founded in the law. They also recognize that attorneys have a professional responsibility not to bring indefensible claims before the court.

Work of Non-Attorneys and Expert Witnesses

Only attorneys, not "lay advocates," may be paid under IDEA, which speaks only about attorneys' fees and not about any other kind of fees (*Arons v. New Jersey State Bd. of Educ.*, 1988). In addition, the courts are split on whether an attorney who represents his or her own child can collect fees, with *Rappaport v. Vance* (1993) disallowing recovery but *Miller v. West Lafayette Community School Corp.* (1996) allowing recovery. Some courts avoid this conflict by holding that if the law concerning self-representation and attorneys'-fees recovery is unsettled at the time the attorney–parent represents his or her child, awarding of attorneys' fees is permissible (*Kattan v. District of Columbia*, 1993). It is unclear whether the rule established by these cases will survive under the 2004 reauthorization.

The U.S. Supreme Court has ruled that IDEA does not authorize courts to award expert witness fees to a prevailing parent (*Arlington Cent. Sch. Dist. v. Murphy*, 2006).

SUMMARY

In this chapter, we discussed IDEA's new enforcement provisions, paying close attention to those provisions that require the U.S. Department of Education to monitor, provide technical assistance to, and then sanction state and local educational agencies that default under IDEA or are unable to comply with their progress and correction plans. We also discussed remedies under IDEA, Section 504, ADA, and Section 1983 of the Civil Rights Act. We concluded by examining IDEA's new provisions related to attorneys' fees.

The most important means for enforcing IDEA still remains the expensive, protracted, and emotionally fraught procedural due process that we discussed in chapter 8. Congress, however, has attempted to deter parents and LEAs from due process by providing for the mediation and mandatory resolution sessions (chapter 8) and by tightening up parents' ability to recover attorneys' fees and making it clear that an LEA may recover attorneys' fees (chapter 8).

Moreover, Congress has significantly strengthened the federal–state–local monitoring responsibilities, basically tracking the approach it used in NCLB but also creating a greater wall of separation (or, if you will, a stronger wall requiring arms-length dealing) between the federal Department of Education, the SEA, and the LEAs. Finally, there remain the convoluted uses of Section 504, ADA, and Section 1983 to enforce IDEA rights and, even beyond these, the highly tenuous educational malpractice/damages routes.

More and more obviously, Congress is reflecting, in IDEA, a policy that discourages the use of the courts by individuals who believe they are aggrieved by state or local agencies or by private or not-for-profit entities. This policy direction is called *tort reform*. The word "tort" means a legal wrong, such as by deliberate and intentional action or by negligence and careless action. The policy direction is reflected most clearly in debates about whether a physician should be held liable to pay huge damages for medical malpractice or a corporation can be held liable to pay huge damages for activities such as environmental harm. The policy also reflects antipathy to "plaintiffs' attorneys" who recover large contingent fees whenever they win a case. It is not hard to detect that policy in IDEA's attorneys'-fees provisions.

Is it defensible to regard IDEA, as reauthorized in 2004, as a leading edge of a general policy of tort reform and of insulating governments from accountability to the citizens to whom they have duties? Yes. But that "yes" is qualified.

As we point out in chapter 11, IDEA still rests on a theory of accountability. After all—as we have stated several times in this chapter—a right is meaningless unless it also leads to a remedy.

But IDEA rests on concepts other than just accountability. Indeed, 17 other concepts—18 in all—are core to IDEA. It's now time to discuss those core concepts.

Chapter 11

The Core Concepts of Disability Policy

DEFINING AND UNDERSTANDING THE CORE CONCEPTS

No single Case on Point can make the point of this chapter. All of the cases we have discussed, whether as a Case on Point or in the text of the preceding chapters, relate in one way or another to the core concepts of disability.

What do we mean by "core concepts of disability"? The word *concept* means an abstract or generic idea generalized from particular instances (*Merriam-Webster*, 1996). Thus, a concept relating to disability policy is one that derives from statutes and court decisions. The word *core* means central and foundational (*Merriam-Webster*, 1996). So a core concept of disability policy is one that is utterly indispensable to the policy framework. It is an integral part of our understanding about disability policy.

The word *policy* refers to the statutes we have discussed—principally IDEA but also Section 504, the Americans with Disabilities Act, and the Family Educational Rights and Privacy Act—and the court decisions we have analyzed. Thus, the core concepts of disability policy are those essential abstract or generic ideas that derive from the statutes and cases.

Presenting the Core Concepts

As a result of analyzing nearly every federal statute dealing with disability and all of the decisions of the U.S. Supreme Court interpreting those statutes or the federal Constitution and many lower-court decisions doing the same, and after extensive interviews with the nation's leading policy-makers and policy researchers, two of the authors of this book identified 18 core concepts of disability policy (Turnbull, Beegle, & Stowe, 2001). In this chapter we

- identify each concept by name;
- state the most obvious issues related to it so you will understand why the concept is indeed core;
- explain the nature of the claim that students and other individuals with disabilities make so you will have a still firmer grasp on why the concept is core; and
- relate the concept, issues, and claims to IDEA, Section 504, ADA, FERPA, and the cases, as appropriate, to back up our statement that IDEA is a superb example of the core concepts of disability policy.

Identifying the Beneficiaries of the Core Concepts

You soon will learn that some of the core concepts apply more directly to individuals with disabilities than to their families. For example, the core concept called antidiscrimination arguably is more important to individuals or students with disabilities than to their families, whereas the core concept called family-centeredness arguably is equally important to individuals with disabilities and their families.

Does the primary–secondary beneficiary distinction make a significant difference in how we understand the core concepts? We think not. Policy that affects an individual with a disability (including children) also affects his or her family as long as they are involved with each other in the sense of performing any family functions together. These functions relate to affection, self-esteem, economics, daily care, socialization, recreation, and education (Turnbull, Turnbull, Erwin, & Soodak, 2006). As IDEA acknowledges, parents exercise their children's rights to a free appropriate public education until the children become adults. At that point, IDEA transfers most of those right to the student (as we pointed out in chapter 9 in the discussion of IDEA's transition provisions and its devolution-of-rights approach).

Also bear in mind that IDEA itself seeks to benefit more than one group of people. Its beneficiaries are

- students with disabilities,
- their family members,
- the professionals who are charged with educating the students, and
- "the public" (other students and members of the communities where students with disabilities learn and live).

When one of the core concepts benefits families more than students with disabilities or benefits still other individuals and the public as well as students with disabilities and their families, we draw that to your attention. In doing so, we help you understand just how valuable IDEA is as an instrument of social stability and change.

Understanding the Function of the Law and the Core Concepts

The law is itself an instrument of social stability and change. It preserves that which the governed value, and thus promotes stability and predictability in the relationships that people have with each other and with their governments. But the law also changes the circumstances of the governed to meet their needs and desires. The law authorizes new activities; legislators often appropriate funds to support those activities; and the law creates new rights and duties. Two of the law's principal roles, then, are stability and change as needed.

Think of the law as a type of "social engineering"—a technique to engineer (design) society in certain ways. Or think of the law as a type of "behavior modification"—a technique for shaping the behavior of people toward each other and of the government toward the governed. Given this understanding of the law, it behooves you to know just how IDEA reflects core concepts of disability policy, how it implements the social-engineering/behavior-modification function that laws play, and just how worthy IDEA is of being preserved and implemented faithfully and effectively.

THE CORE CONCEPTS

Now you will learn more about each core concept by our

- defining the core concept,
- discussing the issues it raises,
- discussing the claims that students and their families or other IDEA beneficiaries make, and
- connecting the core concepts to each other.

Antidiscrimination

The core issue is discrimination based on disability. The core concept holds that discrimination on the basis of disability alone violates an individual's rights to equal protection under the federal Constitution and to equal treatment and equal opportunity. We begin with the core concept of antidiscrimination because it has been the focus of a substantial amount of disability policy and, indeed, was one of the original foundations on which progressive policy was based. It also is the foundation for IDEA, Section 504, and ADA, as we explained in chapter 3 ("IDEA, Antidiscrimination Laws, and General Education Law") and also chapter 4 ("Zero Reject").

One purpose of antidiscrimination is to require educators to make decisions about a student objectively and on the basis of a fair evaluation of the student's strengths and needs (chapter 5, "Nondiscriminatory Evaluation"). Another purpose is to advance the constitutional doctrine of equal protection by promoting equal opportunity to participate and benefit. For example, the claim of students with disabilities to a free appropriate public education is a claim to be treated as students and thus to have access to education, just as nondisabled students have a right to go to school (chapter 4).

The same logic applies to the students' claims to participate in federally assisted programs or in the public and private sectors, as assured by Section 504 and ADA. In both IDEA and the 504–ADA situation, some accommodations—indeed, even extensive ones—are necessary when students attend schools, especially in the general curriculum. Accordingly, Section 504 and ADA provide that an individual with a disability (a) may not be subjected to discrimination solely on the basis of disability, (b) is entitled to reasonable accommodations (not affirmative action) to qualify and participate, and (c) thereby is protected under the Fourteenth Amendment's equal protection clause.

Having a right against discrimination and to equal opportunity is meaningless unless services are available to implement that right. The next core concepts—individualized and appropriate services, classification, and capacity-based services—implement the antidiscrimination and equal opportunity claim and deal with who gets what, why, and under what kinds of eligibility standards and processes.

Individualized and Appropriate Services

The central issue is how to translate the antidiscrimination claim—the claim to equal opportunity—into reality. The response? Individualized and appropriate services (chapter 5). The claim is to education that is genuine (is a "real" service), effective and efficacious (it actually does for the person what its providers say it will do), and meaningful (that is, valuable to the beneficiary). Those are the guts of appropriate education when the word *appropriate* means "beneficial," as *Rowley* and IDEA require (chapter 6, "Individualized and Appropriate Education," and chapter 7, "Least Restrictive Environment").

For a service to meet those three standards, it must be based on a fair (nondiscriminatory) evaluation of the student (chapter 5). Finally (as we explain later), individualized and appropriate services incorporate the least drastic means of intervention and education, known as education in the least restrictive environment (chapter 7). The principal methods to achieve individualized and appropriate services include classification (chapter 5), capacity-based services (appropriate education through the IEP or IFSP, chapter 6), empowerment and participatory decision making (chapters 5, 6, 7, and 9, "Parent Participation"), and service coordination and collaboration (chapter 6). Let's first turn to classification, which is the heart of the question: Who is entitled to get IDEA benefits?

Classification

The core issue is whether a student qualifies for IDEA benefits, especially the individualized and appropriate services of the IEP and IFSP, based on IDEA's eligibility standards. The student's claim is to a fair distribution of limited resources through qualification or prioritization based upon measurable criteria that are applied nondiscriminatorily. A related claim is to receive services that prevent a disability from occurring or that prevent an existing disability from becoming more impairing. As a good illustration of a prevention policy, Part C of IDEA authorizes federal assistance for state and local services to infants and toddlers who have developmental delays or have physical or mental conditions that carry a high probability of causing developmental delays.

As we pointed out in chapter 5, the term *classification* refers to the processes (ways) and the standards (criteria) by which a person with a disability or the person's family qualifies (becomes eligible) to benefit from certain laws (antidiscrimination or other rights or entitlements). A child qualifies for IDEA benefits when he or she cannot benefit from general education and therefore needs special education.

Capacity-Based Services

Once a student is determined to be eligible for a service, how should it be provided? Although classification often is based on need and priority related to severity, services nevertheless should not be focused narrowly on only the person's needs but also should take into account the person's capacities. The student's and family's claim is to services that regard them holistically by taking into account their limitations and capacities.

As we point out in chapter 6 and especially (but not exclusively) with respect to Part C (early intervention), the term "capacity-based services" refers to evaluation of the unique strengths and needs of the child and the family and to a family-directed evaluation of the resources, priorities, and concerns and family-based identification of the services necessary to carry out Part C's purposes with respect to the child and family. The claim has two parts: to remediate the child's disability and to build on the family's resources and strengths.

To remediate disability and build on strength is a powerful way to reduce the "fix it," or pathology-based, approach that has rendered individuals with disabilities and their families subservient to professionals (as we pointed out in chapter 9, where we discussed the roles that families have played, willingly or not). Indeed, building on strength is one way of overcoming the power relationship that traditionally has favored the professional over the person or family.

Capacity-based services recognize that the goal is to improve the student's or family's quality of life rather than solely to ameliorate the effects of a disability. Services must be person centered and grow from the strengths of the individual or family. That is why IDEA requires a multidisciplinary and comprehensive evaluation of the student's strengths and needs and why, in early intervention, it also requires a family-directed assessment of the family's resources, priorities, and concerns, to identify supports and services necessary to enhance the capacity of the individual and family to meet the needs of the infant or toddler. When families and students participate in making decisions about supports and services, they do so under the auspices of the core concept that we call participatory decision making and empowerment.

Participatory Decision Making/Empowerment

The core issue here is how to assure that an SEA or LEA delivers the services in a way that is individualized, appropriate, and capacity-based while simultaneously respecting the family's and student's autonomy. Their claim is to shared decision-making power between the provider/professional and the beneficiary/recipient. These people should decide jointly, with appropriate deference to each other's expertise, preferences, and roles, whether the student has a disability (chapter 5) and, if so, what services and supports will be effective for educating the student (chapter 6), where they will be delivered (chapter 7), and how they will be accounted for (chapter 8, "Procedural Due Process," and chapter 10, "Compliance, Rights, and Remedies") and decided on (chapter 9). That is why, under IDEA, planning, developing, delivering/ implementing, and evaluating services is a joint activity involving parents and professionals alike.

This kind of participatory decision making brings another core concept into play: empowerment. Empowerment—getting what a person or family wants and doing so in the way the person or family wants—is context-based and is greater or lesser depending on various circumstances, professionals, settings, and policies (Turnbull & Turnbull, 2001). Empowerment is also dynamic and affects a person or family differently at different times and in different circumstances. Most of all, empowerment is both a result of participatory decision making and a principle that supports participatory decision making.

It does not, however, ensure that the supports and services are effective to satisfy a student's or family's needs or desires. For that to happen, other core concepts come into play.

Service Coordination and Collaboration

The core issue is that students with disabilities and their families usually have needs that cut across various domains of their life, yet the services designed for them too often disregard that fact. The challenge is to satisfy their horizontal needs (those that cut across the domains) through traditionally vertical service-delivery sectors such as general education, special education, related services, and health-care services. (We discussed those needs and IDEA's responses in chapters 4, 5, 6, and 7.) Their claim is services that are coordinated, for professionals who collaborate with each other, and for funding streams that are "braided" with each other. Like a braided belt, each stream retains its own identity but is tightly associated with others to create a whole, and therefore more useful, river of money (we discussed IDEA's funding in chapter 10).

The typical techniques include various forms of partnerships between or among service-delivery professionals and different forms of service delivery. These are known variously as school-linked, community-linked, unified, coordinated, intrasector/-agency, intersector/-agency, seamless service delivery, one-stop shopping, and integrated or braided services and funding streams.

Note how IDEA and NCLB align with each other (chapter 3) and that the alignment is one way of coordinating and collaborating between general and special education. Note also how powerfully the student's NDE and IEP/IFSP support the student's education in the least restrictive environment of the general curriculum or "natural" or other settings (chapter 7). Coordination and collaboration assist SEAs and LEAs to deliver effective services across general and special education and also in alliance with professionals in related and health-care services. When educators, related-services personnel, and health-care professionals coordinate and collaborate in serving a student and a family, they protect them from the harm of being excluded from education and other services. Let's look at that concept of protection from harm.

Protection From Harm

One issue is how to ensure that the student and family experience no harm as a result of being involved in general and special education. Their claim is negative in nature. It is a claim to be protected against what SEAs, LEAs, and individual professionals might do. IDEA advances this claim by creating protections related to discipline and a presumption in favor of positive behavioral interventions (chapter 4) and by presuming that the least restrictive placement is better than a more segregated one (chapter 7).

A related but different claim is to have services and supports that ameliorate any harms their current education may create. That is why both NCLB and IDEA require educators to assess a student's progress as they implement the student's IEP (chapter 6). This claim is positive and rests on prevention (itself a core concept) and the argument that government has a duty to benefit the governed by providing for them to be educated appropriately and in the least restrictive setting and with the least drastic interventions. When we use the terms "least restrictive" and "least drastic," we begin to talk about the next core concept, liberty.

Liberty

The issue is that students with disabilities have been unjustifiably denied their liberty (their physical freedom). The core concept is the right to liberty, to be free from unwarranted state confinement and intrusion. Of course, this core concept relates to another one—integration (the right to be included in the world that people without a disability take for granted). Because the interest in liberty is distinct from the interest in integration, it deserves its own separate place as a core concept.

Liberty here has a negative connotation, consisting of a right against unjustified state action. It is a right to a protective wall. IDEA reflects this liberty claim in two ways:

1. Its discipline provisions (chapter 4) balance a student's interest in education against the interests of other students and professionals to learn and teach in a safe environment (also an NCLB principle).
2. Whenever the state is justified in acting, it must do so consistent with the doctrine of the least restrictive alternative (chapter 7). That doctrine, which

IDEA calls "least restrictive environment," balances the student's rights to an education in certain environments against the rights of other students not to be harmed by being educated with a student with a disability.

As we pointed out in chapter 7, the LRE doctrine in IDEA reflects the legal precept that whenever the state has a legitimate reason to act (to deprive a person of his or her liberty), it must act in the way that is least restrictive of the person's freedom. Do liberty and freedom relate only to physical freedom? What about the issues of privacy and confidentiality that we discussed when describing FERPA in chapter 8? We are about to acquire another understanding about liberty and freedom, which has to do with autonomy.

Autonomy

The issue of autonomy is whether the student with a disability and his or her family legally may exercise control over the state's and professionals' actions. Their claim is to make decisions about their lives and to be able to require educators to honor those decisions. The claim is to personal autonomy and is achieved through the legal right to give, refuse, or withdraw consent.

Autonomy supports the right of a student or family to say "yes" or "no" and then to withdraw that yes (consent) or no (refusal to consent) in making decisions with educators. As we noted in chapters 6, 7, 8, and 9, IDEA expresses the concept of autonomy under the term *consent.* You may know that term by words such as choice, control, self-determination, self-direction, self-responsibility, or person-directed services (also called "consumer-directed," "participant-directed," or "client-directed" services).

You probably link autonomy to "empowerment and participatory decision making." After all, both value the opportunity for individuals to have power to affect what happens to them. But these two core concepts are not identical.

Autonomy refers to the state of being self-governed and to act in chosen ways. Empowerment and participatory decision making refer to the ways by which a person or family acts after deciding to act. The consent—the autonomous action—precedes the person's participation with professionals in educational decision-making processes, and it terminates that participation, too. A person may consent/chose to participate or not and may withdraw from participating. That consent/choice is the autonomous action, and the participation is its manifestation.

If a person or family is incompetent to exercise the legal rights of consent, a duly appointed surrogate may do so. Closely related to autonomy and empowerment–participatory decision making is the core concept of privacy and confidentiality.

Privacy and Confidentiality

The issue is whether, and, if so, to what extent, do students with disabilities and their families control the arguably public aspects of their lives. There are two claims: privacy and confidentiality (chapter 8).

The first claim is to privacy, to a zone into which the state, professionals, and private entities may not enter without consent of the student or parents. The student and family have a right to make certain decisions without state or professional oversight and without the possibility of state or professional veto. Typically, these decisions are of a purely or predominately private nature and include, for example, whether to avail themselves of certain interventions or services. That is why IDEA requires separate consent for special education services.

The second claim is to the confidentiality of information and records. What families and students will find as they deal with schools is that, for each of them, "I am my record." That is why families and students seek to control what educators do with information that the students and families have disclosed (voluntarily or compulsorily), such as in a nondiscriminatory evaluation (chapter 5) or an IFSP or IEP (chapter 6). The essence of their claim is to be able to have access and to correct, expunge, and consent to, or prevent, the publication (dissemination) of information that relates to those protected zones of privacy (chapter 8).

Privacy and confidentiality enhance autonomy by putting substance behind this core concept, acknowledging that "I am my record" is a true statement, and making sure that information and the records containing it lead to individualized and appropriate services (and accompanying cooperation and collaboration). In addition, these claims have a therapeutic basis. If students and their families fear that their privacy and confidentiality will be breached and, therefore, choose not to disclose information that is relevant to their claims to effective services, they undermine their claim to individualized and appropriate service delivery in the least restrictive environment—that is, in the general curriculum and in integrated settings.

Integration

The issue is whether individuals with disabilities have a right to be in the community and to participate in its typical activities, such as attending schools, even neighborhood schools (chapter 7). They claim integration (not segregation), inclusion (not exclusion), and participation (not limitation). They want to be with, in, of, and among people (other students) who do not have disabilities. Their claim also is to liberty—the interest in being free from unwarranted physical confinement—because liberty advances integration. One cannot be integrated unless one experiences liberty.

The claim to integration and against segregation derives directly from the core concept of antidiscrimination (chapter 4). Similarly, integration implicates the legal doctrine of the least restrictive environment (chapter 7).

The claim to integration (to community membership and to participation, fully or partially, in the three domains of the general curriculum) consists of two elements:

1. The negative claim to be free from unjustified deprivation of liberty and unwarranted segregation (as, for example, by unwarranted placement in restrictive educational environments, measured along IDEA's continuum of services)

2. The positive claim to be part of a community's typical activities, to participate in the general curriculum; this is an affirmative claim—to be a member of, and to participate in, the generic, typical, normal activities of education

Inclusion—the term that educators use to describe IDEA's LRE principle and access to the general curriculum—is how educators implement the core concept of integration. The core concept is integration; the implementing technique is inclusion.

Inclusion requires educators to teach a student with a disability in the general curriculum by being sure that they align IDEA with NCLB and provide individualized education with related services and supplementary aids and services in the general curriculum. It is not just that the student's physical environment is to be inclusive and least restrictive. It is also that the educators' methods of inclusion are to be the least drastic to meet the person's needs and most typical of the setting.

Thus, "least restrictive" and "least drastic" are expressions of the concepts of liberty, autonomy, and integration. Although these and other core concepts are valued in their own rights as intrinsically worthwhile, they also are instrumental to various outcomes. What are the outcomes for which they are the means?

Productivity and Contribution

The issue is whether students with disabilities and their families will have the opportunity to lead lives that produce and contribute value to themselves and to their communities. Their claim is to have the opportunities, with accommodations, to be productive and contributory.

There is a distinction between productivity and contribution. Productivity usually refers to income-producing work or other unpaid work that contributes to a household or community. IDEA and ADA refer to productivity when they declare that the nation's disability policy goals include economic self-sufficiency, and IDEA advances it through the IEP provisions related to transition (chapter 6).

Productivity, in this sense, reflects the fact that our culture values a work ethic. Yet, as ADA and Section 504 acknowledge (and as we noted in chapters 3 and 4), discrimination prevents people with disabilities from having a job, earning part or all of their living, and being economically self-reliant and independent (in whole or in part). So their claim is to a free appropriate public education in the least restrictive environment that allows them to have meaningful, productive lives. Productive people contribute to the nation's economic health even while they simultaneously avoid the stigma of being a dependent, and stigma is precisely the condition that creates the discrimination that Section 504 and ADA prohibit.

By contrast, contribution acknowledges the psychological value of contributing to the well-being of oneself, one's family and friends, or one's community. Contribution recognizes that students with disabilities contribute to the moral, ethical, spiritual, and social fabric of their schools. Contribution reflects the social dynamics that occur when students go to school together. That's why the "associational value" of the LRE principle (chapter 7) is one of LRE's essential components. When students with and without disabilities are educated together, they contribute to each other, educationally and otherwise.

Both productivity and contribution depend on access to services and thus relate to the core concept of antidiscrimination (chapter 4). Also, individualized and appropriate services (chapter 6) promote productivity and contribution.

Earlier we said that IDEA benefits families and that its core concepts are not only intrinsically valuable but also means to various outcomes. Let's consider just how some of the core concepts value families and outcomes related to families.

Family Integrity and Unity

The issue is whether policy and practice advance or impede the integrity and unity of the family of the student with a disability. The family's and student's claim is to have state support—through education—that makes it possible for the family to raise a child with a disability and for the child to have the benefits of being raised in, and living with, a family for as long as the family and child chose to or can remain as a single unit. IDEA's Part C explicitly advances the core concept of family integrity and unity by declaring the goal of enhancing families' capacities to meet their children's special needs.

The core concept called family integrity and unity refers to preserving and strengthening the family as the core unit of society. It is reflected in services that maintain the family intact, respond to all family members, and take into account the family's cultural, ethnic, linguistic, or other socioeconomic traits and choices. Both Part C through the IFSP and Part B through the IEP and related services respond to the traits and choices of families—all members of the family under Part C.

Family-Centeredness: Services to the Whole Family

The issue is whether policy and practice encourage services to be provided to the entire family. The student's and family's claim is to services that respond to the needs of the child and thereby the entire family, fairly (chapter 5), appropriately (chapter 6), and inclusively (chapter 7). Obviously, the core concept of family-centered services relates to two other core concepts: cultural responsiveness and individualized appropriate services. Yet, it stands on its own because it emphasizes that services to the entire family advance the family's interests even as they also advance the student's interests.

Cultural Responsiveness

The issue is that some families, especially those from cultural, linguistic, and ethnically diverse backgrounds, those from various socioeconomic groups, and those who exemplify other cultural traits (e.g., same-sex partnerships or disability culture), may have different values than their children's educators. Their claim is to services or supports that are provided in a manner that responds to their needs in culturally sensitive ways and thereby increase the likelihood of benefit to the family, child, or both.

Through the Part C and the IFSP, and less so by Part B's IEP (chapter 6), IDEA requires educators to respond to families' cultural, linguistic, and ethnic characteristics. More importantly, and as we pointed out when we discussed the core concept that we call autonomy, IDEA permits families to consent or not, and to protest, to evaluations, services, and other educational decisions (chapters 5, 8, and 9).

Having rights that rest on core concepts means having remedies when a government violates those rights. There are no meaningful rights without effective remedies. So let's now consider rights, remedies, and the core concept of accountability.

Accountability

The issue is whether the policies and services indeed achieve the outcomes they seek. The students' and families' claim is to those techniques that hold policy-makers and policy implementers accountable to those who are affected by their actions.

As we made clear when discussing discipline (chapter 4), evaluations (chapter 5), procedural due process (chapter 8), parent participation (chapter 9), and enforcement (chapter 10), accountability includes a variety of techniques, including

- procedural safeguards (legal accountability via procedural due process), direct or proxy representation by attorneys or others at the individual and system level, and recovery of actual or punitive damages and attorney fees;
- fiscal incentives and disincentives built into services;
- highly qualified educators using evidence-based techniques of education and measuring their results by various assessment and standards techniques;
- independent evaluations;
- administrative and budgetary oversight processes;
- financial management and reporting;
- independent SEA advisory councils;
- management techniques (e.g., service linkages, service coordination, "care/case" management); and
- capacity-building and program-improvement activities (e.g., personnel development, research, technical assistance, model development, information and training, and similar activities, all as provided by IDEA Part D).

The core concept of participatory decision making also advances accountability at the system and individual levels. Accountability, then, involves the student, the family, policy-makers, professionals, and various governments. By holding educators accountable, IDEA makes it likely that the student's disabilities will have less effect on the student, family, and society. It really prevents disability from playing a role. Let's see why IDEA provides an example of prevention policy.

Prevention

Given that some disabilities or the effects of some disabilities can be prevented or reduced, the issue is how to benefit society as a whole (social utilitarianism) and individuals (individual utilitarianism) by preventing or reducing the effects of disabilities. The students' and families' claim, as well as that of the public generally, is to policies and practices that seek primary, secondary, and tertiary prevention of disability (see the discussion of individualized and appropriate services in chapter 6).

1. Primary prevention refers to an intervention that prevents a disability from ever occurring; a good example is fetal surgery.
2. Secondary prevention refers to an intervention that nips a disability in the bud and prevents it from persisting; PKU screening/treatment is a good example.
3. Tertiary prevention refers to an intervention that mitigates the effects of an existing disability; special education and rehabilitation services are good examples.

   IDEA supports the core concept of prevention through Part C (early intervention) and its authority for educators to serve students who are at risk (chapter 4). Also, IDEA stimulates prevention by providing appropriate services (chapter 6) and promoting inclusive and integrated programs (chapter 7). As more students with disabilities attend schools with peers who do not have disabilities, communities and their leaders may become more aware of the importance of prevention. In advancing prevention, IDEA obviously builds the capacity of families to care for their children with disabilities and the capacities of the students themselves to attain the nation's disability policy goals.

Family, Student, and System Capacity Building

By now, you should clearly see that IDEA seeks to build the capacities of the families and their children to attain the four national policy goals of equal opportunity, full participation, independent living, and economic self-sufficiency (chapter 2; 20 U.S.C. Sec. 1400(c)(1)).

- By involving families in evaluations, individualized program development, placement decisions, dispute resolution, and other means (chapters 4 through 9), IDEA gives them rights and responsibilities (as we argued in chapter 9) and also the opportunity to be trustworthy and trusting partners with educators.
- By granting students various rights (included in the six principles, chapters 4 through 9) and setting the conditions under which general and special educators provide a free appropriate public education in the least restrictive environment, IDEA puts a tremendous amount of resources into their education and also guides how they should learn and behave in school.

By creating rights and allocating resources (money and professionals), IDEA carries out the principle of dual accommodations. (You may remember that principle from chapter 3.)

This principle requires educators to accommodate to the disability-related aspects of all students and to their families' disability-related needs. It also requires the students and families to be responsible by conducting themselves in ways that make it possible for educators to carry out those duties (chapter 4, regarding discipline; chapters 5, 6, and 7, regarding NDE, appropriate education, and LRE; and chapters 8 and 9, regarding procedural due process and parent participation).

In short, IDEA develops the capacities of educators and the schools and the capacities of the students and their families. And as it does so, it declares that there can be no rights without responsibilities. The right to services entails the responsibility to maximize the services' benefits.

SUMMARY AND ADMONITION

A core concept is the specific idea, derived from particular instances, that is indispensable to public policy. In a variety of independent or overlapping provisions and through each of its six principles, IDEA advances each of the 18 core concepts of disability policy.

As you now come to the end of this book, you should have learned about IDEA and some other laws and about the core concepts that IDEA advances. More than that, you should have recognized how values—call them core concepts, if you will—permeate special education and IDEA. If there ever were a value-driven law, one so fundamentally aligned with what Americans cherish—education, fairly and effectively delivered and organized and administered by and for professionals and families on behalf of children with disabilities—it must be IDEA.

Whatever role you may play in general or special education, we ask you simply to hold true to IDEA's core concepts, to affirm its values, and to comply rigorously with its provisions. If you discharge those duties, you will render an immeasurable service to students with disabilities, their families and educators, and the future of our country. To do this much is to do great work and be a great person, without regard to any other measure of greatness. To do less is to be less than a great person. It's your choice. We hope we have guided you to making the right choice.

Appendix A

Brown v.
Board of Education

(excerpts from the Supreme Court's unanimous opinion, with only Footnote 11 included)

OLIVER BROWN, et al., Appellants,

v.

BOARD OF EDUCATION OF TOPEKA, Shawnee County,
Kansas, et al. (No. 1.)

Mr. Chief Justice Warren delivered the opinion of the Court.

These cases come to us from the States of Kansas, South Carolina, Virginia, and Delaware. They are premised on different facts and different local conditions, but a common legal question justifies their consideration together in this consolidated opinion.[1]

In each of the cases, minors of the Negro race, through their legal representatives, seek the aid of the courts in obtaining admission to the public schools of their community on a nonsegregated basis. In each instance, they had been denied admission to schools attended by white children under laws requiring or permitting segregation according to race. This segregation was alleged to deprive the plaintiffs of the equal protection of the laws under the Fourteenth Amendment....

The plaintiffs contend that segregated public schools are not "equal" and cannot be made "equal," and that hence they are deprived of the equal protection of the laws....

The most avid proponents of the post-War Amendments undoubtedly intended them to remove all legal distinction among "all persons born or naturalized in the United States." Their opponents, just as certainly, were antagonistic to both the letter and the spirit of the Amendments and wished them to have the most limited effect. What others in Congress and the state legislatures had in mind cannot be determined with any degree of certainty.

An additional reason for the inconclusive nature of the Amendment's history, with respect to segregated schools, is the status of public education at that time.[4] In the South, the movement toward free common schools, supported by general taxation, had not yet taken hold. Education of white children was largely in the hands of private groups. Education of Negroes was almost nonexistent, and practically all of the race were illiterate. In fact, any education of Negroes was forbidden by law in some states. Today, in contrast, many Negroes have achieved outstanding success in the arts and sciences as well as in the business and professional world. It is true that public school education at the time of the Amendment had advanced further in the North, but the effect of the Amendment on Northern States was generally ignored in the congressional debates. Even in the North, the conditions of public education did not approximate those existing today. The curriculum was usually rudimentary; ungraded schools were common in rural areas; the school term was but three months a year in many states; and compulsory school attendance was virtually unknown. As a consequence, it is not surprising that there should be so little in the history of the Fourteenth Amendment relating to its intended effect on public education.

In the first cases in this Court construing the Fourteenth Amendment, decided shortly after its adoption, the Court interpreted it as proscribing all state-imposed discriminations against the Negro race.[5] The doctrine of "separate but equal" did not make its appearance in this Court until 1896 in the case of Plessy v. Ferguson,... involving not education but transportation.[6]... In more recent cases, all on the graduate school level, inequality was found in that specific benefits enjoyed by white students were denied to Negro students of the same educational qualifications.... In none of these cases was it necessary to reexamine the doctrine to grant relief to the Negro plaintiff. And in Sweatt v. Painter..., the Court expressly reserved decision on the question whether Plessy V. Ferguson should be held inapplicable to public education.

In the instant cases, that question is directly present. Here, unlike Sweatt v. Painter, there are findings below that the Negro and white schools involved have been equalized, or are being equalized, with respect to buildings, curricula, qualifications and salaries of teachers, and other "tangible" factors.[9] Our decision, therefore, cannot turn on merely a comparison of these tangible factors in the Negro and white schools involved in each of the cases. We must look instead to the effect of segregation itself on public education.

In approaching this problem, we cannot turn the clock back to 1868 when the Amendment was adopted, or even to 1896 when Plessy v. Ferguson was written. We must consider public education in the light of its full development and its present place in American life throughout the Nation. Only in this way can it be determined if segregation in public schools deprives these plaintiffs of the equal protection of the laws.

Today, education is perhaps the most important function of state and local governments. Compulsory school attendance laws and the great expenditures for education both demonstrate our recognition of the importance of education to our democratic society. It is required in the performance of our most basic public responsibilities, even service in the armed forces. It is the very foundation of good citizenship. Today it is a principal instrument in awakening the child to cultural values, in preparing him for later professional training, and in helping him to adjust normally to his environment. In these days, it is doubtful that any child may reasonably be expected to succeed in life if he is denied the opportunity of an education. Such an opportunity, where the state has undertaken to provide it, is a right which must be made available to all in equal terms.

We come then to the question presented: Does segregation of children in public schools solely on the basis of race, even though the physical facilities and other "tangible" factors may be equal, deprive the children of the minority group of equal education opportunities? We believe that it does.

In Sweatt v. Painter..., in finding that a segregated law school for Negroes could not provide them equal educational opportunities, this Court relied in large part on "those qualities which are incapable of objective measurement but which make for greatness in a law school." In McLaurin v. Oklahoma State Regents,....the Court, in requiring that a Negro admitted to a white graduate school be treated like all other students, again resorted to intangible considerations: "...his ability to study, to engage in discussions and exchange views with other students, and, in general, to learn his profession." Such considerations apply with added force to children in grade and high schools. To separate them from others of similar age and qualifications solely because of their race generates a feeling of inferiority as to their status in the community that may affect their hearts and minds in a way unlikely ever to be undone. The effect of this separation on their educational opportunities was well stated by a finding in the Kansas case by a court which nevertheless felt compelled to rule against the Negro plaintiffs:

"Segregation of white and colored children in public schools has a detrimental effect upon the colored children. The impact is greater when it has the sanction of the law; for the policy of separating the races is usually interpreted as denoting the inferiority of the Negro group. A sense of inferiority affects the motivation of a child to learn. Segregation with the sanction of the law, therefore, has a tendency to [retard] the educational and mental development of Negro children and to deprive them of some of the benefits they would receive in a racial[ly] integrated school system."[10]

Whatever may have been the extent of psychological knowledge at the time of Plessy v. Ferguson, this finding is amply supported by modern authority.[11] Any language in Plessy v. Ferguson contrary to this finding is rejected.

We conclude that in the field of public education the doctrine of "separate but equal" has no place. Separate educational facilities are inherently unequal. Therefore, we hold that the plaintiffs and others similarly situated for whom the actions have been brought are, by reason of the segregation complained of, deprived of the equal protection of the laws guaranteed by the Fourteenth Amendment. This disposition makes unnecessary any discussion whether such segregation also violates the Due Process Clause of the Fourteenth Amendment.[12]...

NOTES

11. K.B. Clark, Effect of Prejudice and Discrimination on Personality Development (Midcentury White House Conference on Children and Youth, 1950); Witmer and Kotinsky, Personality in the Making (1952), ch VI; Deutscher and Chein, The Psychological Effects of Enforced Segregation: A Survey of Social Science Opinion, 26 J Psychol 259 (1948); Chein, What are the Psychological Effects of Segregation Under Conditions of Equal Facilities?, 3 Int J Opinion and Attitude Res 229 (1949); Brameld, Educational Costs, in Discrimination and National Welfare (MacIver, ed., 1949), 44–48; Frazier, The Negro in the United States (1949), 674–681. And see generally, Myrdal, An American Dilemma (1944).

Appendix B

Southeastern Community College v. Davis

SOUTHEASTERN COMMUNITY COLLEGE

v.

FRANCIS B. DAVIS.

Mr. Justice Powell delivered the opinion of the Court.

This case presents a matter of first impression for this Court: Whether § 504 of the Rehabilitation Act of 1973, which prohibits discrimination against an "otherwise qualified handicapped individual" in federally funded programs "solely by reason of his handicap," forbids professional schools from imposing physical qualifications for admission to their clinical training programs.

I

Respondent, who suffers from a serious hearing disability, seeks to be trained as a registered nurse. During the 1973–1974 academic year she was enrolled in the College Parallel program of Southeastern Community College, a state institution that receives federal funds. Respondent hoped to progress to Southeastern's Associate Degree Nursing program, completion of which would make her eligible for state certification as a registered nurse. In the course of her application to the nursing program, she was interviewed by a member of the nursing faculty. It became apparent that respondent had difficulty understanding questions asked, and on inquiry she acknowledged a history of hearing problems and dependence on a hearing aid. She was advised to consult an audiologist.

On the basis of an examination at Duke University Medical Center, respondent was diagnosed as having a "bilateral, sensori-neural loss." App. 127a. A change in her hearing aid was recommended, as a result of which it was expected that she would be able to detect sounds "almost as well as a person would who has normal hearing." App. 127a 128a. But this improvement would not mean that she could discriminate among sounds sufficiently to understand normal spoken speech. Her lipreading skills would remain necessary for effective communication: "While wearing the hearing aid, she is well aware of gross sounds occurring in the listening environment. However, she can only be responsible for speech spoken to her, when the talker gets her attention and allows her to look directly at the talker." App. 128a.

Southeastern next consulted Mary McRee, Executive Director of the North Carolina Board of Nursing. On the basis of the audiologist's report, McRee recommended that respondent not be admitted to the nursing program. In McRee's view, respondent's hearing disability made it unsafe for her to practice as a nurse.[1] In addition, it would be impossible for respondent to participate safely in the normal clinical training program, and those modifications that would be necessary to enable safe participation would prevent her from realizing the benefits of the program: "To adjust patient learning experiences in keeping with [respondent's] hearing limitations could, in fact, be the same as denying her full learning to meet the objectives of your nursing programs." App. 132a–133a.

After respondent was notified that she was not qualified for nursing study because of her hearing disability, she requested reconsideration of the decision. The entire nursing staff of Southeastern was assembled, and McRee again was consulted. McRee repeated her conclusion that on the basis of the available evidence, respondent "has hearing limitations which could interfere with her safely caring for patients." App. 139a. Upon further deliberation, the staff voted to deny respondent admission.

Respondent then filed suit in the United States District Court for the Eastern District of North Carolina, alleging both a violation of § 504 of the Rehabilitation Act of 1973, 87 Stat. 394, as amended. 29 U.S.C. § 794[2] and a denial of equal protection and due process. After a bench trial, the District Court entered judgment in favor of Southeastern. 424 F Supp. 1341 (1976). It confirmed the findings of the audiologist that even with a hearing aid respondent cannot understand speech directed to her except through lipreading, and further found that,

> "[1] in many situations such as an operation room, intensive care unit, or post-natal care unit, all doctors and nurses wear surgical masks which would make lip-reading impossible. Additionally, in many situations a Registered Nurse would be required to instantly follow the physician's instructions concerning procurement of various types of instruments and drugs where the physician would be unable to get the nurse's attention by other than vocal means." *Id.*, at 1342.

Accordingly, the Court concluded that:

> '[Respondent's] handicap actually prevents her from safely per-
> forming in both her training program and her proposed profes-
> sion. The trial testimony indicated numerous situations where
> [respondent's] particular disability would render her unable to
> function properly. Of particular concern to the court in this case
> is the potential danger to future patients in such situations." *Id.,*
> at 1345.

Based on these findings, the District Court concluded that respondent was not
an "otherwise qualified handicapped individual" protected against discrimination by
§ 504. In its view, "[o]therwise qualified, can only be read to mean otherwise able to
function sufficiently in the position sought in spite of the handicap, if proper training and facilities are suitable and available." *Ibid.* Because respondent's disability
would prevent her from functioning "sufficiently" in Southeastern's nursing program, the Court held that the decision to exclude her was not discriminatory within
the meaning of § 504.[3]

On appeal, the Court of appeals for the Fourth Circuit reversed. 574 F 2d 1158
(1978). It did not dispute the District Court's findings of fact, but held that the Court
had misconstrued § 504. In light of administrative regulations that had been promulgated while the appeal was pending, see 42 Fed. Reg. 22676 (May 4, 1977),[4] the
appellate court believed that § 504 required Southeastern to "reconsider plaintiffs
application for admission to the nursing program without regard to her hearing ability." *Id.,* at 1160. It concluded that the District Court had erred in taking respondent's
handicap into account in determining whether she was "otherwise qualified" for the
program, rather than confining its inquiry to her "academic and technical qualifications." *Id.,* at 1161. The Court of appeals also suggested that § 504 required "affirmative conduct" on the part of Southeastern to modify its program to accommodate
the disabilities of applicants, "even when such modifications become expensive." *Id.,*
at 1162.

Because of the importance of this issue to the many institutions covered by §
504, we granted certiorari. 439 U.S._____ (1979). We now reverse.[5]

II

This is the first case in which this Court has been called upon to interpret § 504. It
is elementary that "[t]he starting point in every case involving the construction of a
statute is the language itself." *Blue Chip Stamps v. Manor Drug Stores,* 421 U.S. 723,
756 (1975) (Powell, J., concurring); see *Greyhound Corp. v. Mt. Hood Stages, Inc.,*
437 U.S. 322, 330 (1978); *Santa Fe Industries, Inc. v. Green,* 430 U.S. 462, 472
(1977). Section 504 by its terms does not compel educational institutions to disregard the disabilities of handicapped individuals or to make substantial modifications

in their programs to allow disabled persons to participate. Instead, it requires only that an "otherwise qualified handicapped individual" not be excluded from participation in a federally funded program "solely by reason of his handicap," indicating only that mere possession of a handicap is not a permissible ground for assuming an inability to function in a particular context.[6]

The court below, however, believed that the "otherwise qualified" persons protected by § 504 include those who would be able to meet the requirements of a particular program in every respect except as to limitations imposed by their handicap. See 574 F 2d. at 1160. Taken literally, this holding would prevent an institution from taking into account any limitation resulting from the handicap, however disabling. It assumes, in effect, that a person need not meet legitimate physical requirements in order to be "otherwise qualified." We think the understanding of the District Court is closer to the plain meaning of the statutory language. An otherwise qualified person is one who is able to meet all of a program's requirements in spite of his handicap.

The regulations promulgated by the Department of Health, Education, and Welfare (HEW) to interpret § 504 reinforce, rather than contradict, this conclusion. According to these regulations, a "[q]ualified handicapped person" is, "[w]ith respect to postsecondary and vocational education services, a handicapped person who meets the academic and technical standards requisite to admission or participation in the [school's] education program or activity...." 45 CFR § 84.3 (k)(3) (1978). An explanatory note states:

> "The term 'technical standards' refers to all nonacademic admissions criteria that are essential to participation in the program in question." 45 CFR pt. 84, App. A, at p. 405 (emphasis supplied).

A further note emphasizes that legitimate physical qualifications may be essential to participation in particular programs.[7] We think it clear, therefore, that HEW interprets the "other" qualifications which a handicapped person may be required to meet as including necessary physical qualifications.

III

The remaining question is whether the physical qualifications Southeastern demanded of respondent might not be necessary for participation in its nursing program. It is not open to dispute that, as Southeastern's Associate Degree Nursing program currently is constituted, the ability to understand speech without reliance on lipreading is necessary for patient safety during the clinical phase of the program. As the District Court found, this ability also is indispensable for many of the functions that a registered nurse performs.

Respondent contends nevertheless that § 504, properly interpreted, compels Southeastern to undertake affirmative action that would dispense with the need for effective oral communication. First, it is suggested that respondent can be given individual supervision by faculty members whenever she attends patients directly. Moreover, certain required courses might be dispensed with altogether for respondent. It is not necessary, she argues, that Southeastern train her to undertake all the tasks a registered nurse is licensed to perform. Rather, it is sufficient to make § 504 applicable if respondent might be able to perform satisfactorily some of the duties of a registered nurse or to hold some of the positions available to a registered nurse.[8]

Respondent finds support for this argument in portions of the HEW regulations discussed above. In particular, a provision applicable to postsecondary educational programs requires covered institutions to make "modifications" in their programs to accommodate handicapped persons, and to provide "auxiliary aids" such as sign-language interpreters.[9] Respondent argues that this regulation imposes an obligation to ensure full participation in covered programs by handicapped individuals and, in particular, requires Southeastern to make the kind of adjustments that would be necessary to permit her safe participation in the nursing program.

We note first that on the present record it appears unlikely respondent could benefit from any affirmative action that the regulation reasonably could be interpreted as requiring. Section 84.44 (d)(2), for example, explicitly excludes "devices or services of a personal nature" from the kinds of auxiliary aids a school must provide a handicapped individual. Yet the only evidence in the record indicates that nothing less than close, individual attention by a nursing instructor would be sufficient to ensure patient safety if respondent took part in the clinical phase of the nursing program. See 424 F Supp., at 1346. Furthermore, it also is reasonably clear that § 84.44 (a) does not encompass the kind of curricular changes that would be necessary to accommodate respondent in the nursing program. In light of respondent's inability to function in clinical courses without close supervision, Southeastern with prudence could allow her to take only academic classes. Whatever benefits respondent might realize from such a course of study, she would not receive even a rough equivalent of the training a nursing program normally gives. Such a fundamental alteration in the nature of a program is far more than the "modification" the regulation requires.

Moreover, an interpretation of the regulations that required the extensive modifications necessary to include respondent in the nursing program would raise grave doubts about their validity. If these regulations were to require substantial adjustments in existing programs beyond those necessary to eliminate discrimination against otherwise qualified individuals, they would do more than clarify the meaning of § 504. Instead, they would constitute an unauthorized extension of the obligations imposed by that statute.

The language and structure of the Rehabilitation Act of 1973 reflect a recognition by Congress of the distinction between the evenhanded treatment of qualified handicapped persons and affirmative efforts to overcome the disabilities caused by handicaps. Section 501 (b), governing the employment of handicapped individuals by the Federal Government, requires each federal agency to submit "an affirmative action program plan for the hiring, placement, and advancement of handicapped individuals...." These plans "shall include a description of the extent to which and methods whereby the special needs of handicapped employees are being met." Similarly, § 503 (a), governing hiring by federal contractors, requires employers to "take affirmative action to employ and advance in employment qualified handicapped individuals...." The President is required to promulgate regulations to enforce this section.

Under § 501 (c) of the Act, by contrast, state agencies such as Southeastern are only "encourage[d]...to adopt such policies and procedures." Section 504 does not refer at all to affirmative action, and except as it applies to federal employers it does not provide for implementation by administrative action. A comparison of these provisions demonstrates that Congress understood accommodation of the needs of handicapped individuals may require affirmative action and knew how to provide for it in those instances where it wished to do so.[10]

Although an agency's interpretation of the statute under which it operates is entitled to some deference, "this deference is constrained by our obligation to honor the clear meaning of a statute, as revealed by its language, purpose and history." *International Brotherhood of Teamsters v. Daniel,* 439 U.S. ____, ____ n. 20 (1979). Here neither the language, purpose, nor history of § 504 reveals an intent to impose an affirmative action obligation on all recipients of federal funds." Accordingly, we hold that even if HEW has attempted to create such an obligation itself, it lacks the authority to do so.

IV

We do not suggest that the line between a lawful refusal to extend affirmative action and illegal discrimination against handicapped persons always will be clear. It is possible to envision situations where an insistence on continuing past requirements and practices might arbitrarily deprive genuinely qualified handicapped persons of the opportunity to participate in a covered program. Technological advances can be expected to enhance opportunities to rehabilitate the handicapped or otherwise to qualify them for some useful employment. Such advances also may enable attainment of these goals without imposing undue financial and administrative burdens upon a State. Thus situations may arise where a refusal to modify an existing program might become unreasonable and discriminatory. Identification of those instances where a refusal to accommodate the needs of a disabled person amounts to discrimination against the handicapped continues to be an important responsibility of HEW.

In this case, however, it is clear that Southeastern's unwillingness to make major adjustments in its nursing program does not constitute such discrimination. The uncontroverted testimony of several members of Southeastern's staff and faculty established that the purpose of its program was to train persons who could serve the nursing profession in all customary ways. See, *e.g.,* App. 35a, 52a, 53a, 7 la, 74a. This type of purpose, far from reflecting any animus against handicapped individuals, is shared by many if not most of the institutions that train persons to render professional service. It is undisputed that respondent could not participate in Southeastern's nursing program unless the standards were substantially lowered. Section 504 imposes no requirement upon an educational institution to lower or to effect substantial modifications of standards to accommodate a handicapped person.[12]

One may admire respondent's desire and determination to overcome her handicap and there well may be various other types of service for which she can qualify. In this case, however, we hold that there was no violation of § 504 when Southeastern concluded that respondent did not qualify for admission to its program. Nothing in the language or history of § 504 reflects an intention to limit the freedom of an educational institution to require reasonable physical qualifications for admission to a clinical training program. Nor has there been any showing in this case that any action short of a substantial change in Southeastern's program would render unreasonable the qualifications it imposed.

V

Accordingly, we reverse the judgment of the court below, and remand for proceedings consistent with this opinion.

So ordered.

NOTES

1. McRee also wrote that respondent's hearing disability could preclude her practicing safely in "any setting" allowed by a "a license as L[icensed] P[ractical] N[urse]." App. 132a. Respondent contends that inasmuch as she already was licensed as a practical nurse, McRee's opinion was inherently incredible. But the record indicates that respondent had "not worked as a practical nurse except to do a little bit of night duty," App. 32a, and had not done that for several years before applying to Southeastern. Accordingly, it is at least possible to infer that respondent in fact could not work safely as a practical nurse in spite of her license to do so. In any event, we note the finding of the District Court that "a Licensed Practical Nurse, unlike a Licensed Registered Nurse, operates under constant supervision and is not allowed to perform medical tasks which require a great degree of technical sophistication." 424 F Supp., 1341, 1342–1343 (EDNC 1976).
2. The statute provides in full: "No otherwise qualified handicapped individual in the United States, as defined in section 706 (6) of this title, shall, solely by reason of his handicap, be excluded from the participation in, or be denied the benefits of, or be subjected to discrimination under any program or activity receiving Federal financial assistance *or under any program or activity conducted by any Executive agency or by the United States Postal Service. The head of each such agency shall promulgate such regulations as may be necessary to carry out the amendments to this section made by the Rehabilitation, Comprehensive Services, and Developmental Disabilities Act of 1978. Copies of any proposed regulation shall be submitted to appropriate authorizing committees of the Congress, and such regulation may take effect no*

earlier than the thirtieth day after the date on which such regulation is so submitted to such committees." The italicized portion of the section was added by § 119 of the Rehabilitation, Comprehensive Services, and Developmental Disabilities Act of 1978, 92 Stat. 2982. Respondent asserts no claim under this portion of the statute.

3. The District Court also dismissed respondent's constitutional claims. The Court of appeals affirmed that portion of the order, and respondent has not sought review of this ruling.

4. Relying on the plain language of the Act, the Department of Health, Education, and Welfare (HEW) at first did not promulgate any regulations to implement § 504. In a subsequent suit against HEW, however, the United States District Court for the District of Columbia held that Congress had intended regulations to be issued and ordered HEW to do so. *Cherry v. Mathews,* 419 F Supp. 922 (1976). The ensuing regulations currently are embodied in 45 CFR pt. 84.

5. In addition to challenging the construction of § 504 by the Court of appeals, Southeastern also contends that respondent cannot seek judicial relief for violations of that statute in view of the absence of any express private right of action. Respondent asserts that whether or not § 504 provides a private action, she may maintain her suit under 42 U.S.C. § 1983. In light of our disposition of this case on the merits, it is unnecessary to address these issues and we express no views on them. See *Norton v. Mathews,* 427 U.S. 524, 529–531 (1976); *Moor v. County of Alameda,* 411 U.S. 693, 715 (1973): *United States v. Augenblick,* 393 U.S. 348, 351–352 (1969).

6. The Act defines "handicapped individual" as follows: "The term 'handicapped individual' means any individual who (A) has a physical or mental disability which for such individual constitutes or results in a substantial handicap to employment and (B) can reasonably be expected to benefit in terms of employability from vocational rehabilitation services provided pursuant to subchapters I and III of this chapter. For the purposes of subchapters IV and V of this chapter, such term means any persons who (A) has a physical or mental impairment which substantially limits one or more of such person's major life activities, (B) has a record of such an impairment, or (C) is regarded as having such an impairment." Section 7 of the Rehabilitation Act of 1973, 87 Star. 359, as amended, 88 Stat. 1619, 89 Stat. 2, 29 U.S.C. § 706 (6). This definition comports with our understanding of § 504. A person who has a record of or is regarded as having an impairment may at present have no actual incapacity at all. Such a person would be exactly the kind of individual who could be "otherwise qualified" to participate in covered programs. And a person who suffers from a limiting physical or mental impairment still may possess other abilities that permit him to meet the requirements of various programs. Thus it is clear that Congress included among the class of "handicapped" persons covered by § 504 a range of individuals who could be "otherwise qualified." See S. Rep. No. 1297, 93d Cong., 2d Sess., 38–39 (1974).

7. The note states: "Paragraph (k) of § 84.3 defines the term 'qualified handicapped person.' Throughout the regulation, this term is used instead of the statutory term 'otherwise qualified handicapped person.' The Department believes that the omission of the word 'otherwise' is necessary in order to comport with the intent of the statute because, read literally, 'otherwise' qualified handicapped persons include persons who are qualified except for their handicap, rather than in spite of their handicap. Under such a literal reading, a blind person possessing all the qualifications for driving a bus except sight could be said to be 'otherwise qualified' for the job of driving. Clearly, such a result was not intended by Congress. In all other respects, the terms 'qualified' and 'otherwise qualified' are intended to be interchangeable." 45CFR pt. 84, App. A, at p. 405.

8. The court below adopted a portion of this argument: "[Respondent's] ability to read lips aids her in overcoming her hearing disability; however, it was argued that in certain situations such as in an operating room environment where surgical masks are used this ability would be unavailing to her. "Be that as it may, in the medical community, there does appear to be a number of settings in which the plaintiff could perform satisfactorily as an RN, such as in industry

or perhaps a physician's office. Certainly [respondent] could be viewed as possessing extraordinary insight into the medical and emotional needs of those with hearing disabilities. "I [respondent] meets all the other criteria for admission in the pursuit of her RN career, under the relevant North Carolina statues, N.C. Gen. Star. §§ 90–158, *et seq.,* it should not be foreclosed to her simply because she may not be able to function effectively in all the roles which registered nurses may choose for their careers." 574 F 2d 1158, 1161 n. 6 (CA4 1978).

9. This regulation provides in full: "(a) *Academic requirements.* A recipient [of federal funds] to which this subpart applied shall make such modifications to its academic requirements as are necessary to ensure that such requirements do not discriminate or have the effect of discriminating, on the basis of handicap, against a qualified handicapped applicant or student. Academic requirements that the recipient can demonstrate are essential to the program of instruction being pursued by such student or to any directly related licensing requirement will not be regarded as discriminatory within the meaning of this section. Modifications may include changes in the length of time permitted for the completion of degree requirements, substitution of specific courses required for the completion of degree requirements, and adaptations of the manner in which specific courses are conducted. "(d) *Auxiliary aids.* (1) A recipient to which this subpart applied shall take such steps as are necessary to ensure that no handicapped student is denied the benefits of, excluded from participation in, or otherwise subjected to discrimination under the education program or activity operated by the recipient because of the absence of educational auxiliary aids for students with impaired sensory, manual, or speaking skills. "(2) Auxiliary aids may include taped texts, interpreters or other effective methods of making orally delivered materials available to students with hearing impairments, readers in libraries for students with visual impairments, classroom equipment adapted for use by students with manual impairments, and other similar services and actions. Recipients need not provide attendants, individually prescribed devices, readers for personal use or study, or other devices or services of a personal nature." 45 CFR § 84.44.

10. § 115(a) of the Rehabilitation Act of 1978 added to the 1973 Act a section authorizing grants to state units for the purpose of providing "such information and technical assistance (including support personnel such as interpreters for the deaf) as may be necessary to assist those entities in complying with this Act, particularly the requirements of § 504." 92 Stat. 2971, codified at 29 U.S.C. § 775. This provision recognizes that on occasion the elimination of discrimination might involve some costs; it does not imply that the refusal to undertake substantial changes in a program by itself constitutes discrimination. Whatever effect the availability of these funds might have on ascertaining the existence of discrimination in some future case, no such funds were available to Southeastern at the time respondent sought admission to its nursing program.

11. The Government, in a brief *amicus curiae* in support of respondent, cites a report of the Senate Committee on Labor and Public Welfare on the 1974 amendments to the 1973 Act and several statements by individual Members of Congress during debate on the 1978 amendments, some of which indicate a belief that § 504 requires affirmative action. See Brief for the Government as *Amicus Curiae* 44–50. But these isolated statements by individual Members of Congress or its committees, all made after the enactment of the statute under consideration, cannot substitute for a clear expression of legislative intent at the time of enactment. *Quern v. Mandley,* 436 U.S. 725, 736 n. 10 (1978); *Los Angeles Dept. of Water & Power v. Manhart,* 435 U.S. 702, 714 (1978). Nor do these comments, none of which represents the will of Congress as a whole, constitute subsequent "legislation" such as this Court might weigh in construing the meaning of an earlier enactment. Cf. *Red Lion Broadcasting Co. v. FCC,* 395 U.S. 367, 380 381(1969). The Government also argues that various amendments to the 1973 Act contained in the Rehabilitation Act of 1978 further reflect Congress' approval of the affirmative action obligation created by HEWs regulations. But the amendment most directly on point undercuts this position. In amending § 504, Congress both extended that section's prohibition of discrimination to "any program or activity conducted by an Executive agency or by the United Postal

Service" and authorized administrative regulations to implement only *this amendment*. See n. 2, *supra*. The fact that no other regulations were mentioned supports an inference that no others were approved. Finally, we note that the assertion by HEW of the authority to promulgate any regulations under § 504 has been neither consistent nor long-standing. For the first three years after the section was enacted, HEW maintained the position that Congress had not intended any regulations to be issued. It altered its stand only after having been enjoined to do so. See n. 4, *supra*. This fact substantially diminishes the deference to be given to HEW's present interpretation of the statute. See *General Electric Co. v. Gilbert,* 429 U.S. 125, 143 (1976).

12. Respondent contends that it is unclear whether North Carolina law requires a registered nurse to be capable of performing all functions open to that profession in order to obtain a license to practice, although McRee, the Executive Director of the state Board of nursing, had informed Southeastern that the law did so require. See App. 138a–139a. Respondent further argues that even if she is not capable of meeting North Carolina's present licensing requirements, she still might succeed in obtaining a license in another jurisdiction. Respondent's argument misses the point. Southeastern's program, structured to train persons who will be able to perform all normal roles of a registered nurse, represents a legitimate academic policy and is accepted by the State. In effect it seeks to ensure that no graduate will pose a danger to the public in any professional role he or she might be cast. Even if the licensing requirements of North Carolina or some other State are less demanding, nothing in the Act requires an educational institution to lower its standards.

Appendix C

Board of
Education v. Rowley

(excerpts from Court's majority opinion only; concurring and dissenting opinions are omitted, as are some footnotes from the majority opinion)

BOARD OF EDUCATION OF THE HENDRICK HUDSON CENTRAL
SCHOOL DISTRICT BD. OF ED., WESTCHESTER COUNTY, ET AL.,
PETITIONERS
v.
AMY ROWLEY, BY HER PARENTS AND NATURAL GUARDIANS,
CLIFFORD AND NANCY ROWLEY, ETC.

Justice Rehnquist delivered the opinion of the court.

I

The Education for All Handicapped Children Act of 1975 (Act), 20 U.S. C. § 1401 *et seq.,* provides federal money to assist state and local agencies in educating handicapped children, and conditions such funding upon a State's compliance with extensive goals and procedures. The Act represents an ambitious federal effort to promote the education of handicapped children, and was passed in response to Congress' perception that a majority of handicapped children in the United States "were either totally excluded from schools or [were] sitting idly in regular classrooms awaiting the time when they were old enough to 'drop out.'" H.R. Rep. No. 94-332, p. 2 (1975). The Act's evolution and major provisions shed light on the questions of statutory interpretation which is at the heart of this case.

Congress first addressed the problem of educating the handicapped in 1966 when it amended the Elementary and Secondary Education Act of 1965 to establish a grant program "for the purpose of assisting the States in the initiation, expansion, and improvement of programs and projects ... for the education of handicapped children." Pub. L. No. 89-750, § 161, 80 Stat. 1204 (1966). That program was repealed in 1970 by the Education for the Handicapped Act, Pub. L. No. 91-230, 84 Stat. 175, Part B of which established a grant program similar in purpose to the repealed legislation. Neither the 1966 nor the 1970 legislation contained specific guidelines for state use of the grant money; both were aimed primarily at stimulating the States to develop educational resources and to train personnel for educating the handicapped.[1]

Dissatisfied with the progress being made under these earlier enactments, and spurred by two district court decisions holding that handicapped children should be given access to a public education,[2] Congress in 1974 greatly increased federal funding for education of the handicapped and for the first time required recipient States to adopt "a goal of providing full educational opportunities to all handicapped children." Pub. L. 93-380, 88 Stat. 579, 583 (1974) (the 1974 statute). The 1974 statute was recognized as an interim measure only, adopted "in order to give the Congress an additional year in which to study what if any additional Federal assistance [was] required to enable the States to meet the needs of handicapped children." H. R. Rep. No. 94-332, *supra*, p. 4. The ensuing year of study produced the Education for All Handicapped Children Act of 1975.

In order to qualify for federal financial assistance under the Act, a State must demonstrate that it "has in effect a policy that assures all handicapped children the right to a free appropriate public education." 20 U.S.C. § 1412(1). That policy must be reflected in a state plan submitted to and approved by the Commissioner of Education,[3] § 1413, which describes in detail the goals, programs, and timetables under which the State intends to educate handicapped children within its borders. §§ 1412, 1413. States receiving money under the Act must provide education to the handicapped by priority, first "to handicapped children who are not receiving an education" and second "to handicapped children...with the most severe handicaps who are receiving an inadequate education," § 1412(3), and "to the maximum extent appropriate" must educate handicapped children "with children who are not handicapped." § 1412(5).[4] The Act broadly defines "handicapped children" to include "mentally retarded, hard of hearing, deaf, speech impaired, visually handicapped, seriously emotionally disturbed, orthopedically impaired, [and] other health impaired children, [and] children with specific learning disabilities." § 1401(1).[5]

The "free appropriate public education" required by the Act is tailored to the unique needs of the handicapped child by means of an "individualized educational program" (IEP). § 1401(18). The IEP, which is prepared at a meeting between a qualified representative of the local educational agency, the child's teacher, the child's parents or guardian, and, where appropriate, the child, consists of a written document containing

"(A) a statement of the present levels of educational performance of the child, (B) a statement of annual goals, including short-term instructional objectives, (C) a statement of the specific educational services to be provided to such child, and the extent to which such child will be able to participate in regular educational programs, (D) the projected date for initiation and anticipated duration of such service, and (E) appropriate objective criteria and evaluation procedures and schedules for determining, on at least an annual basis, whether instructional objectives are being achieved." § 1401(19).

Local or regional educational agencies must review, and where appropriate revise, each child's IEP at least annually. § 1404(a)(5). See also §§ 1413(a)(11), 1414(a)(5).

In addition to the state plan and the IEP already described, the Act imposes extensive procedural requirements upon States receiving federal funds under its provisions. Parents or guardians of handicapped children must be notified of any proposed change in the "identification, evaluation, or educational placement of the children of the provision of a free appropriate public education to the child," and must be permitted to bring a complaint about "any matter relating to" such evaluation and education. § 1415(b)(1)(D) and (E).[6] Complaints brought by parents or guardians must be resolved at "an impartial due process hearing," and appeal to the State educational agency must be provided if the initial hearing is held at the local or regional level. § 1415(b)(2) and (c).[7] Thereafter, "[a]ny party aggrieved by the findings and decisions" of the state administrative hearing has "the right to bring a civil action with respect to the complaint ... in any State court of competent jurisdiction or in a district court of the United States without regard to the amount in controversy." § 1415(e)(2).

Thus, although the Act leaves to the States the primary responsibility for developing and executing educational programs for handicapped children, it imposes significant requirements to be followed in the discharge of that responsibility...

II

This case arose in connection with the education of Amy Rowley, a deaf student at the Furnace Woods School in the Hendrick Hudson Central School District, Peekskill, New York. Amy has minimal residual hearing and is an excellent lipreader. During the year before she began attending Furnace Woods, a meeting between her parents and school administrators resulted in a decision to place her in a regular kindergarten class in order to determine what supplemental services would be necessary to her education. Several members of the school administration prepared for Amy's arrival by attending a course in sign-language interpretation, and a teletype machine was installed in the principal's office to facilitate communication with her parents who are also deaf. At the end of the trail period it was determined that Amy should remain in the kindergarten class, but that she should be provided with an FM hearing aid which would amplify words spoken into a wireless receiver by the teacher or fellow students during certain classroom activities. Amy successfully completed her kindergarten year.

As required by the Act, and IEP was prepared for Amy during the fall of her first-grade year. The IEP provided that Amy should be educated in a regular classroom at Furnace Woods, should continue to use the FM hearing aid, and should receive instruction from a tutor for the deaf for one hour each day and from a speech therapist for three hours each week. The Rowleys agreed with the IEP but insisted that Amy also be provided a qualified sign-language interpreter in all of her academic classes. Such an interpreter had been placed in Amy's kindergarten class for a two-week experimental period, but the interpreter had reported that Amy did not need his services at that time. The school administrators likewise concluded that Amy did not need such an interpreter in her first-grade classroom. They reached this conclusion after consulting the school district's Committee on the Handicapped, which had received expert evidence from Amy's parents on the importance of a sign-language interpreter, received testimony from Amy's teacher and other persons familiar with her academic and social progress, and visited a class for the deaf.

When their request for an interpreter was denied, the Rowleys demanded and received a hearing before an independent examiner. After receiving evidence from both sides, the examiner agreed with the administrators' determination that an interpreter was not necessary because "Amy was achieving educationally, academically, and socially" without such assistance. App. to Pet. for Cert. F-22. The examiner's decision was affirmed on appeal by the New York Commissioner of Education on the basis of substantial evidence in the record.... Pursuant to the Act's provision for judicial review, the Rowleys then brought an action in the United States District Court for the Southern District of New York, claiming that the administrators' denial of the sign-language interpreter constituted a denial of the "free appropriate public education" guaranteed by the Act.

The District Court found that Amy "is a remarkably well-adjusted child" who interacts and communicates well with her classmates and has "developed an extraordinary rapport" with her teachers. 483 E Supp. 528, 53 1. It also found that "she performs better than the average child in her class and is advancing easily from grade to grade," *id.,* at 534, but "that she understands considerably less of what goes on in class than she would if she were not deaf " and thus "is not learning as much, or performing as well academically, as she would without her handicap " *id.,* at 532. This disparity between Amy's achievement and her potential led the court to decide that she was not receiving a "free appropriate public education," which the court defined as "an opportunity to achieve [her] full potential commensurate with the opportunity provided to other children." *Id.,* at 534. According to the District Court, such a standard "requires that the potential of the handicapped child be measured and compared to his or her performance, and that the remaining differential or 'shortfall' be compared to the shortfall experienced by nonhandicapped children." *Ibid.* The District Court's definition arose from its assumption that the responsibility for "giv[ing] content to the requirement of an 'appropriate education'" had "been left entirely to the federal courts and the hearing officer." *Id.,* at 533.[8]

A divided panel of the United States Court of Appeals for the Second Circuit affirmed. The Court of Appeals "agree[d] with the [D]istrict (C)ourt's conclusions of law," and held that its "findings of fact [were] not clearly erroneous." 632 E 2d 945, 947 (1980).

We granted certiorari to review the lower courts' interpretation of the Act. 454 U.S.—1981. Such review requires us to consider two questions: What is meant by the Act's requirement of a "free appropriate public education?" And what is the role of state and federal courts in exercising the review granted by § 1415 of the Act? We consider these questions separately.[9]

III

A

This is the first case in which this Court has been called upon to interpret any provision of the Act. As noted previously, the District Court and the Court of Appeals concluded that "[t]he Act itself does not define 'appropriate education,'" 483 E Supp., at 533, but leaves "to the courts and the hearing officers" the responsibility of "giv[ing] content to the requirement of an appropriate education." *Ibid.* See also 632 E 2d, at 947. Petitioners contend that the definition of the phrase "free appropriate public education" used by the courts below overlooks the definition of that phrase actually found in the Act. Respondents agree that the Act defines "free appropriate public education," but contend that the statutory definition is not "functional" and thus "offers judges no guidance in their consideration of controversies involving the 'identification, evaluation, or educational placement of the child or the provision of a free appropriate public education.'" Brief for Respondents 28. The United States, appearing as *amicus curiae* on behalf of the respondents, states that "[a]lthough the Act includes definitions of 'free appropriate public education' and other related terms, the statutory definitions do not adequately explain what is meant by 'appropriate.'" Brief for United States as *Amicus Curiae* 13.

We are loath to conclude that Congress failed to offer any assistance in defining the meaning of the principal substantive phrase used in the Act. It is beyond dispute that, contrary to the conclusions of the courts below, the Act does expressly define "free appropriate public education":

> "The term 'free appropriate public education' means *special education* and *related services* which (A) have been provided at public expense, under public supervision and direction, and without charge, (B) meet the standards of the State educational agency, (C) include an appropriate preschool, elementary, or secondary school education in the State involved, and (D) are provided in conformity with the individualized education program required under section 1414(a)(5) of this title." § 1401(18) (emphasis added).

"Special education'" as referred to in this definition, means "specially designed instruction, at no cost to parents or guardians, to meet the unique needs of a handicapped child, including classroom instruction, instruction in physical education, home instruction, and instruction in hospitals and institutions." § 1401(16). "Related services" are defined as "transportation, and such developmental, corrective, and other supportive services...as may be required to assist a handicapped child to benefit from special education." § 1401(17).[10]

Like many statutory definitions, this one tends toward the cryptic rather than the comprehensive, but that is scarcely a reason for abandoning the quest for legislative intent. Whether or not the definition is a "functional" one, as respondents contend it is not, it is the principal tool which Congress has given us for parsing the critical phrase of the Act. We think more must be made of it than either respondents or the United States seems willing to admit.

According to the definitions contained in the Act, a "free appropriate public education" consists of educational instruction specially designed to meet the unique needs of the handicapped child, support by such services as are necessary to permit the child "to benefit" from the instruction. Almost as a checklist for adequacy under the Act, the definition also requires that such instruction and services by provided at public expense and under public supervision, meet the State's educational standards, approximate the grade levels used in the State's regular education, and comport with the child's IEP. Thus, if personalized instruction is being provided with sufficient supportive services to permit the child to benefit from the instruction, and the other items on the definitional checklist are satisfied, the child is receiving a "free appropriate public education" as defined by the Act.

Other portions of the statute also shed light upon congressional intent. Congress found that of the roughly eight million handicapped children in the United States at the time of enactment, one million were "excluded entirely from the public school system" and more than half were receiving an inappropriate education. Note to § 1401. In addition, as mentioned in Part 1, the Act requires States to extend educational services first to those children who are receiving no education and second to those children who are receiving and "inadequate education." § 1412(3). When these express statutory findings and priorities are read together with the Act's extensive procedural requirements and its definition of "free appropriate public education," the face of the statute evinces a congressional intent to bring previously excluded handicapped children into the public education systems of the States and to require the States to adopt *procedures* which would result in individualized consideration of and instruction for each child.

Noticeably absent from the language of the statute is any substantive standard prescribing the level of education to be accorded handicapped children. Certainly the language of the statute contains no requirement like the one imposed by the lower courts—that States maximize the potential of handicapped children "commensurate with the opportunity provided to other children." 483 E Supp., at 534. That standard was expounded by the District Court without reference to the statutory definitions or even to the legislative history of the Act. Although we find the statutory definition of "free appropriate public education" to be helpful in our interpretation of the Act, there remains the question of whether the legislative history indicates a congressional intent that such education meet some additional substantive standard. For an answer, we turn to that history."

B

(i). As suggested in Part 1, federal support for education of the handicapped is a fairly recent development. Before passage of the Act some States had passed laws to improve the educational services afforded handicapped children," but many of these children were excluded completely from any form of public education or were left to fend for themselves in classrooms designed for education of their nonhandicapped peers. The House Report begins by emphasizing this exclusion and misplacement, noting that millions of handicapped children "were either totally excluded from schools or [were] sitting idly in regular classrooms awaiting the time when they were old enough to 'drop out.'" H. R. Rep. No. 94-332, supra, at 2. See also S. Rep. No. 94-168, p. 8 (1975). One of the Act's two principal sponsors in the Senate urged its passage in similar terms:

> "While much progress has been made in the last few years, we can take no solace in that progress until all handicapped children are, in fact, receiving an education. The most recent statistics provided by the Bureau of Education for the Handicapped estimate that...1.75 million handicapped children do not receive any educational services, and 2.5 million handicapped children are not receiving an appropriate education." 121 Cong. Rec. 19486 (1975) (remarks of Sen. Williams).

This concern, stressed repeatedly throughout the legislative history,[13] confirms the impression conveyed by the language of the statute: By passing the Act, Congress sought primarily to make public education available to handicapped children. But in seeking to provide such access to public education, Congress did not impose upon the States any greater substantive educational standard than would be necessary to make such access meaningful. Indeed, Congress expressly "recognize[d] that in many instances the process of providing special education and related services to handicapped children is not guaranteed to produce any particular outcome." S. Rep. No. 94-168, *supra,* at 11. Thus, the intent of the Act was more to open the door of public education to handicapped children on appropriate terms than to guarantee any particular level of education once inside.

Both the House and the Senate reports attribute the impetus for the Act and its predecessors to two federal court judgments rendered in 1971 and 1972. As the Senate Report states, passage of the Act "followed a series of landmark court cases establishing in law the right to education for all handicapped children

Mills and *PARC* both held that handicapped children must be given *access* to an adequate, publicly supported education. Neither case purports to require any particular substantive level of education.[15] Rather, like the language of the Act, the cases set forth extensive procedures to be followed in formulating personalized educational programs for handicapped children. See 348 F. Supp., at 878–883; 334 F. Supp., at 1258–1267." The fact that both *PARC* and *Mills* are discussed at length in the legislative reports" suggests that the principles which they established are the principles which, to a significant extent, guided the drafters of the Act. Indeed, immediately after discussing these cases the Senate Report describes the 1974 statute as having "incorporated the major principles of the right to education cases." S. Rep. No. 94-168, *supra,* at 8. Those principles in turn became the bases of the Act, which itself was designed to effectuate the purposes of the 1974 statute. H. R. Rep. No. 94-332, *supra,* at 5.[18]

That the Act imposes no clear obligation upon recipient States beyond the requirement that handicapped children receive some form of specialized education is perhaps best demonstrated by the fact that Congress, in explaining the need for the Act, equated an "appropriate education" to the receipt of some specialized educational services....

It is evident from the legislative history that the characterization of handicapped children as "served" referred to children who were receiving some form of specialized educational services from the States, and that the characterization of children as "unserved" referred to those who were receiving no specialized educational services.... By characterizing the 3.9 million handicapped children who were "served" as children who were "receiving an appropriate education," the Senate and House reports unmistakably disclose Congress' perception of the type of education required by the Act: an "appropriate education" is provided when personalized educational services are provided.[21]

(ii). Respondents contend that "the goal of the Act is to provide each handicapped child with an equal educational opportunity." Brief for Respondents 35. We think, however, that the requirement that a State provide specialized educational services to handicapped children generates no additional requirement that the services so provided be sufficient to maximize each child's potential "commensurate with the opportunity provided other children." Respondents and the United States correctly note that Congress sought "to provide assistance to the States in carrying out their responsibilities under ... the Constitution of the United States to provide equal protection of the laws." S. Rep. No. 94-168, *supra,* at 13.[22] But we do not think that such statements imply a congressional intent to achieve strict equality of opportunity or services.

The educational opportunities provided by our public school systems undoubtedly differ from student to student, depending upon a myriad of factors that might affect a particular student's ability to assimilate information presented in the classroom. The requirement that States provide "equal" educational opportunities would thus seem to present an entirely unworkable standard requiring impossible measurements and comparisons. Similarly, furnishing handicapped children with only such services as are available to nonhandicapped children would in all probability fall short of the statutory requirement of "free appropriate public education"; to require, on the other hand, the furnishing of every special service necessary to maximize each handicapped child's potential is, we think, further than Congress intended to go. Thus to speak in terms of "equal" services in one instance gives less than what is required by the Act and in another instance more. The theme of the Act is "free appropriate public education," a phrase which is too complex to be captured by the word "equal" whether one is speaking of opportunities or services.

The legislative conception of the requirements of equal protection was undoubtedly informed by the two district court decisions referred to above. But cases such as *Mills* and *PARC* held simply that handicapped children may not be excluded entirely from public education.... The right of access to free public education enunciated by these cases is significantly different from any notion of absolute equality of opportunity regardless of capacity. To the extent that Congress might have looked further than these cases which are mentioned in the legislative history, at the time of enactment of the Act this Court had held at least twice that the Equal Protection Clause of the Fourteenth Amendment does not require States to expend equal financial resources on the education of each child. *San Antonio School District v. Rodriguez,* 411 U.S. 1 (1975); *McInnis v. Shapiro,* 293 E Supp. 327 (ND Ill. 1968), *aff'd sub nom, McInnis v. Ogilvie,* 394 U.S. 322 (1969).

In explaining the need for federal legislation, the House Report noted that "no congressional legislation has required a precise guarantee for handicapped children, i.e., a basic floor of opportunity that would bring into compliance all school districts with the constitutional right of equal protection with respect to handicapped children." H. R. Rep. No. 94-332, *supra,* at 14. Assuming that the Act was designed to fill the need identified in the House Report-neither the Act nor its history persuasively demonstrates that Congress thought that equal protection required anything more than equal access. Therefore, Congress' desire to provide specialized educational services, even in furtherance of "equality," cannot be read as imposing any particular substantive educational standard upon the States.

The District Court and the Court of Appeals thus erred when they held that the Act requires New York to maximize the potential of each handicapped child commensurate with the opportunity provided nonhandicapped children. Desirable though that goal might be, it is not the standard that Congress imposed upon States which receive funding under the Act. Rather, Congress sought primarily to identify and evaluate handicapped children, and to provide them with access to a free public education.

(iii). Implicit in the congressional purpose of providing access to a "free appropriate public education" is the requirement that the education to which access is provided be sufficient to confer some educational benefit upon the handicapped child. It would do little good for Congress to spend millions of dollars in providing access

to a public education only to have the handicapped child receive no benefit from that education. The statutory definition of "free appropriate public education," in addition to requiring that States provide each child with "specially designed instruction," expressly requires the provision of "such...supportive services...as may be required to assist a handicapped child *to benefit* from special education." § 1401(17) (emphasis added). We therefore conclude that the "basic floor of opportunity" provided by the Act consists of access to specialized instruction and related services which are individually designed to provide educational benefit to the handicapped child.[23]

The determination of when handicapped children are receiving sufficient educational benefits to satisfy the requirements of the Act presents a more difficult problem. The Act requires participating States to educate a wide spectrum of handicapped children, from the marginally hearing-impaired to the profoundly retarded and palsied. It is clear that the benefits obtainable by children at one end of the spectrum will differ dramatically from those obtainable by children at the other end, with infinite variations in between. One child may have little difficulty competing successfully in an academic setting with nonhandicapped children while another child may encounter great difficulty in acquiring even the most basic of self-maintenance skills. We do not attempt today to establish any one test for determining the adequacy of educational benefits conferred upon all children covered by the Act. Because in this case we are presented with a handicapped child who is receiving substantial specialized instruction and related services, and who is performing above average in the regular classrooms of a public school system, we confine our analysis to that situation.

The Act requires participating States to educate handicapped children with nonhandicapped children whenever possible." When that "mainstreaming" preference of the Act has been met and a child is being educated in the regular classrooms of a public school system, the system itself monitors the educational progress of the child. Regular examinations are administered, grades are awarded, and yearly advancement to higher grade levels is permitted for those children who attain an adequate knowledge of the course material. The grading and advancement system thus constitutes an important factor in determining educational benefit. Children who graduate from our public school systems are considered by our society to have been "educated" at least to the grade level they have completed, and access to an "education" for handicapped children is precisely what Congress sought to provide in the Act.[25]

C

When the language of the Act and its legislative history are considered together, the requirements imposed by Congress become tolerably clear. Insofar as a State is required to provide a handicapped child with a "free appropriate public education," we hold that it satisfies this requirement by providing personalized instruction with sufficient support services to permit the child to benefit educationally from that instruction. Such instruction and services must be provided at public expense, must meet the State's educational standards, must approximate the grade levels used in the State's regular education, and must comport with the child's IEP. In addition, the IEP, and therefore the personalized instruction, should be formulated in accordance with the requirements of the Act and, if the child is being educated in the regular classrooms of the public education system, should be reasonably calculated to enable the child to achieve passing marks and advance from grade to grade.[26]

D

In assuring that the requirements of the Act have been met, courts must be careful to avoid imposing their view of preferable educational methods upon the States.[29] The primary responsibility for formulating the education to be accorded a handicapped child, and for choosing the educational method most suitable to the child's needs, was left by the Act to state and local educational agencies in cooperation with the parents or guardian of the child. The Act expressly charges States with the responsibility of "acquiring and disseminating to teachers and administrators of programs for handicapped children significant information derived from educational research, demonstration, and similar projects and [of] adopting, where appropriate, promising educational practices and materials." Section 1413(a)(3). In the face of such a clear statutory directive, it seems highly unlikely that Congress intended courts to overturn a State's choice of appropriate educational theories in a proceeding conducted pursuant to § 1415(c)(2).[30]

We previously have cautioned that courts lack the "specialized knowledge and experience" necessary to resolve "persistent and difficult questions of educational policy." *San Antonio School District v. Rodriguez,* 411 U.S. 1, 42 (1973). We think that Congress shared that view when it passed the Act. As already demonstrated, Congress' intention was not that the Act displace the primacy of States in the field of education, but that States receive funds to assist them in extending their educational systems to the handicapped. Therefore, once a court determines that the requirements of the Act have been met, questions of methodology are for resolution by the States.

V

Entrusting a child's education to state and local agencies does not leave the child without protection. Congress sought to protect individual children by providing for parental involvement in the development of State plans and policies, *supra,* at 4-5 and n. 6, and in the formulation of the child's individual educational program. As the Senate Report states:

> "The Committee recognizes that in many instances the process of providing special education and related services to handicapped children is not guaranteed to produce any particular

> outcome. By changing the language [of the provision relating to individualized educational programs] to emphasize the process of parent and child involvement and to provide a written record of reasonable expectations, the Committee intends to clarify that such individualized planning conferences are a way to provide parent involvement and protection to assure that appropriate services are provided to a handicapped child." S. Rep. No. 94-168, *supra,* at 11-12. See also S. Conf. Rep. No. 94-445, p. 30 (1975); 45 CFR § 121a.345 (1980).

As this very case demonstrates, parents and guardians will not lack ardor in seeking to ensure that handicapped children receive all of the benefits to which they are entitled by the Act.[31]

NOTES

4. Despite this preference for "mainstreaming" handicapped children-educating them with non-handicapped children—Congress recognized that regular classrooms simply would not be a suitable setting for the education of many handicapped children. The Act expressly acknowledges that "the nature or severity of the handicap [may be] such that education in regular classes with the use of supplementary aids and services cannot be achieved satisfactorily." § 1412(5). The Act thus provides for the education of some handicapped children in separate classes or institutional settings. See *ibid.;* § 1413(a)(4).

6. The requirements that parents be permitted to file complaints regarding their child's education, and be present when the child's IEP is formulated, represent only two examples of Congress' effort to maximize parental involvement in the education of each handicapped child....

15. The only substantive standard which can be implied from these cases comports with the standard implicit in the Act. *PARC* states that each child must receive "access to a free public program of education and training *appropriate to his learning capacities,*" 334 F. Supp., at 1258, and that further state action is required when it appears that "the needs of the mentally retarded child are not being *adequately* served," *id.,* at 1266. (Emphasis added.) *Mills* also speaks in terms of "adequate" educational services, 348 E Supp., at 878, and sets a realistic standard of providing some educational services to each child when every need cannot be met.

21. In seeking to read more into the Act than its language or legislative history will permit, the United States focuses upon the word "appropriate," arguing that "the statutory definitions do not adequately explain what [it means]." Brief for the United States as *Amicus Curiae* 13. Whatever Congress meant by an "appropriate" education, it is clear that it did not mean a potential-maximizing education.
The term as used in reference to educating the handicapped appears to have originated in the *PARC* decision, where the District Court required that handicapped children be provided with "education and training appropriate to [their] learning capacities." 334 F. Supp., at 1258. The word appears again in the *Mills* decision, the District Court at one point referring to the need for "an appropriate educational program," 348 F. Supp., at 879, and at another point speaking of a "suitable publicly-supported education," *id.,* at 878. Both cases also refer to the need for an "adequate" education. See 334 F. Supp., at 1266; 348 F. Supp., at 878.
The use of "appropriate" in the language of the Act, although by no means definitive, suggests that Congress used the word as much to describe the settings in which handicapped children should be educated as to prescribe the substantive content or supportive services of

their education. For example, § 1412(5) requires that handicapped children be educated in classrooms with nonhandicapped children "to the maximum extent appropriate." Similarly, § 1401(19) provides that, "whenever appropriate," handicapped children should attend and participate in the meeting at which their IEP is drafted. In addition, the definition of the "free appropriate public education" itself states that instruction given handicapped children should be at an "appropriate preschool, elementary, or secondary school" level. § 1401(18)(C). The Act's use of the word "appropriate" thus seems to reflect Congress' recognition that some settings simply are not suitable environments for the participation of some handicapped children. At the very least, these statutory uses of the word refute the contention that Congress used "appropriate" as a term of art which concisely expresses the standard found by the lower courts.

23. This view is supported by the congressional intention, frequently expressed in the legislative history, that handicapped children be enabled to achieve a reasonable degree of self sufficiency. After referring to statistics showing that many handicapped children were excluded from public education, the Senate Report states: "The long range implications of these statistics are that public agencies and taxpayers will spend billions of dollars over the lifetimes of these individuals to maintain such persons as dependents and in a minimally acceptable lifestyle. With proper education services, many would be able to become productive citizens, contributing to society instead of being forced to remain burdens. Others, through such services, would increase their independence, thus reducing their dependence on society." S. Rep. No. 94-168, *supra,* at 9. See also H. R. Rep. No. 94-332, *supra,* at 11. Similarly, one of the principal Senate sponsors of the Act stated that "providing appropriate educational services now means that many of these individuals will be able to become a contributing part of our society, and they will not have to depend on subsistence payments from public funds." 121 Cong. Rec. 19492 (1975) (remarks of Sen. Williams). See also 121 Cong. Rec. 25541 (1975) (remarks of Rep. Harkin); 121 Cong. Rec. 37024-37025 (1975) (remarks of Rep. Brademas); 121 Cong. Rec. 37027 (1975) (remarks of Rep. Gude); 121 Cong. Rec. 37410 (1975) (remarks of Sen. Randolph); 121 Cong. Rec. 37416 (1975) (remarks of Sen. Williams).

The desire to provide handicapped children with an attainable degree of personal independence obviously anticipated that state educational programs would confer educational benefits upon such children. But at the same time, the goal of achieving some degree of self sufficiency in most cases is a good deal more modest than the potential-maximizing goal adopted by the lower courts.

Despite its frequent mention, we cannot conclude, as did the dissent in the Court of Appeals, that self sufficiency was itself the substantive standard which Congress imposed upon the States. Because many mildly handicapped children will achieve self sufficiency without state assistance while personal independence for the severely handicapped may be an unreachable goal, "self sufficiency" as a substantive standard is at once an inadequate protection and an overly demanding requirement. We thus view these references in the legislative history as evidence of Congress' intention that the services provided handicapped children be educationally beneficial, whatever the nature or severity of their handicap.

25. We do not hold today that every handicapped child who is advancing from grade to grade in a regular public school system is automatically receiving a "free appropriate public education." In this case, however, we find Amy's academic progress, when considered with the special services and professional consideration accorded by the Furnace Woods school administrators, to be dispositive.

29. In this case, for example, both the state hearing officer and the District Court were presented with evidence as to the best method for educating the deaf, a question long debated among scholars. See Large, Special Problems of the Deaf Under the Education for All Handicapped Children Act of 1975, 58 Washington UL.Q. 213, 229 (1980). The District Court accepted the testimony of respondents' experts that there was "a trend supported by studies showing the greater degree of success of students brought up in deaf households using [the method of communication used by the Rowleys]." 483 F Supp., at 535.

30. It is clear that Congress was aware of the States' traditional role in the formulation and execution of educational policy. "Historically, the States have had the primary responsibility for the education of children at the elementary and secondary level." 121 Cong. Rec. 19498 (1975) (remarks of Sen. Dole). See also *Epperson v. Arkansas,* 393 U.S. 97, 104 (1968) ("[b]y and large, public education in our Nation is committed to the control of state and local authorities").

31. In addition to providing for extensive parental involvement in the formulation of state and local policies, as well as the preparation of individual educational programs, the Act ensures that States will receive the advice of experts in the field of educating handicapped children. As a condition for receiving federal funds under the Act, States must create "an advisory panel, appointed by the Governor or any other official authorized under State law to make such appointments, composed of individuals involved in or concerned with the education of handicapped children, including handicapped individuals, teachers, parents or guardians of handicapped children, State and local education officials, and administrators of programs for handicapped children, which (A) advises the State educational agency of unmet needs within the State in the education of handicapped children, [and] (B) comments publicly on any rules or regulations proposed for issuance by the State regarding the education of handicapped children." § 1413(a)(12).

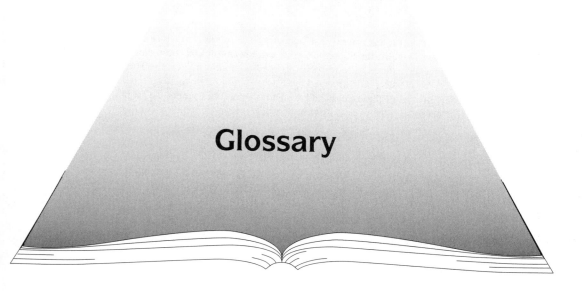

Glossary

AAMR an abbreviation for the American Association on Mental Retardation

ADA an abbreviation for the Americans with Disabilities Act

affirmed (aff'd.) a word that indicates in a citation to a case that a higher court has agreed with the result, and usually the reasoning, of a lower court and approved the judgment of the lower court. Sometimes a higher court can affirm part of a lower court's judgment and reverse part of it, depending on the nature of the judgment.

amicus curiae a Latin term indicating an individual or organization that is neither plaintiff nor defendant in a civil case but, because of special expertise or interest, is allowed by a court to become involved in the case as a "friend of the court." The involvement usually consists of submitting a brief (written presentation) containing supporting legal arguments and special facts to the court.

appeal the process whereby a court of appeals reviews the record of proceedings and judgment of a lower court to determine if errors of law or fact were made which might lead to a reversal or modification of the lower court's decision. If substantial errors are not found, the lower court's decision will be affirmed. If they are, its decision will be reversed or modified.

BIP an abbreviation for *behavior intervention plan*

C.F.R. an abbreviation for *Code of Federal Regulations,* a publication of the U.S. government that contains the regulations of the executive agencies of government (e.g., U.S. Department of Education) implementing laws (statutes) passed by Congress (e.g., PL 97–142).

cert. den. an abbreviation that indicates in a citation to a case that a higher court (usually, the Supreme Court) has declined to order a lower court to send the case to it for review. By contrast, *cert. granted* means the higher court has ordered a lower court to send a case to it for review.

certiorari (cert.) a Latin term that indicates in a citation to a case that an order from an appeals court (usually, the Supreme Court) to a lower court has been entered, either requiring or declining to require the lower court to send up a case for review. The right-to-education cases decided by the U.S. Supreme Court usually go to that court on a petition (request) for *certiorari* by one of the parties (and the Court sometimes grants the request and orders the lower court to send the case to it for review).

CIC an abbreviation for *clean intermittent catheterization*

civil case a lawsuit brought by one or more individuals to seek redress of some legal injury (or aspect of an injury) for which there are civil (non-criminal) remedies. In right-to-education cases, these remedies are based on the federal or state constitutions, federal or state statutes, or federal or state agency regulations, or a combination of federal and state constitutions, statutes and regulations. Right-to-education cases are always civil suits.

class action a civil case brought on behalf of the plaintiffs who are named in the suit, as well as on behalf of all other persons similarly situated, to vindicate their legally protected interests. *Mills v. D. C Board of Education* was brought on behalf of 12-year-old Peter Mills and six other school-age children who were named in the complaint, as well as all other exceptional children in the District. By contrast, *Board v. Rowley* was not a class action lawsuit because it was brought on behalf of only one person, who sued to protect only her rights, not the rights of other people.

competing equities a term describing a situation in which two or more people or groups of people have rights or privileges that cannot be fully satisfied without infringing on the rights or privileges of each other. For example, children with disabilities have some rights to be integrated with nondisabled children, but nondisabled children also have rights to an education that is not disrupted by children with disabilities (see chapter 6). In such a case, the competing equities of both children must be weighed against each other and a decision made by a court or other policy maker as to which claims prevail. Another way of thinking about competing equities is to ask: Whose rights or privileges are to be reduced for the benefit of other people?

complaint a legal document submitted to the court by plaintiffs, in which they inform the court and the defendants that they are bringing a lawsuit and set out the underlying reasons for which they sue and the relief they want.

concur a term that indicates in a citation to a case that one court agrees with the judgment of another and follows the precedent of that court's decision.

consent agreement an out-of-court agreement reached by the parties to a suit, which is formally approved by the court. In *Pennsylvania Association for Retarded Children v. Pennsylvania,* a court entered an order that it adopted pursuant to a consent agreement between plaintiffs and defendants.

constitutional right a legal right based on provisions of the U.S. Constitution or a state constitution. Equal protection and the due process of law are the federal constitutional rights most relevant to the right to education. The Fourteenth Amendment applies to state (and therefore, local) governments and guarantees the rights of due process and equal protection. (See chapters 2 through 8.)

damages money awarded by a court to someone who has been injured (the plaintiff), which must be paid by the one who is responsible for the injury (the defendant).

de facto a Latin term that means, literally, "by reason of the fact." Integration by race and disability now is required by law (*de jure* integration), but may not actually occur in some schools or among some students (*de facto* segregation).

defendant the person against whom a lawsuit is brought for redress of a violation of one or more of a plaintiffs legally protected interests.

defense a reason cited by a defendant why a lawsuit against him or her is without merit or why he or she is not responsible for the injury or violation of rights as alleged by the plaintiff.

de jure a Latin term that means, literally, "by law." Segregation of the schools by race or disability was required by laws of some states; thus, *de jure* segregation was enforced. Present law requires *de jure* integration.

dicta a Latin term describing language in a judicial opinion that is not essential to the disposition of the case or to the court's reasoning and that is regarded as gratuitous. *Dicta* are persuasive but not binding on other courts, whereas the court's holding and reasoning are.

discovery the process by which one party to a civil suit can find out about matters relevant to the case, including information about what evidence the other side has, what witnesses will be called, and so on. Discovery devices for obtaining information include depositions and interrogatories to obtain testimony, requests for documents or other tangibles, and requests for physical or mental examinations.

DOE an abbreviation for the Department of Education

due process of law a right to have any law applied by the federal or state government reasonably and with sufficient safeguards, such as hearings and notice, to ensure that an individual is dealt with fairly. Due process is guaranteed under the Fifth and Fourteenth Amendments to the federal Constitution.

EHA an abbreviation for the Education for All Handicapped Children Act of 1975

EHLR an abbreviation for the works of a commercial publisher that report the opinions and judgments of many of the special education cases decided by state and federal courts in reports cited as *Education for the Handicapped Law Reporter (EHLR)*. In this book, the citation is stated in this way: *EHLR* 552:104-indicating that the report begins at section 552 of *EHLR* and at page 104. The case name precedes the *EHLR* citation, and the abbreviation of the court and date of judgment are set out in parentheses after the page reference.

Eighth Amendment the Eighth Amendment to the federal Constitution guarantees that the federal government will not impose a cruel and unusual punishment upon conviction of a crime. The amendment does not forbid the use of corporal punishment on students. It is not a factor in right-to-education cases.

EMR an abbreviation for *educable mentally retarded*

en banc a Latin term referring to a situation in which a court consisting of more than one member (such as the federal appeals courts) hears a case with all of its members present at the hearing and participating in the decision. Usually, federal courts of appeals are divided into panels (or groups) of judges; a panel hears a case and normally makes the judgment of the court by itself, without participation of the other members of the court. Sometimes, however, a case is so difficult or important that all members of the court hear the case and decide the outcome. The court then sits *en banc*—all together.

equal protection of law a right not to be discriminated against for any unjustifiable reason, such as because of race or handicap. Equal protection is guaranteed under the Fourteenth Amendment. (See chapters 2 and 3.)

ESEA an abbreviation for the Elementary and Secondary Education Act of 1965

ESY an abbreviation for *extended school year*

et seq. a Latin term that means "and following" (et means "and"; *seq.* is an abbreviation for *sequens,* which means "following"). The phrase always follows a noun (e.g., Vol. 20, United States Code, Sections 1401 *et seq.*—hence, "and the following sections").

ex rel. a Latin term that indicates a lawsuit is brought on behalf of one person by another (e.g., the attorney general of a state may sue on behalf of an individual; thus, the case is captioned *"State of Kansas, ex rel. Jane Doe, an incompetent, v. Superintendent, State Hospital"*). The lawsuit normally is one in which the state attorney general seeks to vindicate a legal position that is favorable to the state and its citizens on behalf of a person not able to bring a lawsuit directly.

expert witness a person called to testify because he or she has a recognized competence in an area. For example, experts in the *PARC* right-to-education case had doctoral degrees in the field of special education, were authors of numerous professional publications pertaining to exceptional children, and were consultants to advisory committees on education.

FAPE an abbreviation for *free appropriate public education*

FBA an abbreviation for *functional behavioral assessment*

F.2d an abbreviation, in a citation to a lawsuit's reported judgment and order, that indicates that the case was decided by a federal court of appeals and is reported in a certain volume of the reports of the federal courts of appeals (shown as "Cir." for Circuit Court(s) of Appeal(s)). The volume of the reports precedes the *F 2d (Federal Report, 2d Series)* designation; the page at which the report begins follows the F 2d designation; and the identity of the court and the date of the judgment are set out in parentheses after the page number. Thus, *Smuck v. Hobson,* 408 R 2d 175 (D.C. Cir. 1969), shows that the appellate judgment (in the case involving school classification practices of the District of Columbia Board of Education) is reported at volume 408 of the *Federal Reports, 2d Series,* beginning at page 175, and is a decision of the federal court of appeals (D.C. Circuit Court of Appeals) for the District of Columbia in 1969.

F. Supp. an abbreviation, in a citation to a lawsuit's reported judgment and order, that indicates that the case was decided by a federal trail court (a "district" court) and is reported in a certain volume of the reports of the federal trail courts. The volume of the reports precedes the *F. Supp. (Federal Supplement)* designation; the page at which the report begins follows the *F. Supp.* designation; and the identity of the court and the date of the judgment are set out in parentheses after the page. Thus, in *PARC v. Commonwealth of Pennsylvania,* 343 F Supp. 279 (E.D. Pa. 1972), the case is reported at volume 343 of the *Federal Supplement,* beginning at page 279, and is a decision of the federal district court for the Eastern District (section) of Pennsylvania in 1972.

Fed. Reg. an abbreviation for *Federal Register,* a daily publication of Congress that contains the text of new laws and regulations and comments by members of Congress on matters of public policy.

FERPA an abbreviation for the Family Educational Rights and Privacy Act of 1974

Fifth Amendment the amendment to the federal Constitution that guarantees that the rights of life, liberty, and property will not be taken from a citizen by the federal government without due process of law. Due process guarantees apply to state and local governments under the Fourteenth Amendment.

First Amendment the amendment to the federal Constitution that guarantees free speech, assembly, worship, and petition for redress of grievances.

Fourteenth Amendment the amendment to the federal Constitution that applies to the states (not the federal government, which is bound by the first 10 amendments) and guarantees the rights of due process and equal protection to the citizens of each state.

HOUSSE an abbreviation for *high objective uniform state standards for evaluation*

IAES an abbreviation for *interim alternative educational setting*

IDEA an abbreviation for the Individuals with Disabilities Education Act

IEP an abbreviation for *individualized education program*

IEU an abbreviation for *intermediate educational unit*

IFSP an abbreviation for *individualized family service plan*

in re a Latin term in a captioned title of a case that indicates "in the matter of" and always is followed by the name of a party to a lawsuit (e.g., In Re: John Doe, a minor-here, the caption/title to the lawsuit reads "in the matter of John Doe, a minor/child").

infra a Latin word in a citation to a case that indicates that the same case is referred to in a later part of the same article, chapter, book, judicial opinion, or other writing (e.g., the court may refer to the *Rowley* case, *infra,* meaning later, or, literally, within, its opinion).

injunctive relief a remedy granted by the court forbidding or requiring some action by the defendant. Injunctive relief includes temporary restraining orders and preliminary and final injunctions. The difference among these types of relief is that they are issued for varying lengths of time, at various stages of the litigation process, and on the basis of varying degrees of proof

judgment an order by a court after a verdict has been reached. The judgment declares the relief to be granted.

LEA an abbreviation for *local education agency*

LEP an abbreviation for *limited English proficient*

LRE an abbreviation for *least restrictive environment*

MOU an abbreviation for *memorandum of understanding*

NCLB an abbreviation for the No Child Left Behind Act of 2001

NDE an abbreviation for *nondiscriminatory evaluation*

OCR an abbreviation for the Office of Civil Rights

on remand a reference in a citation to a case that indicates that a lower court has entered a judgment, for at least a second time, when it received the case from a higher court with a judgment and order to act in a particular way (e.g., the court's initial judgment is appealed, the appeals court enters a judgment to reverse in part and affirm in part and directs the lower court to change its original order, and the lower court then does so when the case is "on remand" to it from the higher court).

OSEP an abbreviation for the Office of Special Education Programs

P&A an abbreviation for *protection and advocacy*

parens patriae a Latin term that means, literally, "father of the country," and that refers nowadays to the doctrine that a state may act in a paternalistic way on behalf of its citizens, especially those who are children or who are mentally disabled and therefore less effective than other people in protecting themselves. The *parens patriae* doctrine justifies compulsory education, which is regarded as beneficial to children and the state alike but, because of its benefit to children, can be required for their own good.

PBS an abbreviation for *positive behavioral supports*

per curiam a Latin term in a citation to a case that refers to the judgment of a court entered "by the court" (rather than by a judge who writes the opinion for the court). *Per curiam* cases normally do not have opinions of the judges, only the court's disposition of the case (e.g., affirmed, petition denied, etc.).

P.L. an abbreviation for "Public Law," referring to a statute passed by Congress as a public law. Every public law has a number that follows the P.L. designation thus, P.L. 94–142 refers to Public Law 142 of the 94th Congress.

plaintiff a person who brings a suit to redress a violation of one or more of his or her legal rights.

precedent a decision by a judge or court that serves as a rule of guide to support other judges in deciding future cases involving similar or analogous legal questions. In the early right-to-education cases, courts cited some famous education decisions as precedents, including *Brown v. Board of Education,* outlawing segregated schools, and *Hobson v. Hansen,* outlawing the track system in the District of Columbia. Just as *PARC* and *Mills* were cited as precedent by other courts for finding a constitutional right to education, so *Rowley* is now cited on various legal issues (see chapter 5).

private action a case brought on behalf of one or more individuals to vindicate violation of their own legally protected interests. As distinguished from a class action, where the relief applies to all persons similarly situated or within the class represented by the plaintiffs (e.g., *PARC*), any relief granted in private action applies only to those plaintiffs actually before the court (e.g., *Rowley*).

procedural right a right that relates to the process of enforcing substantive rights or to obtaining relief, such as the right to a hearing, the right to present evidence in one's defense, and the right to counsel.

PTC an abbreviation for *parent training centers*

PTI centers an abbreviation for *parent training and information centers*

quid pro quo a Latin term that literally means "something for something" and indicates an exchange of money and/or goods (e.g., a school district provides inservice training in exchange for—as a *quid pro quo* for—state aid to defray expenses).

relief a remedy for some legal wrong. Relief is requested by a plaintiff to be granted by a court, against a defendant.

reversed (rev'd.) a word that indicates in a citation to a case that a higher court has overturned the result, and usually the reasoning, of a lower court and entered (or ordered the lower court to enter) a different judgment. Sometimes a higher court can reverse part of a lower court's judgment and affirm part of it, depending on the nature of the judgment.

SEA an abbreviation for *state education agency*

settlement an out-of-court agreement among parties to a suit, which resolves some or all of the issues involved in a case.

statutory right a right based on a statute or law passed by a unit of federal, state, or local governments (see chapter 1).

sub nom. a Latin abbreviation in a citation to a case that indicates the case was decided by another court under a different name (*sub* meaning "under," and *nom.* being an abbreviation for the Latin word *nomine,* meaning "name").

substantive right a right such as the right to an education, usually granted by statutes and constitutions.

supra a Latin word in a citation to a case that indicates that the same case has been referred to in an earlier part of the same article, chapter, book, judicial opinion, or other writing. It means the opposite of *infra.*

U.S. an abbreviation, in a citation to a decision of the U.S. Supreme Court, that indicates that a judgment of that Court is reported at a certain volume of the *United States Reports,* which contain only the judgments and other orders of the US. Supreme Court. The volume number precedes the *U.S.* designation, the page number follows it, and the date of judgment is set out in parentheses after the page reference.

U.S.C. (also U.S.C.A.) an abbreviation for *United States Code,* and official publication of the United States government (or *United States Code Annotated,* a commercial publication) that contains the codified acts of Congress.

U.S.L.W. a commercial publication that reports the judgments of various courts in *United States Law Week.* The volume of *USLW* precedes the USLW designation, and the page of the report follows it, with the identity of the court and date of judgment set out in parentheses after the page number.

vacated an abbreviation that indicates in a citation to a case that a higher court has set aside the judgment of a lower court.

verdict a decision by a judge or jury in favor of one side or the other in a case.

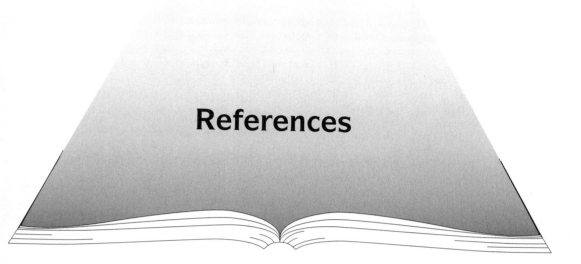

References

CITATIONS

American Association on Mental Retardation (AAMR). (2002). *Mental retardation: Definition, classification, and systems of support.* Washington, DC: Author.

American Psychiatric Association. (1994). *Diagnostic and Statistical Manual of Mental Disorders, Fourth Edition (DSM-IV).* Washington, DC: American Psychiatric Association.

Blatt, B., & Kaplan, F. (1974*). Christmas in Purgatory.* Boston: Allyn and Bacon.

Center on Human Policy. (2006). A statement of common principles on life-sustaining care and treatment of people with disabilities. Retrieved on April 3, 2006, from http://thechp.syr.edu/endorse/index.htm

Chambers, D. (1972). Alternatives to civil commitment of the mentally ill: Practical guides and constitutional imperatives. *Michigan Law Review 70, 1108.*

Erickson, K. (1966). *The wayward Puritans: A study in the sociology of deviance.* New York: John Wiley and Sons.

Finn, C., Rotherham, A., & Hokanson, C. (2001). *Rethinking special education for a new century.* Washington, DC: Fordham Foundation.

Gliedman, J., & Roth, W. (1980). *The unexpected minority: Handicapped children in America.* New York: Harcourt Brace Jovanovich.

Merriam-Webster's collegiate dictionary (10th ed.). (1996). Springfield, MA: Merriam-Webster.

Morse, S. (1978). Crazy behavior, morals, and science: An analysis of mental health law. *Southern California Law Review, 51*(4), 528–654.

National Institute for Disability and Rehabilitation Research (NIDRR). (2002). *Long-range plan* (1999–2003). Washington, DC: Author.

National Research Council. (2002). *Minority students in special education and gifted education.* Washington, DC: National Academy Press.

President's Commission on Excellence in Special Education. (2002, July). A new era: Revitalizing special education for children and their families. Retrieved Jan. 19, 2006, from http://www.ed.gov/inits/commissionsboards/whspecialeducation/reports/letter.html

Sarason, S., & Doris, J. (1975). *Educational handicap, public policy, and social history: A broadened perspective on mental retardation.* New York: Free Press.

Stone, A. (1976). *Mental health and law: A system in transition.* Washington, DC: National Institute of Mental Health.

Stowe, M. J., Turnbull, H. R., & Sublet, C. (2006). The Supreme Court, "Our Town," and disability policy: Boardrooms and bedrooms, courtrooms and cloakrooms. *Mental Retardation, 44,* 83–99.

Trilling, L., quoted in Rothman, D. (1980). *Convenience and conscience: The asylum and its alternatives in progressive America.* Boston: Little Brown.

Turnbull, A. P., and Turnbull, H. R. (1997). *Families, professionals, and exceptionality: A special partnership.* Columbus, OH: Merrill/Prentice Hall.

Turnbull, A. P., & Turnbull, H. R. (2001). *Families, professionals, and exceptionality* (4th ed.). Upper Saddle River, NJ: Merrill/Prentice Hall.

Turnbull, A. P., Turnbull, H. R., Erwin, E., & Soodak, L. (2006). *Families, professionals, and exceptionality: Positive outcomes through partnerships and trust* (5th ed.). Upper Saddle River, NJ: Merrill/Prentice Hall.

Turnbull, A. P., Turnbull, R., & Wehmeyer, M. (2006). *Exceptional lives: Special education in today's schools* (5th ed.). Upper Saddle River, NJ: Merrill/Prentice Hall.

Turnbull, H. R. (2005). Testimony to the Senate. Committee on Health, Education, Labor, and Pensions. *Research and Practice for Persons with Severe Disabilities, 30*(1), 38–41.

Turnbull, H. R., Beegle, G., & Stowe, M. J. (2001). The core concepts of disability policy affecting families who have children with disabilities. *Journal of Disability Policy Studies, 12*(3), 133–143.

Turnbull, H. R., Brotherson, M. J., Czyzewski, M., Esquith, D. S., Otis, A. K., Summers, J. A., et al. (1983). A policy analysis of "least restrictive" education of handicapped children. *Rutgers Law Journal 14*(3), 489–540.

Turnbull, H. R., & Stowe, M. J. (2001). Five models for thinking about disability: Implications for policy responses. *Journal of Disability Policy Studies, 12*(3), 198–205.

Turnbull, H. R., & Turnbull, A. P. (1985). *Parents speak out: Now and then.* Columbus, OH: Charles E. Merrill.

Turnbull, H. R., Wilcox, B. L., Turnbull, A. P., Sailor, W., & Wickham, D. (2001). IDEA, positive behavioral supports, and school safety. *Journal of Law and Education, 30*(3), 445–504.

U.S. Congress. (2004). *Conference Report 779.* 108th Cong., 2nd Sess. 232 (2004).

U.S. Department of Education (USDOE). (1999, March 12). *Analysis of comments and changes, attachment to the final Part B regulations.* 64 Fed. Reg. at 12548.

U.S. Department of Education. (2003). Press Release: Paige Releases Principles for Reauthorizing Individuals with Disabilities Education Act (IDEA). Washington, DC. Retrieved Jan. 19, 2006, from http://www.ed.gov/news/pressreleases/2003/02/02252003.html

Wald, P. (1976). Basic personal and civil rights. In M. Kindred, J. Cohen, D. Penrod, & T. Shaffer (Eds.), *The mentally retarded citizen and the law* (pp 3–28). New York: Free Press.

Wright, P., & Wright, P. (2003). *Wrightslaw: From emotions to advocacy* (2nd ed.). Hartford, VA: Harbor House Law Press.

TABLE OF LAWS

Adoption Assistance and Child Welfare Act (P.L. 96-272, 1980), 42 U.S.C. Secs. 620 *et seq.*, including Promoting Safe and Stable Families Program, 42 U.S.C. Secs. 629 *et seq.*

Americans with Disabilities Act of 1990 (ADA) (P.L. 101-336), 42 U.S.C. Secs. 12101 *et seq.*

Child Abuse Prevention and Treatment Act (CAPTA) (P.L. 93-247), 42 U.S.C. Sec. 5101, originally enacted in 1974; amended several times; most recently amended and reauthorized by the Keeping Children and Families Safe Act of 2003 (P.L. 108-36).

Children's and Communities Mental Health Systems Improvement Act of 1991, 42 U.S.C. Secs. 290ff *et seq.*

Children's Health Act of 2000 (P.L. 106-310), 42 U.S.C. Secs. 290bb-39 *et seq.*

Civil Rights Act of 1964 (P.L. 88-352), 42 U.S.C. Sec. 1971.

Civil Rights Act of 1991 (P.L. 102-166), 42 U.S.C. Sec. 1981 (*see also* Title VII of Civil Rights Act of 1991).

Developmental Disabilities Assistance and Bill of Rights Act of 1975 and 2000 (P.L. 106-402), 42 U.S.C. Secs. 1500 *et seq.*

Early & Periodic Screening Diagnosis and Treatment (EPSDT), 42 U.S.C. Sec. 1396d.

Education of All Handicapped Children Act of 1975 (P.L. 94-142), 20 U.S.C. Sec. 1400(d).

Elementary and Secondary Education Act of 1965 (ESEA), originally 20 U.S.C. Secs. 3801–3900, now 20 U.S.C. Sec. 7801.

Emergency Medical Treatment and Active Labor Act (EMTALA), 42 U.S.C. Sec. 1395dd, passed as part of the Consolidated Omnibus Budget Reconciliation Act of 1986 (COBRA).

Employee Retirement Income Security Act (ERISA, 1974), 29 U.S.C. Secs. 1181 *et seq.*

Equal Protection Clause: U.S.C. Const. Amend. 14, Sec. 1.

Family and Medical Leave Act of 1993 (FMLA) (P.L. 103-3), 29 U.S.C. Secs. 2601 *et seq.*

Family Educational Rights and Privacy Act of 1974 (FERPA) (P.L. 93-380), 20 U.S.C. Sec. 1232g, FERPA: 34 C.F.R. 99.1 *et seq.*

Health Insurance Portability and Accountability Act of 1996 (HIPAA) (P.L. 104-191), 42 U.S.C. Secs. 300gg *et seq.*

Individuals with Disabilities Education Act (IDEA), 20 U.S.C. Sec. 1400 *et seq.*, 34 C.F.R. 300 *et seq.*

IDEA Amendments of 1997 (P.L. 105-17).

IDEA Amendments of 2004 (P.L. 108-446).

IDEA Proposed Federal Regs, 34 C.F.R. 300, 301, and 304.

McKinney-Vento Homeless Education Assistance Improvements Act of 2001 in NCLB (P.L. 107-110), 42 U.S.C. Sec. 11434a, 2002.

Medicare Catastrophic Coverage Act of 1988 (MCCA) (P.L. 100-360).

Medicare Catastrophic Coverage Repeal Act of 1989 (P.L. 101-234).

Mental Health Parity Act (P.L. 104-204, 1997), 29 U.S.C. Sec. 1185a.

No Child Left Behind Act of 2001 (NCLB) (P.L. 107-110).

Rehabilitation Act of 1973, as amended in 1974 (P.L. 93-651), 29 U.S.C. Sec. 794, Sec. 504, 34 C.F.R. 104–104.61.

Technology-Related Assistance for Individuals with Disabilities Act of 1988 (P.L. 100-407), 29 U.S.C. Secs. 3001 *et seq.,* as amended in 1994 (P.L. 103-218), and as amended in 1998 by the Assistive Technology Act (P.L. 105-394).

Ticket to Work and Work Incentives Improvement Act of 1999 (P.L. 106-170), 42 U.S.C. Secs. 1320b-19.

Title V SSA: Title V Maternal and Child Health Services Block Grant, 42 U.S.C. 701 *et seq.*

Title VII of Civil Rights Act of 1991 (P.L. 102-166), 42 U.S.C. Sec. 2000e.
Title XVI SSA: Title XVI Supplemental Security Income, 42 U.S.C. 1381 *et seq.*
Title XVIII SSA: Title XVIII Medicare, 42 U.S.C. 1395 *et seq.*
Title XIX SSA: Title XIX Medicaid, 42 U.S.C. 1396 *et seq.*
Title XX SSA: Title XX Social Services Block Grant, 42 U.S.C. 1397 *et seq.*
Title XXI SSA: Title XXI State Child Health Insurance Program, 42 U.S.C. 1397aa.
Workforce Investment Act of 1998 (P.L. 105-220), 29 U.S.C. Secs. 2801 *et seq.*

TABLE OF CASES

Addington v. Texas, 441 U.S. 418 (1979).
Agostini v. Felton, 138 L.Ed.2d 391 (U.S. 1997).
Alexander S. v. Boyd, 876 F. Supp. 773 (D.S.C. 1995).
Amann v. Stow School System, 982 F.2d 644 (1st Cir. 1992).
Anderson v. Creighton, 483 U.S. 635 (1987).
Anderson v. Thompson, 658 F.2d 1205 (7th Cir. 1981).
Anti-Fascist Committee v. McGrath, 341 U.S. 123 (1951).
Arline (see *School Bd. of Nassau County v. Arline*)
Arlington Cent. Sch. Dist. v. Murphy, 548 U.S., 2006.
Armstrong v. Kline, 476 F. Supp. 583 (E.D. Pa. 1979), aff'd in part sub. nom, *Battle v. Commonwealth of Pennsylvania*, 629 F.2d 269 (3rd Cir. 1980), further proceedings, 513 F.Supp. 425 (E.D.Pa. 1980).
Arons v. New Jersey State Bd. of Educ., 842 F.2d 58 (3rd Cir. 1988), cert. denied, 488 U.S. 942 (1988).
Barbara R. v. Tirozzi, 665 F. Supp. 141 (D.Conn. 1987).
Barnett v. Fairfax County Sch. Bd., 721 F. Supp. 757 (E.D.Va. 1989), aff'd, 927 F.2d 146 (4th Cir. 1991), cert. denied, 502 U.S. 859 (1991).
Bd. of County Comm'rs v. Brown, 117 S.Ct. 1382 (U.S. 1997).
Bd. of Educ. of City of Plainfield v. Cooperman, 523 A.2d 655 (N.J. 1987).
Bd. of Educ. of Kiryas Joel Village School Dist. v. Grumet, 618 N.E.2d 94 (N.Y. 1993), aff'd, 512 U.S. 687 (1994).
Bd. of Educ. v. Rowley, 458 U.S. 176, 102 S. Ct. 3034 (1982).
Begay v. Hodel, 730 F. Supp. 1001 (D.Ariz. 1990).
Behavior Research Institute v. Secretary of Administration, 577 N.E.2d 297 (Mass. 1991).
Belanger v. Nashua Sch. Dist., 856 F. Supp. 40 (D.N.H. 1994).
Bevin H. v. Wright, 666 F. Supp. 71 (W.D.Pa 1987).
Blazejewski v. Bd. of Educ., 599 F. Supp. 975 (W.D.N.Y. 1985).
Board of Education v. Arline, 480 U.S. 273, 107 S. Ct. 1123 (1987).
Bonadonna v. Cooperman, 619 F.Supp. 401 (D.N.J. 1985).
Borgna v. Binghampton City School Dist., 18 IDELR 121 (N.D.N.Y. 1991).
Bowen v. Massachusetts, 487 U.S. 879, 108 S. Ct. 2722 (1988).
Bragdon v. Abbott, 118 S.Ct. 2196, 524 U.S. 624 (1998).
Brown v. Board of Education, 349 U.S. 886, 75 S. Ct. 210, (1954).
Brown v. District of Columbia Board of Educ., 551 IDELR 101 (D.D.C. 1978).
Burke County Bd. of Educ. v. Denton, 895 F.2d 973 (4th Cir. 1990).
Burlington Sch. Comm. v. Massachusetts Dept. of Education, 471 U.S. 359 (1985).

Carlisle Area Sch. Dist. v. Scott P., 62 F.3d 520 (3rd Cir. 1995), cert. denied, 116 S.Ct. 1419 (U.S. 1996).

Cedar Rapids Community Sch. Dist. v. Garrett F., 106 F.3d 822 (8th Cir. 1997), 526 U.S. 66, 119 S. Ct. 992 (1999).

Chris D. v. Montgomery County Bd. of Educ., 16 EHLR 1182 (M.D. Ala. 1990).

Christen G. v. Lower Merion Sch. Dist., 919 F. Supp. 793 (E.D.Pa. 1996).

Christopher P. v. Marcus, 915 F.2d 794 (2nd Cir. 1990), cert. denied, 498 U.S. 1123 (1991).

Christopher W. v. Portsmouth School Committee, 877 F.2d 1089 (1st Cir. 1989).

Cleburne v. Cleburne Living Center, Inc., 473 U.S. 432 (1985).

Clovis Unified School Dist. v. California Office of Admin. Hearings, 903 F.2d 635 (9th Cir. 1990).

Colin K. v. Schmidt, 715 F.2d 1 (1st Cir. 1983).

Concerned Parents and Citizens for Continuing Education at Malcolm X (PS 79) v. New York City Bd. of Education, 629 F.2d 751 (2nd Cir. 1980), cert. denied, 449 U.S. 1078 (1981).

Crocker v. Tennessee Secondary School Athletic Ass'n., 873 F.2d 933 (6th Cir. 1989), aff'd. 908 F.2d 972 (6th Cir. 1990).

Daniel R.R. v. State Bd. of Educ., 874 F.2d 1036 (5th Cir. 1989).

Davis v. Monroe County Board of Education, 526 U.S. 629, 119 S. Ct. 1661 (1999).

Day v. Radnor Township School Dist., 20 IDELR 1237 (E.D. Pa. 1994).

DeBord v. Board of Education of the Ferguson-Florissant School Dist. 126 F.3d 1102 (8th Cir., 1997).

Dellmuth v. Muth, 491 U.S. 223 (1989).

Denton (see *Burke County Bd. of Educ. v. Denton*)

Detsel v. Bd. of Educ. of the Auburn Enlarged City School Dist., 820 F.2d 587 (2nd Cir. 1987), cert. denied, 484 U.S. 981 (1987).

Detsel v. Sullivan, 895 F.2d 58 (2nd Cir. 1990).

Dima v. Macchiarola, 513 F.Supp. 565 (E.D.N.Y. 1981).

Dist. 27 Community School Bd. v. Bd. of Educ. of New York City, 502 N.Y.S.2d 325 (Sup. Ct. NY 1986).

Doe v. Bd. of Ed. of Tullahoma City Schools, IDELR 18/1089 (E.D.Tenn. 1992), aff'd, 9 F.3d 455 (6th Cir. 1993), cert. denied, 511 U.S. 1108 (1994).

Doe v. Belleville Public Schools Dist. No. 118, 672 F. Supp. 342 (S.D. Ill. 1987).

Doe v. Defendant I, 898 F.2d 1186 (6th Cir. 1990).

Edelman v. Jordan, 415 U.S. 651 (1974).

Escambia County Bd. Of Educ. V. Benton, U.S. Dist. LEXIS 37931 (S. Dist. of Alabama, 2005).

Estelle v. Gamble, 429 U.S. 97 (1976).

Ezratty v. Commonwealth of Puerto Rico, 648 F.2d 770 (1st Cir. 1981).

Felter v. Cape Girardeau School Dist., 830 F. Supp. 1279 (E.D.Mo. 1993).

Field v. Haddonfield Bd. of Educ., 769 F. Supp. 1313 (D.N.J. 1991).

Fitzpatrick v. Bitzer, 427 U.S. 445 (1976).

Florence County Sch. Dist. Four v. Carter, 510 U.S. 7, 114 S. Ct. 361 (1993).

Franklin v. Gwinnett County Pub. Sch., 503 U.S. 60, 112 S. Ct. 1028 (1992).

Ft. Zumwalt Sch. Dist. v. Missouri State Bd of Ed., 865 F. Supp. 604 (E.D. Mo. 1994), further proceedings, 923 F. Supp. 1216 (E.D.Mo. 1996), aff'd in part, rev'd in part sub nom., *Ft. Zumwalt Sch. Dist. v. Clynes*, Nos. 96-2503/2504, 1997 U.S. App. Lexis 17214 (8th Cir. 1997).

Garrett F. (see *Cedar Rapids Community Sch. Dist. v. Garrett F.*)

Garrity v. Gallen, 522 F.Supp. 171 (D.N.H. 1981).

Geis v. Bd. of Educ. of Parsnippany-Troy Hills, 589 F. Supp. 269 (D.N.J. 1984), aff'd, 774 F.2d 575 (3rd Cir. 1985).

Glenn III v. Charlotte Mecklenburg Sch. Bd. of Educ., 903 F. Supp. 918 (W.D.N.C. 1995).

Goodman v. Georgia, consolidated with and reported under the title *U.S. v. Georgia,* 2006 LEXIS 759 (2006).

Goss v. Lopez, 419 U.S. 565, 95 S. Ct. 729 (1975).

Grace B. v. Lexington Sch. Comm., 762 F. Supp. 416 (D.Mass. 1991).

Greer v. Rome City Sch. Dist., 762 F. Supp 936 (N.D. Ga 1990) aff'd, 950 F.2d 688 (11th Cir. 1991), withdrawn & reinstated in part, 967 F.2d 470 (11th Cir. 1992).

Grinsted v. Houston County Sch. Dist., 826 F. Supp. 482 (M.D.Ga. 1993).

Grumet (see *Bd. of Educ. of Kiryas Joel Village School Dist. v. Grumet*)

Hall v. Shawnee Mission School Dist., 856 F. Supp. 1521 (D. Kan. 1994).

Harlow v. Fitzgerald, 457 U.S. 800 (1982).

Harris v. Campbell, 472 F.Supp. 51 (E.D.Va. 1979).

Harris v. D.C. Bd. of Ed., IDELR 19/105 (D.D.C. 1992).

Harris v. McCarthy, 790 F.2d 753 (9th Cir. 1986).

Heidemann v. Rother, 84 F.3d 1021 (8th Cir. 1996).

Hoekstra v. Indep. Sch. Dist. No. 283, 103 F.3d 624 (8th Cir. 1996); cert. denied 117 S.Ct. 1852 (U.S. 1997).

Holland (see *Sacramento City School District v. Rachel H.*)

Holmes v. Sobol, 18 IDELR 53 (W.D.N.Y. 1991).

Honig v. Doe, 484 U.S. 305, 108 S. Ct. 592 (1988).

Howey v. Tippecanoe School Corp., 734 F. Supp. 1485 (N.D.Ind. 1990).

Hudson v. Wilson, 828 F.2d 1059 (4th Cir. 1987).

Hulme v. Dellmuth, 17 EHLR 940 (E.D. Pa. 1991).

Hunter v. Bd. of Educ. of Montgomery County, 555 EHLR 559 (Md. Ct. App. 1982).

Ingraham v. Wright, 430 U.S. 651, 97 S. Ct. 1401 (1977).

Irving Indep. School Dist. v. Tatro, 703 F.2d 823 (5th Cir. 1983), aff'd in part, rev'd in part, 468 U.S. 883, 104 S. Ct. 3371 (1984).

J.B. v. Indep. Sch. Dist., 21 IDELR 1157 (D.Minn. 1995).

J.G. v. Bd. of Educ., EHLR 554:265 (W.D.N.Y. 1982), EHLR 555:190 (W.D.N.Y. 1983), 648 F.Supp 1452 (W.D.N.Y. 1986), aff'd. in part, modified in part, 830 F.2d 444 (2nd Cir. 1987).

Jackson v. Franklin County Sch. Bd., 606 F. Supp. 152 (S.D.Miss. 1985), aff'd, 765 F.2d 535 (5th Cir. 1985).

Jeanette H. v. Pennsbury School District, No. 91-CV-3273, 1992 U.S. Dist. Lexis 7283 (E.D.Pa. 1992).

Jeremy H. v. Mount Lebanon Sch. Dist., 95 F.3d 272 (3rd Cir. 1996).

John G. v. Bd. of Educ., 891 F. Supp. 122 (S.D.N.Y. 1995).

Johnson v. Ind. Sch. Dist. No. 4, 921 F.2d 1022 (10th Cir. 1990), cert. denied, 500 U.S. 905 (1991).

Johnson v. Westmoreland County School Bd., 19 IDELR 787 (E.D. Va. 1993).

Joiner v. Dist. of Columbia, 16 EHLR 424, 87-3445 (D.D.C. 1990).

Jonathon G. v. Caddo Parish Sch. Bd., 875 F. Supp. 352 (W.D.La. 1994).

Jose P. v. Ambach, 551 EHLR 245 & 412 (E.D.N.Y. 1979), aff'd, 669 F.2d 865 (2nd Cir. 1982), further proceedings, 557 F. Supp. 1230 (E.D.N.Y. 1983).

Kattan v. District of Columbia, 18 IDELR 296 (D.D.C. 1991), aff'd, 995 F.2d 274 (D.C. Cir. 1993), cert. denied, 511 U.S. 1018 (1994).

Kerr Center Parents Association v. Charles, 572 F. Supp. 448 (D.Ore. 1983), aff'd. in part, re'd in part, 897 F.2d 1463 (9th Cir. 1990).

Kiryas Joel Village School (see *Bd. of Educ. of Kiryas Joel Village School Dist. v. Grumet*)

Lake Country Estates Inc. v. Tahoe Regional Planning Agency, 440 U.S. 391 (1979).

Larry P. v. Riles, 793 F. Supp. 969, 1984 U.S. App. LEXIS 26195 (1984).

Lemon v. Kurtzman, 411 U.S. 192 (1973).

Lenn v. Portland School Committee, 998 F.2d 1083 (1st Cir. 1993).

Leo P. v. Board of Education, EHLR 553:644 (N.D.Ill. 1982).

Lester H. v. Gilhool, 916 F.2d 865 (3d Cir. 1990), cert. denied, 499 U.S. 923 (1991).

Levine v. New Jersey, 522 EHLR 163 (N.J.Sup. Ct. 1980).

Loughran v. Flanders, 470 F. Supp. 110 (D.Conn. 1979).

M.B. v. Arlington Central School District et. al., 2002 U.S. Dist. LEXIS 4015, (S.D.N.Y. March 11, 2002).

M.C. v. Central Regional School Dist., 22 IDELR 1036 (D.N.J. 1995).

Maine v. Thiboutot, 448 U.S. 1 (1980).

Martinez v. School Bd. of Hillsborough County, 675 F. Supp. 1574 (M.D.Fla. 1987), vacated, 861 F.2d 1502 (11th Cir. 1988).

Marvin H. v. Austin Indep. Sch. Dist., 714 F.2d 1348 (5th Cir. 1983).

Maynard v. Greater Hoyt Sch. Dist. No. 61-4, 876 F. Supp. 1104 (D.S.D. 1995).

McManus v. Wilmette School Dist. 39 Bd. of Ed., IDELR 19/485, 1992 U.S. Dist. Lexis 18167 (N.D. Ill. 1992).

Metropolitan Nashville & Davidson County Sch. System v. Guest, 900 F. Supp. 905 (M.D.Tenn. 1995).

Miener v. Missouri, 498 F. Supp. 944 (E.D. Mo. 1980), aff'd in part, rev'd in part, 673 F.2d 969 (8th Cir. 1982), cert. denied, 459 U.S. 909, 916 (1982), on remand, *Miener v. Special School District*, 580 F. Supp. 562 (E.D. Mo. 1984), aff'd in part, rev'd in part, 800 F.2d 749 (8th Cir. 1986).

Miller v. West Lafayette Community School Corp., 665 N.E.2d 905 (Ind. 1996).

Mills v. District of Columbia Bd. of Ed., 348 F. Supp. 866 (D.D.C. 1972); contempt proceedings, EHLR 551:643 (D.D.C. 1980).

Molly L. v. Lower Merion School Dist., 194 F.Supp.2d 422, (E.D.Pa.2002).

Monahan v. Nebraska, 491 F. Supp. 1074 (D. Neb. 1980), aff'd in part, vacated in part, 645 F.2d 592 (8th Cir. 1981), aff'd in part, vacated in part, 687 F.2d 1164 (8th Cir. 1982), cert. denied, 460 U.S. 1012 (1983), modified sub nom., *Rose v. Nebraska*, 748 F.2d 1258 (8th Cir. 1984), cert. denied, 474 U.S. 817 (1985).

Monell v. New York Dep't. of Social Services, 436 U.S. 658 (1978).

Monroe v. Pape, 365 U.S. 167 (1961).

Monticello Sch. Dist. No. 25 v. Illinois State Bd. of Educ., 910 F. Supp. 446 (C.D.Ill. 1995), aff'd sub nom., *Monticello Sch. Dist. No. 25 v. George L.*, 102 F.3d 895 (7th Cir. 1996).

Moore v. Dist. of Columbia, 674 F. Supp. 901 (D.D.C. 1987), rev'd, 886 F.2d 335 (D.C.Cir. 1989), vacated, 907 F.2d 165 (D.C. Cir. 1990), cert. denied, 498 U.S. 998 (1990).

Mrs. C. v. Wheaton, 916 F.2d 69 (2nd Cir. 1990).

Mrs. W. v. Tirozzi, 832 F.2d 748 (2nd Cir. 1987).

Murphy v. Timberlane Regional Sch. Dist., 22 F.3d 1186 (1st Cir. 1994), cert. denied, 513 U.S. 987 (1994).

Murphysboro Community Unit School Dist. v. Illinois State Bd. of Educ., 41 F.3d 1162 (7th Cir. 1994).

Natchez-Adams School Dist. v. Searing, 918 F. Supp. 1028 (S.D.Miss. 1996).

Neely v. Rutherford County School, 851 F. Supp. 888 (M.D. Tenn. 1995), rev'd, 68 F.3d 965 (6th Cir. 1995), cert. denied, 116 S.Ct. 1418 (U.S. 1996).

New Mexico Association for Retarded Citizens v. New Mexico, 495 F. Supp. 391 (D.N.M. 1980), rev'd, 678 F.2d 847 (10th Cir. 1982).

Newport v. Fact Concerts, Inc., 453 U.S. 247 (1981).

North v. D.C. Bd. of Ed., 471 F.Supp. 136 (D.D.C. 1979).

O'Connor v. Donaldson, 422 U.S. 563 (1975).

Ojai Unified Sch. Dist. v. Jackson, 4 F.3d 1467 (9th Cir. 1993), cert. denied, 513 U.S. 825 (1994).

Owens v. Independence, 445 U.S. 622 (1980).

Papacoda v. Connecticut, 528 F. Supp. 68 (D.Conn. 1981).

Parents in Action on Special Education (PASE) v. Hannon, No. 74 C 3586 N.D. Ill. (1980).

Parents of Student W. v. Puyallup, 31 F.3d 1489 (9th Cir. 1994).

Parham v. J.R., 442 U.S. 584 (1979).

Parks v. Pavkovic, 536 F. Supp. 296 (N.D. Ill. 1982), further proceedings, 557 F. Supp. 1280 (N.D. Ill. 1983), aff'd in part, rev'd in part, 753 F.2d 1397 (7th Cir. 1985), cert. denied, 473 U.S. 906 (1985).

PASE (see *Parents in Action on Special Education [PASE] v. Hannon*)

Pennhurst State School and Hospital v. Halderman, 446 F. Supp. 1295 (E.D. Pa. 1977), aff'd in part, rev'd in part, 612 F.2d 84 (3rd Cir. 1979), rev'd, 451 U.S.1 (1981), on remand, 673 F.2d 647 (3rd Cir. 1982), rev'd, 465 U.S. 89 (1984).

Pennsylvania Ass'n for Retarded Children (PARC) v. Commonwealth of Pennsylvania, 334 F. Supp. 1257 (E.D. Pa. 1971); 343 F. Supp. 279 (E.D. Pa. 1972).

Pennsylvania Dept. of Corrections v. Yeskey, 524 U.S. 206, 118 S.Ct. 1952 (1998).

Petersen v. Hastings Public Schools, 831 F. Supp. 742 (D.Neb. 1993), aff'd, 31 F.3d 705 (8th Cir. 1994).

Phipps v. New Hannover County Bd. of Educ., 551 F.Supp. 732 (E.D.N.C. 1982).

Plyler v. Doe, 457 U.S. 202 (1982).

Porter v. Board of Trustees of Manhattan Beach Unified Sch. Dist., 307 F.3d 1064, 2002 U.S. App. LEXIS 20997 (9th Cir. Cal. 2002), cert denied, 537 U.S. 1194 (2003).

Pullen v. Cuomo, 18 IDELR 132 (N.D.N.Y. 1991).

Quackenbush v. Johnson City School District, 716 F.2d 141 (2nd Cir. 1983), cert denied, 465 U.S. 1071 (1984).

Quern v. Jordan, 440 U.S. 332 (1979).

Rappaport v. Vance, 812 F. Supp. 609 (D.Md. 1993), appeal dismissed, 14 F.3d 596 (4th Cir. 1994), dismissed, No. 93-1916; 1994 U.S. App. Lexis 80 (4th Cir. 1994).

Raymond S. v. Ramirez, 918 F.Supp. 1280 (N.D. Iowa 1995).

Reid v. Bd. of Educ., Lincolnshire-PrairieView Sch. Dist 103, 765 F. Supp. 965 (N.D.Ill. 1991).

River Forest School Dist. #90 v. Laurel D., No. 95 C 5503, 1996 U.S. Dist. Lexis 4988 (N.D.Ill. 1996).

Robinson v. Pinderhughes, 810 F.2d 1270 (4th Cir. 1987).

Rodgers v. Magnet Cove Pub. Schs., 34 F.3d 642 (8th Cir. 1994).

Roncker v. Walter, 700 F.2d 1058 (6th Cir. 1983), cert. denied, 464 U.S. 864 (1983).

Rowley (see *Bd. of Educ. v. Rowley*)

Russell v. Jefferson Sch. Dist., 609 F. Supp. 605 (N.D.Cal. 1985).

Russman v. Sobol, 85 F.3rd 1050 (2nd Cir. 1996), vacated, 138 L.Ed.2d 1008 (U.S. 1997).

Ruth Ann M. v. Alvin Independent School District, 532 F. Supp. 460 (S.D. Tex. 1982).

Sacramento City School District v. Rachel H., 14 F.3d 1398 (9th Cir. 1994), *cert. denied sub nom., Sacramento City Unified School Dist. v. Holland,* 114 S. Ct. 2679 (1994).

Salley v. St. Tammany Parish Sch. Bd., 57 F.3d 458 (5th Cir. 1995).

Sanger v. Montgomery County Bd. of Ed., 916 F. Supp. 518 (D.Md. 1996).

Schaffer v. Weast, 126 S. Ct. 528 (2005).

School Board of Hillsborough County v. Student 26493257S, 23 IDELR 93 (M.D. Fla 1995).

School Bd. of Nassau County v. Arline, 480 U.S. 273 (1987).

Scituate School Committee v. Robert B., 620 F. Supp. 1224 (D.R.I. 1985), aff'd 795 F.2d 77 (1st Cir. 1986).

Seals v. Loftis, 614 F. Supp. 302 (E.D.Tenn. 1985).

Sean R. v. Bd. of Educ., 794 F. Supp. 467 (D.Conn. 1992).

S.H. v. State-Operated Sch. Dist., 336 F.3d 260 (3d Cir. N.J. 2003).

Smith v. Robinson, 468 U.S. 992, 104 S. Ct. 3457 (1984).

Smith v. Wade, 461 U.S. 30 (1983).

Southeastern Community College v. Davis, 442 U.S. 397, 99 S. Ct. 2361 (1987).

Supreme Court v. Consumers Union of United States, 446 U.S. 719 (1980), on remand sub nom, *Consumers Union of United States v. American Bar Ass'n,* 505 F. Supp. 822 (E.D. Va. 1981), appeal dismissed, 451 U.S. 1012 (1981), aff'd in part, rev'd in part, 688 F.2d 218 (4th Cir. 1982), cert. denied. 462 U.S. 1137 (1983).

Susan N. v. Wilson Sch. Dist., 70 F.3d 751 (2nd Cir. 1995).

Tall v. Board of School Comm'rs of Baltimore City, 28 IDELR 151 (Md. App. Ct. 1998).

Tatro (see *Irving Indep. School Dist. v. Tatro*)

Teague Indep. School Dist. v. Todd L., 999 F.2d 127 (5th Cir. 1993).

Tenney v. Brandhove, 341 U.S. 367 (1951).

Texas State Teachers Ass'n. v. Garland Indep. Sch. Dist., 837 F.2d 190 (5th Cir. 1988), rev'd, 489 U.S. 782 (1989).

Thomas v. Atascadero Unified School Dist., 662 F. Supp. 376 (C.D.Cal. 1986).

Thomas v. Davidson Academy, 846 F. Supp. 611 (M.D. Tenn. 1994).

Thompson v. Bd. of Special Sch. Dist. No. 1, 936 F. Supp. 644 (D.Minn. 1996).

Tilton v. Jefferson County Bd. of Educ., 705 F2d 800 (6th Cir. 1983); cert. denied 465 U.S. 1006 (1984).

Timms v. Metro School Dist., 722 F.2d 1310 (7th Cir. 1983).

Timothy W. v. Rochester School Dist., 559 EHLR 480 (D.N.H. 1988), 875 F.2d 954 (1st Cir. 1989), cert. denied, 493 U.S. 983 (1989).

Todd v. Elkins Sch. Dist. No. 10, 28 IDELR 29 (8th Cir. 1998).

Union School Dist. v. Smith, 15 F.3d 1519 (9th Cir. 1994), cert. denied, 513 U.S. 965 (1994).

United Cerebral Palsy of NYC v. Bd. of Ed. of City of N.Y., 669 F2d 865 (2nd Cir. 1982), further proceedings, 557 F.Supp. 1230 (E.D.N.Y 1983).

Urban v. Jefferson County School Dist R-1, 870 F. Supp. 1558 (D.Co. 1994), aff'd, 89 F.3d 720 (10th Cir. 1996).

Vander Malle v. Ambach, 673 F.2d 49 (2nd Cir. 1982), further proceedings, 667 F. Supp. 1015 (S.D.N.Y. 1987).

W.B. v. Matula, 67 F.3d 484 (3rd Cir. 1995).

Walker v. San Francisco Unified School Dist., 46 F.3d 1449 (9th Cir. 1995).

Wall v. Mattituck-Cutchogue Sch. Dist., 945 F. Supp. 501 (E.D.N.Y. 1996).

Weast (see *Schaffer v. Weast*)

White v. Western School Corporation, 1985 U.S. Dist. LEXIS 16540 (S.D. Ind. 1985).

Whitehead v. Sch. Bd., 918 F. Supp. 1515 (M.D.Fla. 1996).

Will v. Michigan Dep't. of State Police, 491 U.S. 58 (1989).

Windward School v. State, EHLR 551:219 (S.D.N.Y. 1978), aff'd EHLR 551:224 (2nd Cir. 1979).

Wood v. Strickland, 420 U.S. 308 (1975).

Wyatt v. Cole, 504 U.S. 158 (1992).

Wyatt v. Stickney, 344 F. Supp. 373 (M.D. Ala. 1972), aff'd in part, rev'd in part sub nom.

Yeskey (see *Pennsylvania Dept. of Corrections v. Yeskey*)

Youngberg v. Romeo, 457 U.S. 307 (1982).

Zelman v. Simmons-Harris, 536 U.S. 639, 122 S. Ct. 2460 (2002).

Zobrest v. Catalina Foothills School Dist., 963 F.2d 1190 (9th Cir. 1992), rev'd, 509 U.S. 1 (1993).

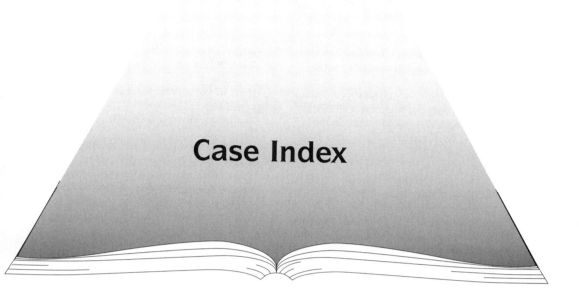

Case Index

Jose P. v. Ambach, 278

K

Kattan v. District of Columbia, 348, 349
Kerr Center Parents Association v. Charles, 278, 279
Kiryas Joel Village School. *See* Bd. of Educ. of Kiryas Joel Village School Dist.

L

Lake Country Estates Inc. v. Tahoe Regional Planning Agency, 340
Larry P. v. Riles, 113–114, 116–117, 118, 119, 120, 136, 151
Lemon v. Kurtzman, 69
Lenn v. Portland School Committee, 306
Leo P. v. Board of Education, 305
Lester H. v. Gilhool, 331
Levine v. New Jersey, 79
Loughran v. Flanders, 278

M

M.B. v. Arlington Central School District et al., 49
M.C. v. Central Regional School Dist., 331, 332
Maine v. Thiboutot, 342
Martinez v. School Bd. of Hillsborough County, 84
Marvin H. v. Austin Indep. Sch. Dist., 346
Maynard v. Greater Hoyt Sch. Dist. No. 61-4, 343
McManus v. Wilmette School Dist. 39 Bd. of Ed., 330
Metropolitan Nashville & Davidson County Sch. System v. Guest, 302
Miener v. Missouri, 277, 331
Miller v. West Lafayette Community School Corp., 349
Mills v. District of Columbia Bd. of Ed., 56, 80, 98, 101, 319
Molly L. v. Lower Merion School Dist., 49
Monahan v. Nebraska, 277, 336, 344, 345
Monell v. New York Dep't of Social Services, 340, 345
Monroe v. Pape, 342
Monticello Sch. Dist. No. 25 v. George L., 348
Moore v. Dist. of Columbia, 348
Mrs. C. v. Wheaton, 331

Mrs. W. v. Tirozzi, 279, 337
Murphy v. Timberlane Regional Sch. Dist., 331
Murphysboro Community Unit School Dist. v. Illinois State Bd. of Educ., 304

N

Natchez-Adams School Dist. v. Searing, 71, 72
Neely v. Rutherford County School, 182
New Mexico Association for Retarded Citizens v. New Mexico, 279
Newport v. Fact Concerts, Inc., 344
North v. D.C. Bd. of Ed., 278

O

O'Connor v. Donaldson, 85
Ojai Unified Sch. Dist. v. Jackson, 305
Owens v. Independence, 341

P

Papacoda v. Connecticut, 185
PARC. *See* Pennsylvania Ass'n for Retarded Children
Parents in Action on Special Education (PASE) v. Hannon, 118, 119, 120, 137
Parents of Student W. v. Puyallup, 332
Parham v. J.R., 104
Parks v. Pavkovic, 305
PASE. *See* Parents in Action on Special Education
Pennhurst State School and Hospital v. Halderman, 339
Pennsylvania Ass'n for Retarded Children (PARC) v. Commonwealth of Pennsylvania, 56, 70, 80, 98, 101, 154, 211, 319
Pennsylvania Dept. of Corrections v. Yeskey, 65
Petersen v. Hastings Public Schools, 306
Phipps v. New Hanover County Bd. of Educ., 279
Plyler v. Doe, 86
Porter v. Board of Trustees of Manhattan Beach Unified Sch. Dist., 279
Pullen v. Cuomo, 182

Q

Quackenbush v. Johnson City School District, 278, 279

Name Index

Subject Index